Waiting for Spring

for Spring

Anashin

8

Waiting
for Spring
vol.8

Presented by
Anashin

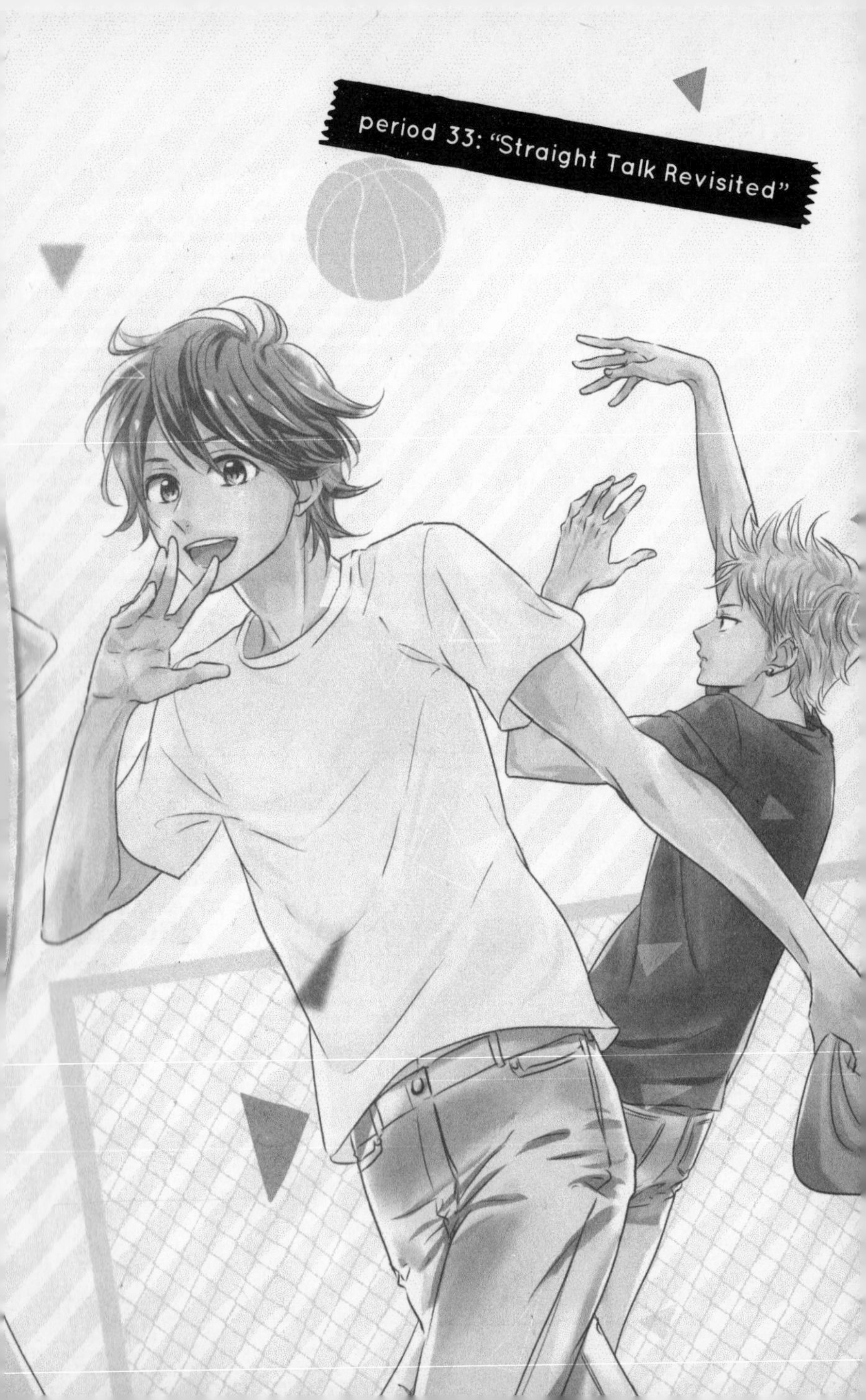
period 33: "Straight Talk Revisited"

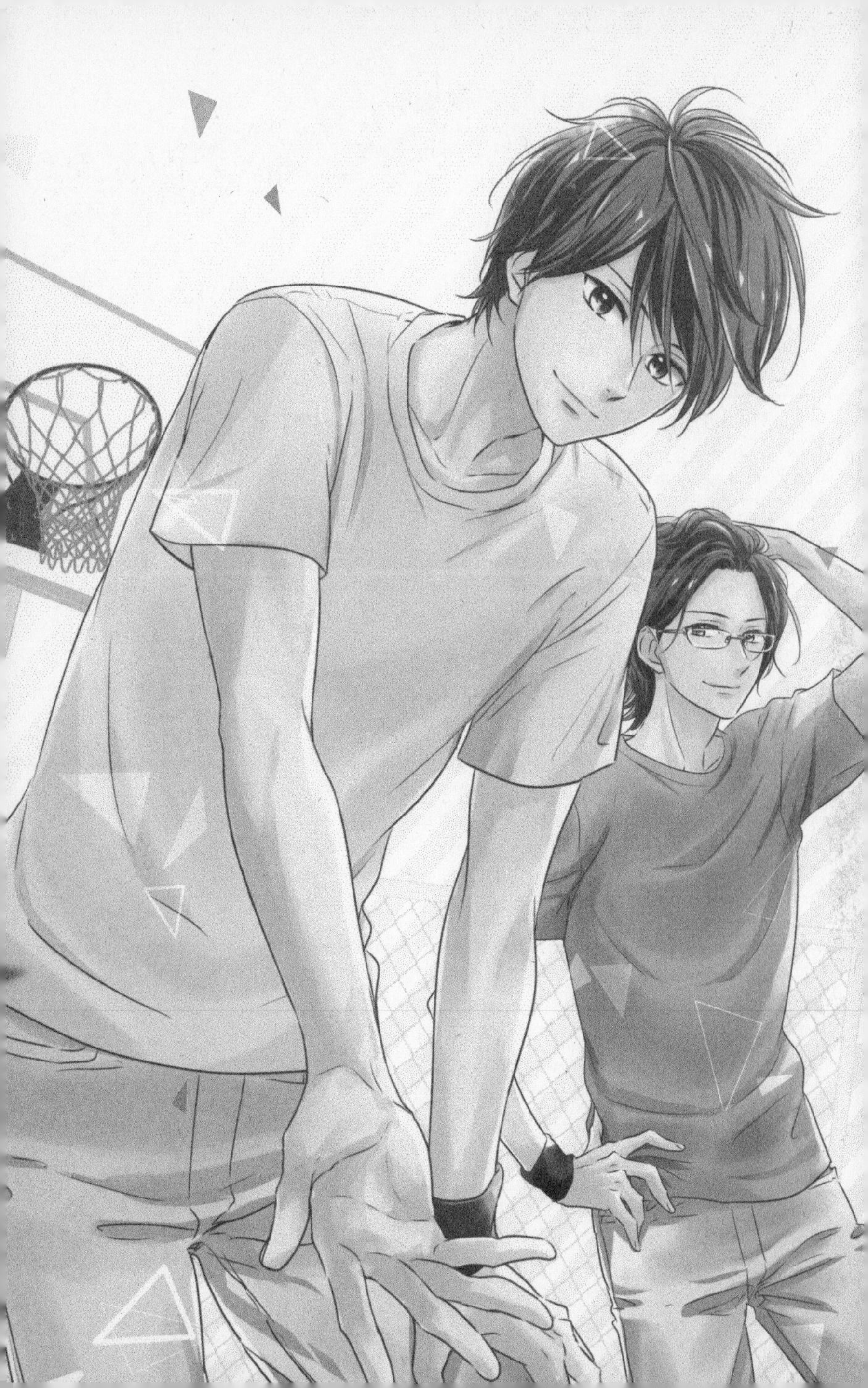

Hello! Anashin here!

Thank you so much for picking up Volume 8!

So the cover ended up being Rui and Mitsuki. And that means the next cover is pretty obvious → 👓 (ha ha)

And that means I have less to talk about here... Darn it...

Okay, let's talk about my private life! ...Or that **would** be an idea, but... that gives me even **less** to talk about!!

By which I mean, my life generally goes like this:

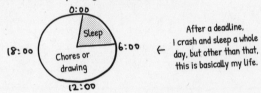

After a deadline, I crash and sleep a whole day, but other than that, this is basically my life.

But that doesn't mean I'm overworking myself. I'm just the type who spends whatever time I have doing my job. I've always drawn slower than most people, and I sit at my desk all day without interruption, so I keep myself stuck inside all day... If this keeps up, it won't be good for my health or my art!! And so, for now I just started exercising, but these days I'm realizing that if I want more stimulation, I have to go outside... And if this helps me get to be more active, then I have this goal now that, if possible, "I want to climb Mt. Fuji...! (with my father)" (ha ha). I want to keep working so that someday, somewhere I can report that I have. (And all of that has absolutely nothing to do with the manga! I hope you won't mind that once in a while.º)

Now, I hope you enjoy Volume 8...

TOWA SAYS HE'S ON HIS WAY HERE NOW.
He just called.
WHAT?!
WHY?
IS MITSUKI COMING?
NO, JUST TOWA.
BUT WAIT. I THOUGHT HE WAS GOING TO WALK HER HOME AND TELL HER HE LIKES HER...
Donny's

Now, I think I will continue from the previous volume and use this space to talk about the characters' early designs and families!

☆ This time, we'll cover these three →

And I think this volume will be the end of this miniseries.

I didn't really have anything to write about for Mitsuki...

Even her name was Mitsuki right from the start...

I'm sorry.

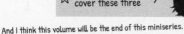

Design from before the series started. →

Her family consists of: her Father, Mother, Mitsuki, and two younger sisters (ages 13 and 10)

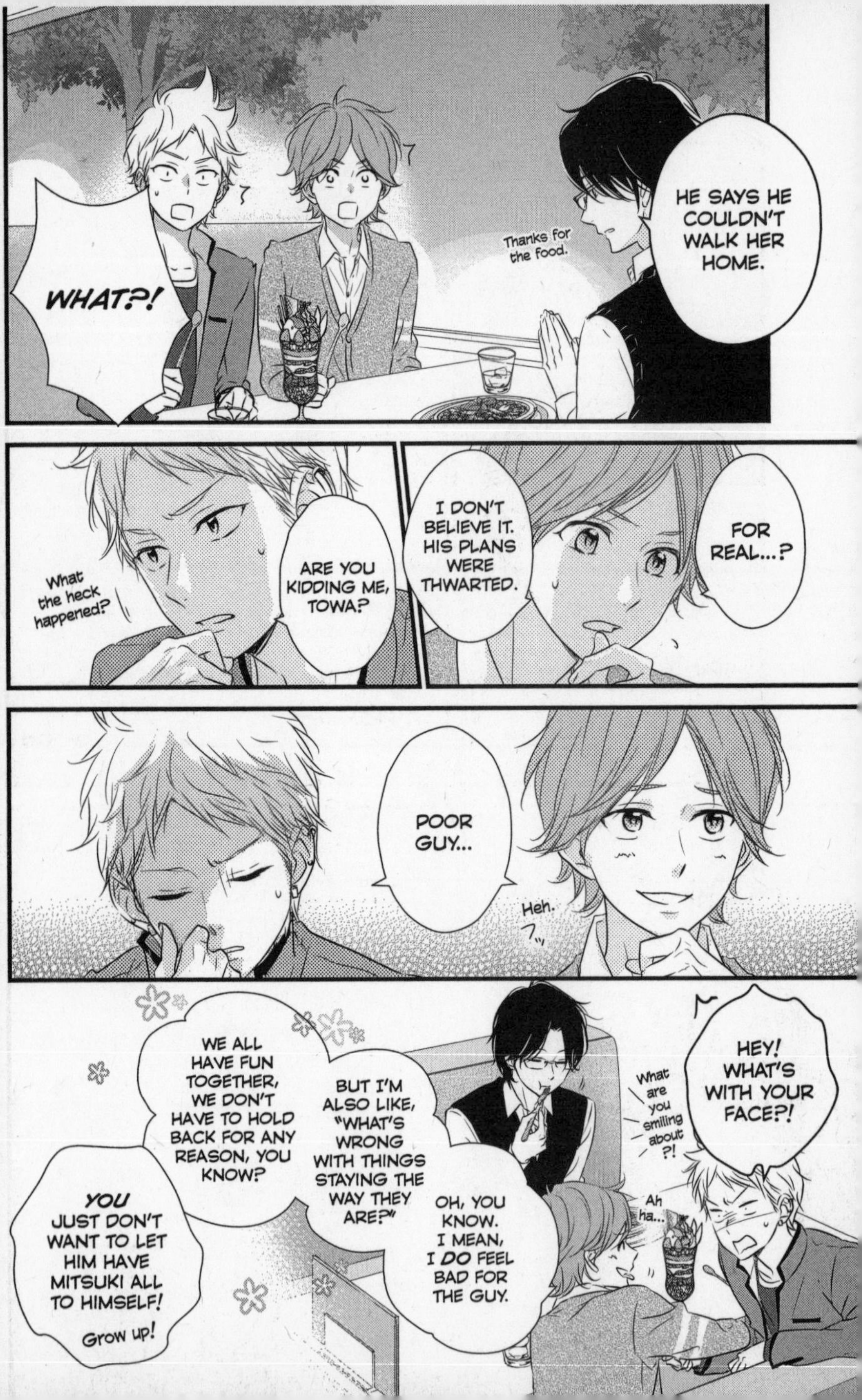
HE SAYS HE COULDN'T WALK HER HOME.
Thanks for the food.
WHAT?!
FOR REAL...?
I DON'T BELIEVE IT. HIS PLANS WERE THWARTED.
ARE YOU KIDDING ME, TOWA?
What the heck happened?
POOR GUY...
Heh.
HEY! WHAT'S WITH YOUR FACE?!
What are you smiling about?!
Ah ha...
OH, YOU KNOW. I MEAN, I DO FEEL BAD FOR THE GUY.
BUT I'M ALSO LIKE, "WHAT'S WRONG WITH THINGS STAYING THE WAY THEY ARE?"
WE ALL HAVE FUN TOGETHER, WE DON'T HAVE TO HOLD BACK FOR ANY REASON, YOU KNOW?
YOU JUST DON'T WANT TO LET HIM HAVE MITSUKI ALL TO HIMSELF!
Grow up!

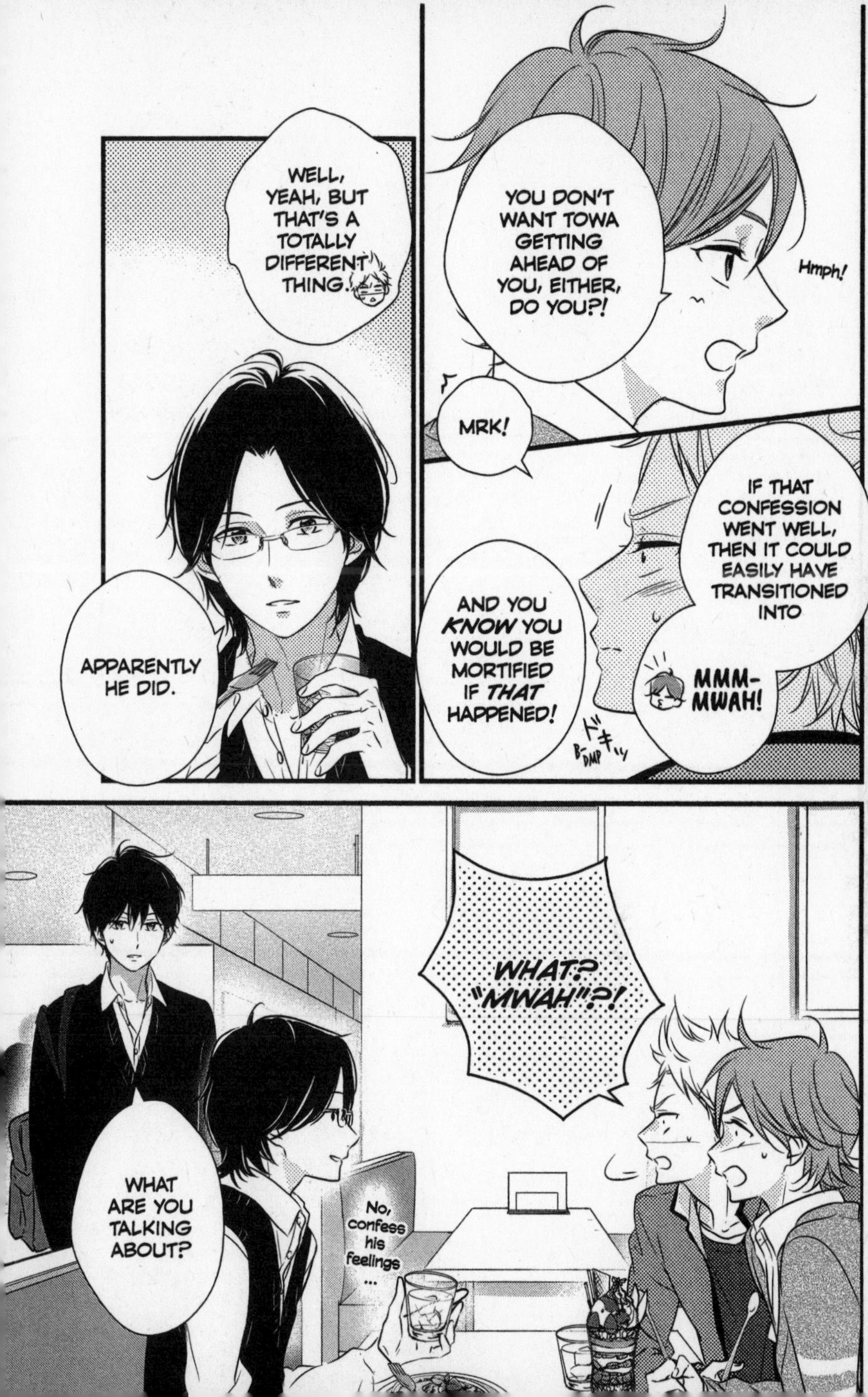
YOU DON'T WANT TOWA GETTING AHEAD OF YOU, EITHER, DO YOU?!
Hmph!
MRK!
IF THAT CONFESSION WENT WELL, THEN IT COULD EASILY HAVE TRANSITIONED INTO
MMM-MWAH!
AND YOU *KNOW* YOU WOULD BE MORTIFIED IF *THAT* HAPPENED!
ドキッ
B-DMP
WELL, YEAH, BUT THAT'S A TOTALLY DIFFERENT THING.
APPARENTLY HE DID.
WHAT? "MWAH"?!
No, confess his feelings ...
WHAT ARE YOU TALKING ABOUT?

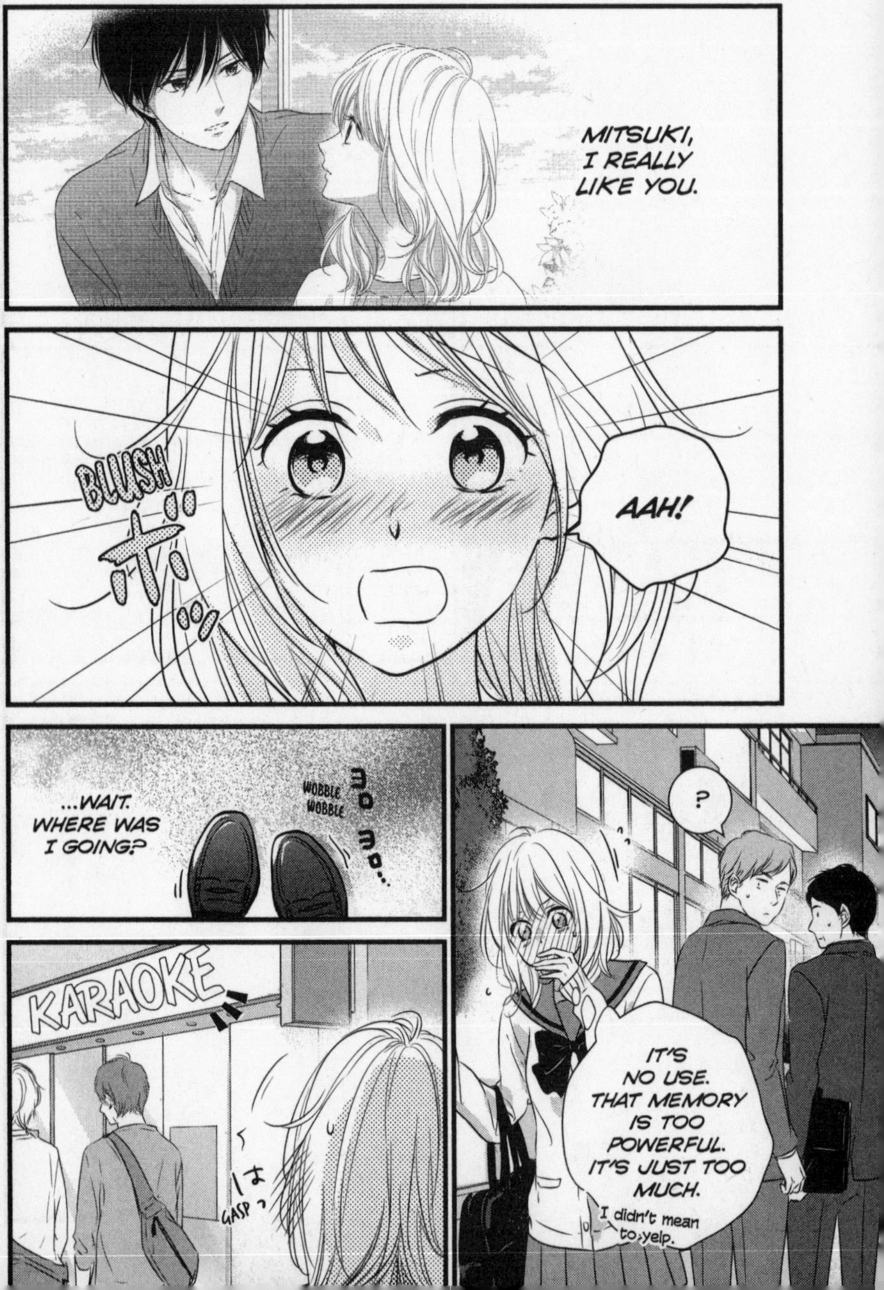

MITSUKI, I REALLY LIKE YOU.
AAH!
BLUSH
ボッ
?
IT'S NO USE. THAT MEMORY IS TOO POWERFUL. IT'S JUST TOO MUCH.
I didn't mean to yelp.
ヨロ ヨロ…
WOBBLE WOBBLE
...WAIT. WHERE WAS I GOING?
KARAOKE
はっ
GASP

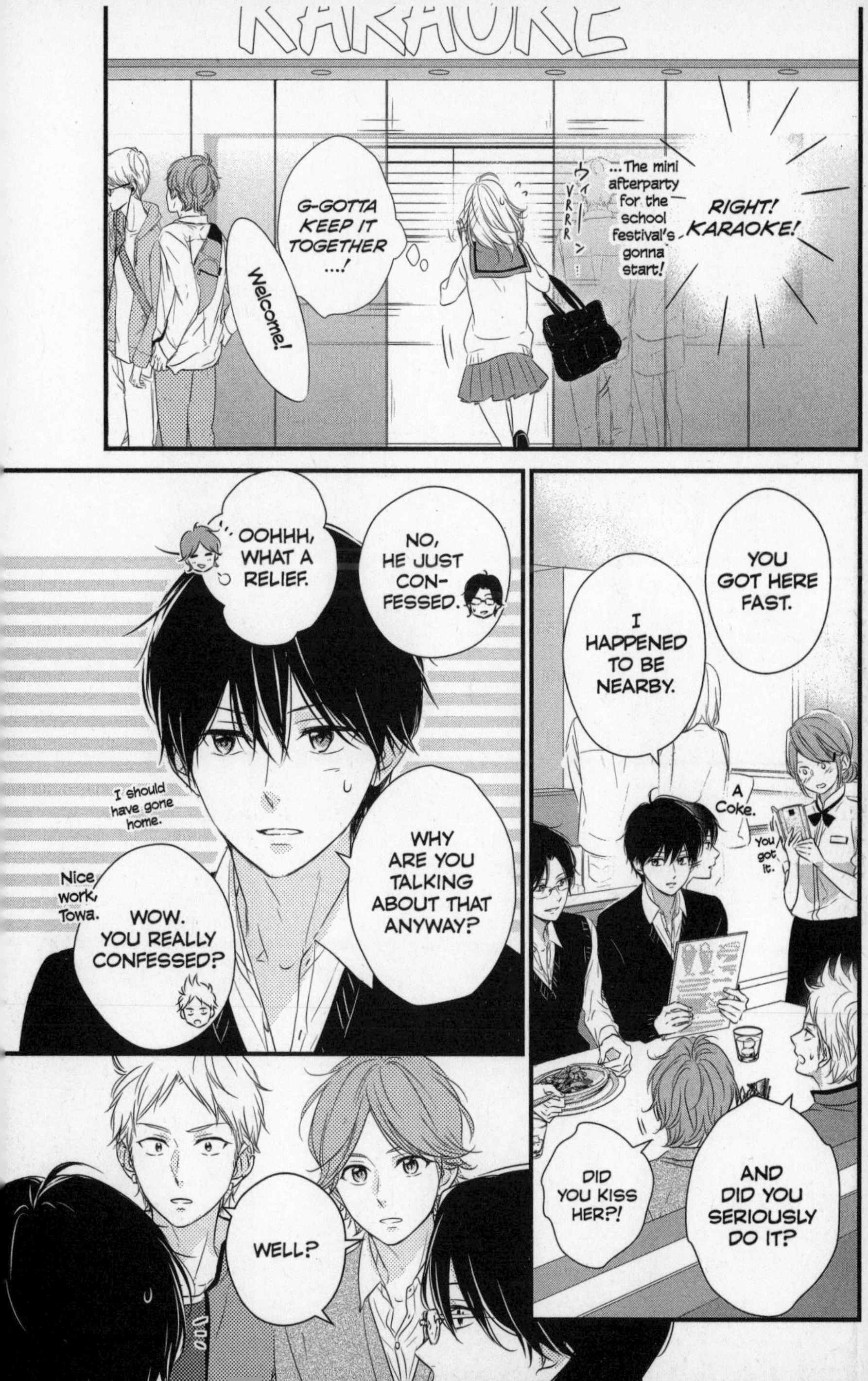
KARAOKE
RIGHT! KARAOKE!
...The mini afterparty for the school festival's gonna start!
VRRR
G-GOTTA KEEP IT TOGETHER ....!
Welcome!
YOU GOT HERE FAST.
I HAPPENED TO BE NEARBY.
A Coke.
You got it.
AND DID YOU SERIOUSLY DO IT?
DID YOU KISS HER?!
NO, HE JUST CON-FESSED.
OOHHH, WHAT A RELIEF.
WHY ARE YOU TALKING ABOUT THAT ANYWAY?
I should have gone home.
WOW. YOU REALLY CONFESSED?
Nice work, Towa.
WELL?

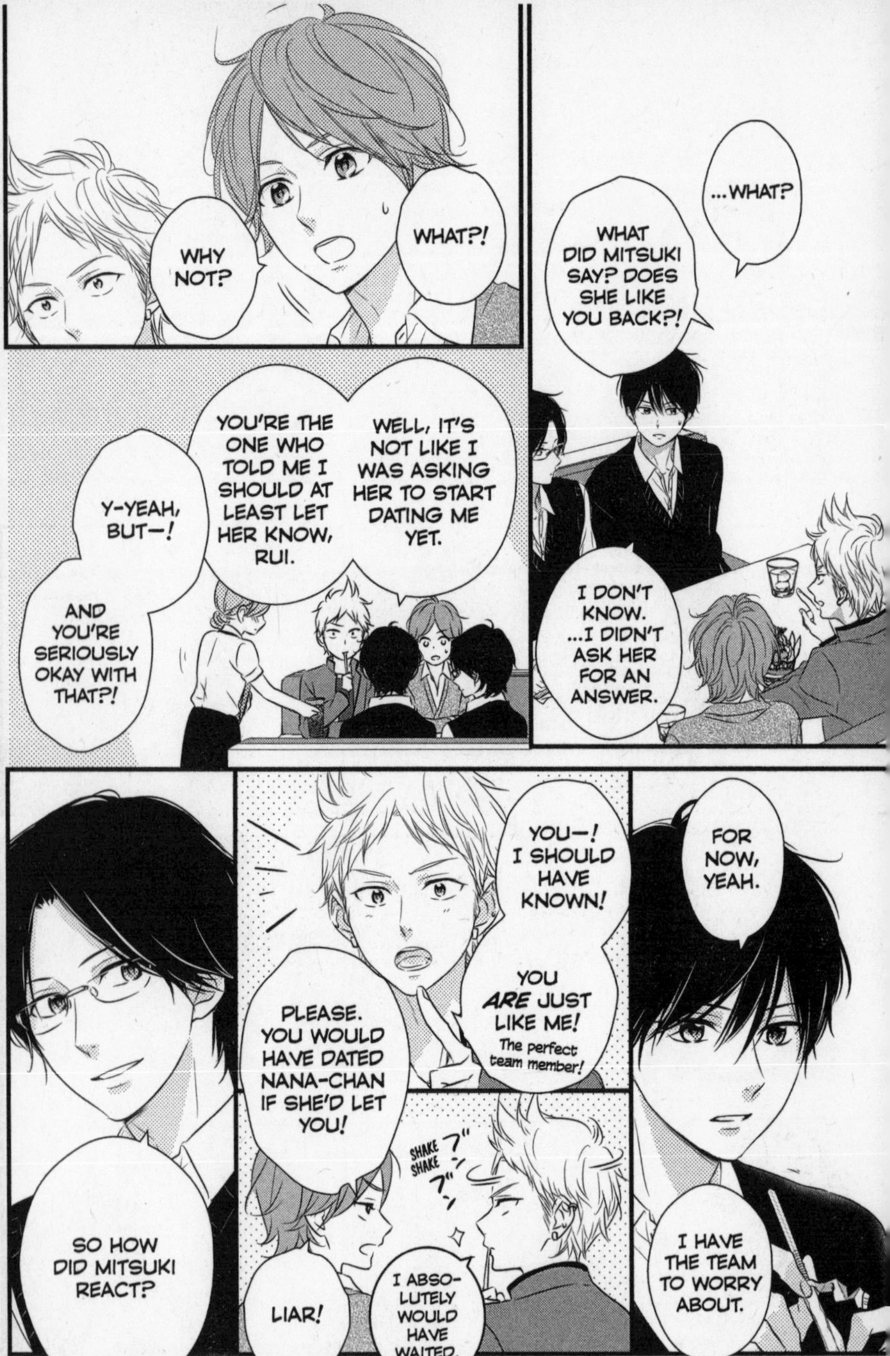
...WHAT?
WHAT DID MITSUKI SAY? DOES SHE LIKE YOU BACK?!
I DON'T KNOW. ...I DIDN'T ASK HER FOR AN ANSWER.
WHAT?!
WHY NOT?
WELL, IT'S NOT LIKE I WAS ASKING HER TO START DATING ME YET.
YOU'RE THE ONE WHO TOLD ME I SHOULD AT LEAST LET HER KNOW, RUI.
Y-YEAH, BUT—!
AND YOU'RE SERIOUSLY OKAY WITH THAT?!
FOR NOW, YEAH.
I HAVE THE TEAM TO WORRY ABOUT.
YOU—! I SHOULD HAVE KNOWN!
YOU *ARE* JUST LIKE ME!
The perfect team member!
PLEASE. YOU WOULD HAVE DATED NANA-CHAN IF SHE'D LET YOU!
SHAKE SHAKE
I ABSO-LUTELY WOULD HAVE WAITED.
LIAR!
SO HOW DID MITSUKI REACT?

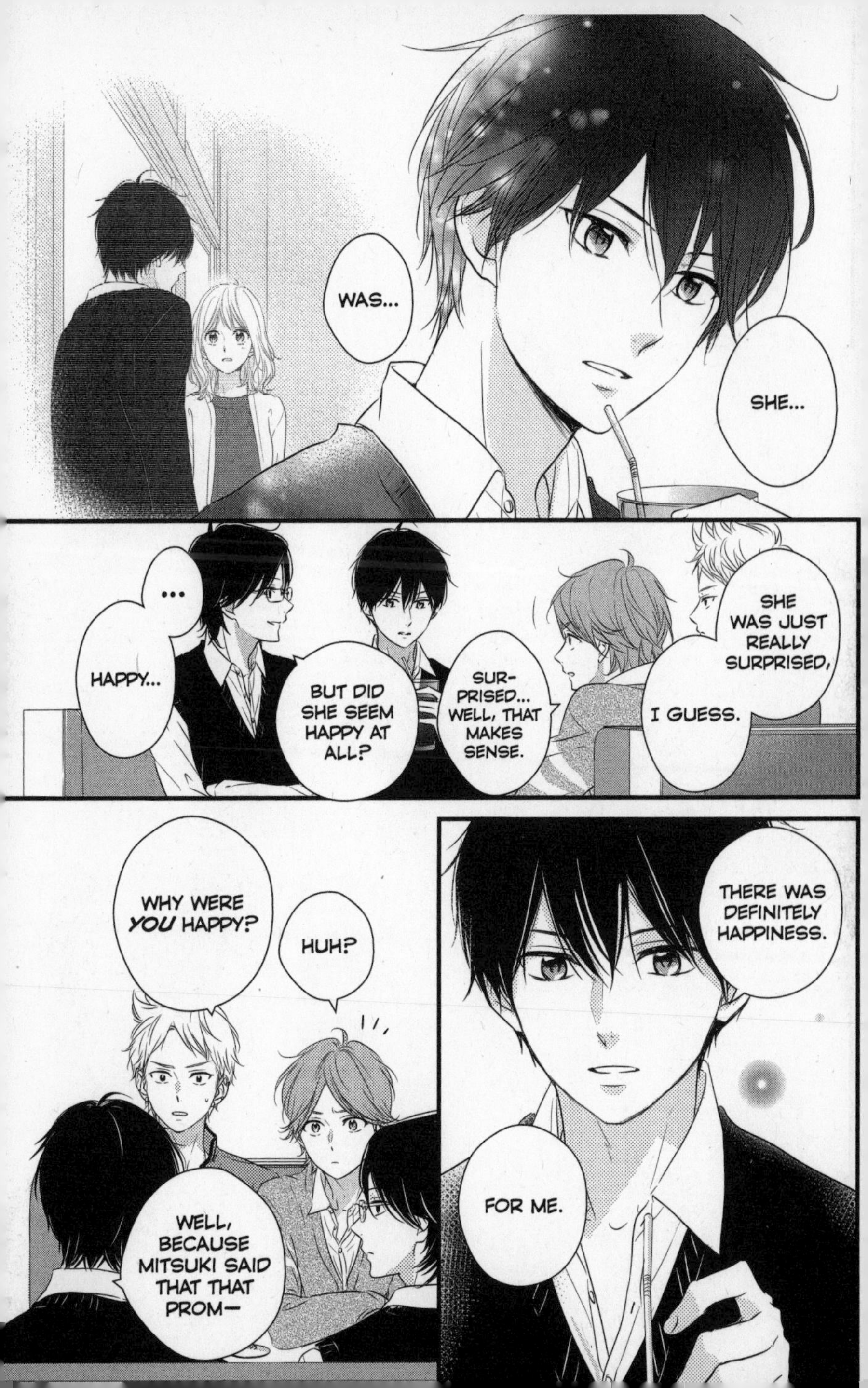
SHE...
WAS...
SHE WAS JUST REALLY SURPRISED,
I GUESS.
SUR-PRISED... WELL, THAT MAKES SENSE.
BUT DID SHE SEEM HAPPY AT ALL?
...
HAPPY...
THERE WAS DEFINITELY HAPPINESS.
FOR ME.
WHY WERE *YOU* HAPPY?
HUH?
WELL, BECAUSE MITSUKI SAID THAT THAT PROM—

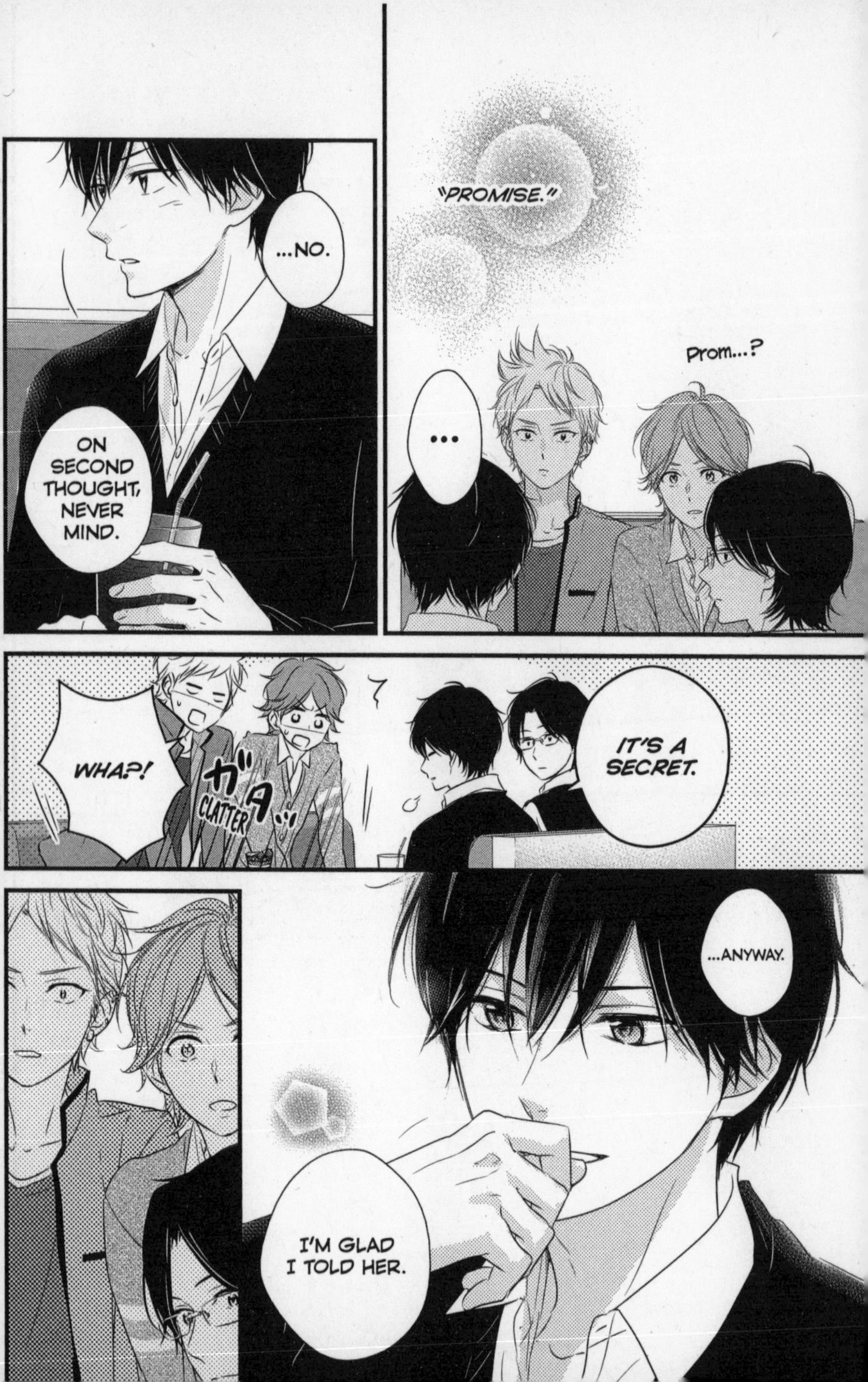
"PROMISE."
Prom...?
...
...NO.
ON SECOND THOUGHT, NEVER MIND.
IT'S A SECRET.
WHA?!
ガタッ
CLATTER
...ANYWAY.
I'M GLAD I TOLD HER.

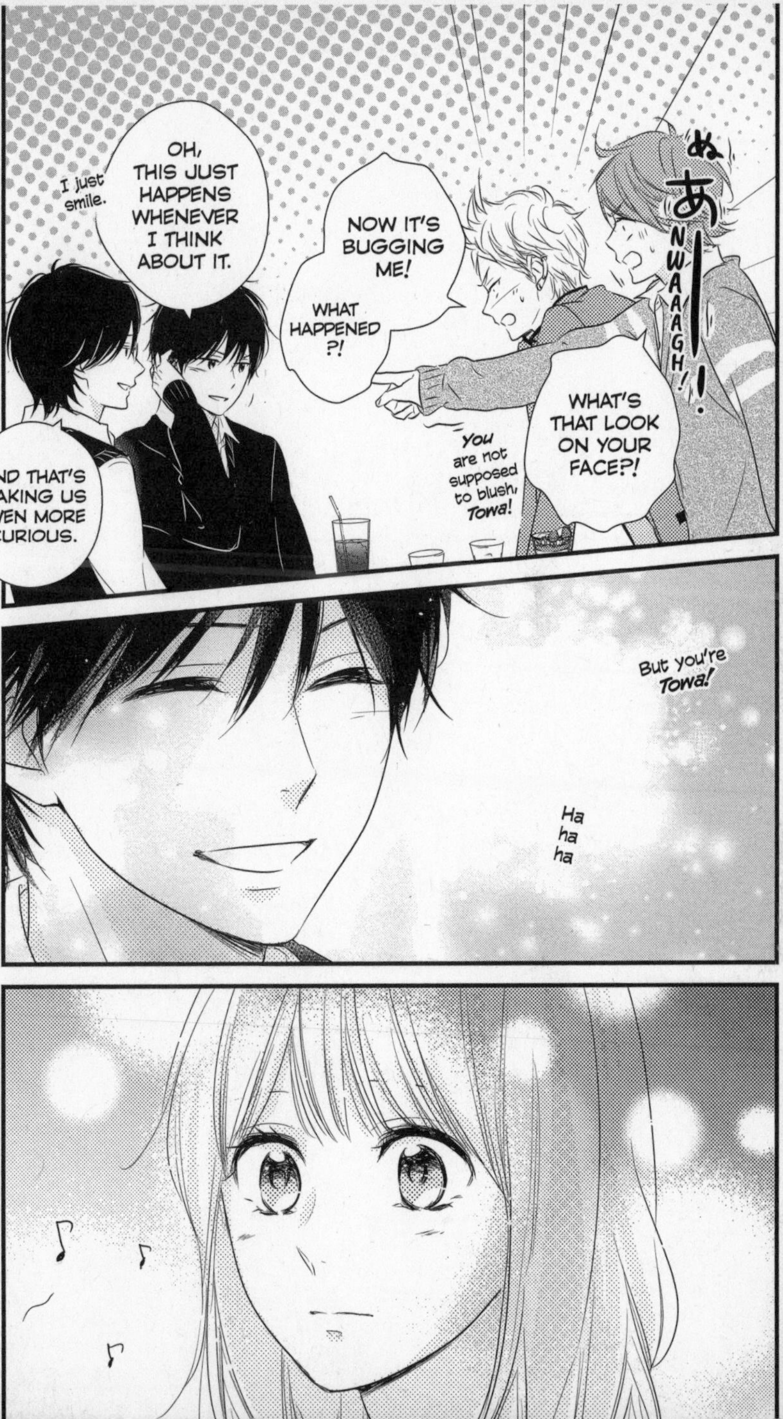
ぬあー!!
NWAAAGH!!
WHAT'S THAT LOOK ON YOUR FACE?!
You are not supposed to blush, Towa!
NOW IT'S BUGGING ME!
WHAT HAPPENED?!
OH, THIS JUST HAPPENS WHENEVER I THINK ABOUT IT.
I just smile.
AND THAT'S MAKING US EVEN MORE CURIOUS.
But you're Towa!
Ha ha ha

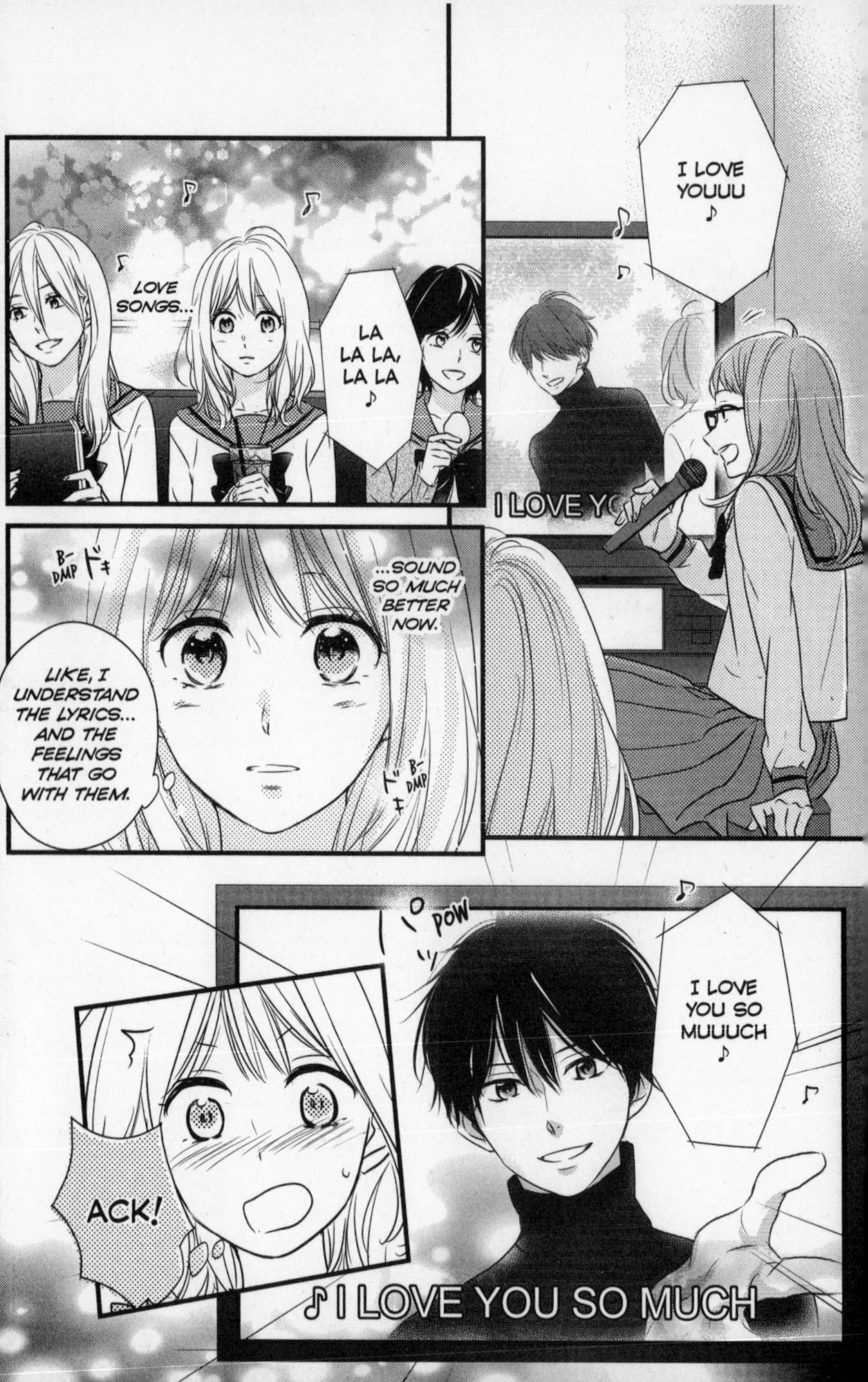

I LOVE YOUUU ♪
I LOVE YO
LA LA LA, LA LA ♪
LOVE SONGS...
B-DMP ドキ
...SOUND SO MUCH BETTER NOW.
LIKE, I UNDERSTAND THE LYRICS... AND THE FEELINGS THAT GO WITH THEM.
B-DMP ドキ
POW
I LOVE YOU SO MUUUCH ♪
♪ I LOVE YOU SO MUCH
ACK!

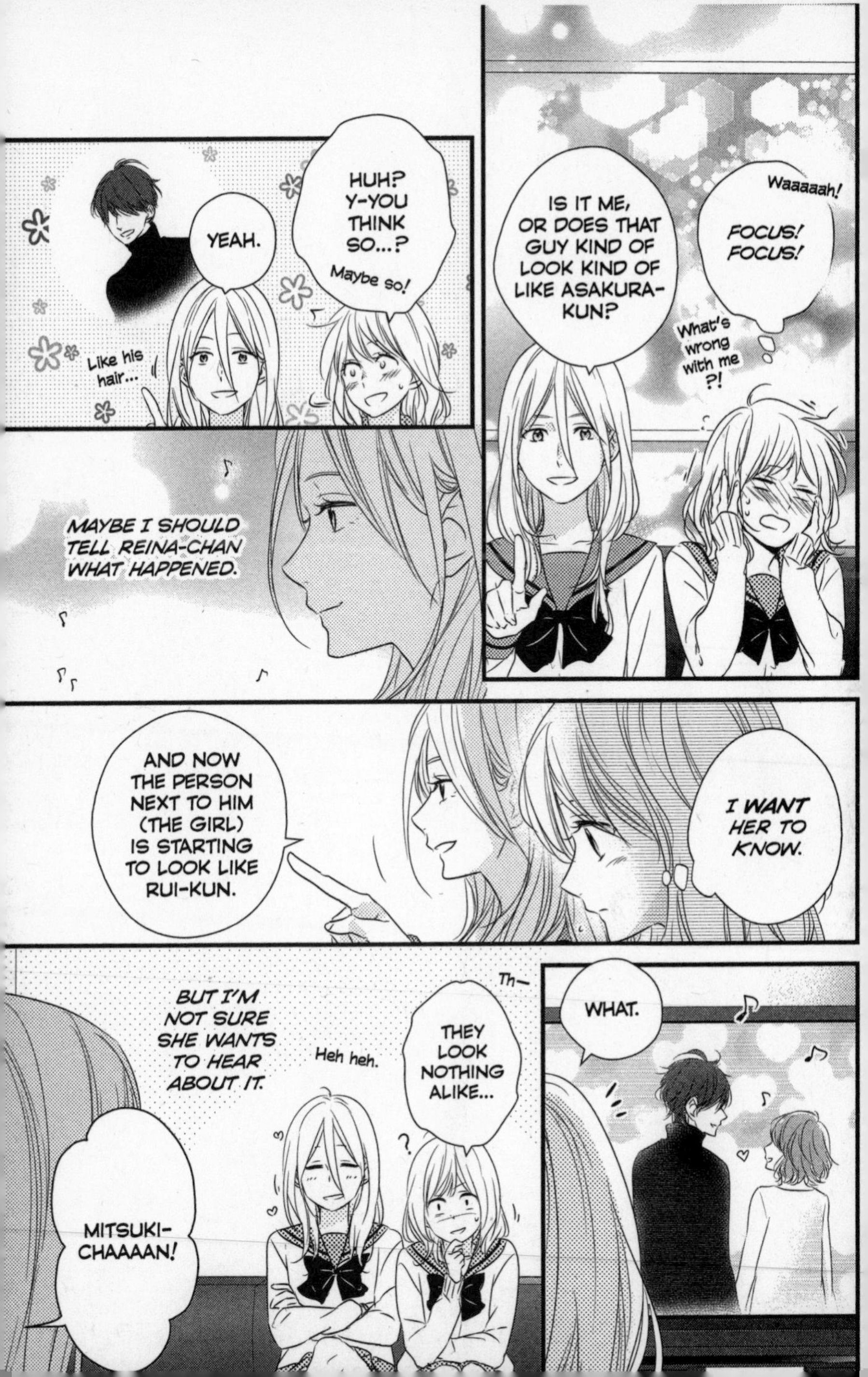
IS IT ME, OR DOES THAT GUY KIND OF LOOK KIND OF LIKE ASAKURA-KUN?
Waaaaah!
FOCUS! FOCUS!
What's wrong with me ?!
HUH? Y-YOU THINK SO...?
Maybe so!
YEAH.
Like his hair...
MAYBE I SHOULD TELL REINA-CHAN WHAT HAPPENED.
I WANT HER TO KNOW.
AND NOW THE PERSON NEXT TO HIM (THE GIRL) IS STARTING TO LOOK LIKE RUI-KUN.
WHAT.
Th—
THEY LOOK NOTHING ALIKE...
Heh heh.
BUT I'M NOT SURE SHE WANTS TO HEAR ABOUT IT.
MITSUKI-CHAAAAN!

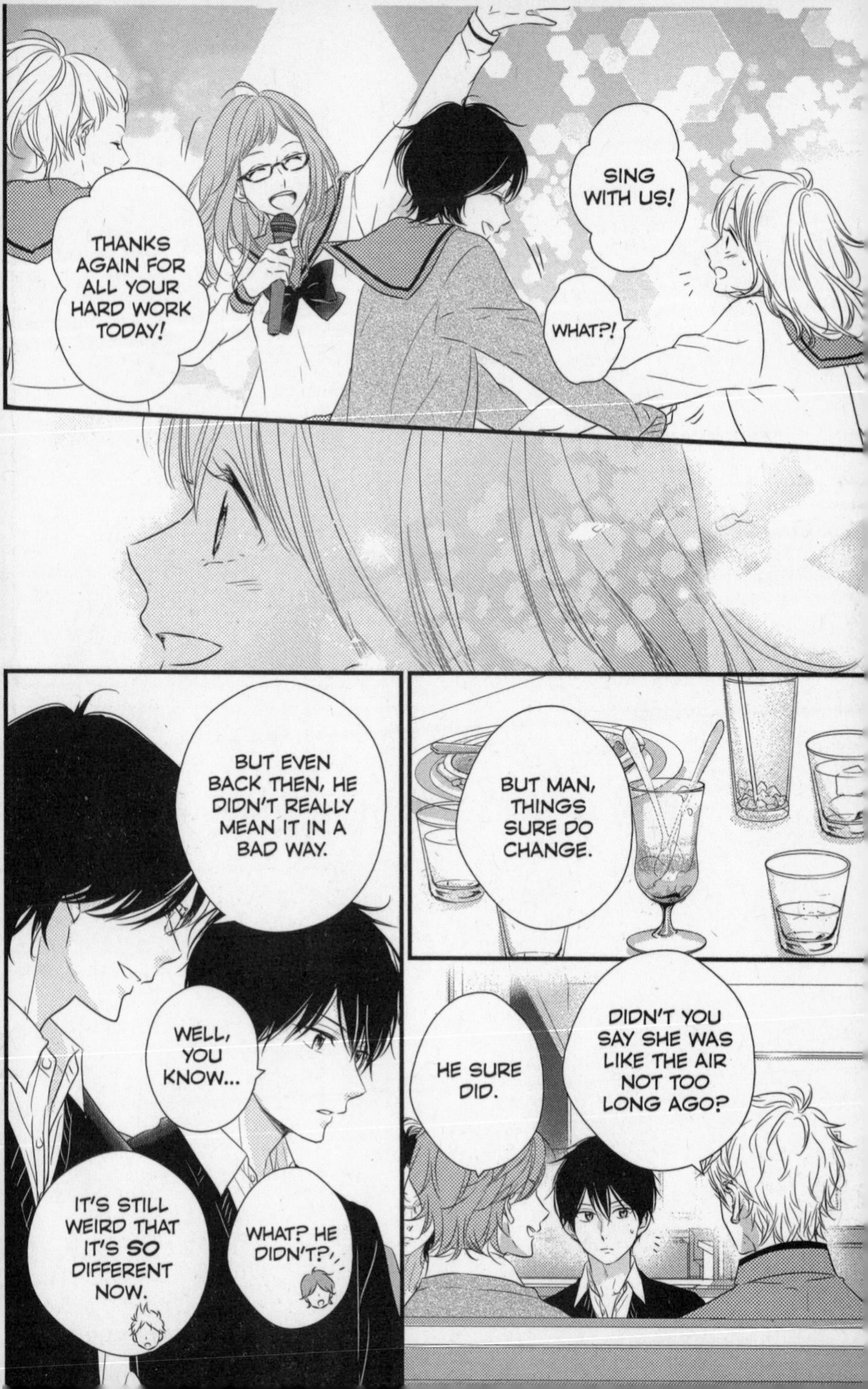
SING WITH US!
WHAT?!
THANKS AGAIN FOR ALL YOUR HARD WORK TODAY!
BUT MAN, THINGS SURE DO CHANGE.
DIDN'T YOU SAY SHE WAS LIKE THE AIR NOT TOO LONG AGO?
HE SURE DID.
BUT EVEN BACK THEN, HE DIDN'T REALLY MEAN IT IN A BAD WAY.
WELL, YOU KNOW...
WHAT? HE DIDN'T?
IT'S STILL WEIRD THAT IT'S **SO** DIFFERENT NOW.

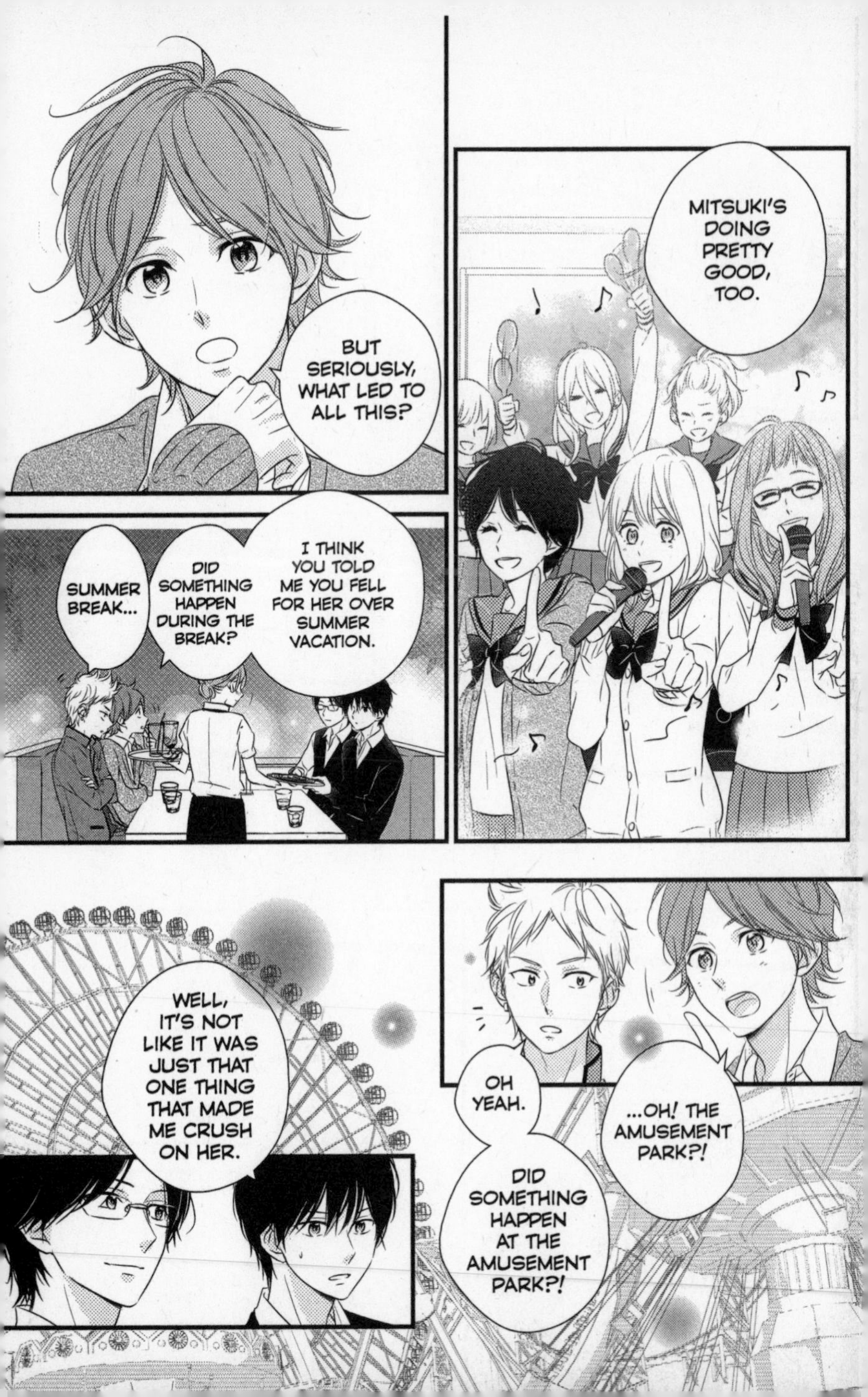
MITSUKI'S DOING PRETTY GOOD, TOO.
BUT SERIOUSLY, WHAT LED TO ALL THIS?
I THINK YOU TOLD ME YOU FELL FOR HER OVER SUMMER VACATION.
DID SOMETHING HAPPEN DURING THE BREAK?
SUMMER BREAK...
...OH! THE AMUSEMENT PARK?!
OH YEAH.
DID SOMETHING HAPPEN AT THE AMUSEMENT PARK?!
WELL, IT'S NOT LIKE IT WAS JUST THAT ONE THING THAT MADE ME CRUSH ON HER.

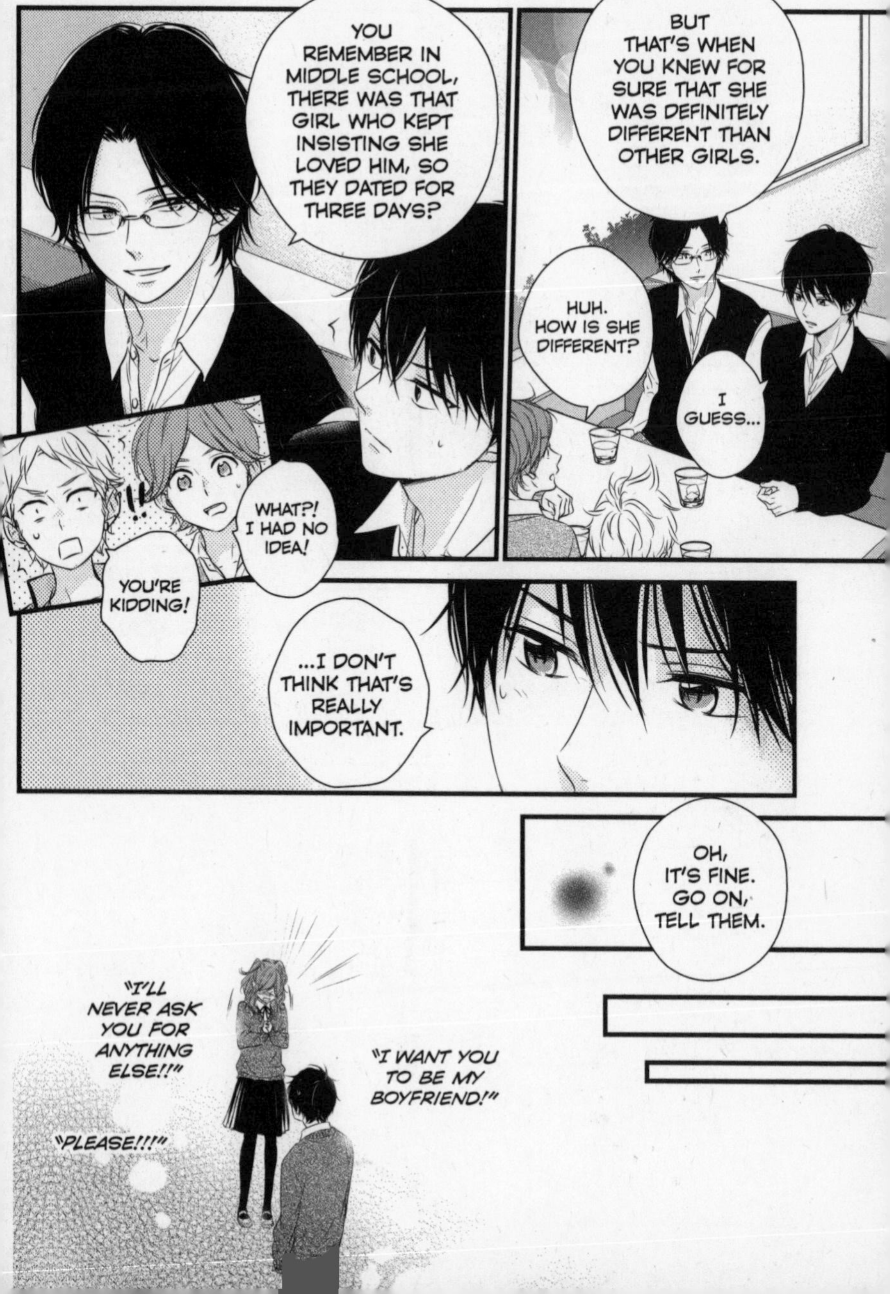
BUT THAT'S WHEN YOU KNEW FOR SURE THAT SHE WAS DEFINITELY DIFFERENT THAN OTHER GIRLS.
HUH. HOW IS SHE DIFFERENT?
I GUESS...
YOU REMEMBER IN MIDDLE SCHOOL, THERE WAS THAT GIRL WHO KEPT INSISTING SHE LOVED HIM, SO THEY DATED FOR THREE DAYS?
!!
WHAT?! I HAD NO IDEA!
YOU'RE KIDDING!
...I DON'T THINK THAT'S REALLY IMPORTANT.
OH, IT'S FINE. GO ON, TELL THEM.
"I WANT YOU TO BE MY BOYFRIEND!"
"I'LL NEVER ASK YOU FOR ANYTHING ELSE!!"
"PLEASE!!!"

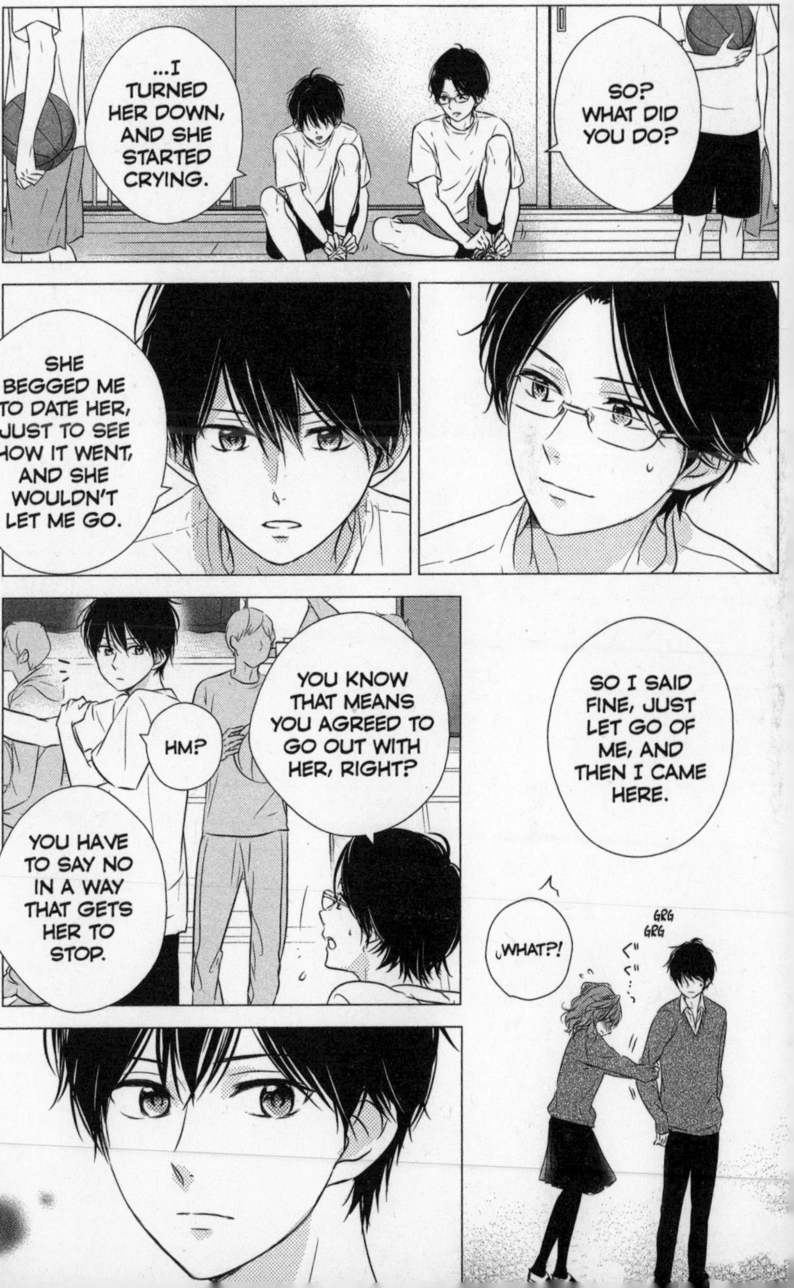
SO? WHAT DID YOU DO?
...I TURNED HER DOWN, AND SHE STARTED CRYING.
SHE BEGGED ME TO DATE HER, JUST TO SEE HOW IT WENT, AND SHE WOULDN'T LET ME GO.
SO I SAID FINE, JUST LET GO OF ME, AND THEN I CAME HERE.
YOU KNOW THAT MEANS YOU AGREED TO GO OUT WITH HER, RIGHT?
HM?
YOU HAVE TO SAY NO IN A WAY THAT GETS HER TO STOP.
WHAT?!
GRG GRG

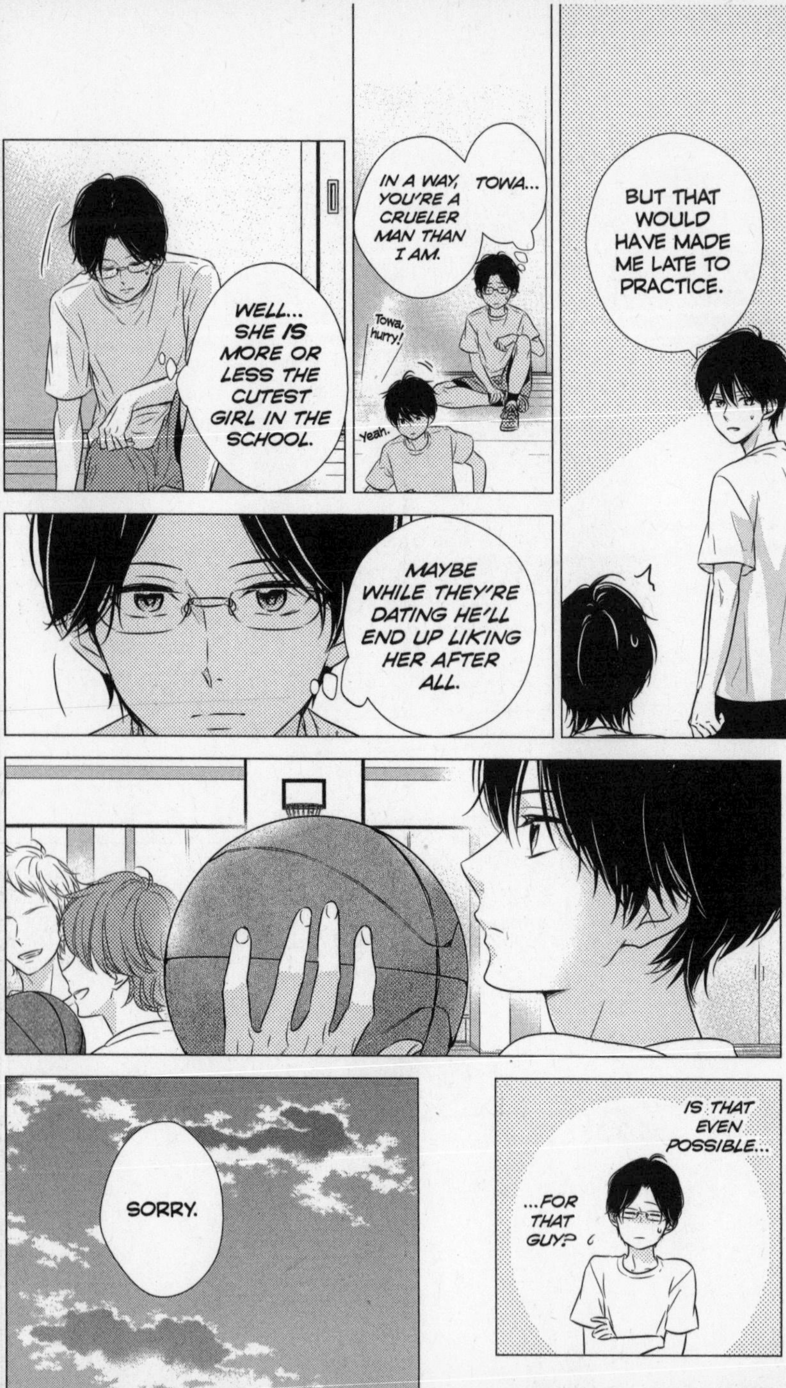
BUT THAT WOULD HAVE MADE ME LATE TO PRACTICE.
TOWA...
IN A WAY, YOU'RE A CRUELER MAN THAN I AM.
Towa, hurry!
Yeah.
WELL... SHE *IS* MORE OR LESS THE CUTEST GIRL IN THE SCHOOL.
MAYBE WHILE THEY'RE DATING HE'LL END UP LIKING HER AFTER ALL.
IS THAT EVEN POSSIBLE...
...FOR THAT GUY?
SORRY.

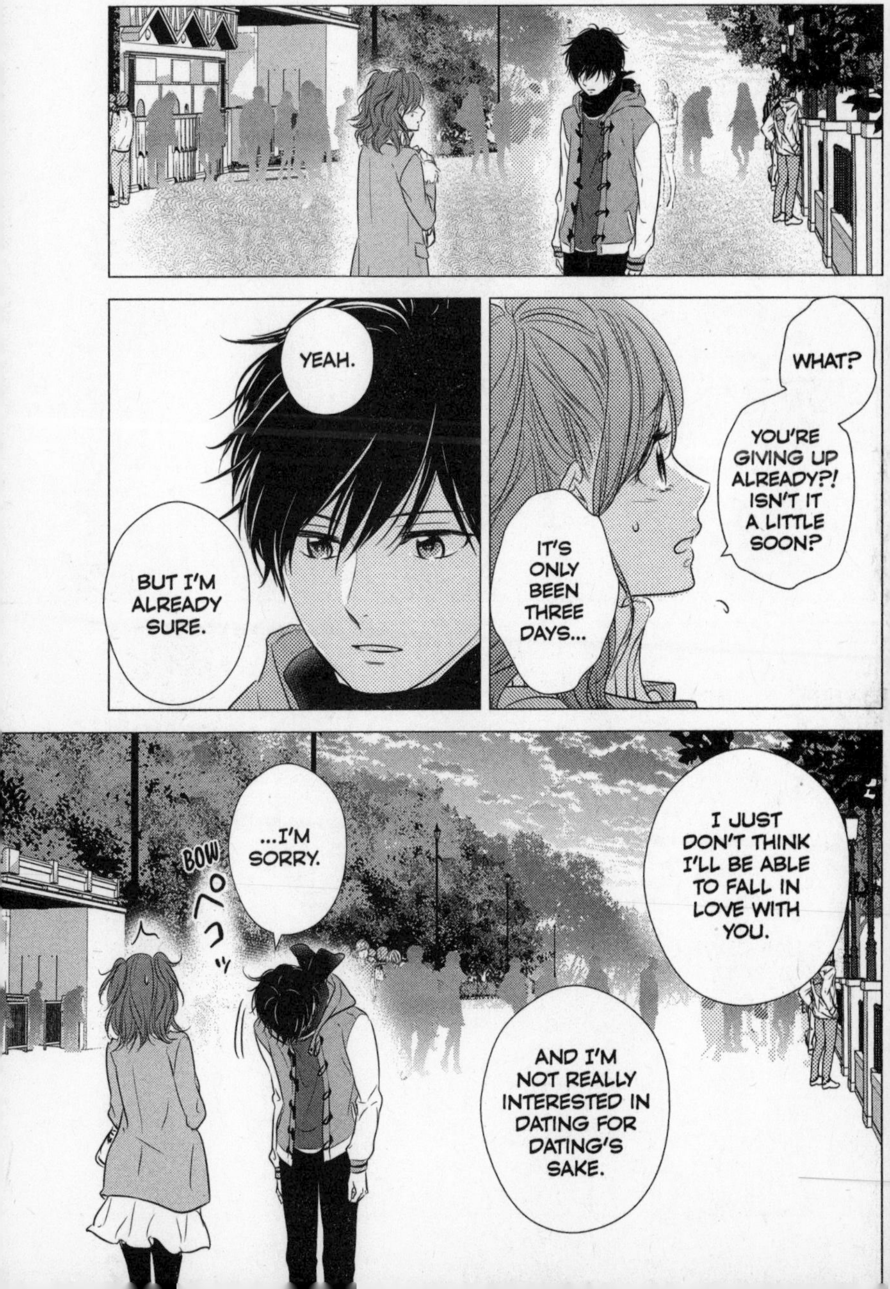
WHAT?
YOU'RE GIVING UP ALREADY?! ISN'T IT A LITTLE SOON?
IT'S ONLY BEEN THREE DAYS...
YEAH.
BUT I'M ALREADY SURE.
I JUST DON'T THINK I'LL BE ABLE TO FALL IN LOVE WITH YOU.
AND I'M NOT REALLY INTERESTED IN DATING FOR DATING'S SAKE.
...I'M SORRY.
BOW
ペコッ

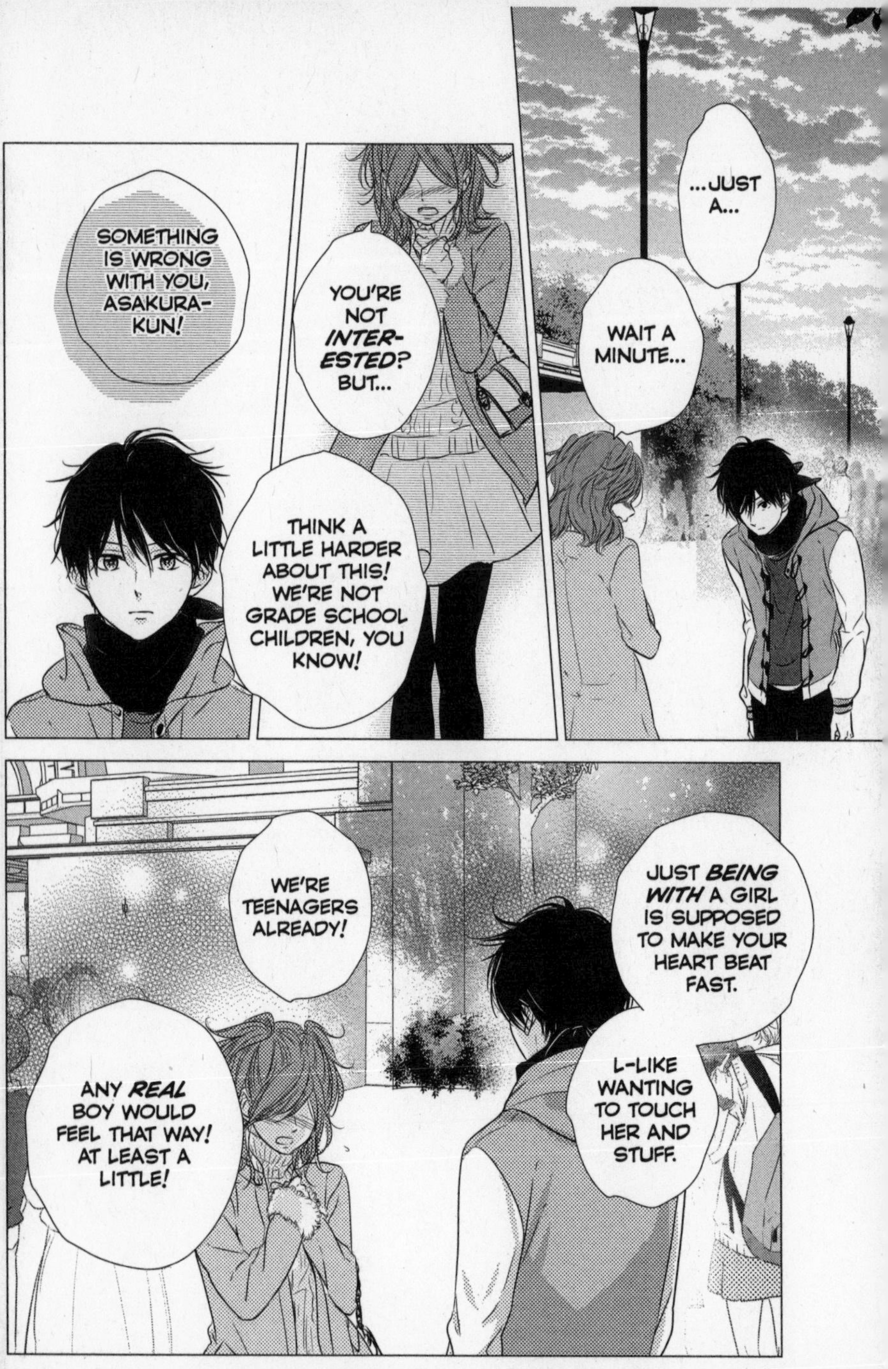
...JUST A...
WAIT A MINUTE...
YOU'RE NOT INTERESTED? BUT...
THINK A LITTLE HARDER ABOUT THIS! WE'RE NOT GRADE SCHOOL CHILDREN, YOU KNOW!
SOMETHING IS WRONG WITH YOU, ASAKURA-KUN!
JUST BEING WITH A GIRL IS SUPPOSED TO MAKE YOUR HEART BEAT FAST.
L-LIKE WANTING TO TOUCH HER AND STUFF.
WE'RE TEENAGERS ALREADY!
ANY REAL BOY WOULD FEEL THAT WAY! AT LEAST A LITTLE!

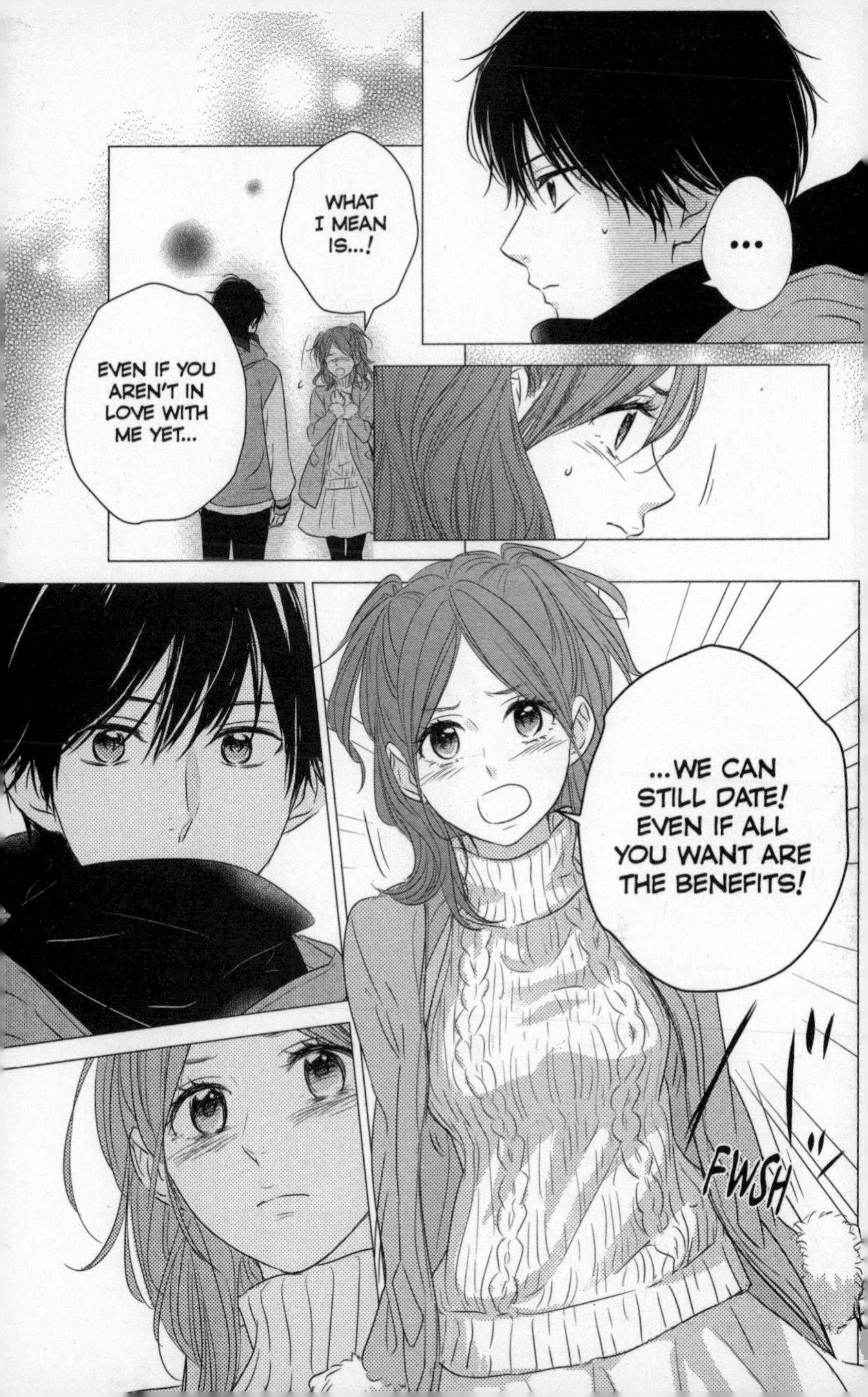
...
WHAT I MEAN IS...!
EVEN IF YOU AREN'T IN LOVE WITH ME YET...
...WE CAN STILL DATE! EVEN IF ALL YOU WANT ARE THE BENEFITS!
FWSH

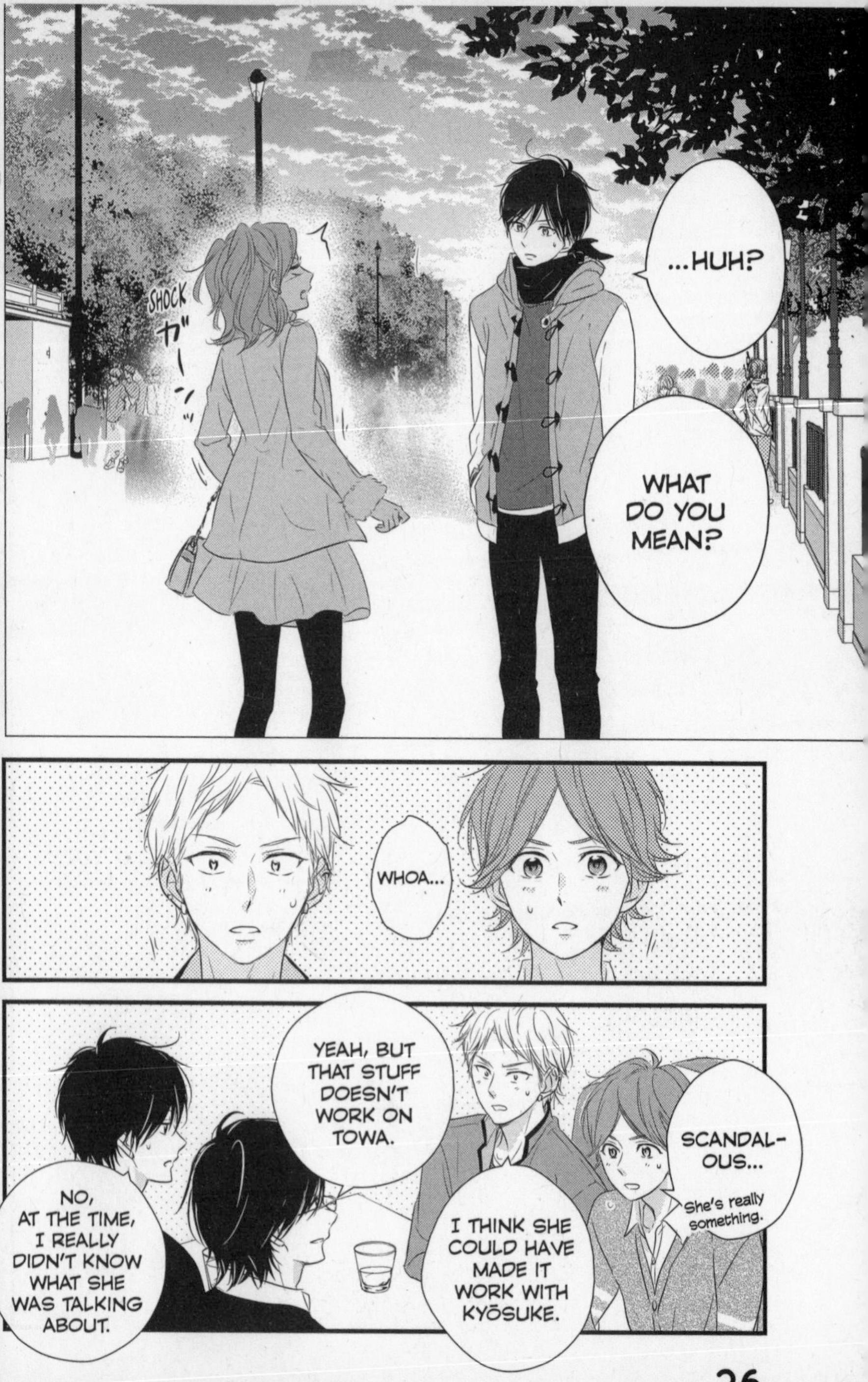
...HUH?
WHAT DO YOU MEAN?
SHOCK
ガーン
WHOA...
SCANDAL-OUS...
She's really something.
YEAH, BUT THAT STUFF DOESN'T WORK ON TOWA.
I THINK SHE COULD HAVE MADE IT WORK WITH KYŌSUKE.
NO, AT THE TIME, I REALLY DIDN'T KNOW WHAT SHE WAS TALKING ABOUT.

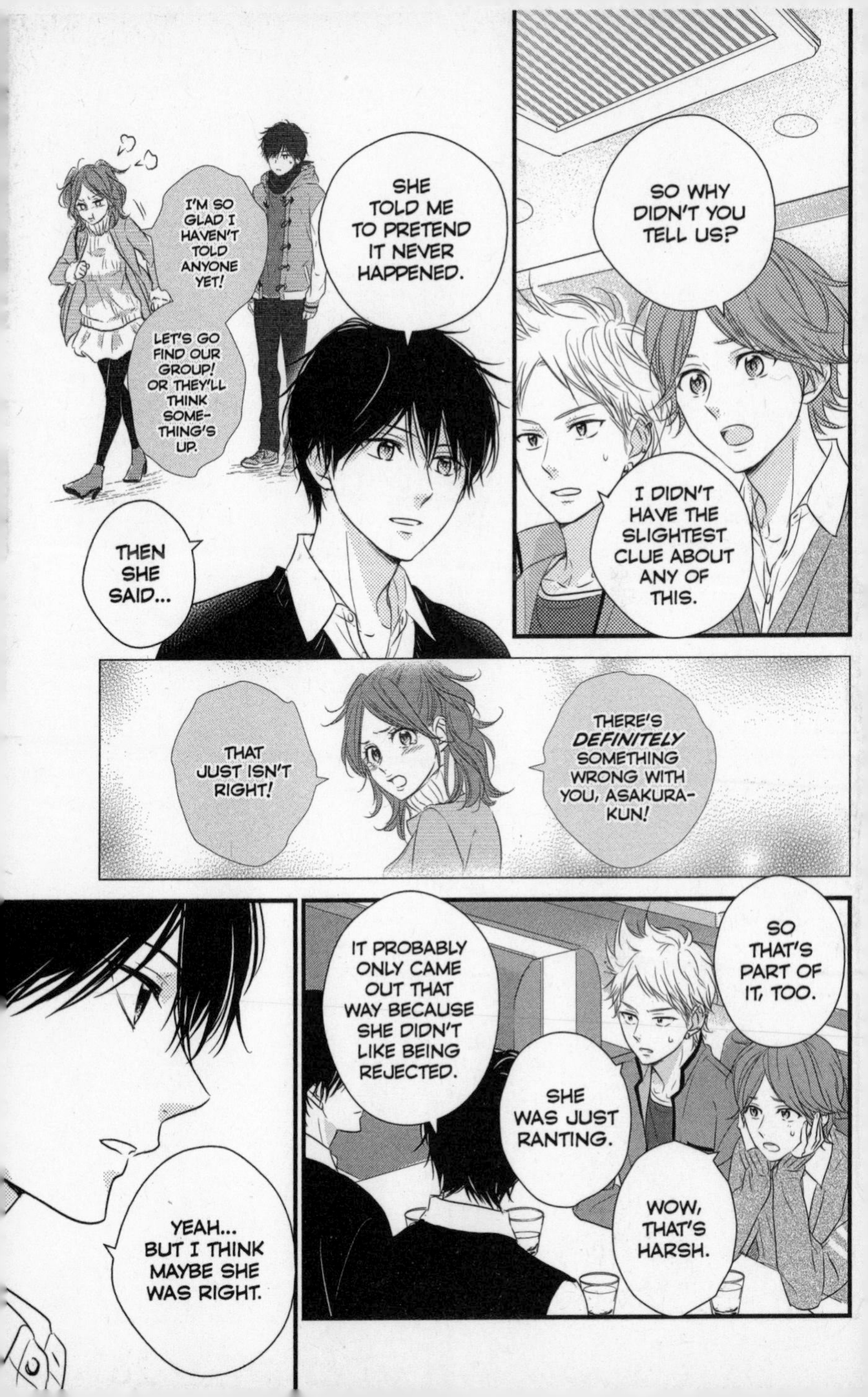
SO WHY DIDN'T YOU TELL US?
I DIDN'T HAVE THE SLIGHTEST CLUE ABOUT ANY OF THIS.
SHE TOLD ME TO PRETEND IT NEVER HAPPENED.
I'M SO GLAD I HAVEN'T TOLD ANYONE YET!
LET'S GO FIND OUR GROUP! OR THEY'LL THINK SOME-THING'S UP.
THEN SHE SAID...
THERE'S *DEFINITELY* SOMETHING WRONG WITH YOU, ASAKURA-KUN!
THAT JUST ISN'T RIGHT!
SO THAT'S PART OF IT, TOO.
IT PROBABLY ONLY CAME OUT THAT WAY BECAUSE SHE DIDN'T LIKE BEING REJECTED.
SHE WAS JUST RANTING.
WOW, THAT'S HARSH.
YEAH... BUT I THINK MAYBE SHE WAS RIGHT.

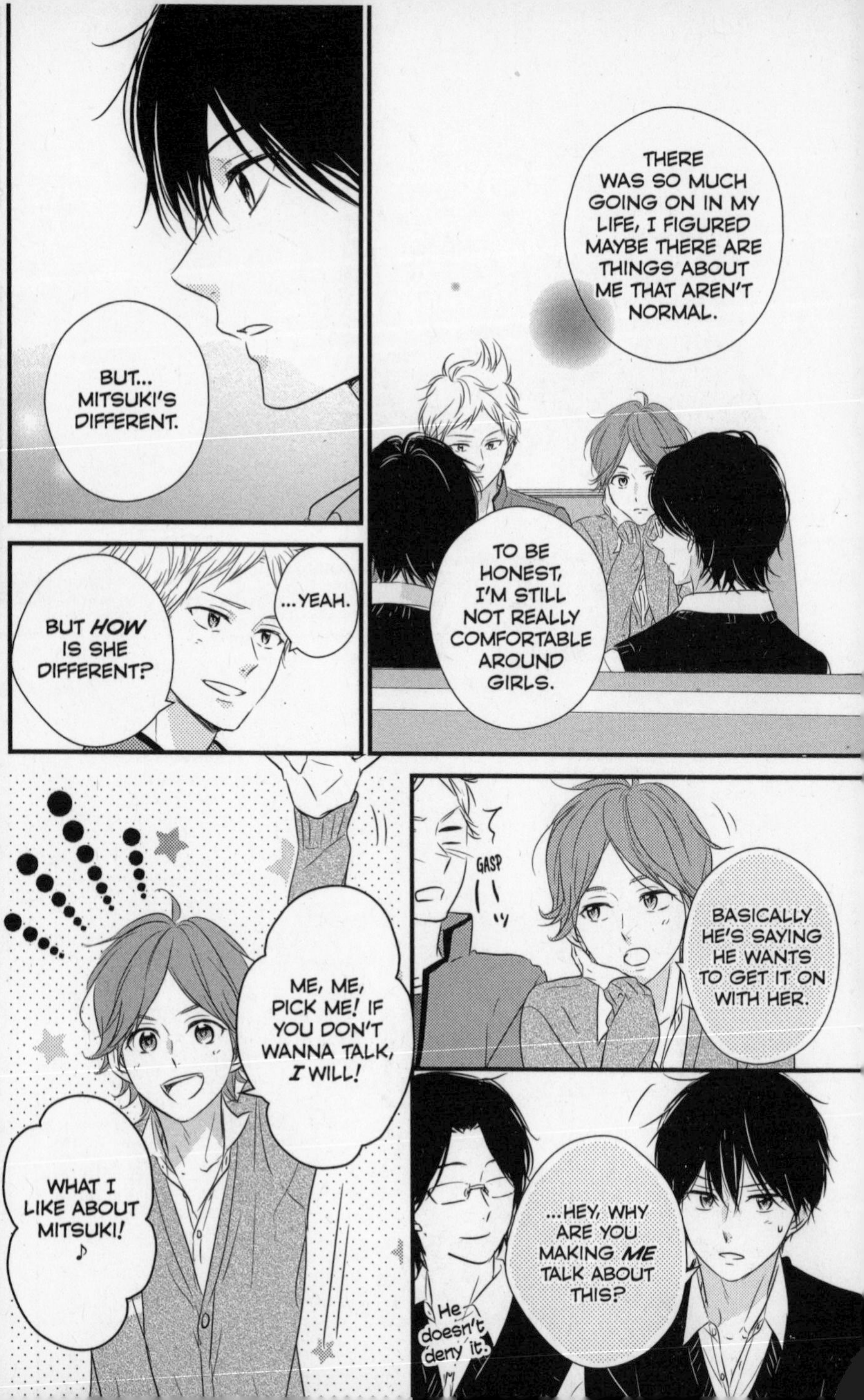
THERE WAS SO MUCH GOING ON IN MY LIFE, I FIGURED MAYBE THERE ARE THINGS ABOUT ME THAT AREN'T NORMAL.
TO BE HONEST, I'M STILL NOT REALLY COMFORTABLE AROUND GIRLS.
BUT... MITSUKI'S DIFFERENT.
...YEAH.
BUT *HOW* IS SHE DIFFERENT?
GASP
BASICALLY HE'S SAYING HE WANTS TO GET IT ON WITH HER.
...HEY, WHY ARE YOU MAKING *ME* TALK ABOUT THIS?
He doesn't deny it.
ME, ME, PICK ME! IF YOU DON'T WANNA TALK, *I* WILL!
WHAT I LIKE ABOUT MITSUKI! ♪

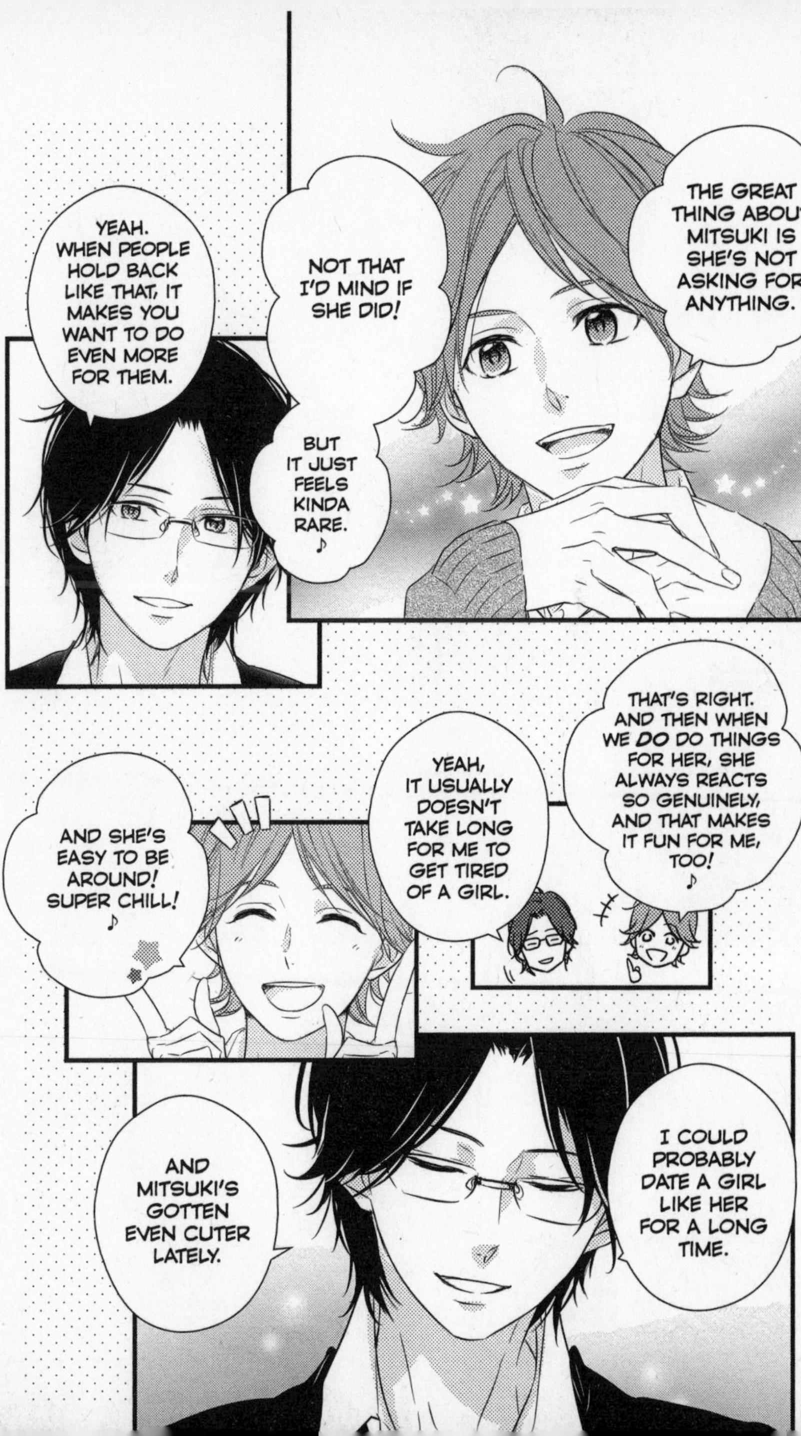
THE GREAT THING ABOUT MITSUKI IS SHE'S NOT ASKING FOR ANYTHING.
NOT THAT I'D MIND IF SHE DID!
BUT IT JUST FEELS KINDA RARE. ♪
YEAH. WHEN PEOPLE HOLD BACK LIKE THAT, IT MAKES YOU WANT TO DO EVEN MORE FOR THEM.
THAT'S RIGHT. AND THEN WHEN WE *DO* DO THINGS FOR HER, SHE ALWAYS REACTS SO GENUINELY, AND THAT MAKES IT FUN FOR ME, TOO! ♪
YEAH, IT USUALLY DOESN'T TAKE LONG FOR ME TO GET TIRED OF A GIRL.
AND SHE'S EASY TO BE AROUND! SUPER CHILL! ♪
I COULD PROBABLY DATE A GIRL LIKE HER FOR A LONG TIME.
AND MITSUKI'S GOTTEN EVEN CUTER LATELY.

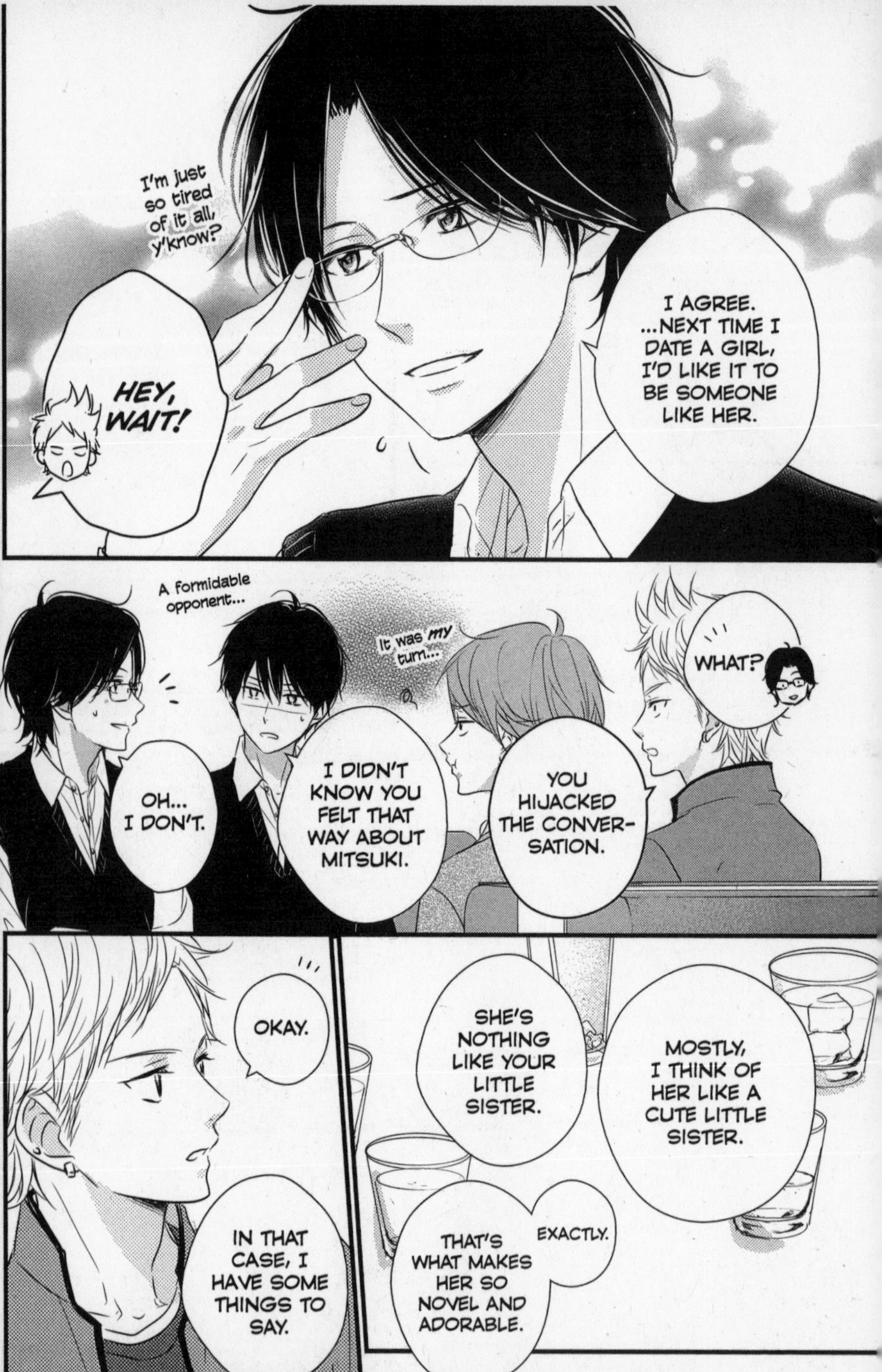
I AGREE. ...NEXT TIME I DATE A GIRL, I'D LIKE IT TO BE SOMEONE LIKE HER.
I'm just so tired of it all, y'know?
HEY, WAIT!
WHAT?
YOU HIJACKED THE CONVER-SATION.
It was *my* turn...
I DIDN'T KNOW YOU FELT THAT WAY ABOUT MITSUKI.
A formidable opponent...
OH... I DON'T.
MOSTLY, I THINK OF HER LIKE A CUTE LITTLE SISTER.
SHE'S NOTHING LIKE YOUR LITTLE SISTER.
EXACTLY.
THAT'S WHAT MAKES HER SO NOVEL AND ADORABLE.
OKAY.
IN THAT CASE, I HAVE SOME THINGS TO SAY.

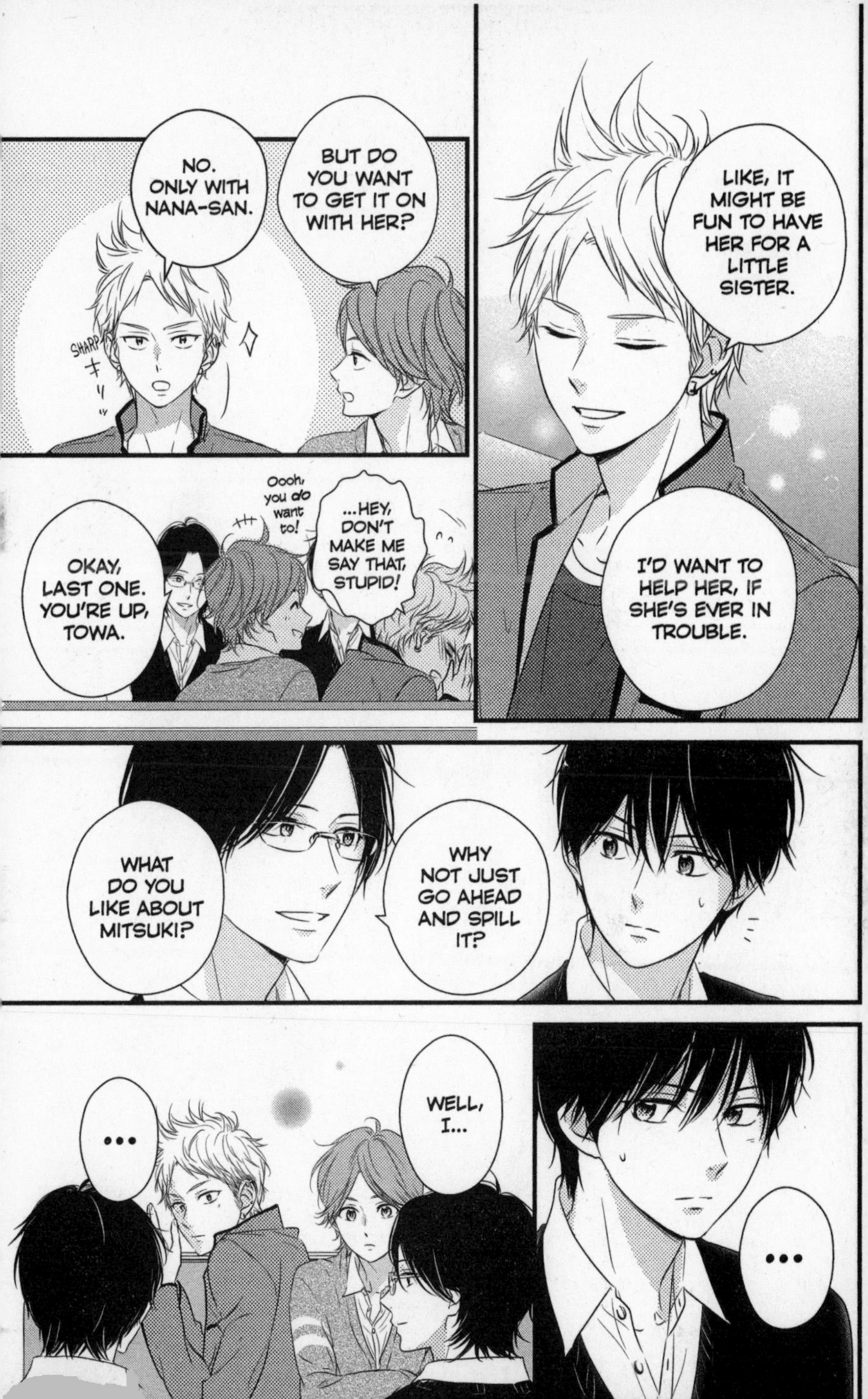
LIKE, IT MIGHT BE FUN TO HAVE HER FOR A LITTLE SISTER.
I'D WANT TO HELP HER, IF SHE'S EVER IN TROUBLE.
BUT DO YOU WANT TO GET IT ON WITH HER?
NO. ONLY WITH NANA-SAN.
SHARP
...HEY, DON'T MAKE ME SAY THAT, STUPID!
Oooh, you do want to!
OKAY, LAST ONE. YOU'RE UP, TOWA.
WHY NOT JUST GO AHEAD AND SPILL IT?
WHAT DO YOU LIKE ABOUT MITSUKI?
...
WELL, I...
...

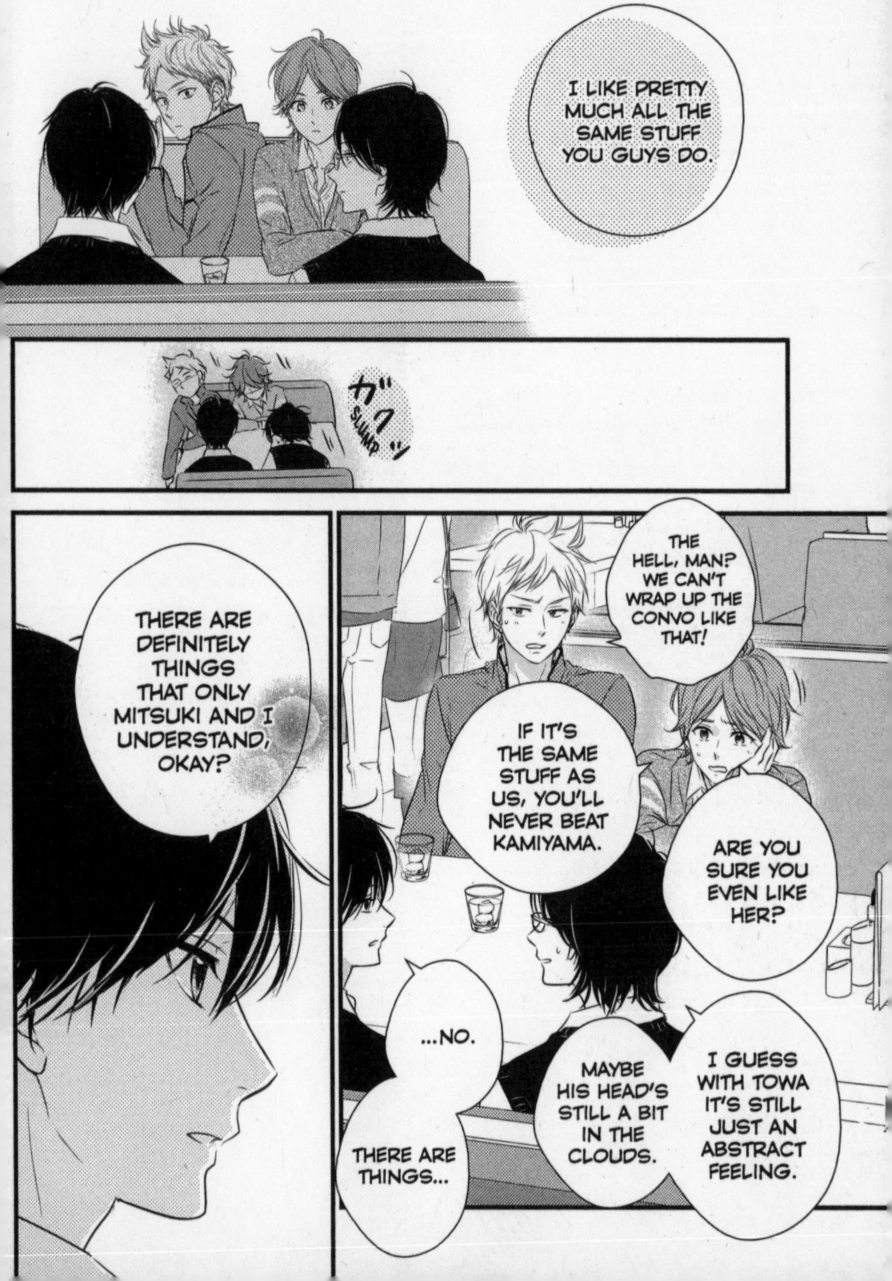
I LIKE PRETTY MUCH ALL THE SAME STUFF YOU GUYS DO.
ガクッ
SLUMP
THE HELL, MAN? WE CAN'T WRAP UP THE CONVO LIKE THAT!
IF IT'S THE SAME STUFF AS US, YOU'LL NEVER BEAT KAMIYAMA.
ARE YOU SURE YOU EVEN LIKE HER?
I GUESS WITH TOWA IT'S STILL JUST AN ABSTRACT FEELING.
MAYBE HIS HEAD'S STILL A BIT IN THE CLOUDS.
...NO.
THERE ARE THINGS...
THERE ARE DEFINITELY THINGS THAT ONLY MITSUKI AND I UNDERSTAND, OKAY?

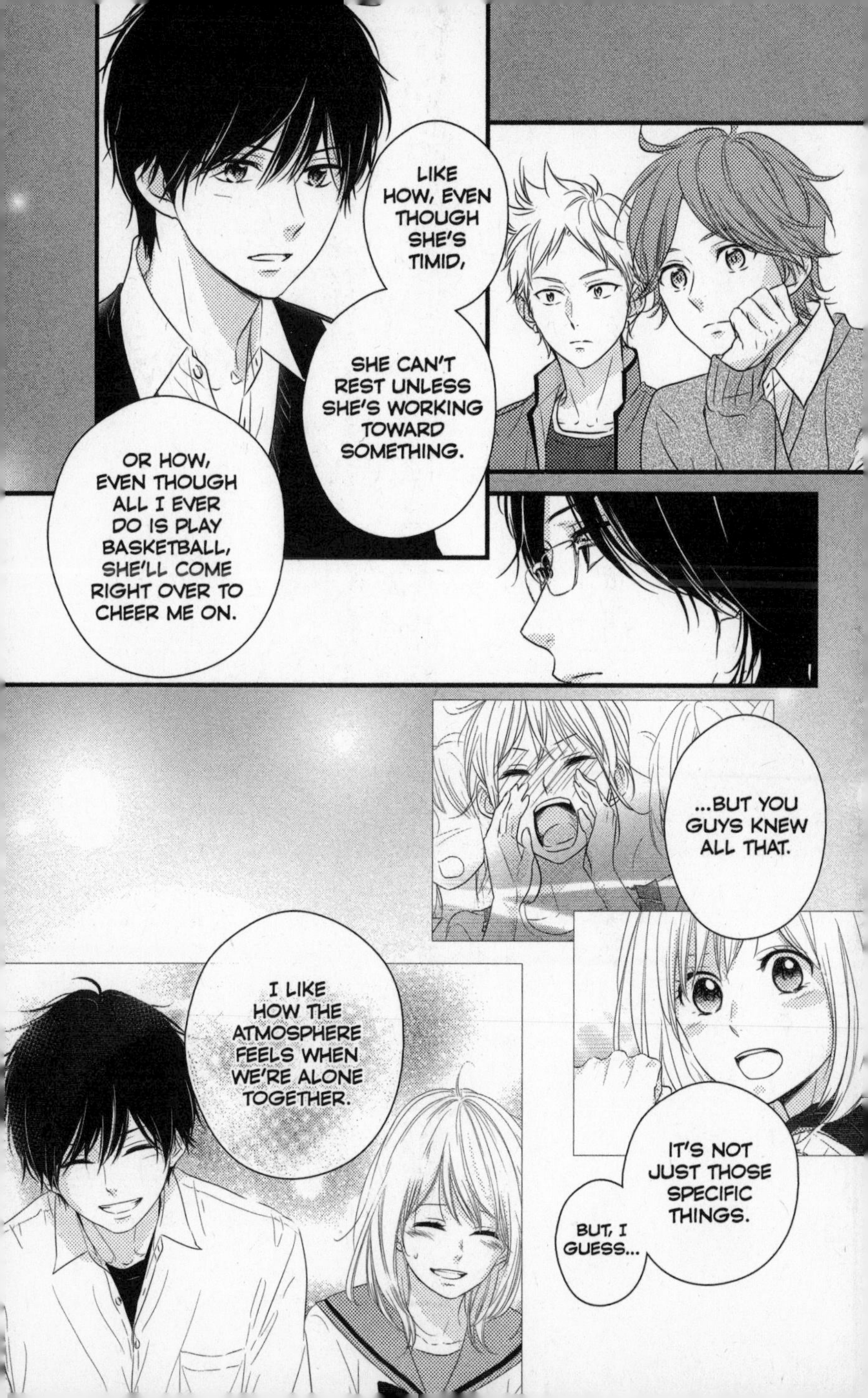
LIKE HOW, EVEN THOUGH SHE'S TIMID,
SHE CAN'T REST UNLESS SHE'S WORKING TOWARD SOMETHING.
OR HOW, EVEN THOUGH ALL I EVER DO IS PLAY BASKETBALL, SHE'LL COME RIGHT OVER TO CHEER ME ON.
...BUT YOU GUYS KNEW ALL THAT.
IT'S NOT JUST THOSE SPECIFIC THINGS.
BUT, I GUESS...
I LIKE HOW THE ATMOSPHERE FEELS WHEN WE'RE ALONE TOGETHER.

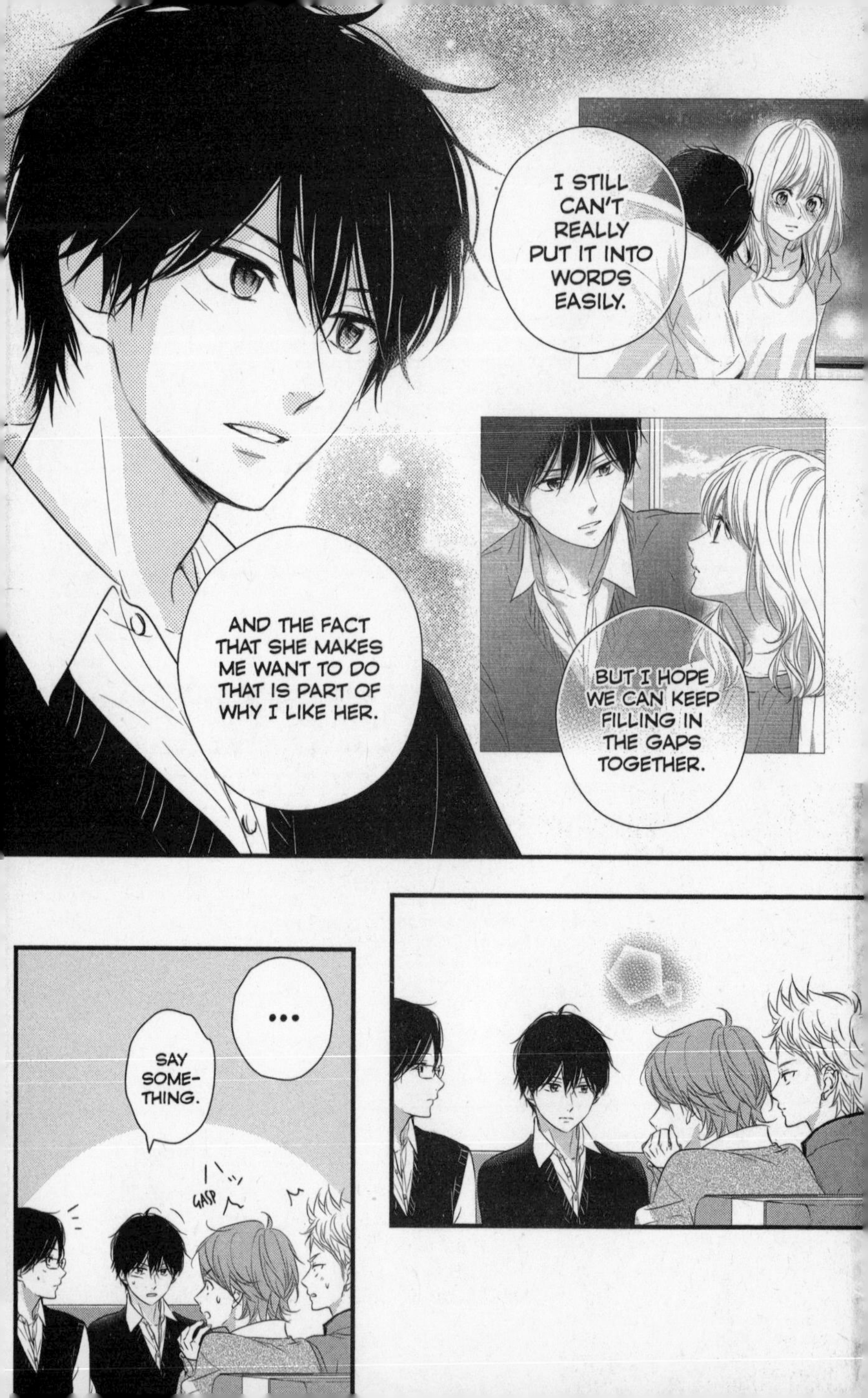
I STILL CAN'T REALLY PUT IT INTO WORDS EASILY.
BUT I HOPE WE CAN KEEP FILLING IN THE GAPS TOGETHER.
AND THE FACT THAT SHE MAKES ME WANT TO DO THAT IS PART OF WHY I LIKE HER.
...
SAY SOME-THING.
GASP

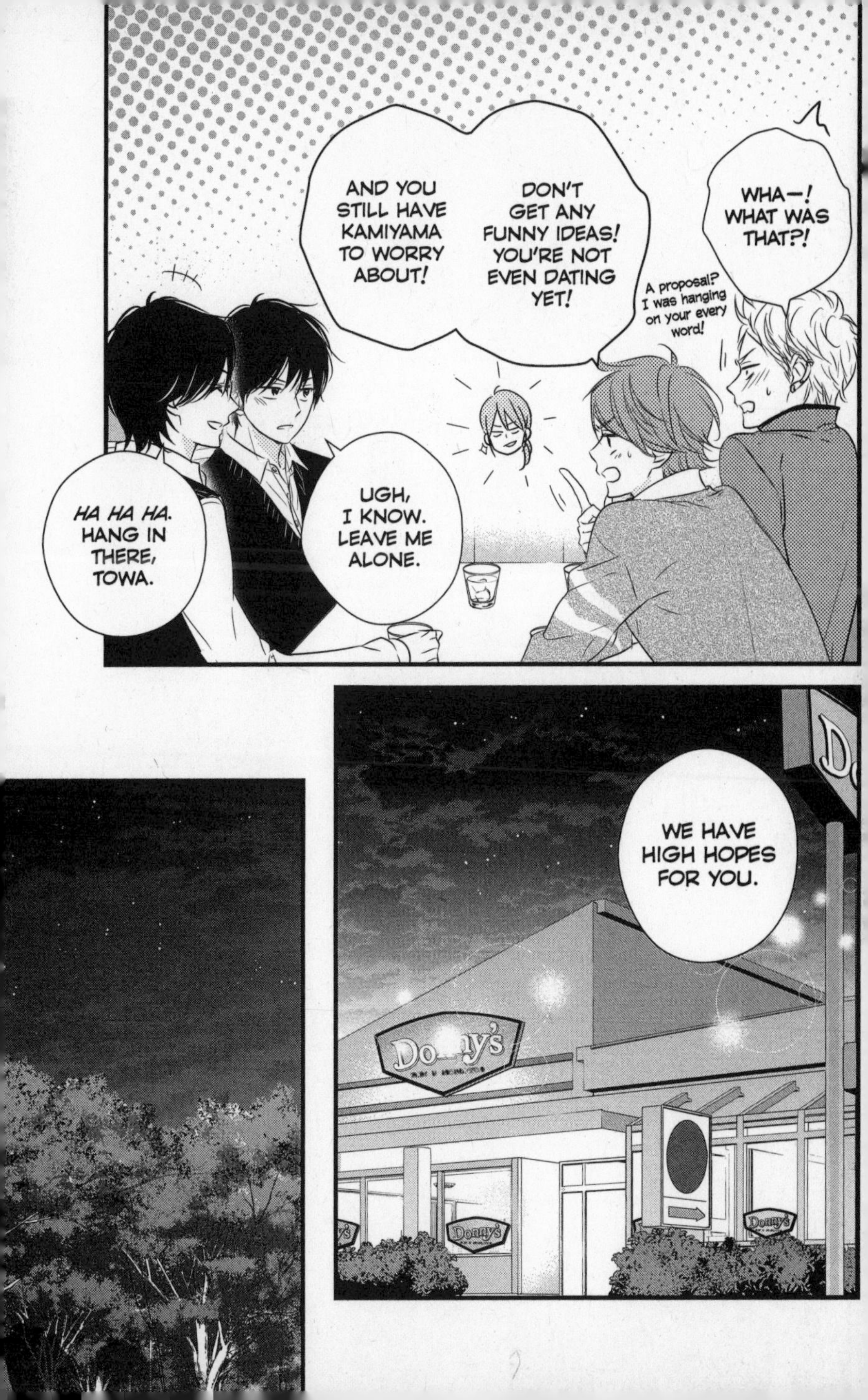
WHA—! WHAT WAS THAT?!
A proposal? I was hanging on your every word!
DON'T GET ANY FUNNY IDEAS! YOU'RE NOT EVEN DATING YET!
AND YOU STILL HAVE KAMIYAMA TO WORRY ABOUT!
UGH, I KNOW. LEAVE ME ALONE.
HA HA HA. HANG IN THERE, TOWA.
WE HAVE HIGH HOPES FOR YOU.

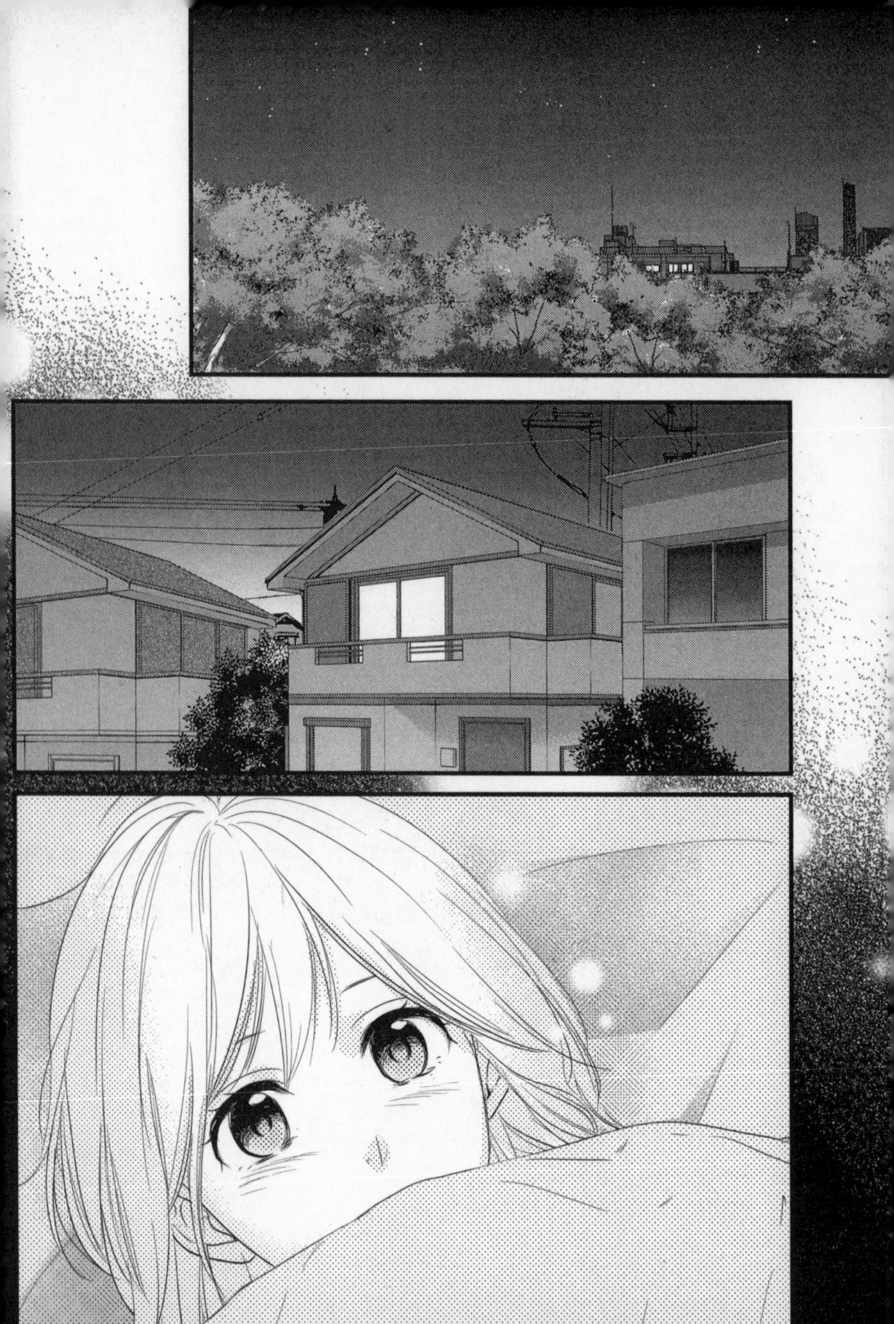

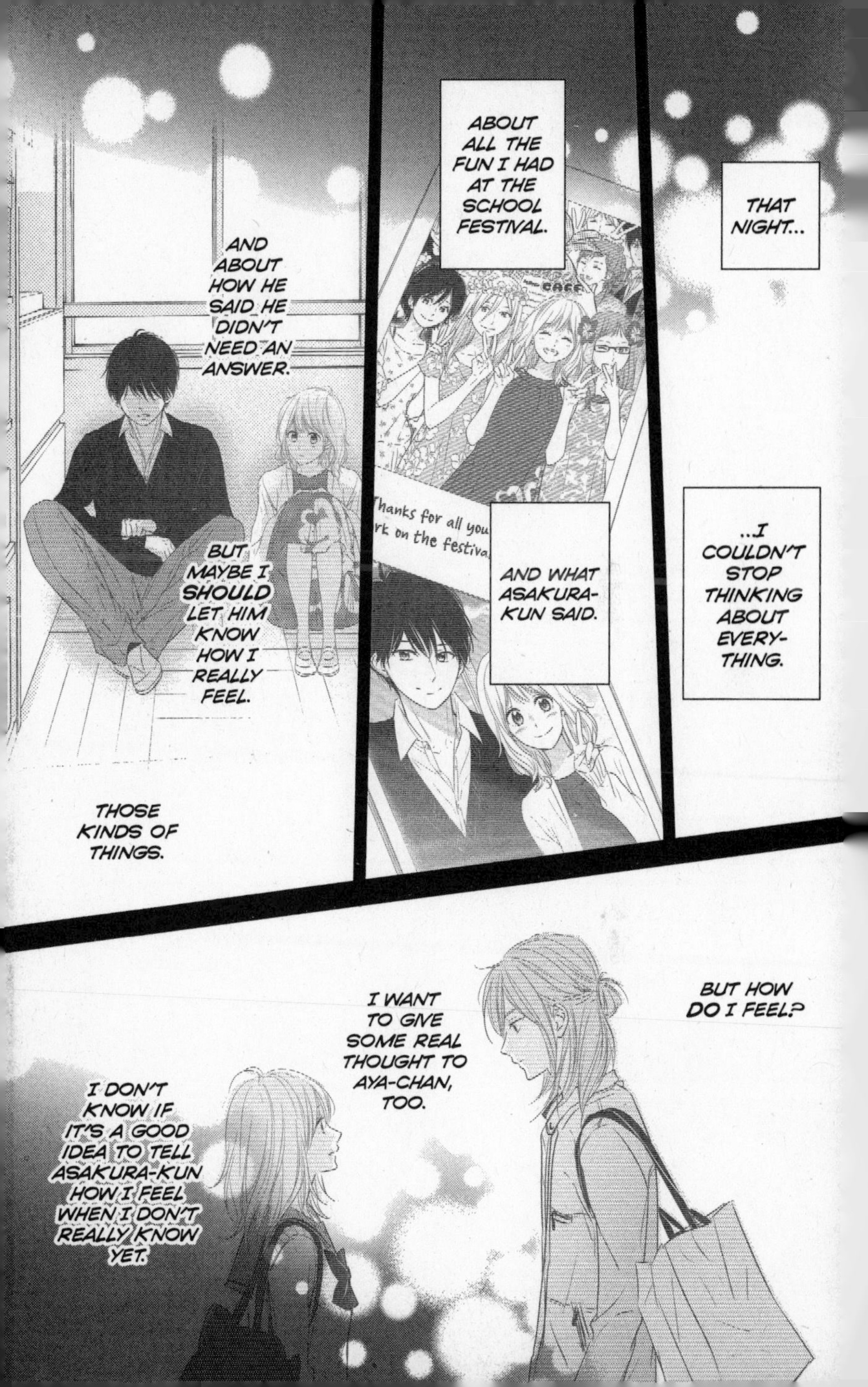
THAT NIGHT...
...I COULDN'T STOP THINKING ABOUT EVERYTHING.
ABOUT ALL THE FUN I HAD AT THE SCHOOL FESTIVAL.
CAFE
Thanks for all you
rk on the festiva
AND WHAT ASAKURA-KUN SAID.
AND ABOUT HOW HE SAID HE DIDN'T NEED AN ANSWER.
BUT MAYBE I SHOULD LET HIM KNOW HOW I REALLY FEEL.
THOSE KINDS OF THINGS.
BUT HOW DO I FEEL?
I WANT TO GIVE SOME REAL THOUGHT TO AYA-CHAN, TOO.
I DON'T KNOW IF IT'S A GOOD IDEA TO TELL ASAKURA-KUN HOW I FEEL WHEN I DON'T REALLY KNOW YET.

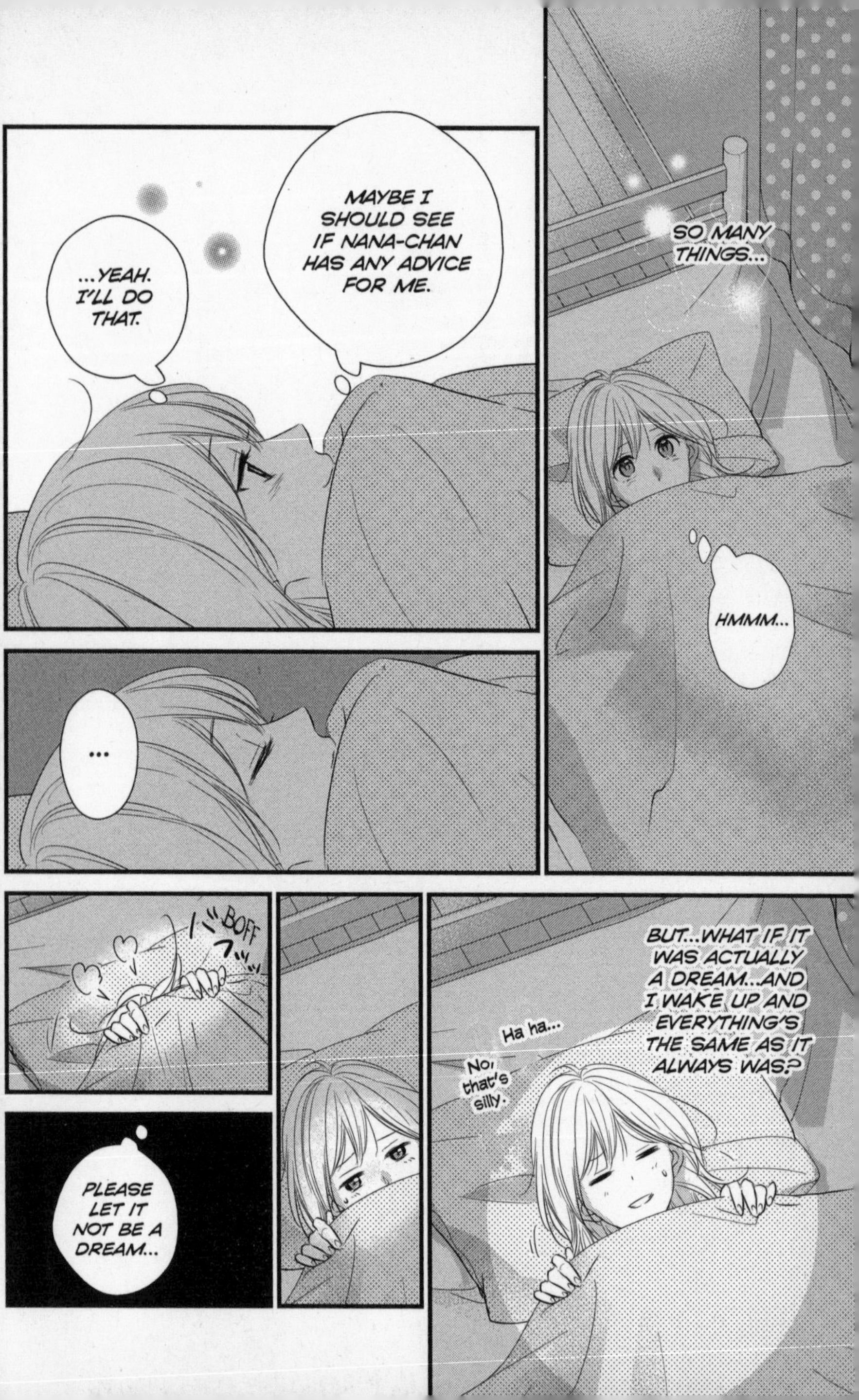
SO MANY THINGS...
HMMM...
MAYBE I SHOULD SEE IF NANA-CHAN HAS ANY ADVICE FOR ME.
...YEAH. I'LL DO THAT.
...
BUT...WHAT IF IT WAS ACTUALLY A DREAM...AND I WAKE UP AND EVERYTHING'S THE SAME AS IT ALWAYS WAS?
Ha ha...
No, that's silly.
BOFF
PLEASE LET IT NOT BE A DREAM...

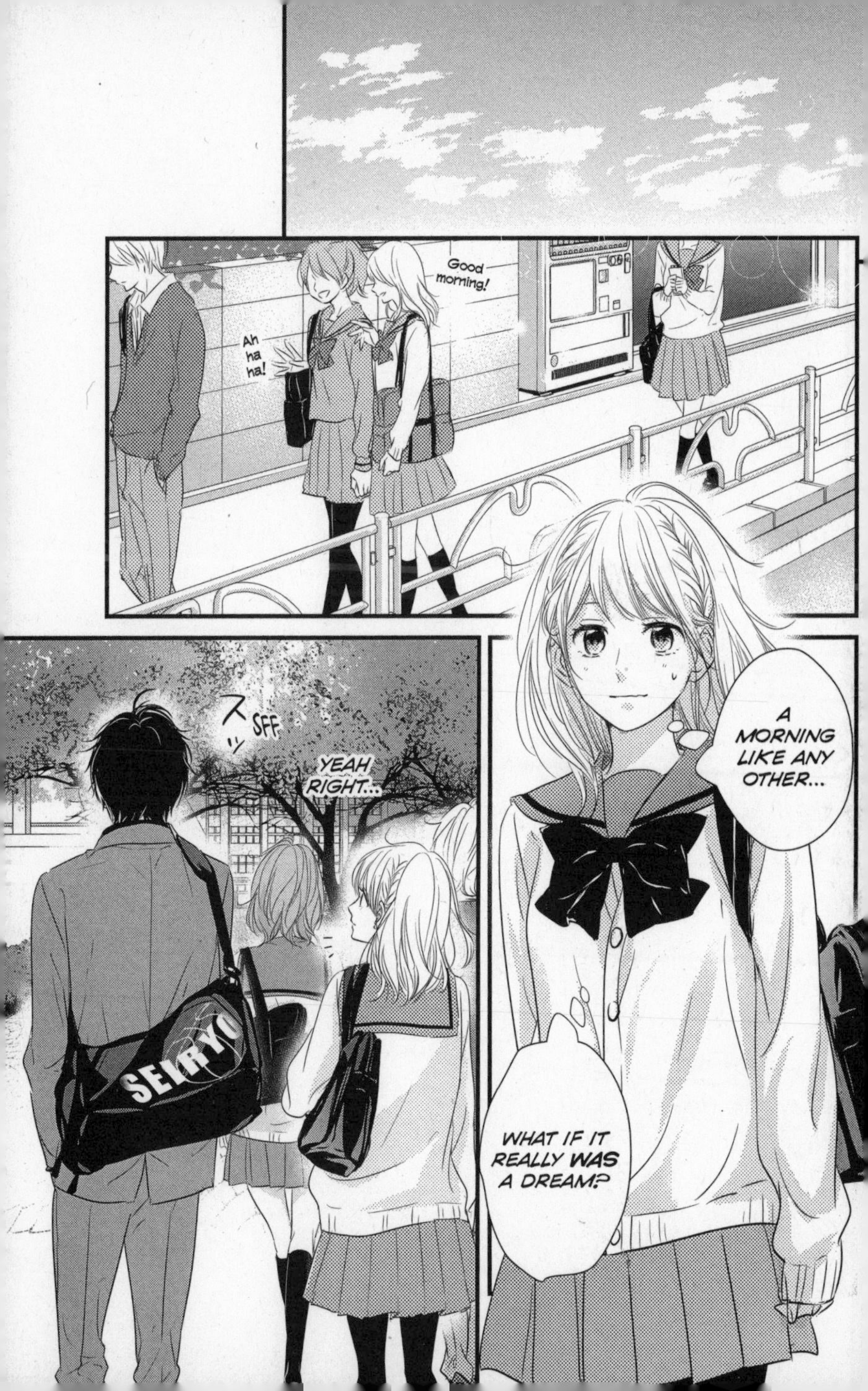
Good morning!
Ah ha ha!
A MORNING LIKE ANY OTHER...
WHAT IF IT REALLY WAS A DREAM?
スッ
SFF
YEAH RIGHT...
SEIRYO

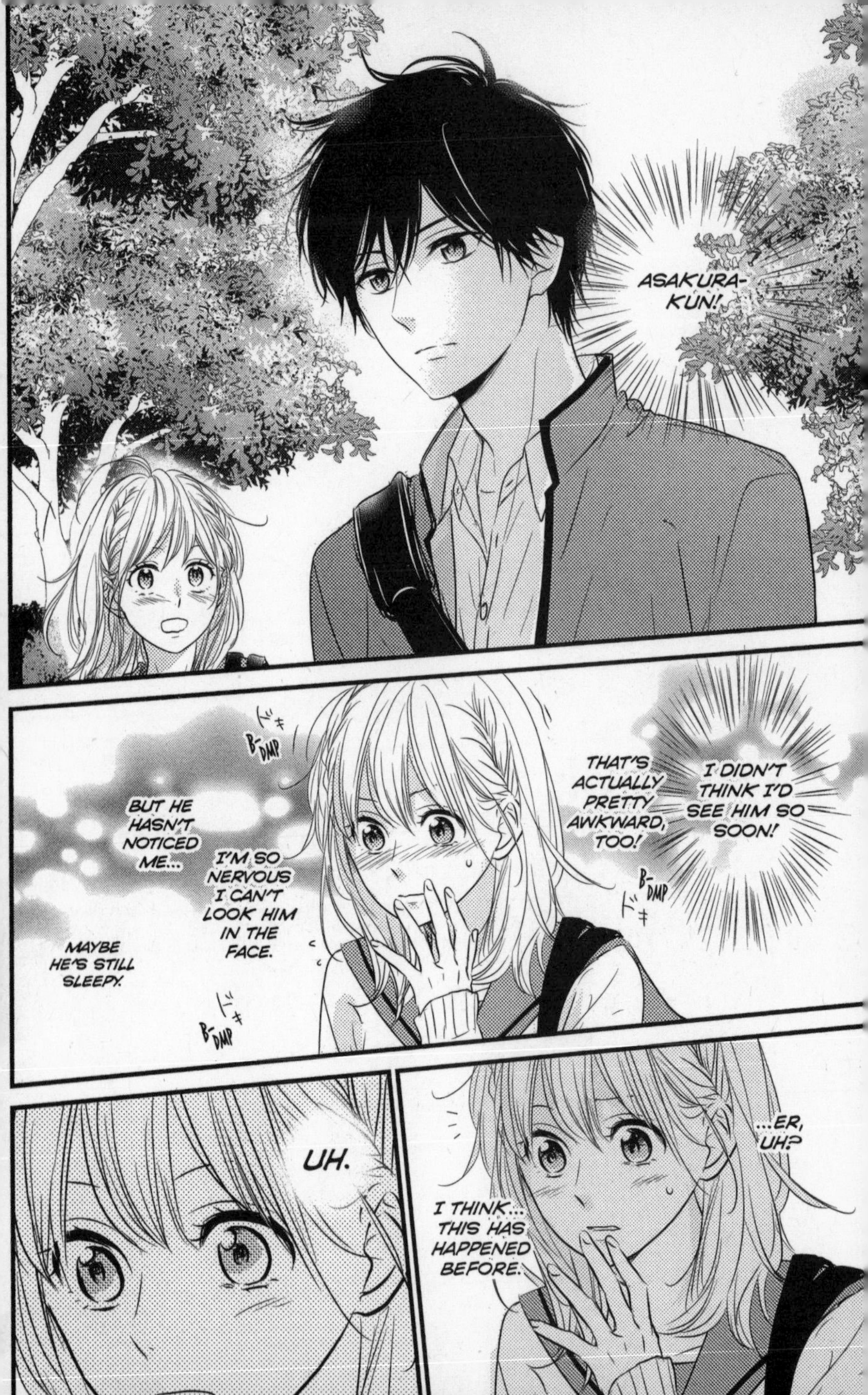
ASAKURA-KUN!
I DIDN'T THINK I'D SEE HIM SO SOON!
THAT'S ACTUALLY PRETTY AWKWARD, TOO!
ドキ B-DMP
ドキ B-DMP
I'M SO NERVOUS I CAN'T LOOK HIM IN THE FACE.
BUT HE HASN'T NOTICED ME...
MAYBE HE'S STILL SLEEPY.
ドキ B-DMP
...ER, UH?
I THINK... THIS HAS HAPPENED BEFORE.
UH.

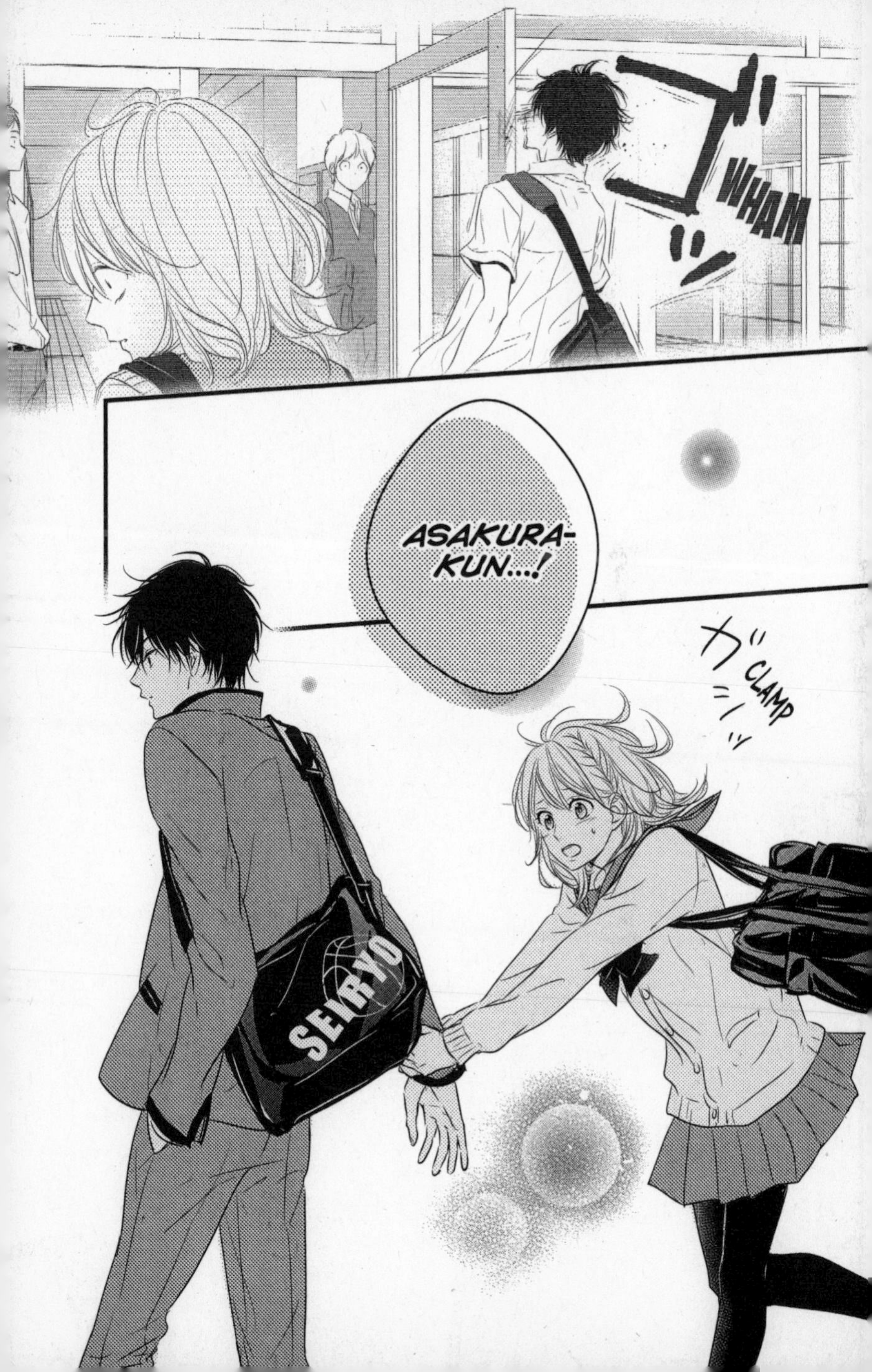
WHAM
ASAKURA-KUN...!
CLAMP

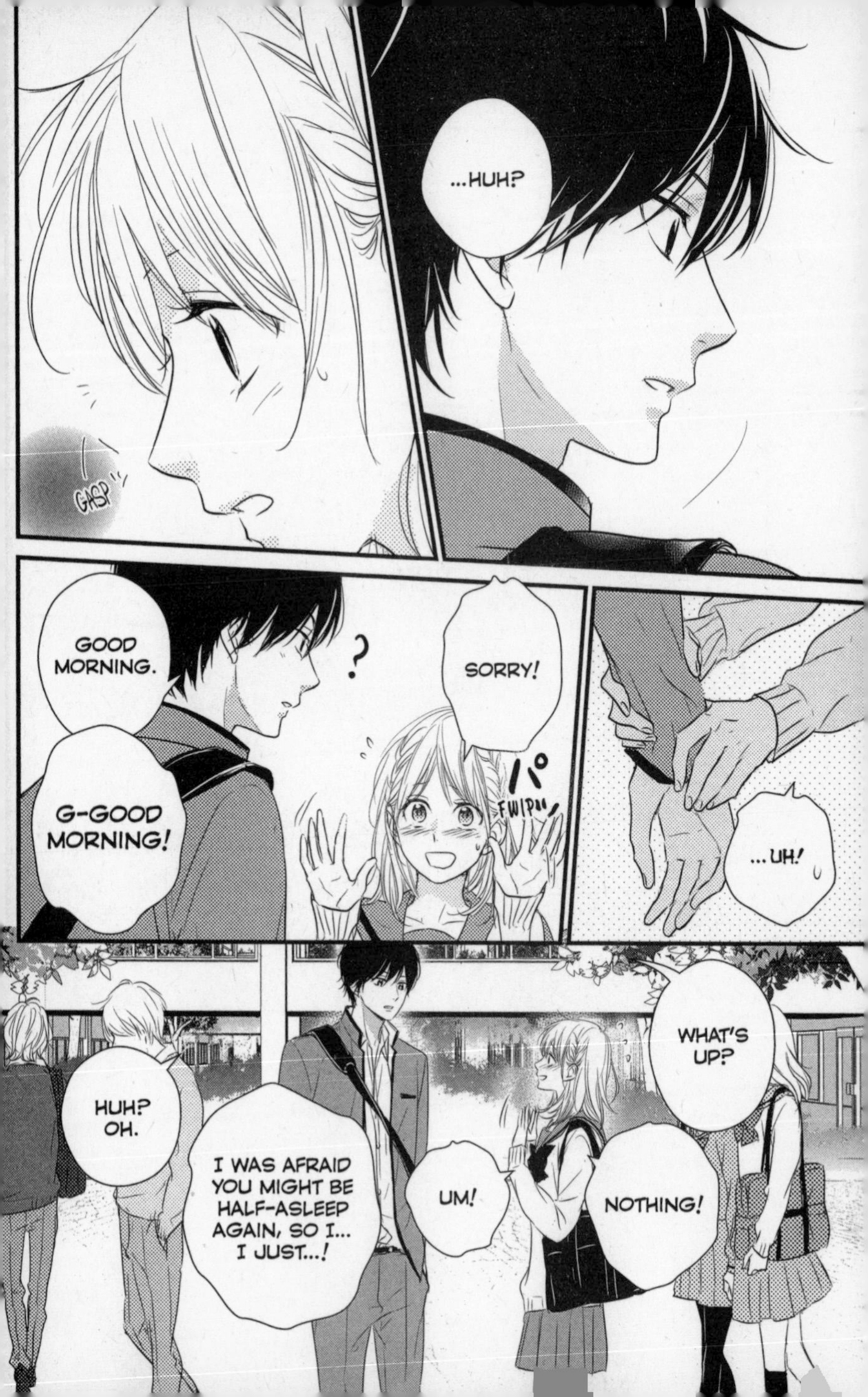
...HUH?
GASP
...UH!
SORRY!
パ
FWIP
GOOD MORNING.
G-GOOD MORNING!
WHAT'S UP?
NOTHING!
UM!
I WAS AFRAID YOU MIGHT BE HALF-ASLEEP AGAIN, SO I... I JUST...!
HUH? OH.

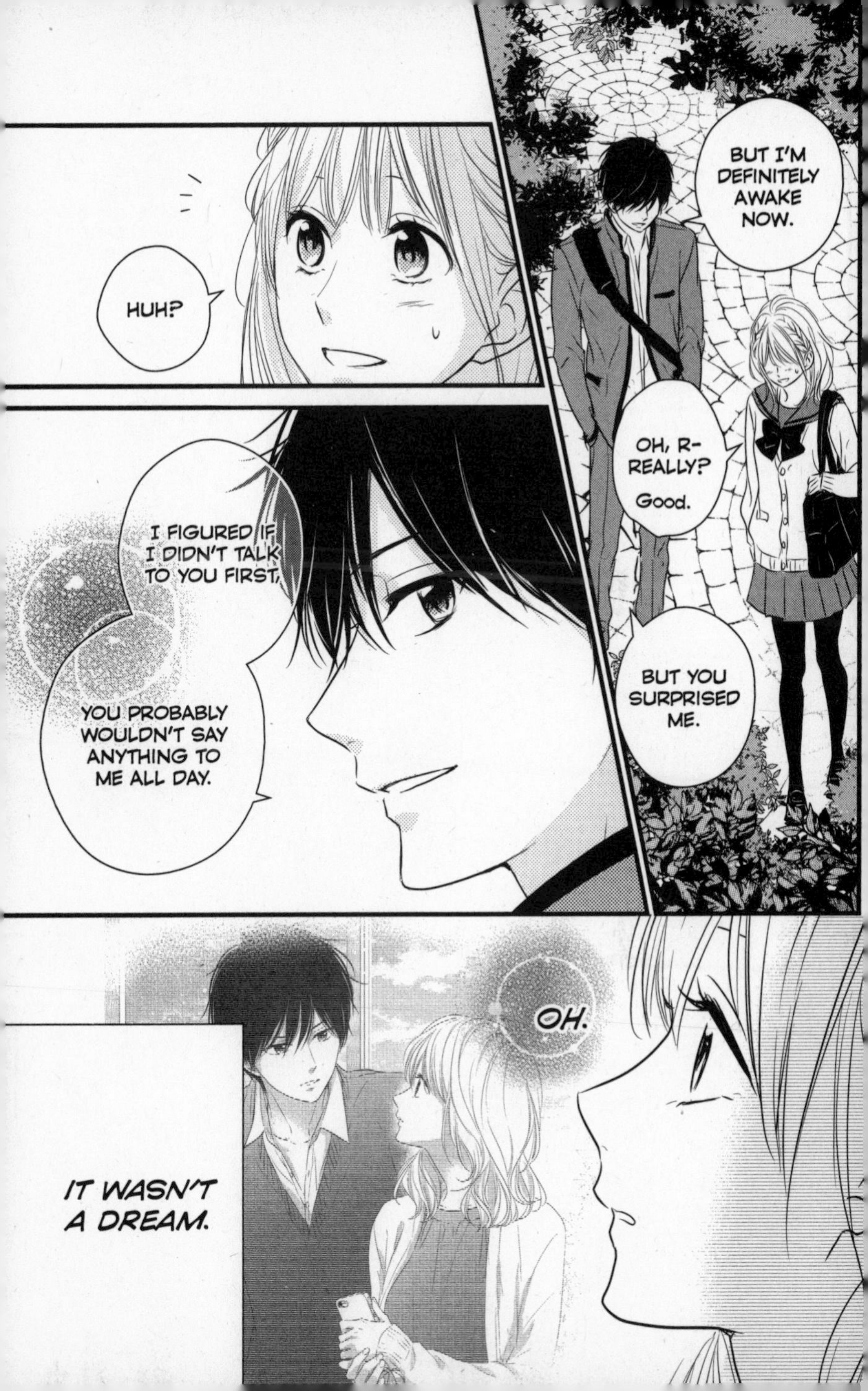
BUT I'M DEFINITELY AWAKE NOW.
OH, R-REALLY? Good.
BUT YOU SURPRISED ME.
HUH?
I FIGURED IF I DIDN'T TALK TO YOU FIRST,
YOU PROBABLY WOULDN'T SAY ANYTHING TO ME ALL DAY.
OH.
IT WASN'T A DREAM.

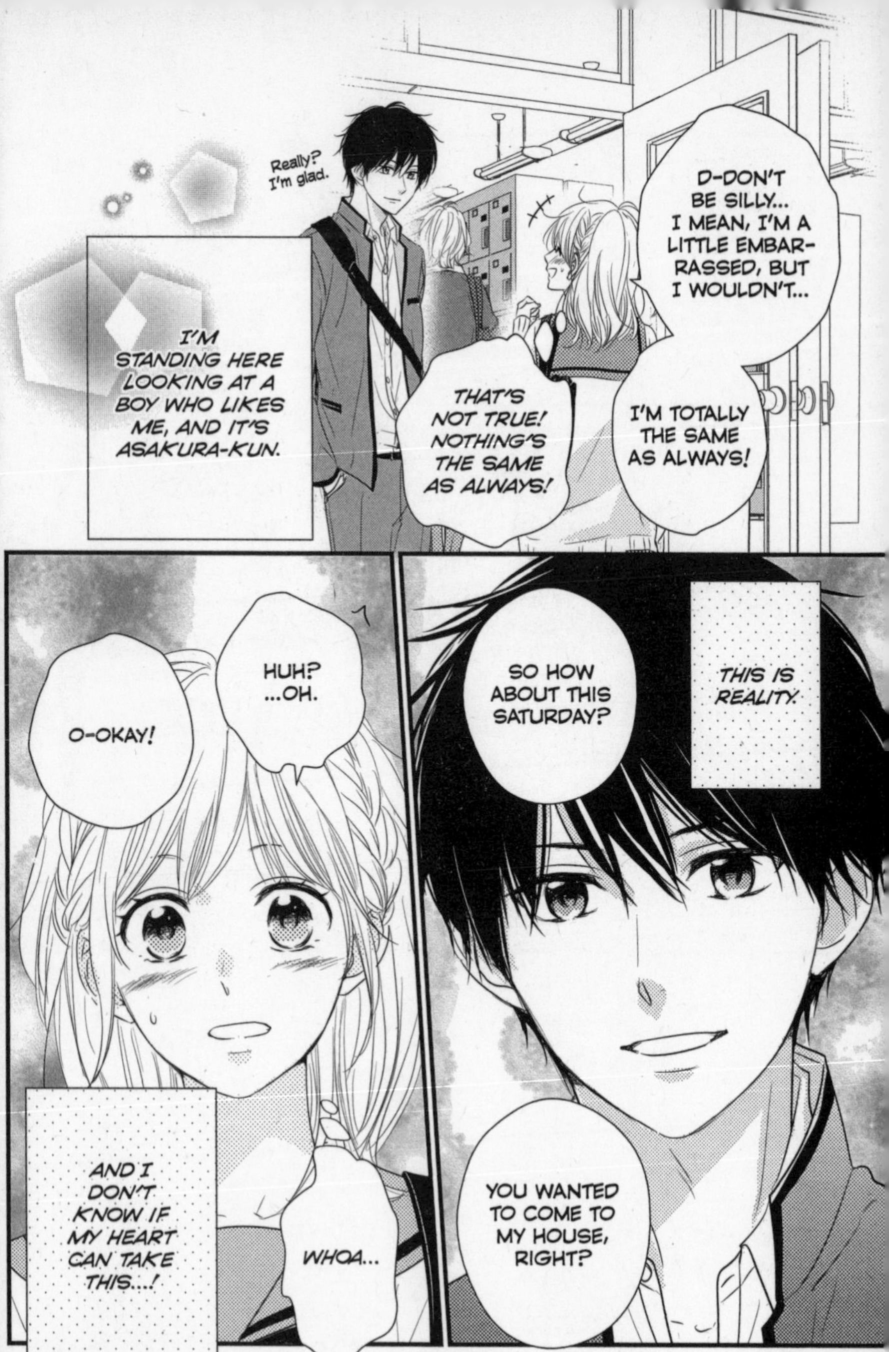
D-DON'T BE SILLY... I MEAN, I'M A LITTLE EMBARRASSED, BUT I WOULDN'T...
Really? I'm glad.
I'M TOTALLY THE SAME AS ALWAYS!
THAT'S NOT TRUE! NOTHING'S THE SAME AS ALWAYS!
I'M STANDING HERE LOOKING AT A BOY WHO LIKES ME, AND IT'S ASAKURA-KUN.
THIS IS REALITY.
SO HOW ABOUT THIS SATURDAY?
YOU WANTED TO COME TO MY HOUSE, RIGHT?
HUH? ...OH.
O-OKAY!
WHOA...
AND I DON'T KNOW IF MY HEART CAN TAKE THIS...!

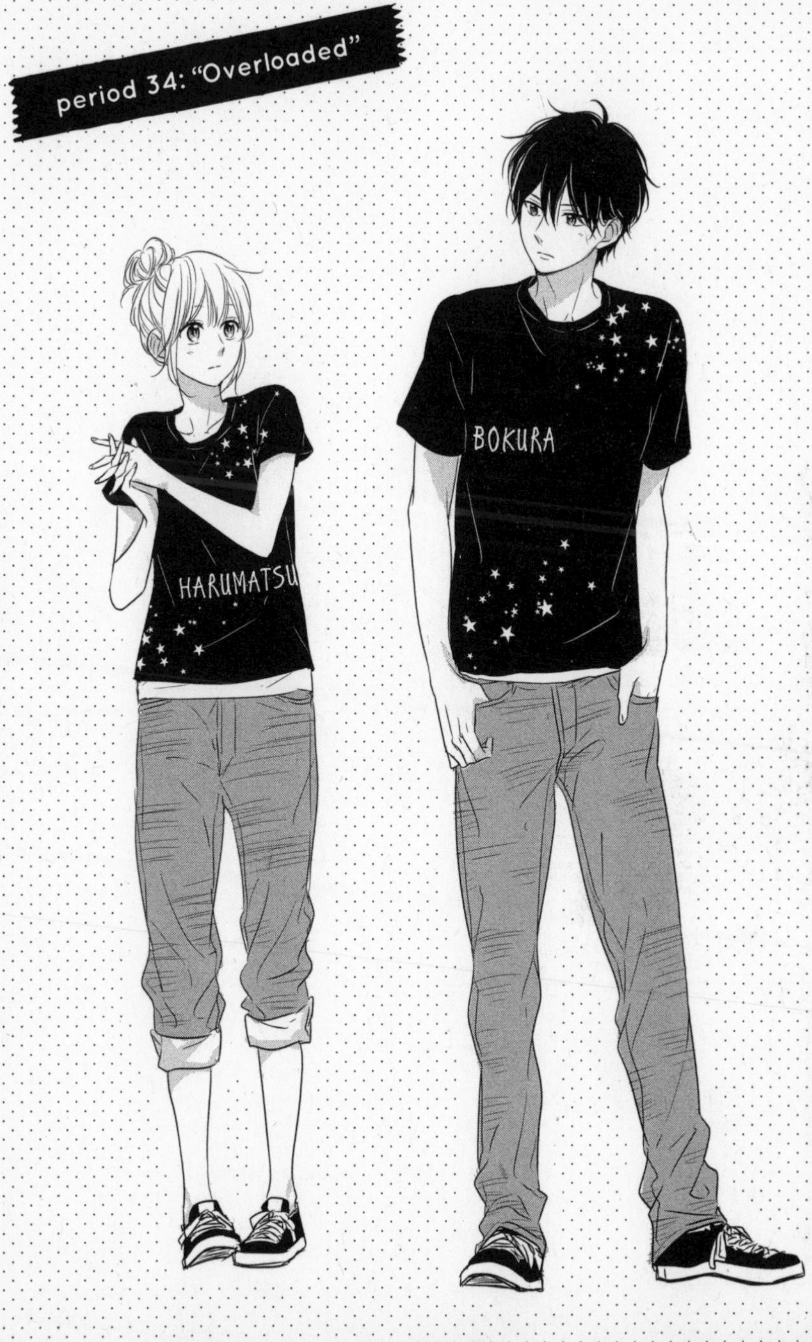
period 34: "Overloaded"
BOKURA
HARUMATSU

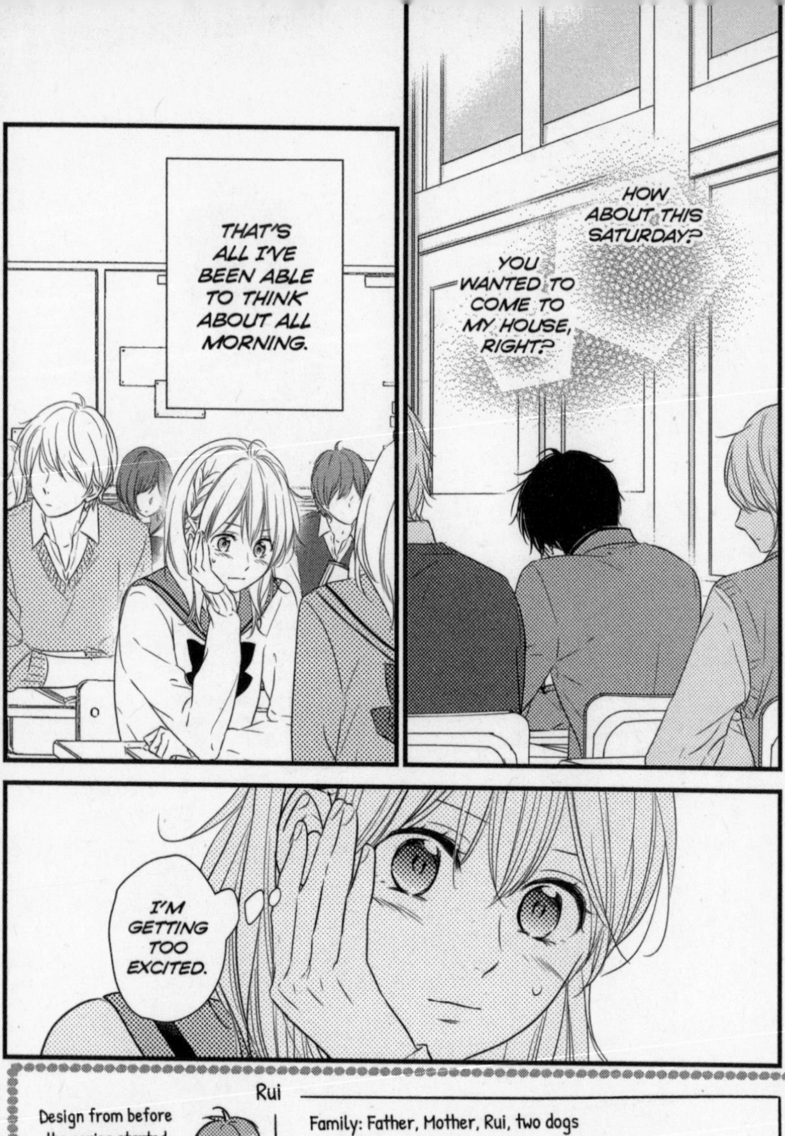
HOW ABOUT THIS SATURDAY?
YOU WANTED TO COME TO MY HOUSE, RIGHT?
THAT'S ALL I'VE BEEN ABLE TO THINK ABOUT ALL MORNING.
I'M GETTING TOO EXCITED.

Rui

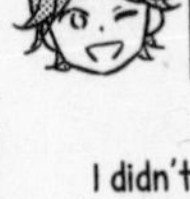

Family: Father, Mother, Rui, two dogs
He's an only child, but he has a lot of relatives, so he grew up loved by many grownups.

Design from before the series started

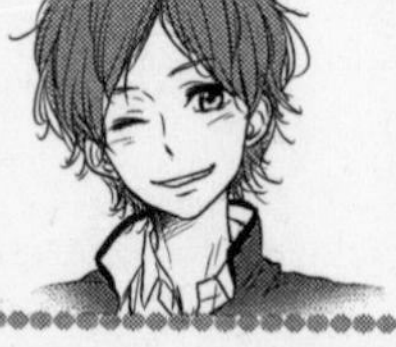

I didn't want Rui to be **just** cute, I wanted him to have his manly side, too. So when he's acting cute, my intention is that he's doing it on purpose, because he knows that's what people expect from him. But I wonder if that comes across...? (ha ha) At first, his name was Leo.

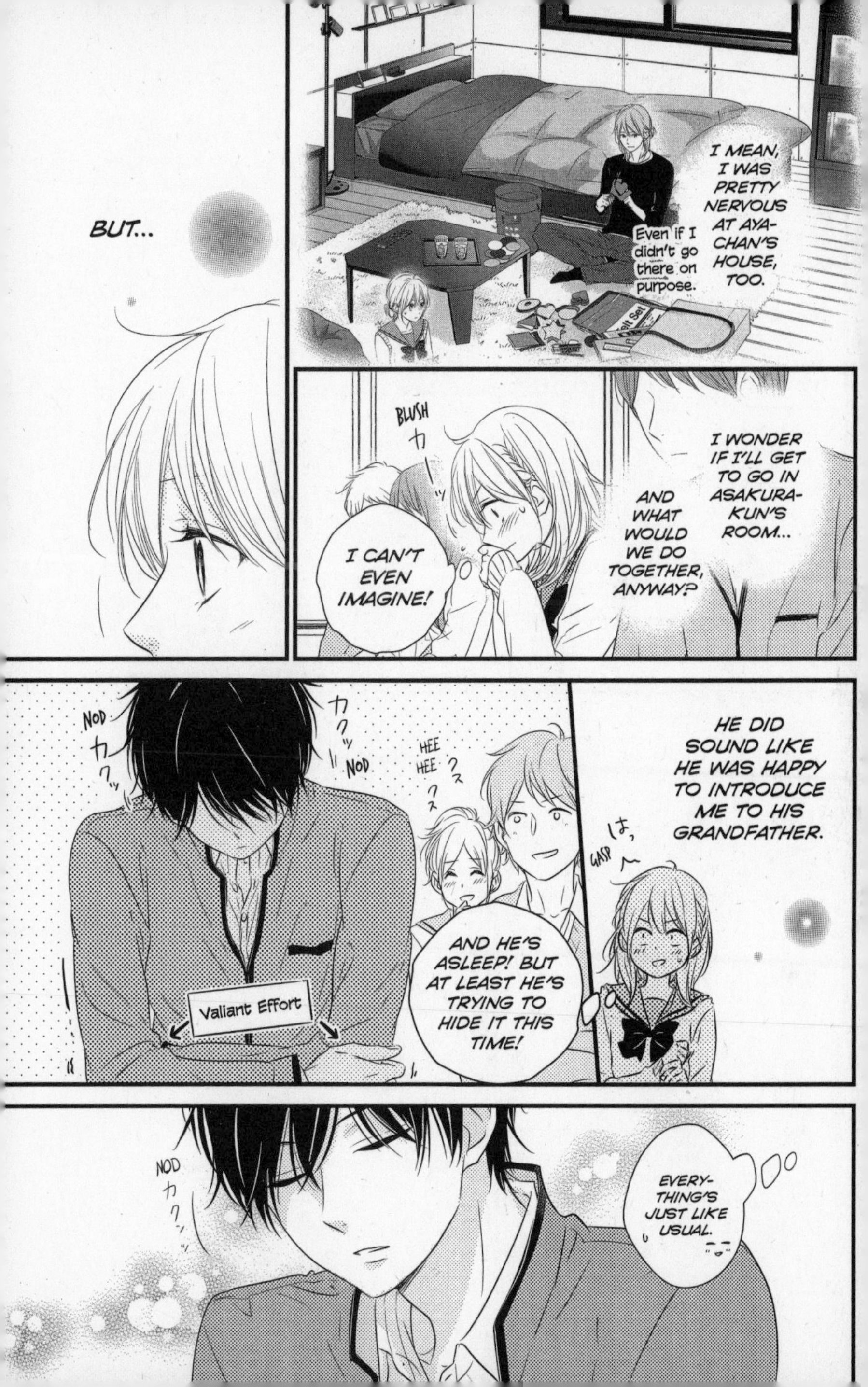
I MEAN, I WAS PRETTY NERVOUS AT AYA-CHAN'S HOUSE, TOO.
Even if I didn't go there on purpose.
I WONDER IF I'LL GET TO GO IN ASAKURA-KUN'S ROOM...
AND WHAT WOULD WE DO TOGETHER, ANYWAY?
BLUSH
I CAN'T EVEN IMAGINE!
BUT...
HE DID SOUND LIKE HE WAS HAPPY TO INTRODUCE ME TO HIS GRANDFATHER.
GASP
HEE HEE
AND HE'S ASLEEP! BUT AT LEAST HE'S TRYING TO HIDE IT THIS TIME!
NOD
NOD
Valiant Effort
EVERY-THING'S JUST LIKE USUAL.
NOD

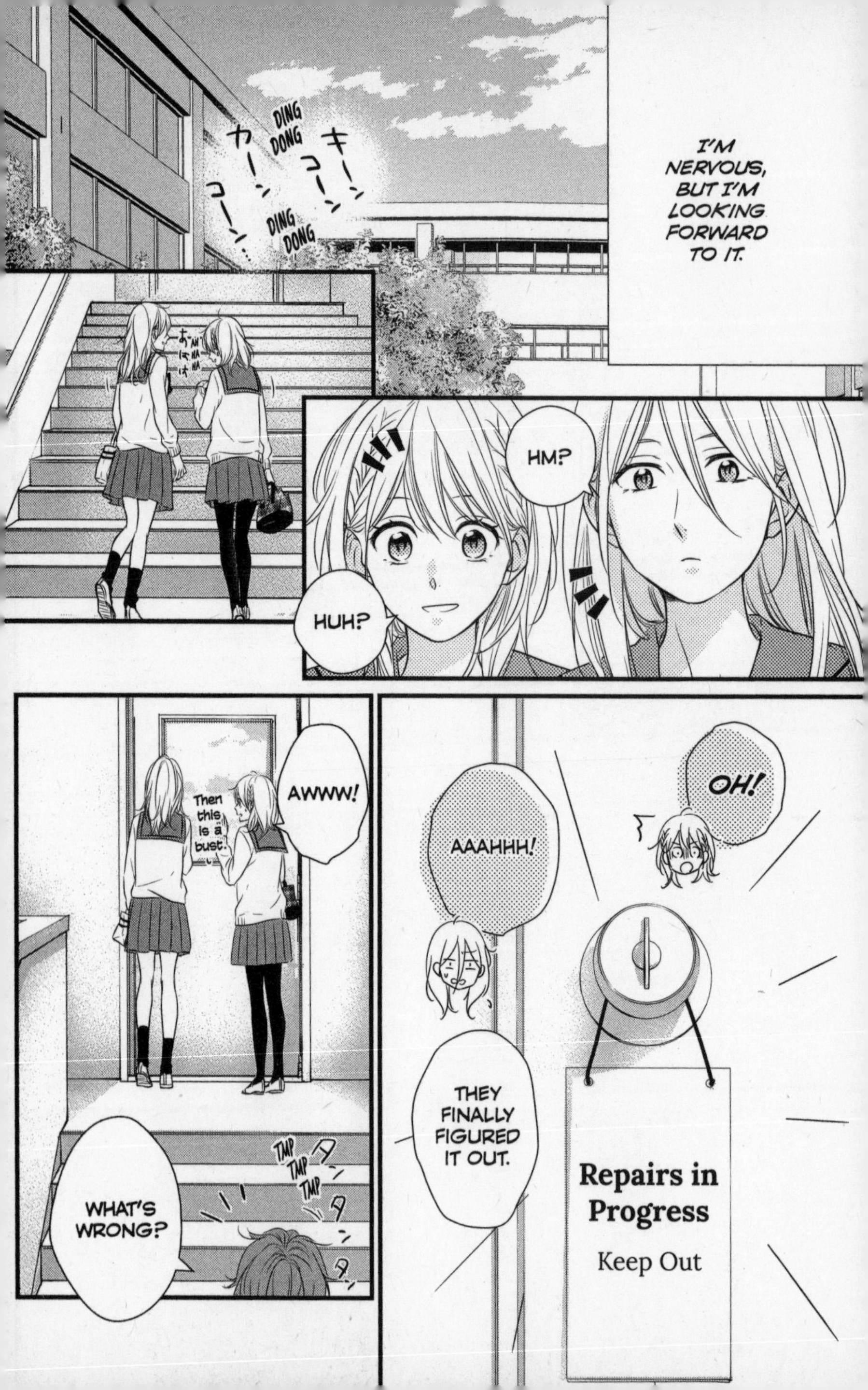
I'M NERVOUS, BUT I'M LOOKING FORWARD TO IT.
キーンコーン
DING DONG
カーンコーン…
DING DONG
HM?
HUH?
AH HA HA
OH!
AAAHHH!
THEY FINALLY FIGURED IT OUT.
Repairs in Progress
Keep Out
AWWW!
Then this is a bust.
TMP TMP TMP
WHAT'S WRONG?

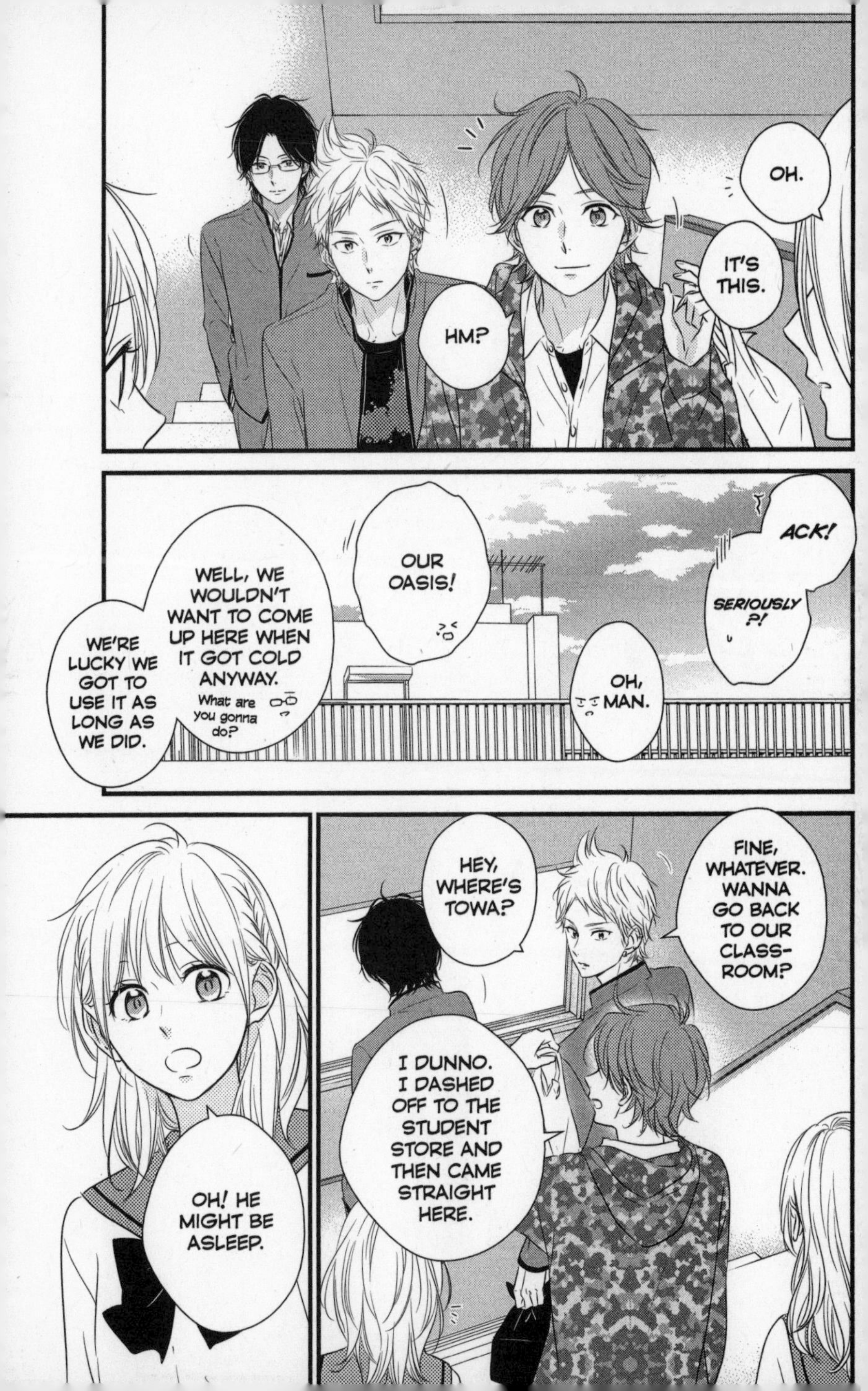
OH.
IT'S THIS.
HM?
ACK!
SERIOUSLY?!
OH, MAN.
OUR OASIS!
WELL, WE WOULDN'T WANT TO COME UP HERE WHEN IT GOT COLD ANYWAY.
What are you gonna do?
WE'RE LUCKY WE GOT TO USE IT AS LONG AS WE DID.
FINE, WHATEVER. WANNA GO BACK TO OUR CLASS-ROOM?
HEY, WHERE'S TOWA?
I DUNNO. I DASHED OFF TO THE STUDENT STORE AND THEN CAME STRAIGHT HERE.
OH! HE MIGHT BE ASLEEP.

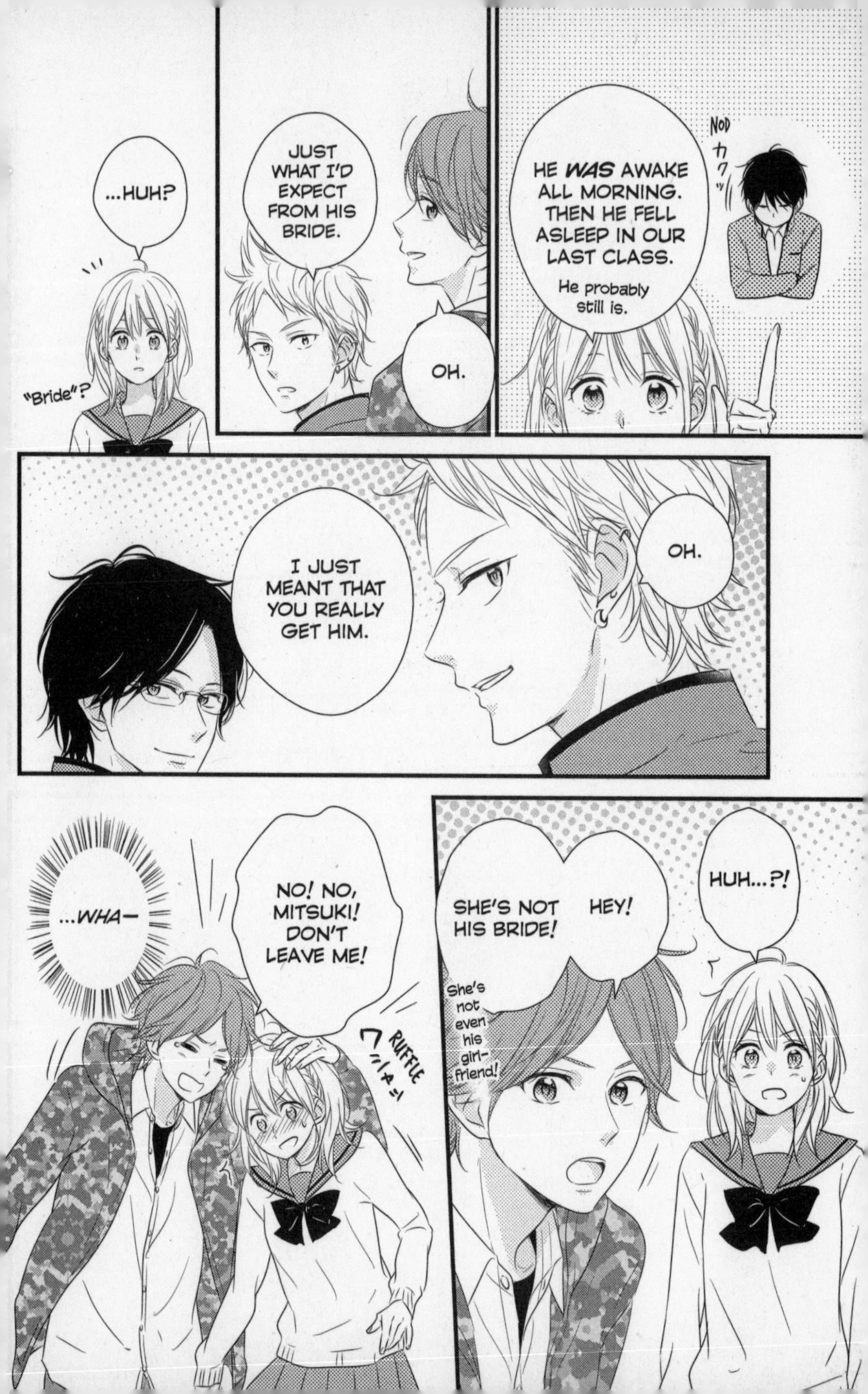
NOD
カクッ
HE WAS AWAKE ALL MORNING. THEN HE FELL ASLEEP IN OUR LAST CLASS.
He probably still is.
JUST WHAT I'D EXPECT FROM HIS BRIDE.
OH.
...HUH?
"Bride"?
OH.
I JUST MEANT THAT YOU REALLY GET HIM.
HUH...?!
HEY!
SHE'S NOT HIS BRIDE!
She's not even his girlfriend!
NO! NO, MITSUKI! DON'T LEAVE ME!
RUFFLE
ワシャッ
...WHA—

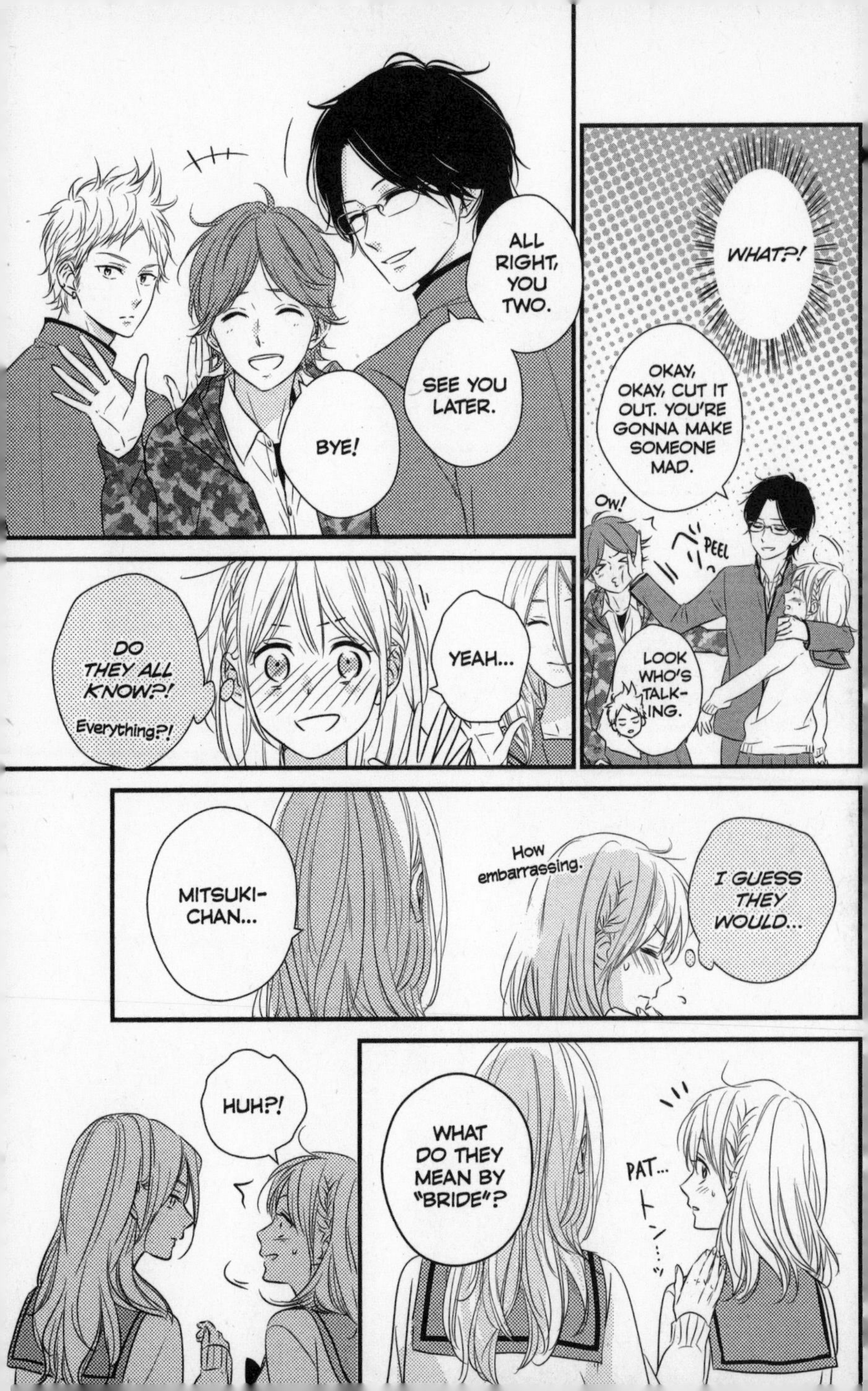
WHAT?!
OKAY, OKAY, CUT IT OUT. YOU'RE GONNA MAKE SOMEONE MAD.
OW!
PEEL
LOOK WHO'S TALK-ING.
ALL RIGHT, YOU TWO.
SEE YOU LATER.
BYE!
YEAH...
DO THEY ALL KNOW?!
Everything?!
I GUESS THEY WOULD...
How embarrassing.
MITSUKI-CHAN...
PAT...
WHAT DO THEY MEAN BY "BRIDE"?
HUH?!

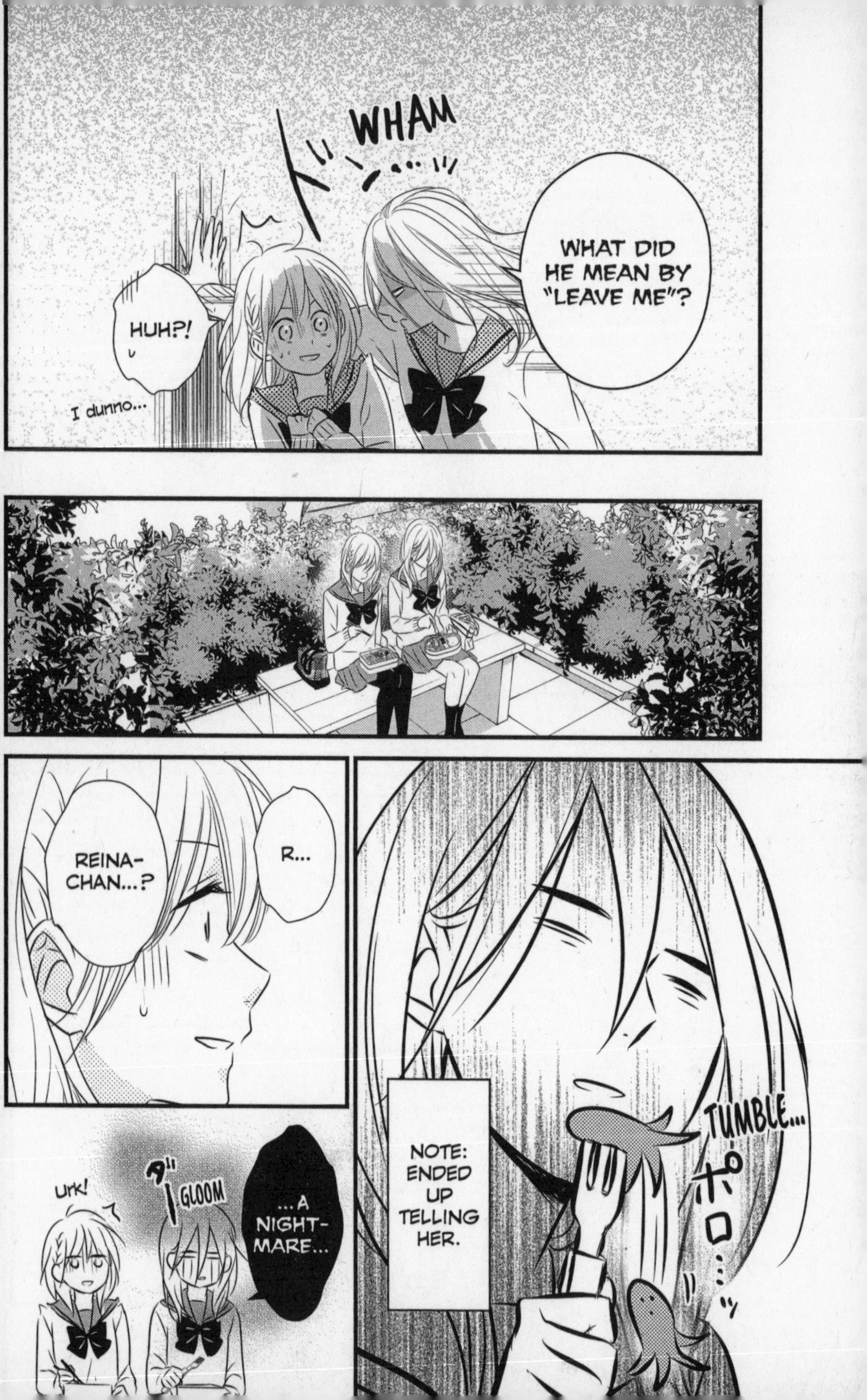
WHAM
WHAT DID HE MEAN BY "LEAVE ME"?
HUH?!
I dunno...
TUMBLE...
ポロ…ッ
NOTE: ENDED UP TELLING HER.
R...
REINA-CHAN...?
...A NIGHT-MARE...
GLOOM
Urk!

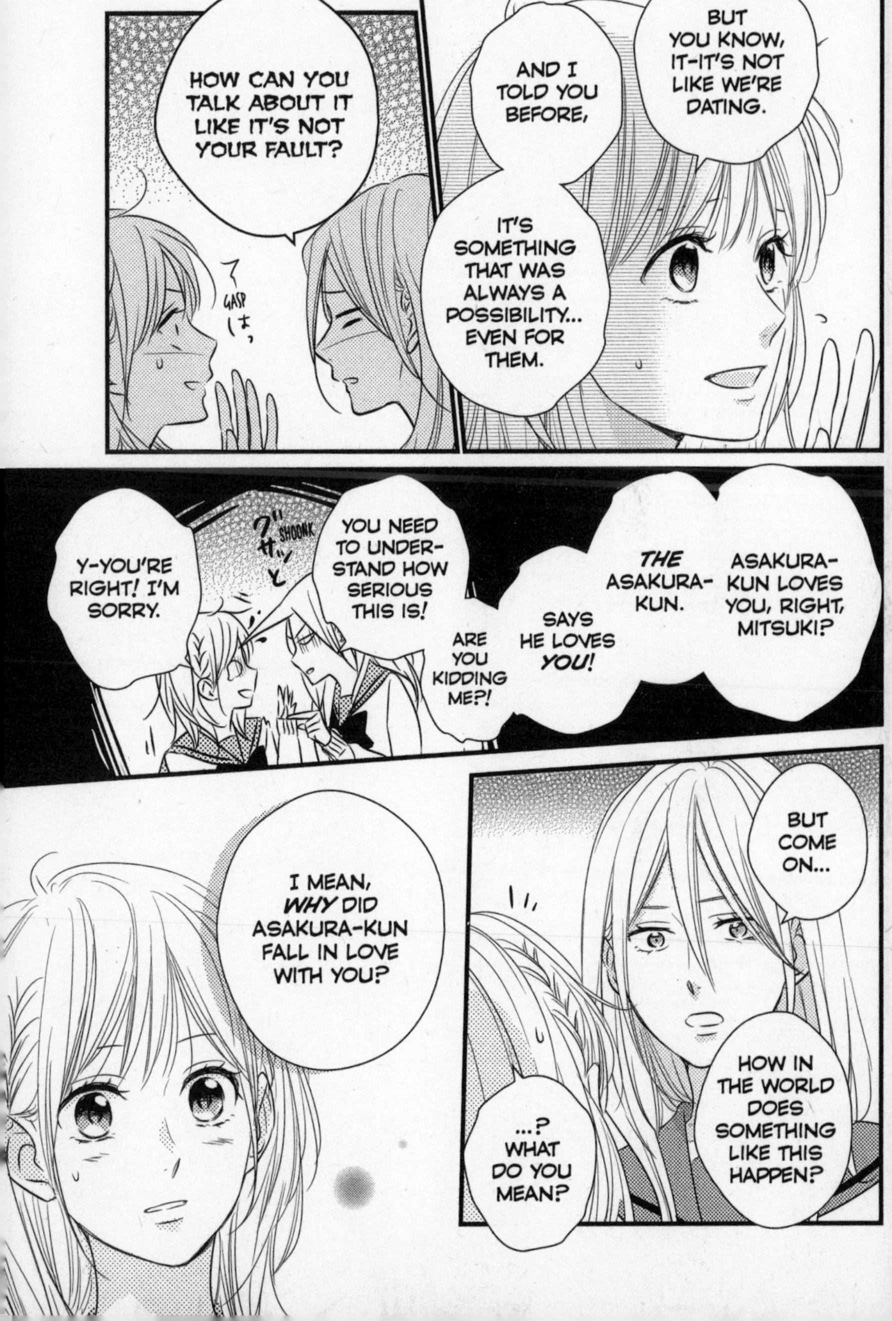
BUT YOU KNOW, IT-IT'S NOT LIKE WE'RE DATING.
AND I TOLD YOU BEFORE,
IT'S SOMETHING THAT WAS ALWAYS A POSSIBILITY... EVEN FOR THEM.
HOW CAN YOU TALK ABOUT IT LIKE IT'S NOT YOUR FAULT?
GASP
ASAKURA-KUN LOVES YOU, RIGHT, MITSUKI?
THE ASAKURA-KUN.
SAYS HE LOVES *YOU*!
ARE YOU KIDDING ME?!
YOU NEED TO UNDERSTAND HOW SERIOUS THIS IS!
SHOONK
Y-YOU'RE RIGHT! I'M SORRY.
BUT COME ON...
HOW IN THE WORLD DOES SOMETHING LIKE THIS HAPPEN?
...? WHAT DO YOU MEAN?
I MEAN, *WHY* DID ASAKURA-KUN FALL IN LOVE WITH YOU?

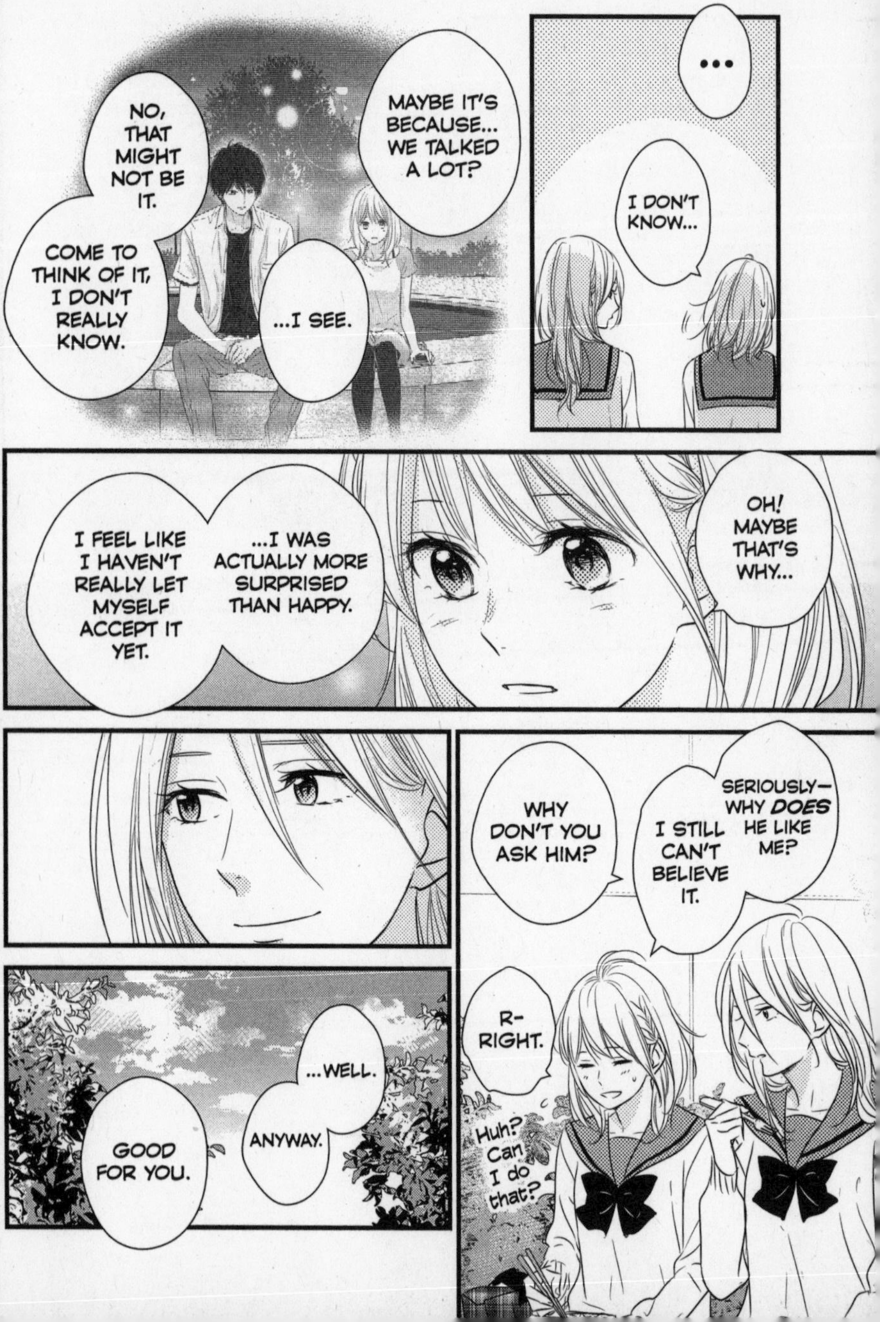
...
I DON'T KNOW...
MAYBE IT'S BECAUSE... WE TALKED A LOT?
NO, THAT MIGHT NOT BE IT.
COME TO THINK OF IT, I DON'T REALLY KNOW.
...I SEE.
OH! MAYBE THAT'S WHY...
...I WAS ACTUALLY MORE SURPRISED THAN HAPPY.
I FEEL LIKE I HAVEN'T REALLY LET MYSELF ACCEPT IT YET.
SERIOUSLY—WHY *DOES* HE LIKE ME?
I STILL CAN'T BELIEVE IT.
WHY DON'T YOU ASK HIM?
R-RIGHT.
Huh? Can I do that?
...WELL.
ANYWAY.
GOOD FOR YOU.

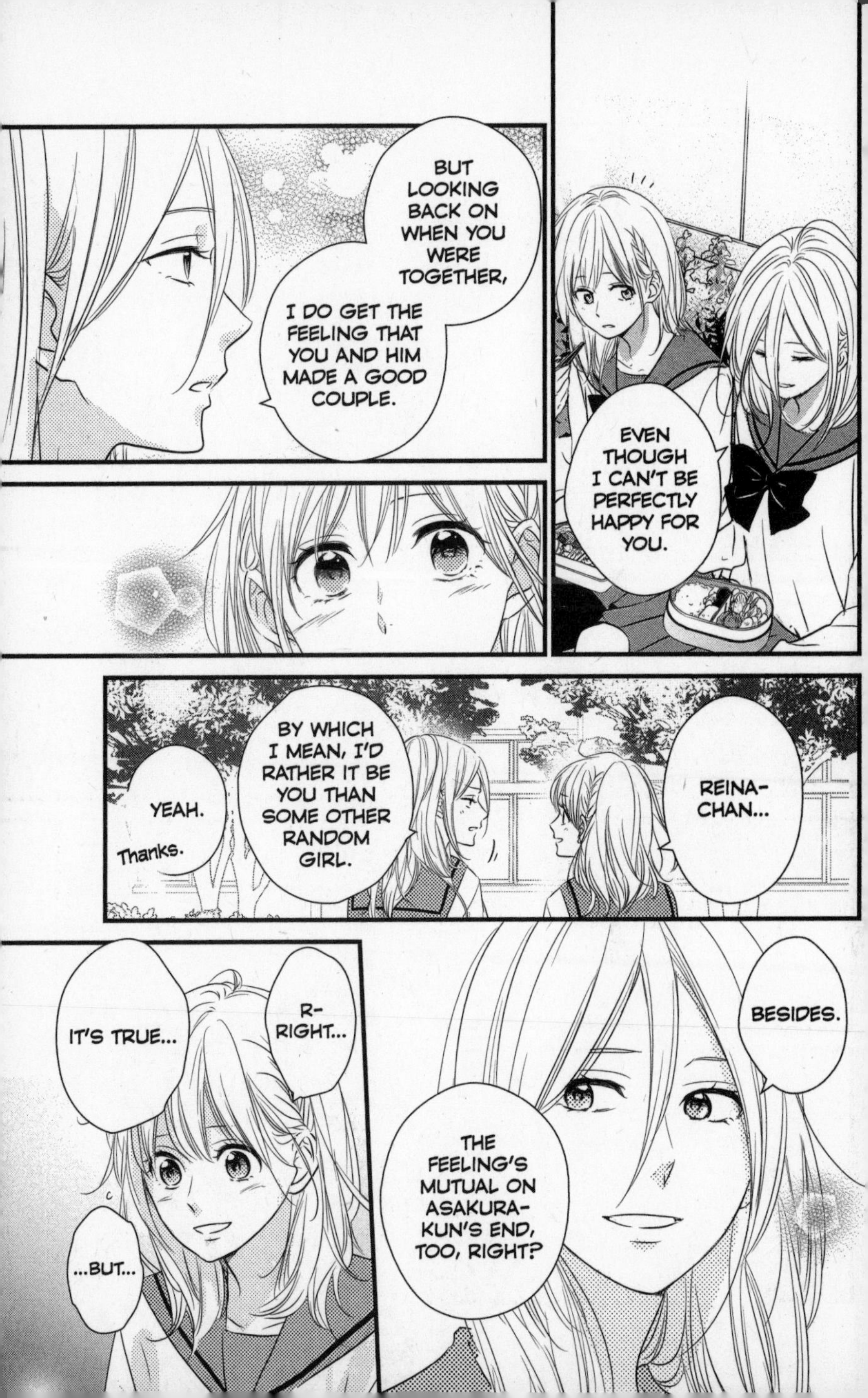
EVEN THOUGH I CAN'T BE PERFECTLY HAPPY FOR YOU.
BUT LOOKING BACK ON WHEN YOU WERE TOGETHER,
I DO GET THE FEELING THAT YOU AND HIM MADE A GOOD COUPLE.
REINA-CHAN...
BY WHICH I MEAN, I'D RATHER IT BE YOU THAN SOME OTHER RANDOM GIRL.
YEAH.
Thanks.
BESIDES.
THE FEELING'S MUTUAL ON ASAKURA-KUN'S END, TOO, RIGHT?
R-RIGHT...
IT'S TRUE...
...BUT...

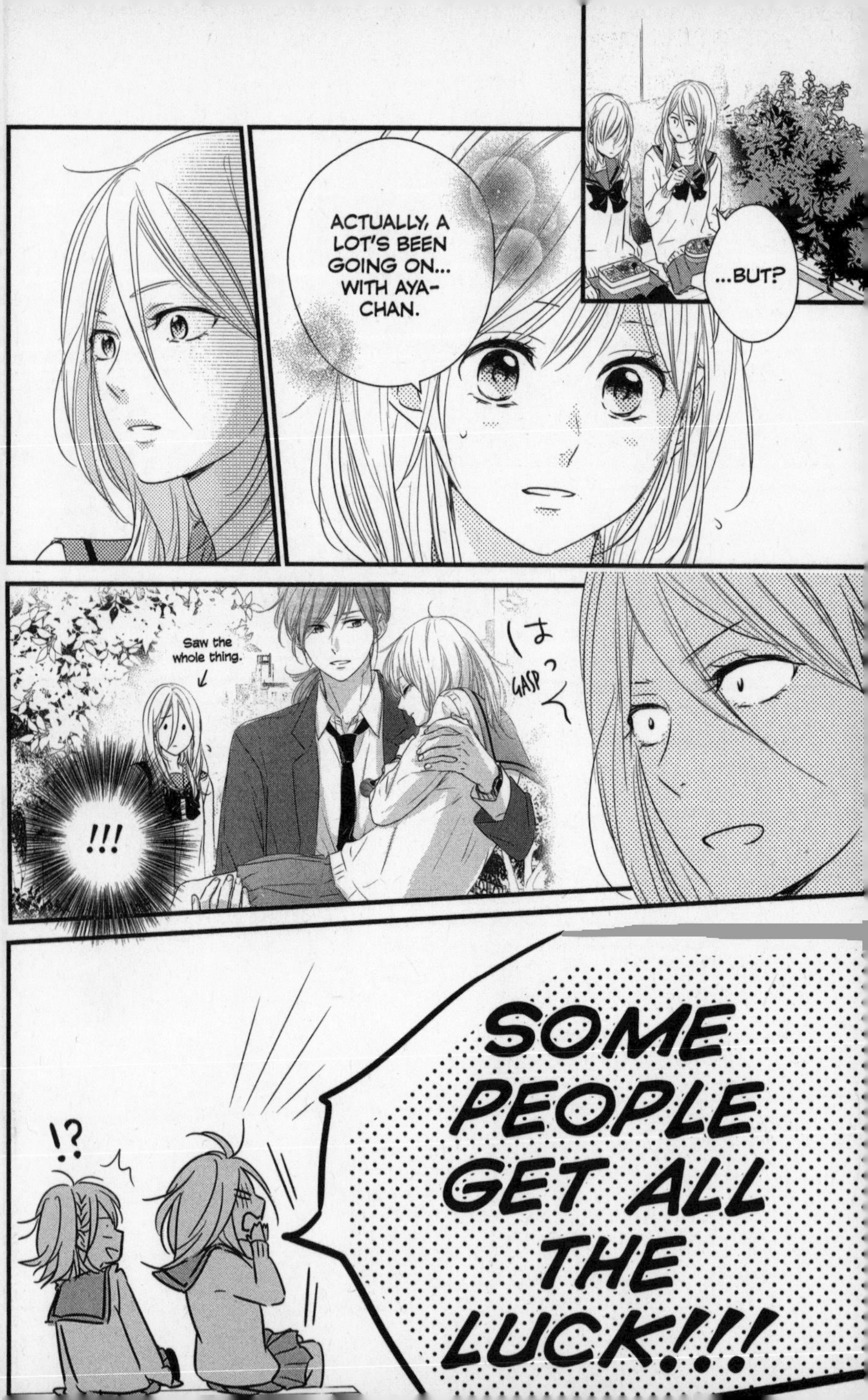
...BUT?
ACTUALLY, A LOT'S BEEN GOING ON... WITH AYA-CHAN.
はっ
GASP
Saw the whole thing.
!!!
SOME PEOPLE GET ALL THE LUCK!!!
!?

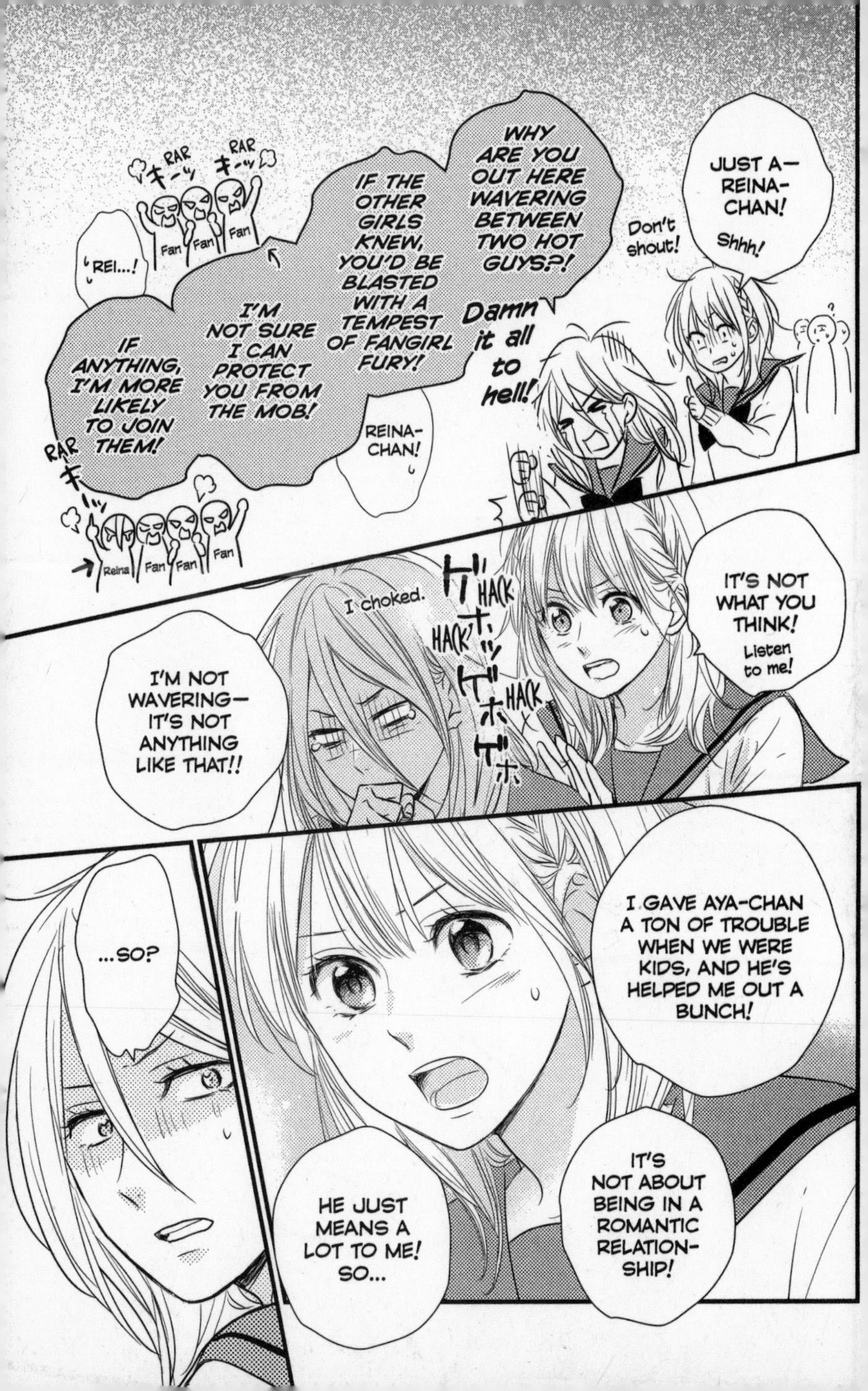
JUST A— REINA-CHAN!
Shhh!
Don't shout!
WHY ARE YOU OUT HERE WAVERING BETWEEN TWO HOT GUYS?!
Damn it all to hell!
IF THE OTHER GIRLS KNEW, YOU'D BE BLASTED WITH A TEMPEST OF FANGIRL FURY!
RAR
RAR
Fan
Fan
Fan
I'M NOT SURE I CAN PROTECT YOU FROM THE MOB!
REINA-CHAN!
IF ANYTHING, I'M MORE LIKELY TO JOIN THEM!
REI...!
RAR
Reina
Fan
Fan
Fan
IT'S NOT WHAT YOU THINK!
Listen to me!
HACK
HACK
HACK
I choked.
I'M NOT WAVERING— IT'S NOT ANYTHING LIKE THAT!!
I GAVE AYA-CHAN A TON OF TROUBLE WHEN WE WERE KIDS, AND HE'S HELPED ME OUT A BUNCH!
IT'S NOT ABOUT BEING IN A ROMANTIC RELATION-SHIP!
HE JUST MEANS A LOT TO ME! SO...
...SO?

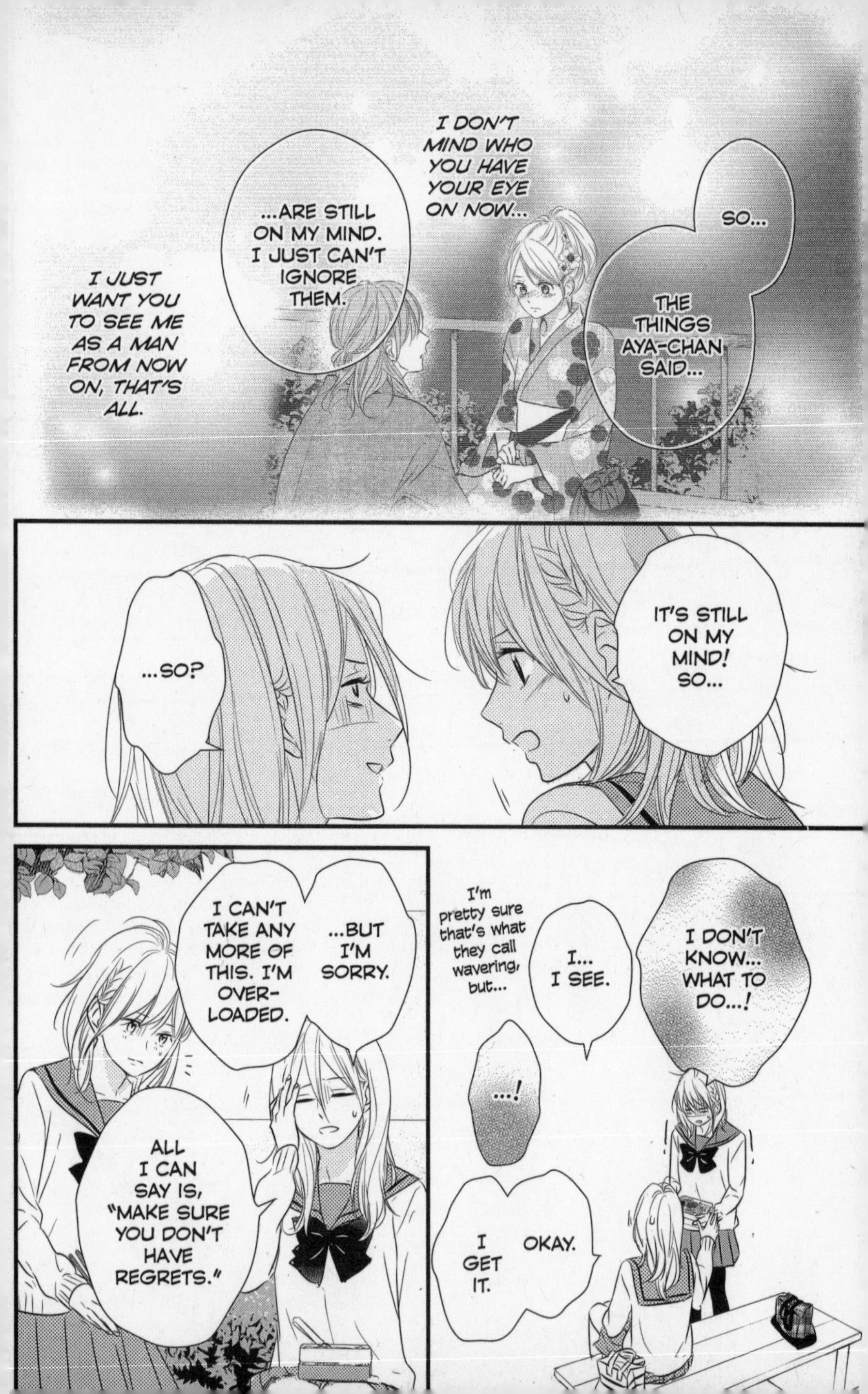
SO...
THE THINGS AYA-CHAN SAID...
I DON'T MIND WHO YOU HAVE YOUR EYE ON NOW...
...ARE STILL ON MY MIND. I JUST CAN'T IGNORE THEM.
I JUST WANT YOU TO SEE ME AS A MAN FROM NOW ON, THAT'S ALL.
IT'S STILL ON MY MIND! SO...
...SO?
I DON'T KNOW... WHAT TO DO...!
I... I SEE.
I'm pretty sure that's what they call wavering, but...
...!
OKAY.
I GET IT.
...BUT I'M SORRY.
I CAN'T TAKE ANY MORE OF THIS. I'M OVER-LOADED.
ALL I CAN SAY IS, "MAKE SURE YOU DON'T HAVE REGRETS."

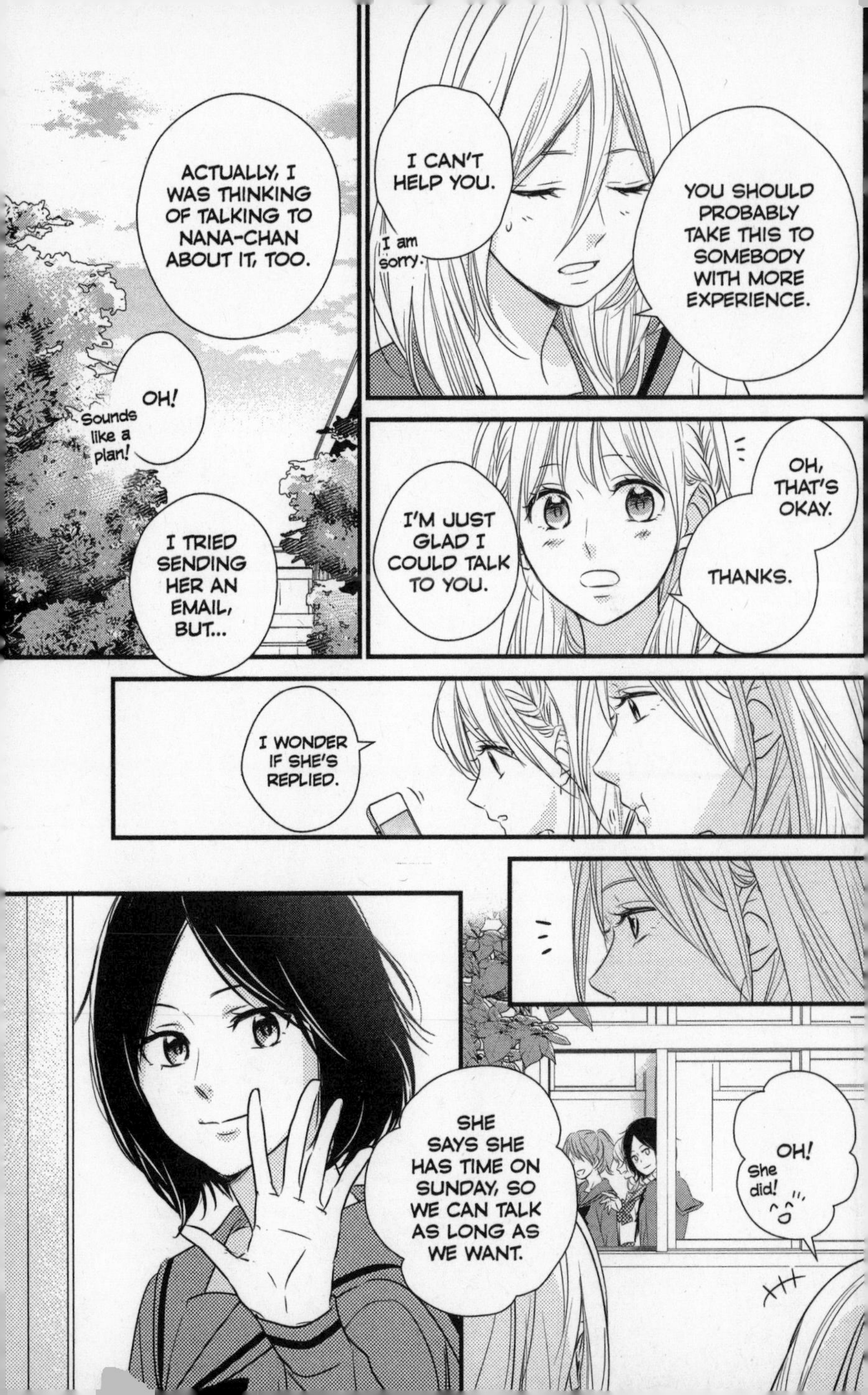

I CAN'T HELP YOU.
I am sorry.
YOU SHOULD PROBABLY TAKE THIS TO SOMEBODY WITH MORE EXPERIENCE.
OH, THAT'S OKAY.
THANKS.
I'M JUST GLAD I COULD TALK TO YOU.
ACTUALLY, I WAS THINKING OF TALKING TO NANA-CHAN ABOUT IT, TOO.
OH!
Sounds like a plan!
I TRIED SENDING HER AN EMAIL, BUT...
I WONDER IF SHE'S REPLIED.
OH!
She did!
SHE SAYS SHE HAS TIME ON SUNDAY, SO WE CAN TALK AS LONG AS WE WANT.

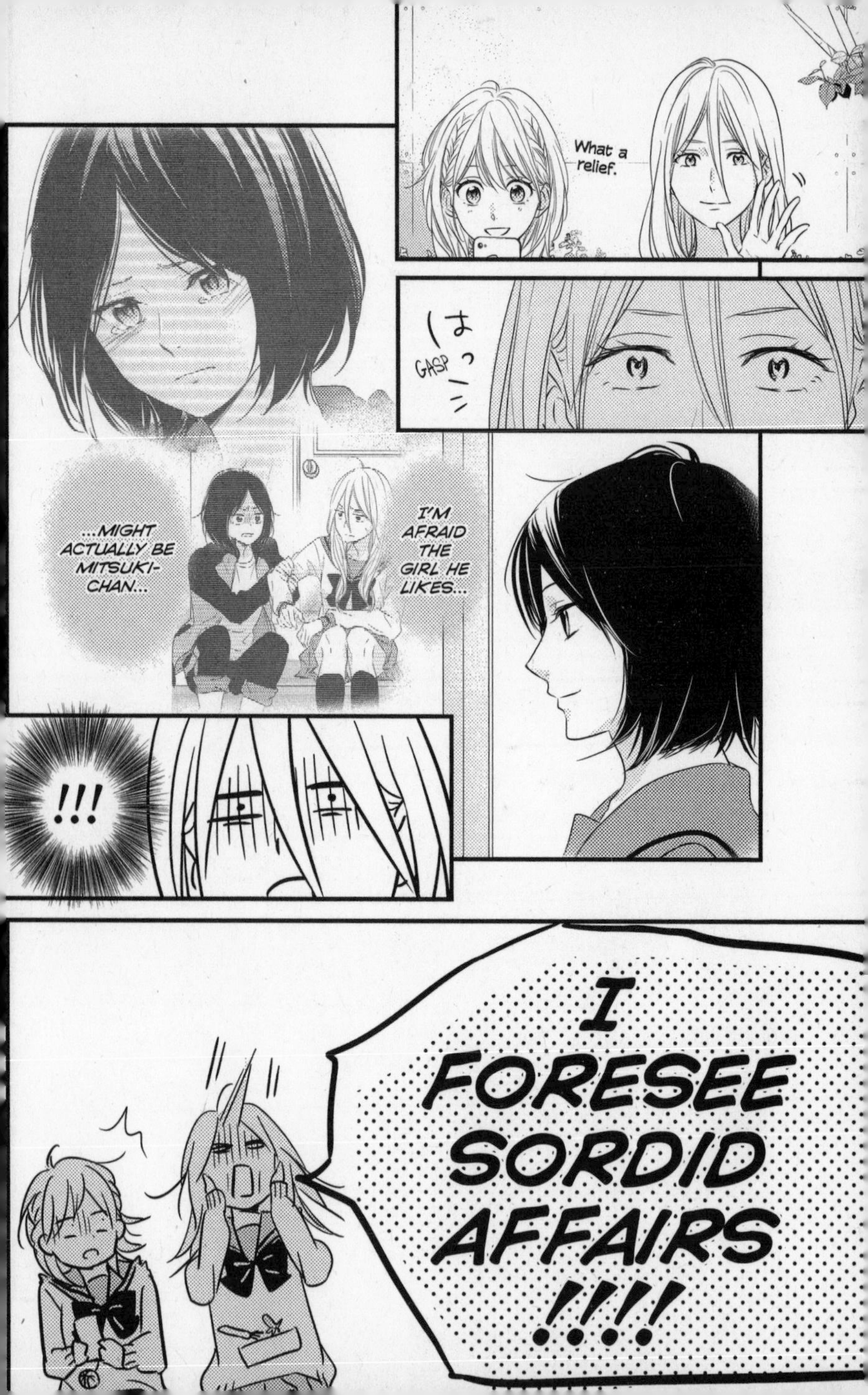
What a relief.
はっ
GASP
I'M AFRAID THE GIRL HE LIKES...
...MIGHT ACTUALLY BE MITSUKI-CHAN...
!!!
I FORESEE SORDID AFFAIRS!!!!

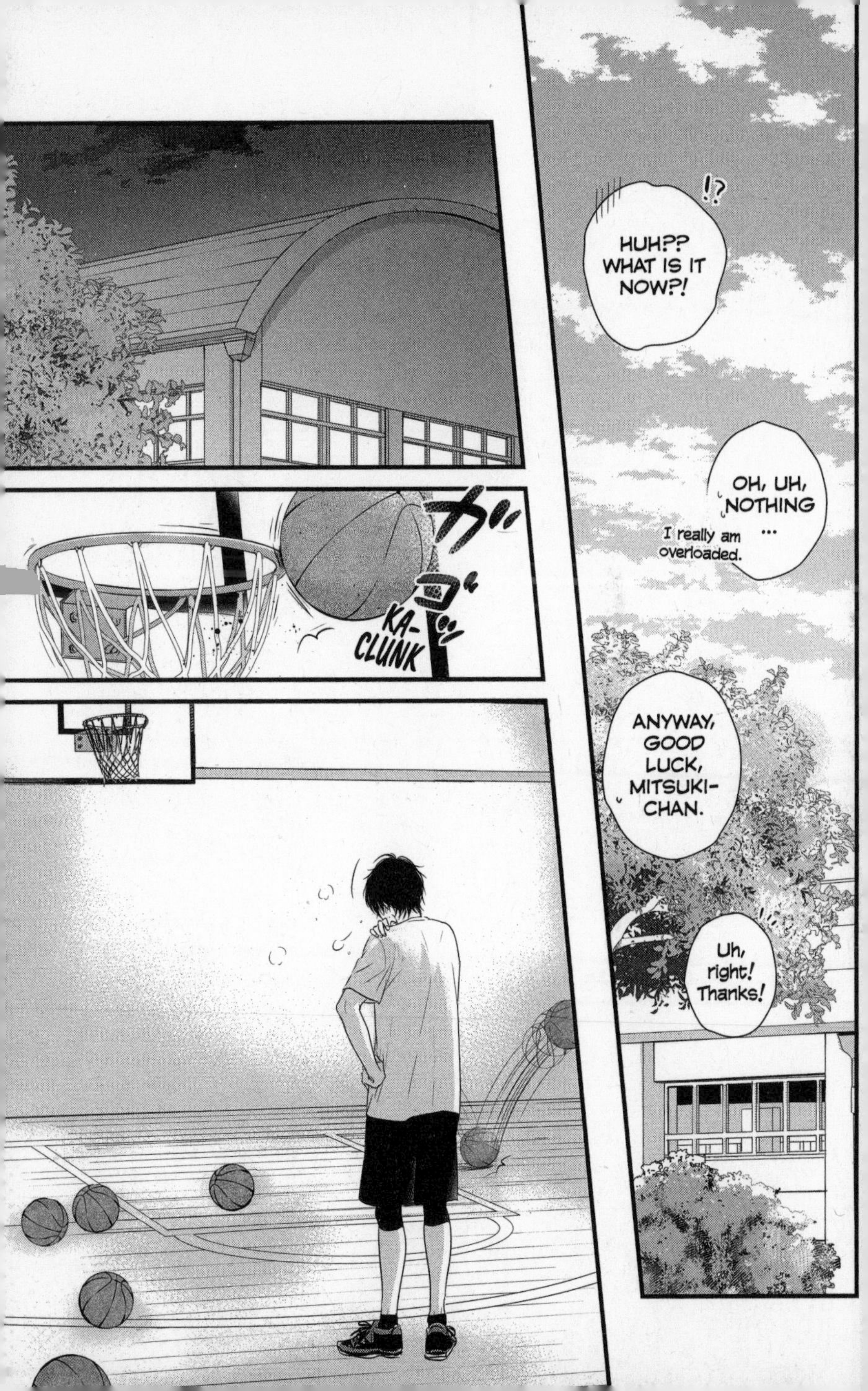
!?
HUH?? WHAT IS IT NOW?!
OH, UH, NOTHING ...
I really am overloaded.
ANYWAY, GOOD LUCK, MITSUKI-CHAN.
Uh, right! Thanks!
KA-CLUNK

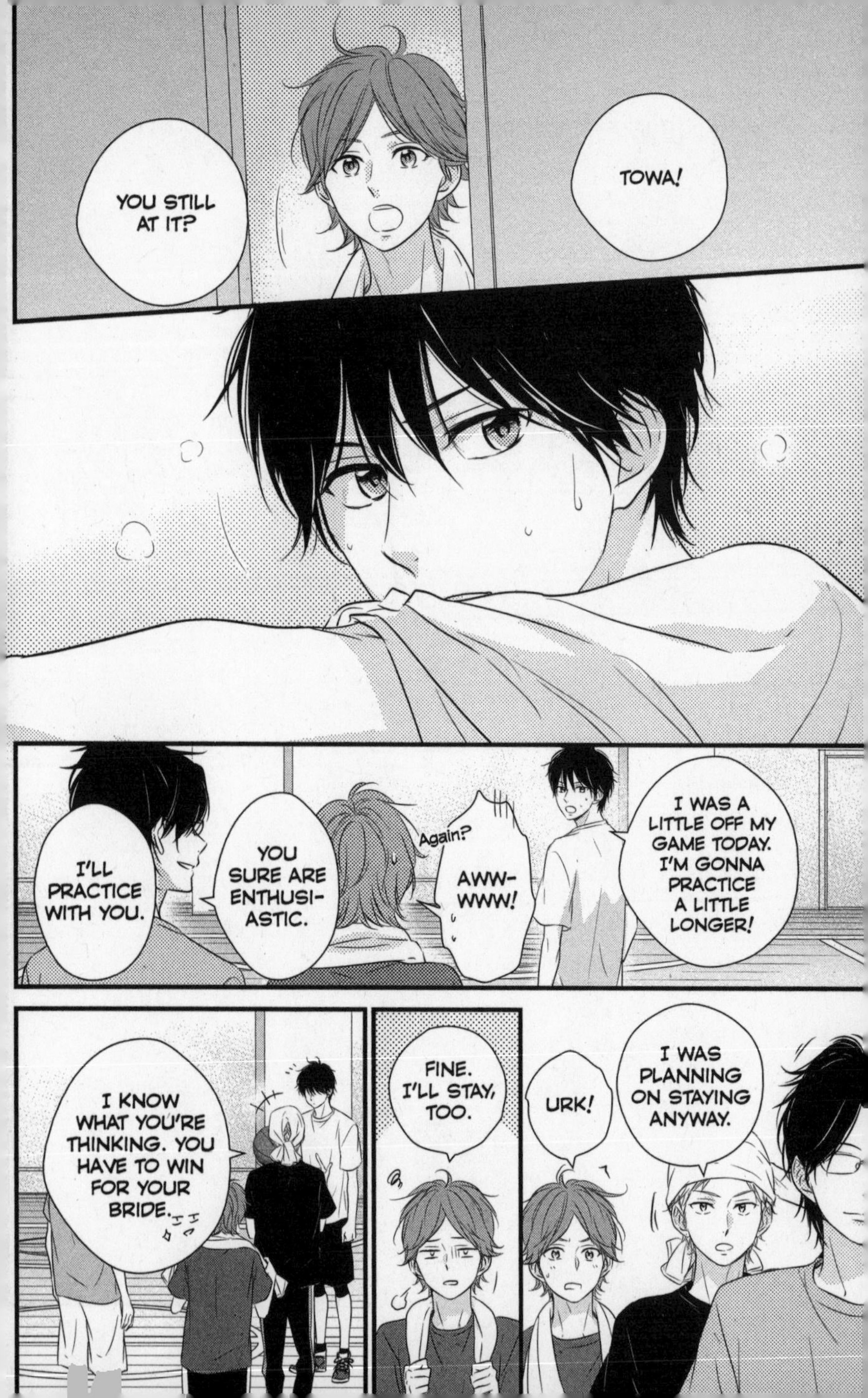
TOWA!
YOU STILL AT IT?
I WAS A LITTLE OFF MY GAME TODAY. I'M GONNA PRACTICE A LITTLE LONGER!
Again?
AWW-WWW!
YOU SURE ARE ENTHUSI-ASTIC.
I'LL PRACTICE WITH YOU.
I WAS PLANNING ON STAYING ANYWAY.
URK!
FINE. I'LL STAY, TOO.
I KNOW WHAT YOU'RE THINKING. YOU HAVE TO WIN FOR YOUR BRIDE.

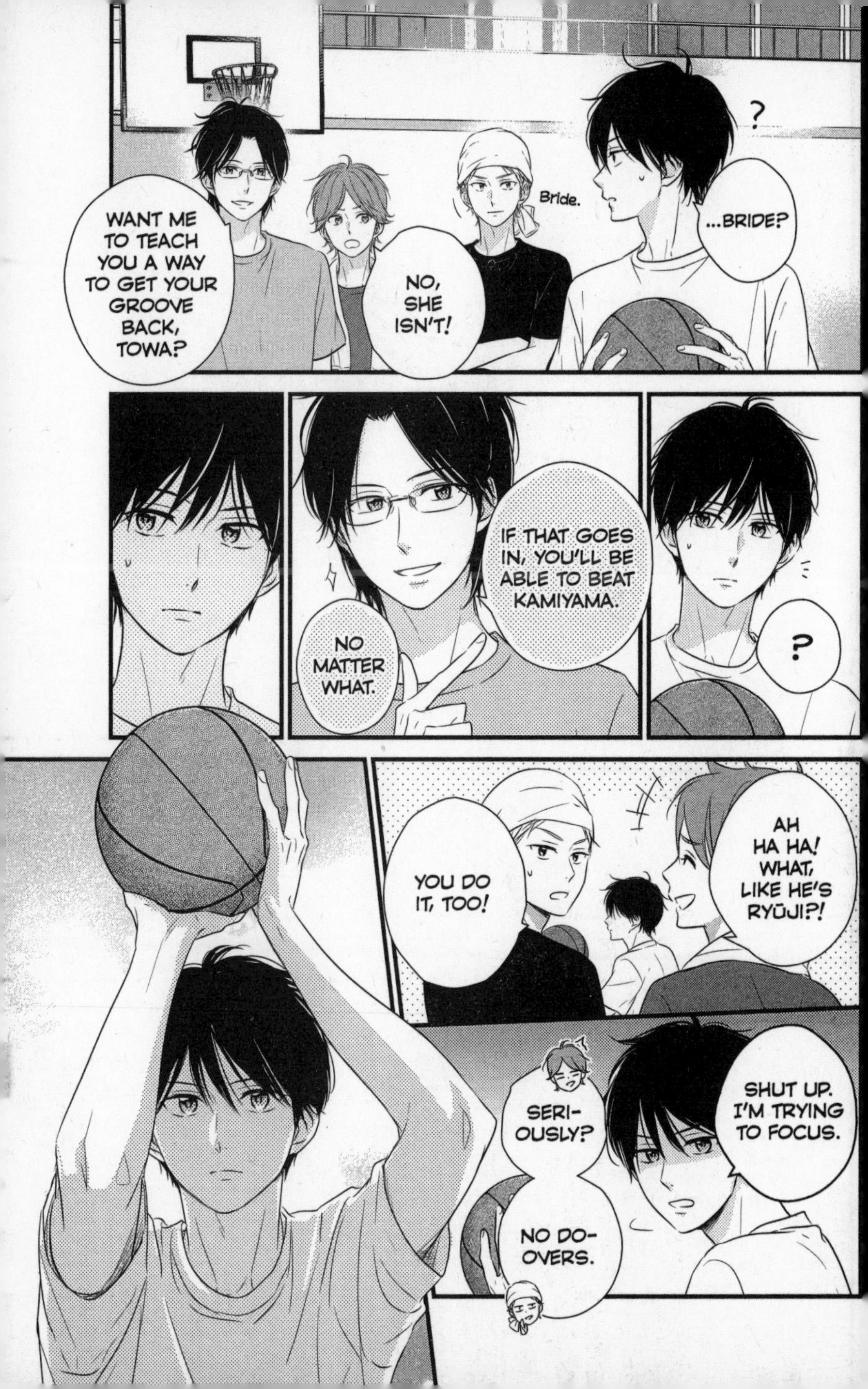
?
...BRIDE?
Bride.
NO, SHE ISN'T!
WANT ME TO TEACH YOU A WAY TO GET YOUR GROOVE BACK, TOWA?
?
IF THAT GOES IN, YOU'LL BE ABLE TO BEAT KAMIYAMA.
NO MATTER WHAT.
AH HA HA! WHAT, LIKE HE'S RYŪJI?!
YOU DO IT, TOO!
SHUT UP. I'M TRYING TO FOCUS.
SERI-OUSLY?
NO DO-OVERS.

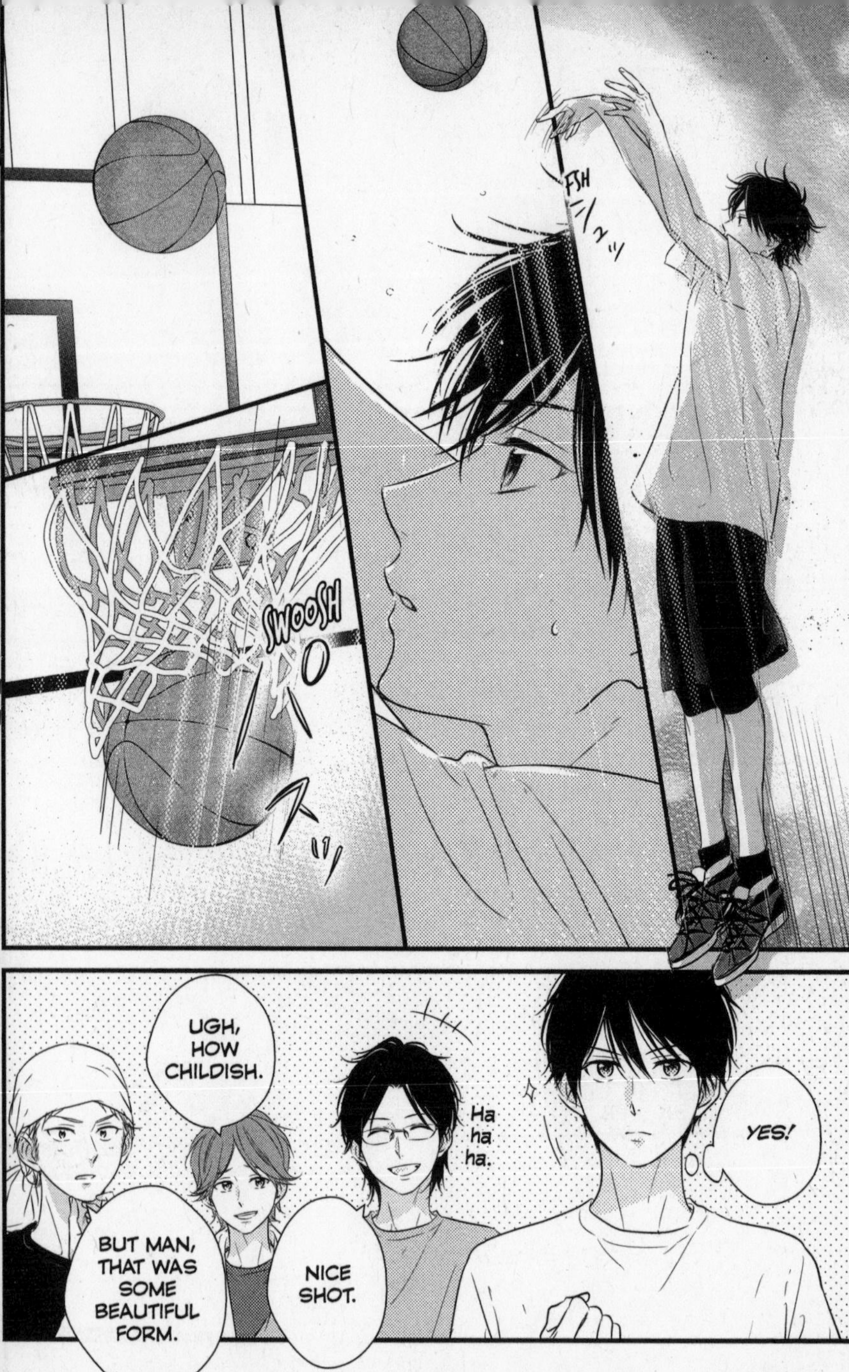
FSH
SWOOSH
YES!
Ha ha ha.
UGH, HOW CHILDISH.
NICE SHOT.
BUT MAN, THAT WAS SOME BEAUTIFUL FORM.

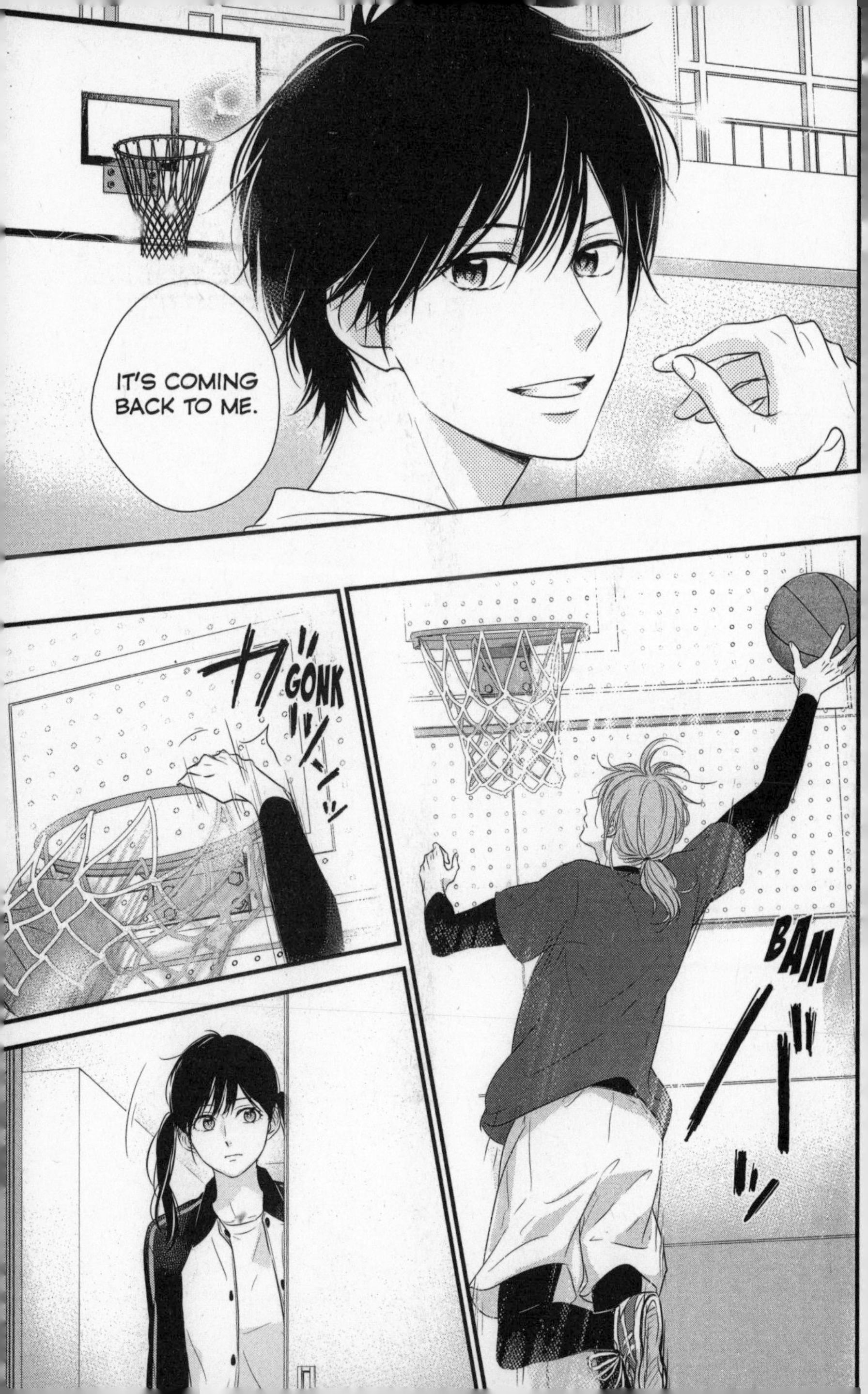
IT'S COMING BACK TO ME.
BAM
GONK

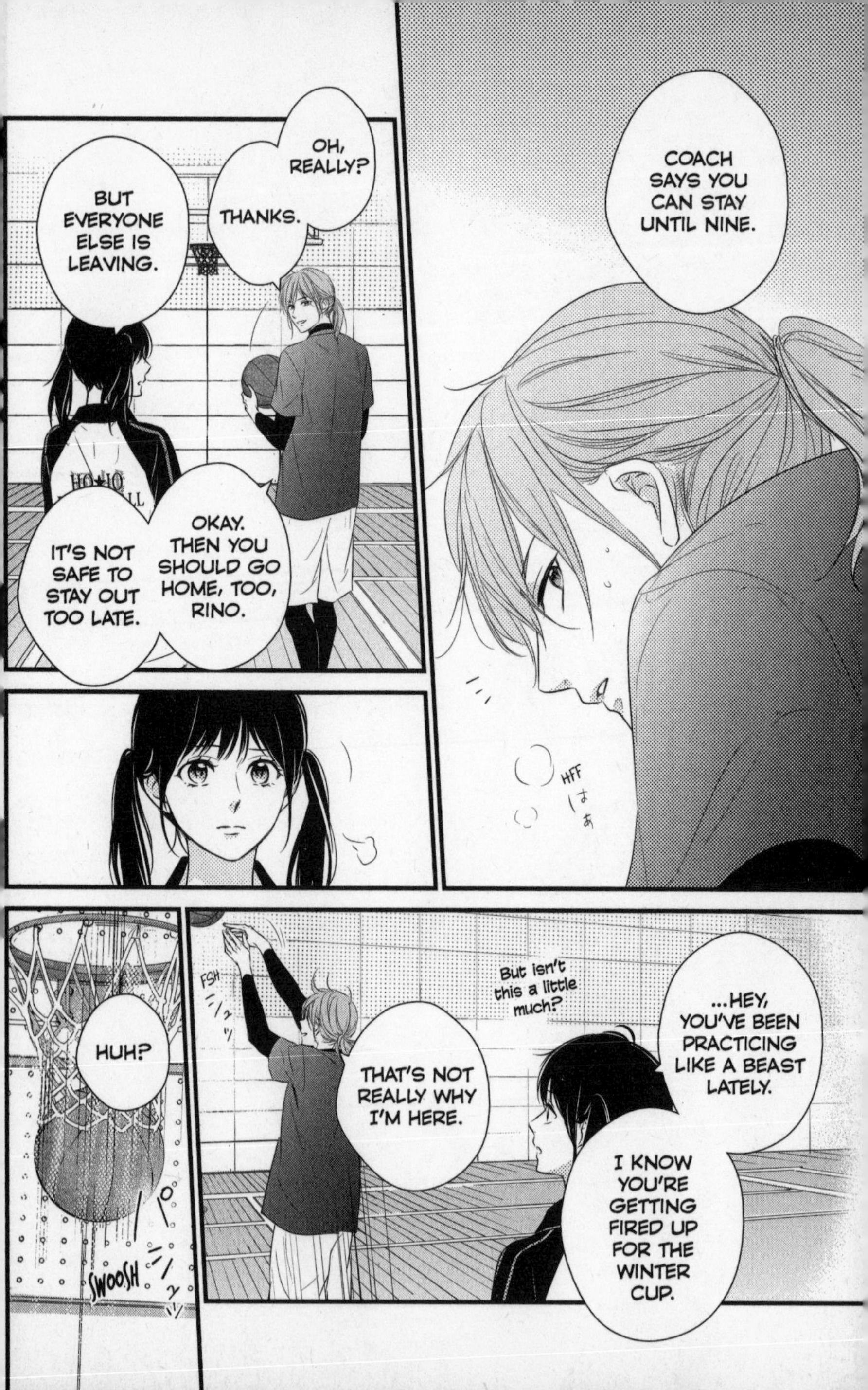
COACH SAYS YOU CAN STAY UNTIL NINE.
HFF
OH, REALLY?
THANKS.
BUT EVERYONE ELSE IS LEAVING.
OKAY. THEN YOU SHOULD GO HOME, TOO, RINO.
IT'S NOT SAFE TO STAY OUT TOO LATE.
...HEY, YOU'VE BEEN PRACTICING LIKE A BEAST LATELY.
I KNOW YOU'RE GETTING FIRED UP FOR THE WINTER CUP.
But isn't this a little much?
THAT'S NOT REALLY WHY I'M HERE.
FSH
HUH?
SWOOSH

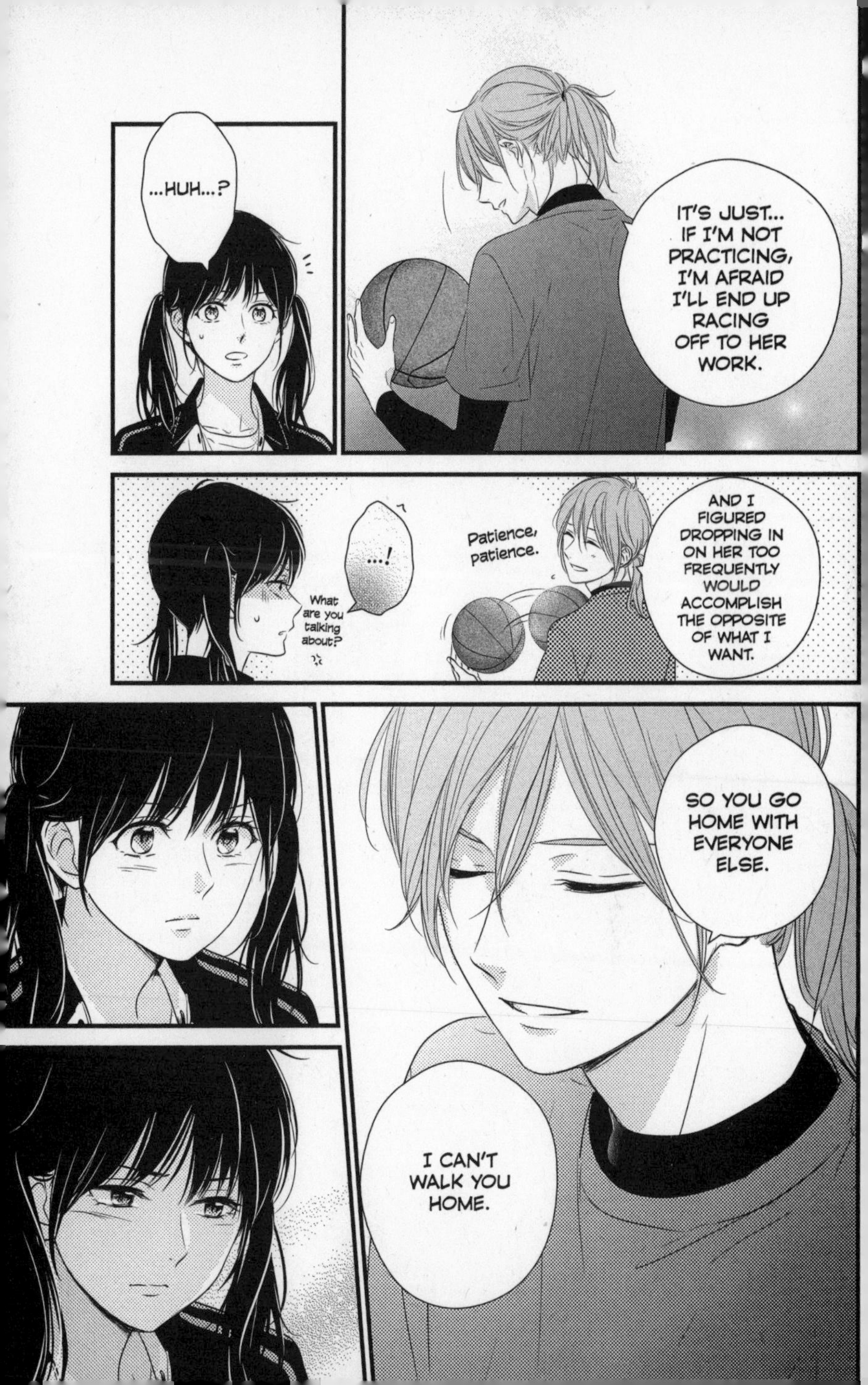
IT'S JUST... IF I'M NOT PRACTICING, I'M AFRAID I'LL END UP RACING OFF TO HER WORK.
...HUH...?
AND I FIGURED DROPPING IN ON HER TOO FREQUENTLY WOULD ACCOMPLISH THE OPPOSITE OF WHAT I WANT.
Patience, patience.
...!
What are you talking about?
SO YOU GO HOME WITH EVERYONE ELSE.
I CAN'T WALK YOU HOME.

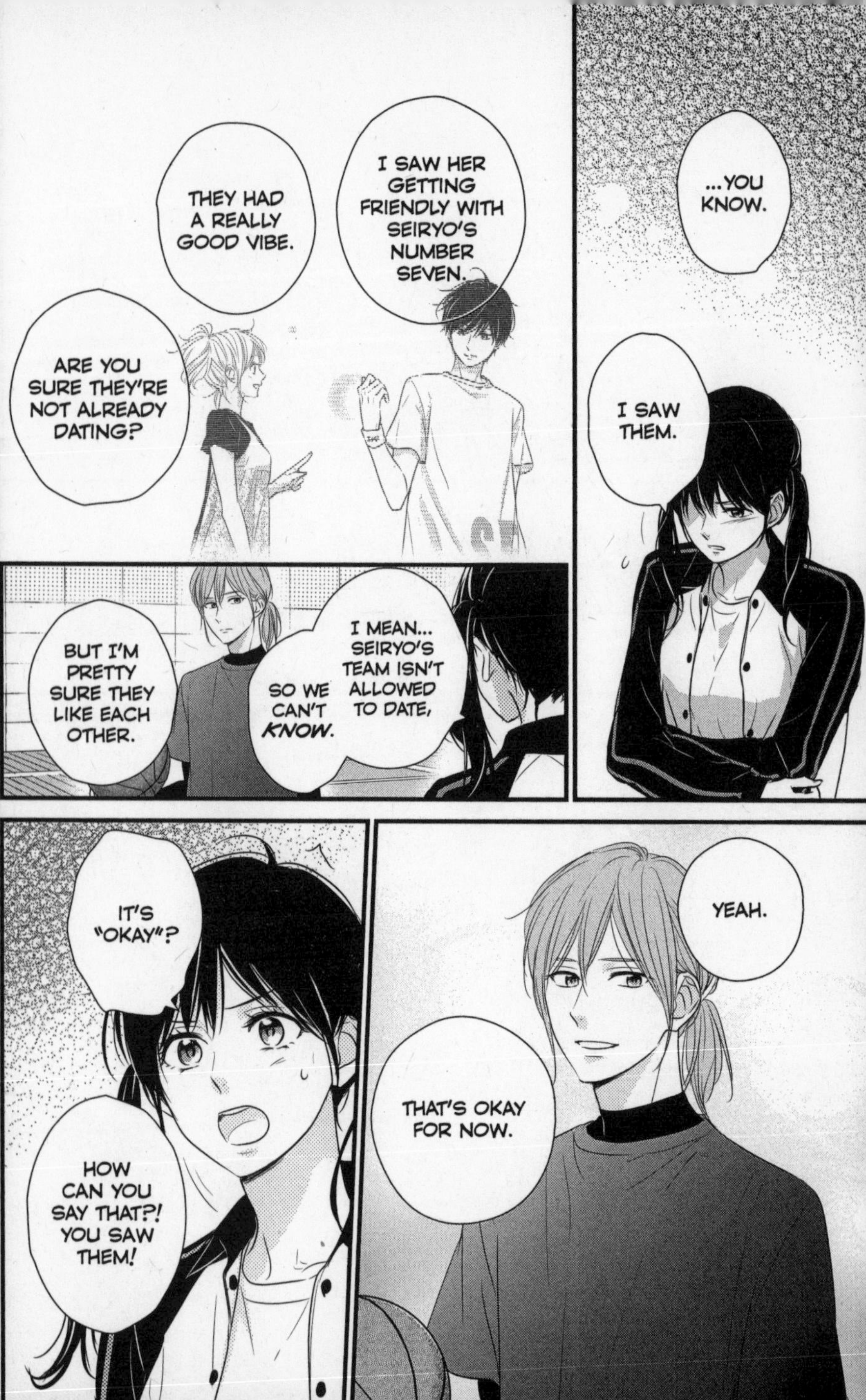
...YOU KNOW.
I SAW THEM.
I SAW HER GETTING FRIENDLY WITH SEIRYO'S NUMBER SEVEN.
THEY HAD A REALLY GOOD VIBE.
ARE YOU SURE THEY'RE NOT ALREADY DATING?
I MEAN... SEIRYO'S TEAM ISN'T ALLOWED TO DATE,
SO WE CAN'T *KNOW*.
BUT I'M PRETTY SURE THEY LIKE EACH OTHER.
YEAH.
THAT'S OKAY FOR NOW.
IT'S "OKAY"?
HOW CAN YOU SAY THAT?! YOU SAW THEM!

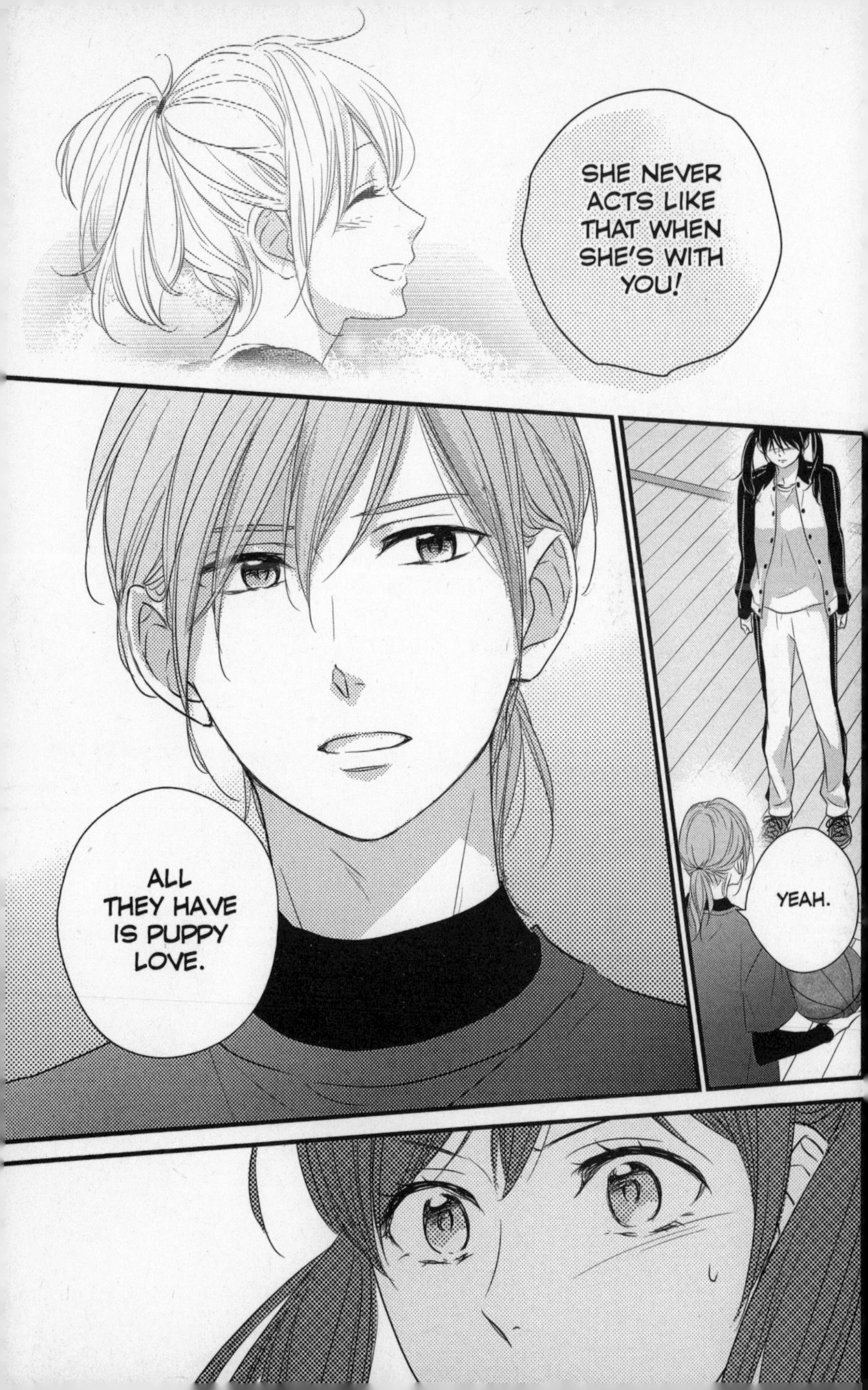
SHE NEVER ACTS LIKE THAT WHEN SHE'S WITH YOU!
YEAH.
ALL THEY HAVE IS PUPPY LOVE.

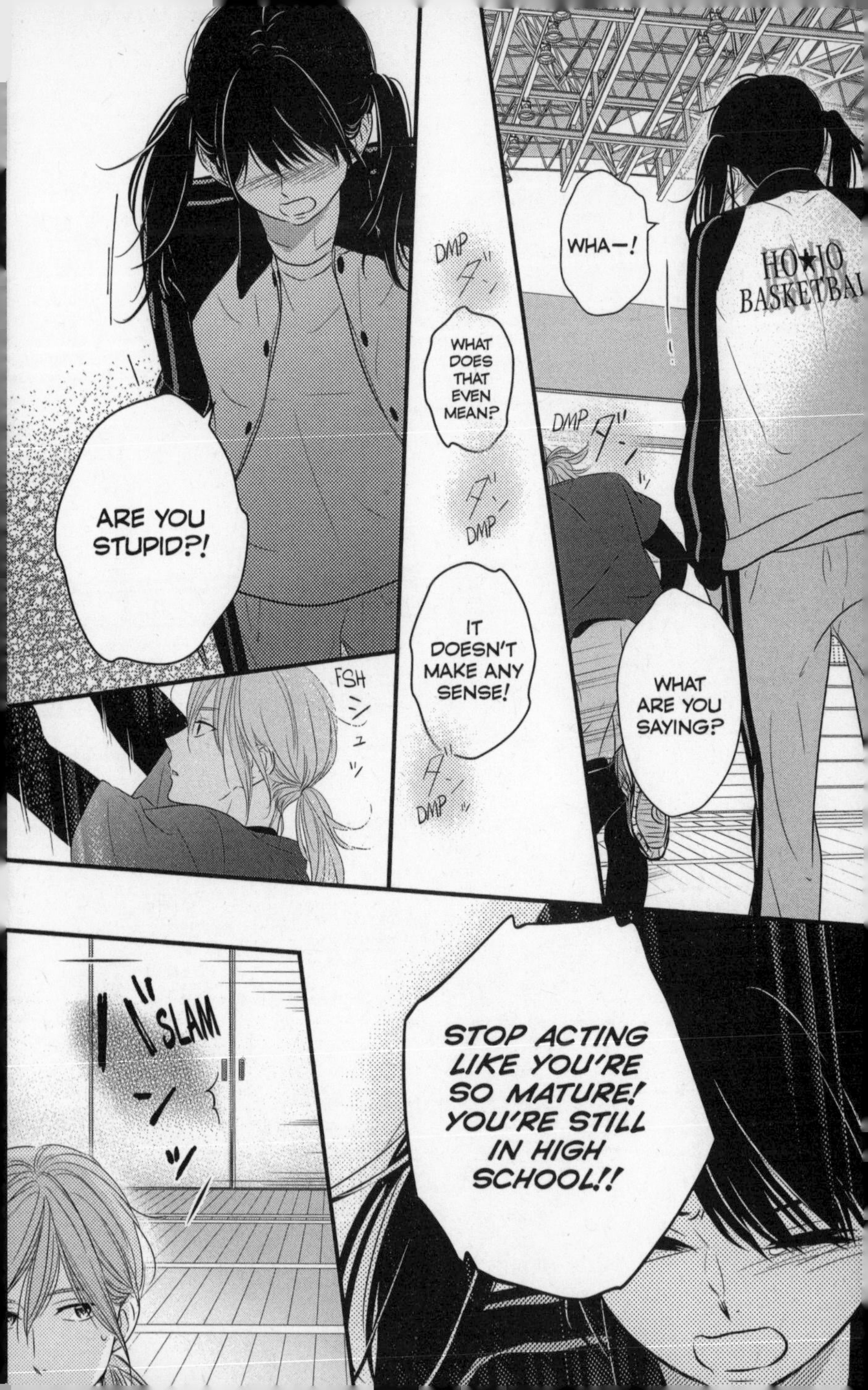
WHA—!
DMP
WHAT ARE YOU SAYING?
DMP
WHAT DOES THAT EVEN MEAN?
DMP
IT DOESN'T MAKE ANY SENSE!
DMP
ARE YOU STUPID?!
FSH
STOP ACTING LIKE YOU'RE SO MATURE! YOU'RE STILL IN HIGH SCHOOL!!
SLAM

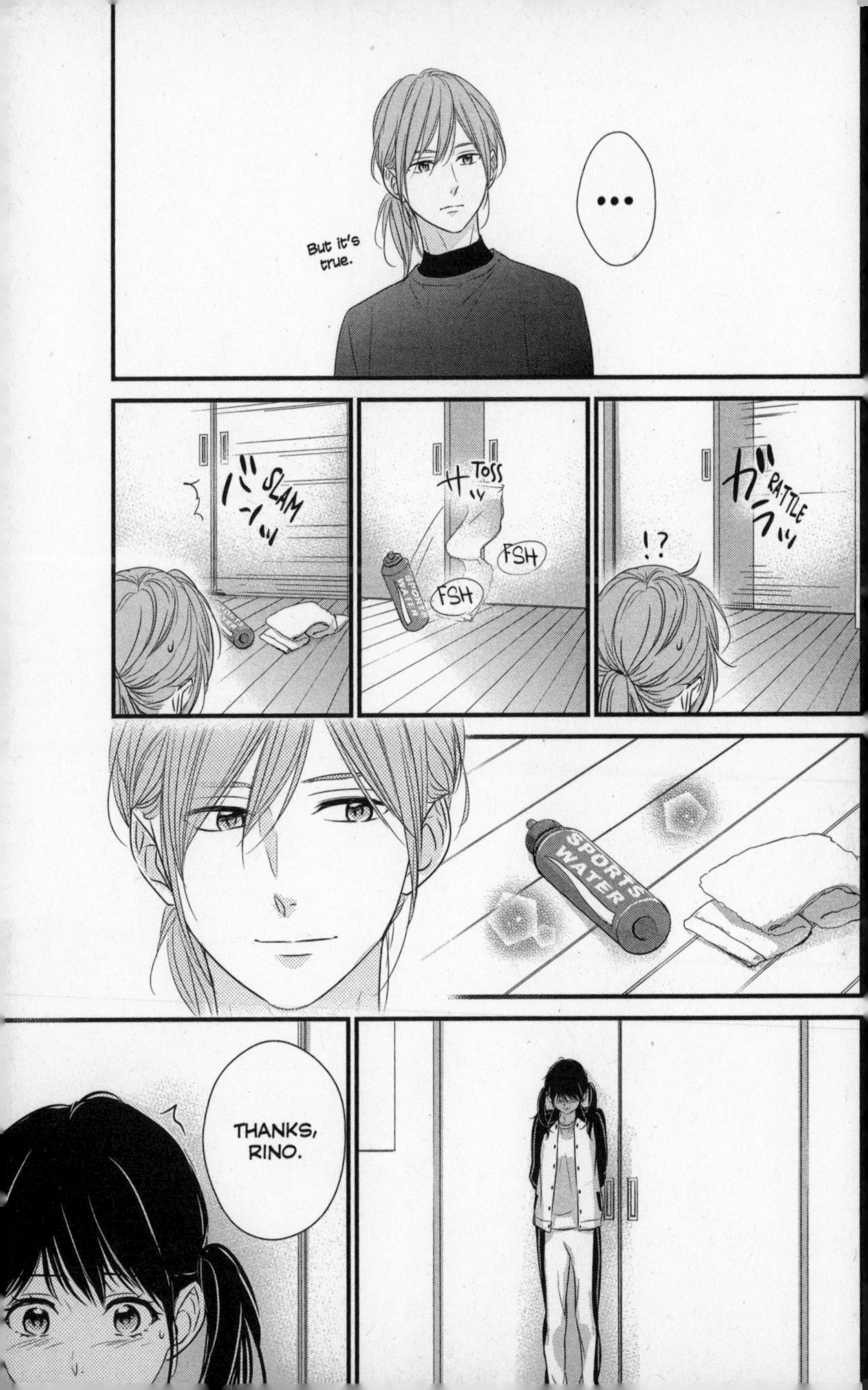
...
But it's true.
RATTLE
!?
TOSS
FSH
FSH
SLAM
SPORTS WATER
THANKS, RINO.

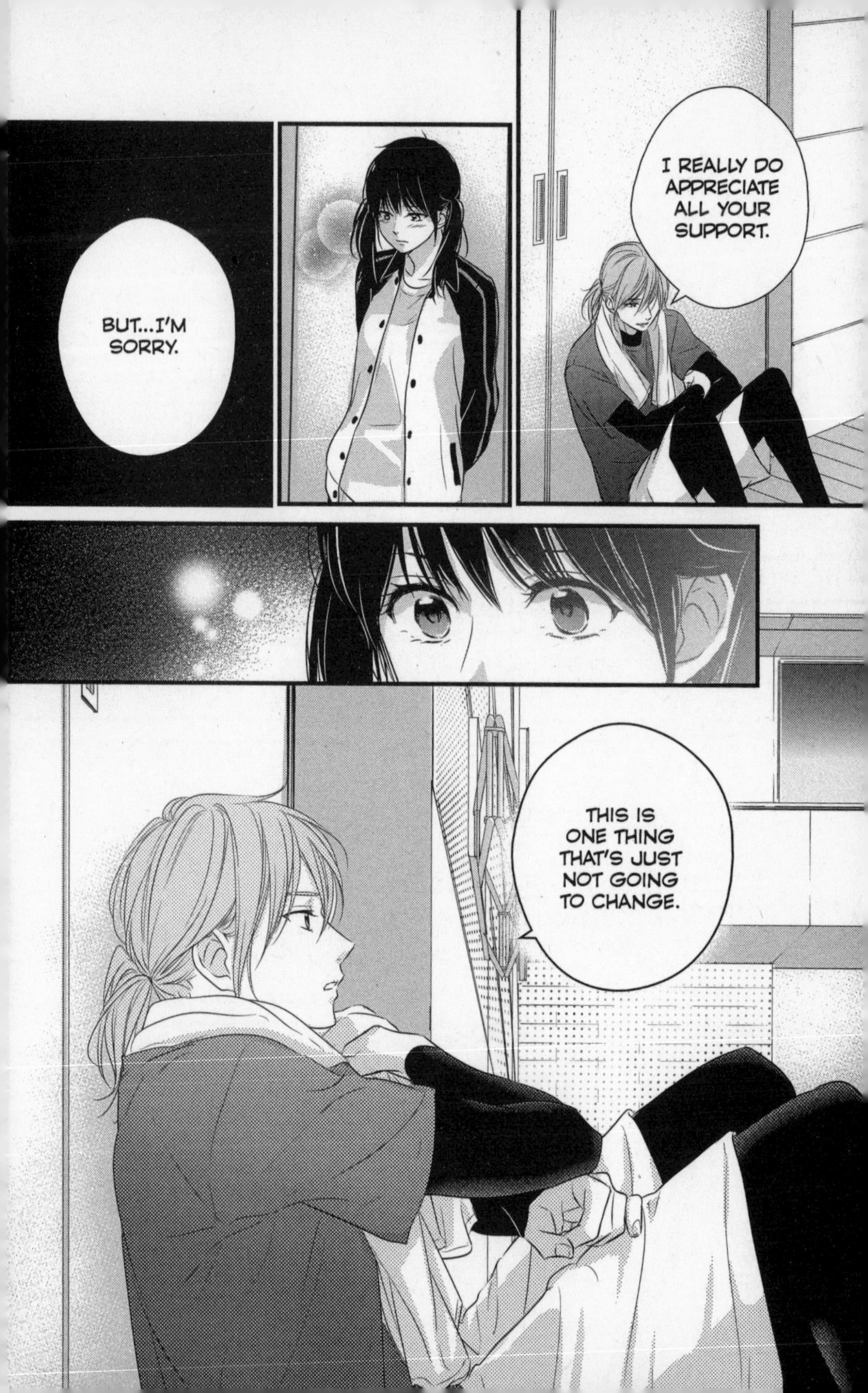
I REALLY DO APPRECIATE ALL YOUR SUPPORT.
BUT...I'M SORRY.
THIS IS ONE THING THAT'S JUST NOT GOING TO CHANGE.

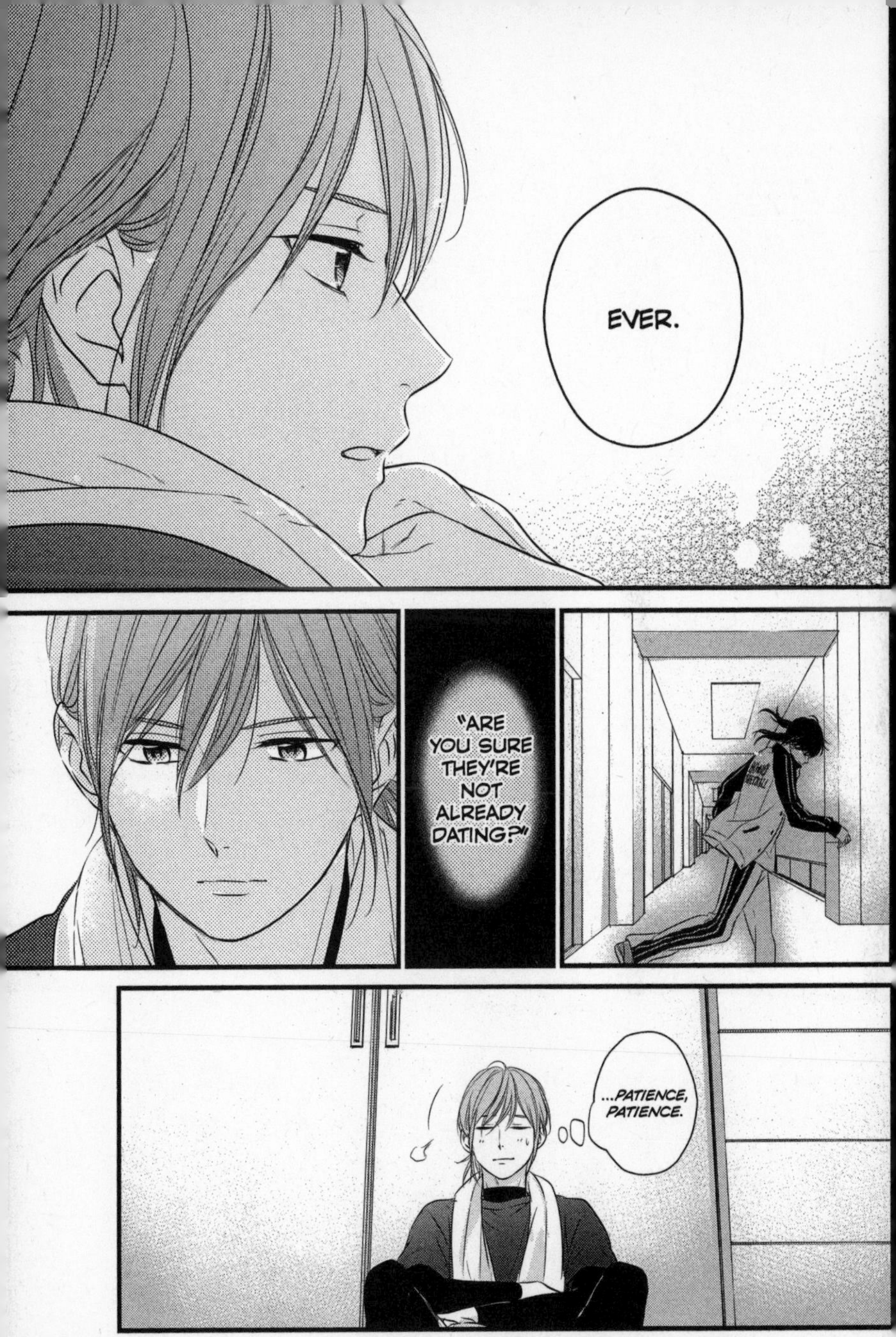
EVER.
"ARE YOU SURE THEY'RE NOT ALREADY DATING?"
...PATIENCE, PATIENCE.

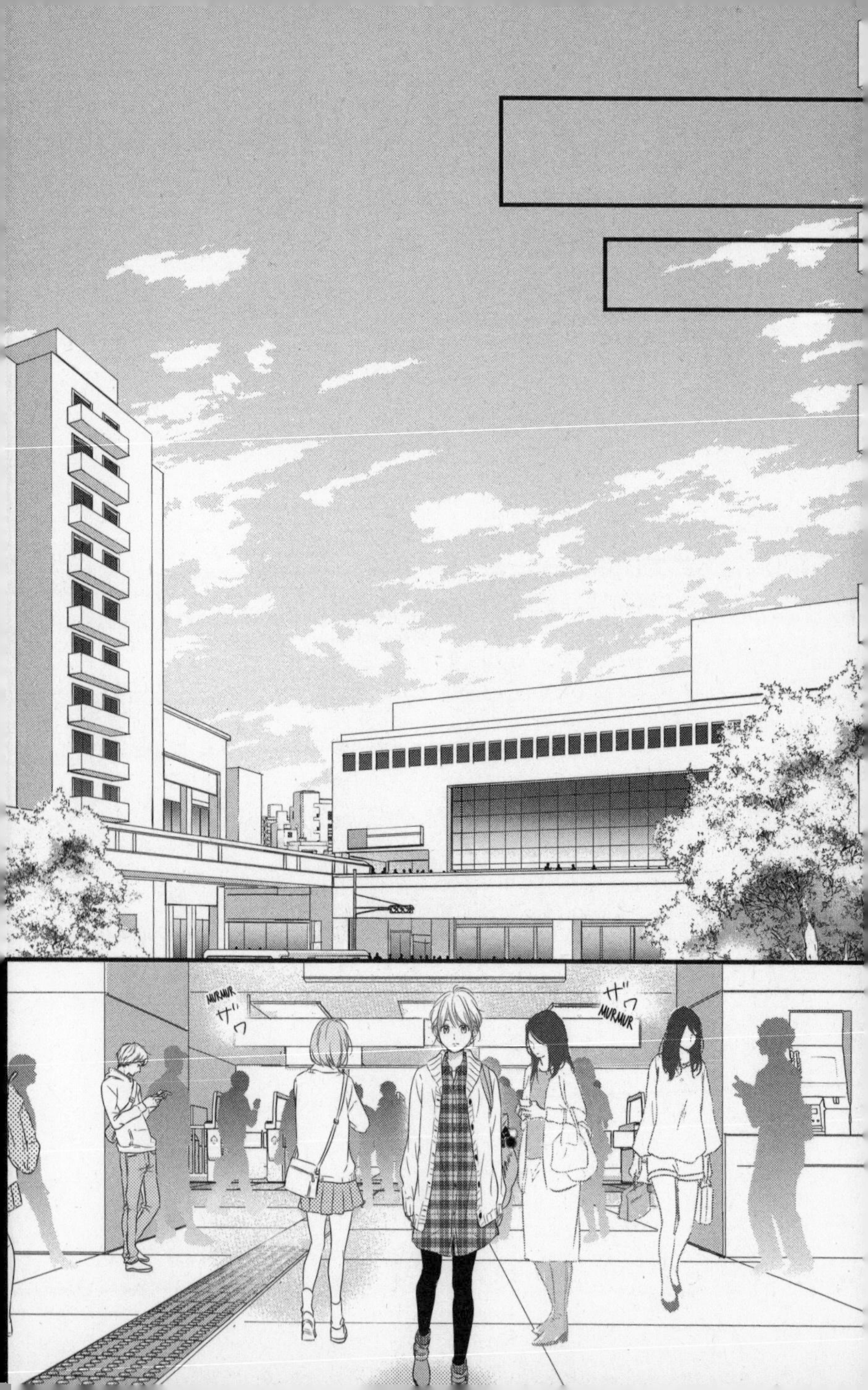
ザワ
MURMUR
MURMUR
ザワ

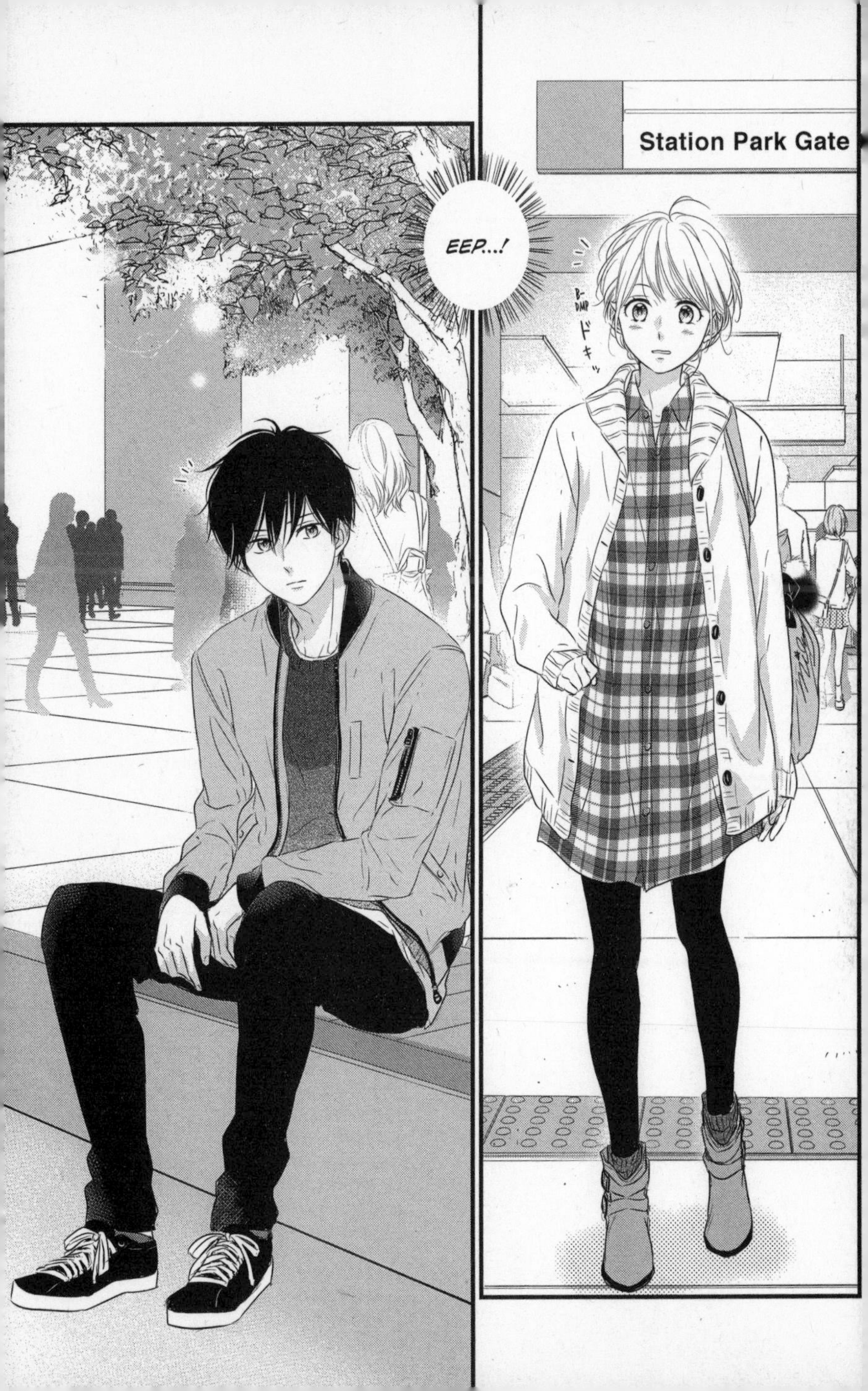
Station Park Gate
EEP...!
B-DMP
ドキッ

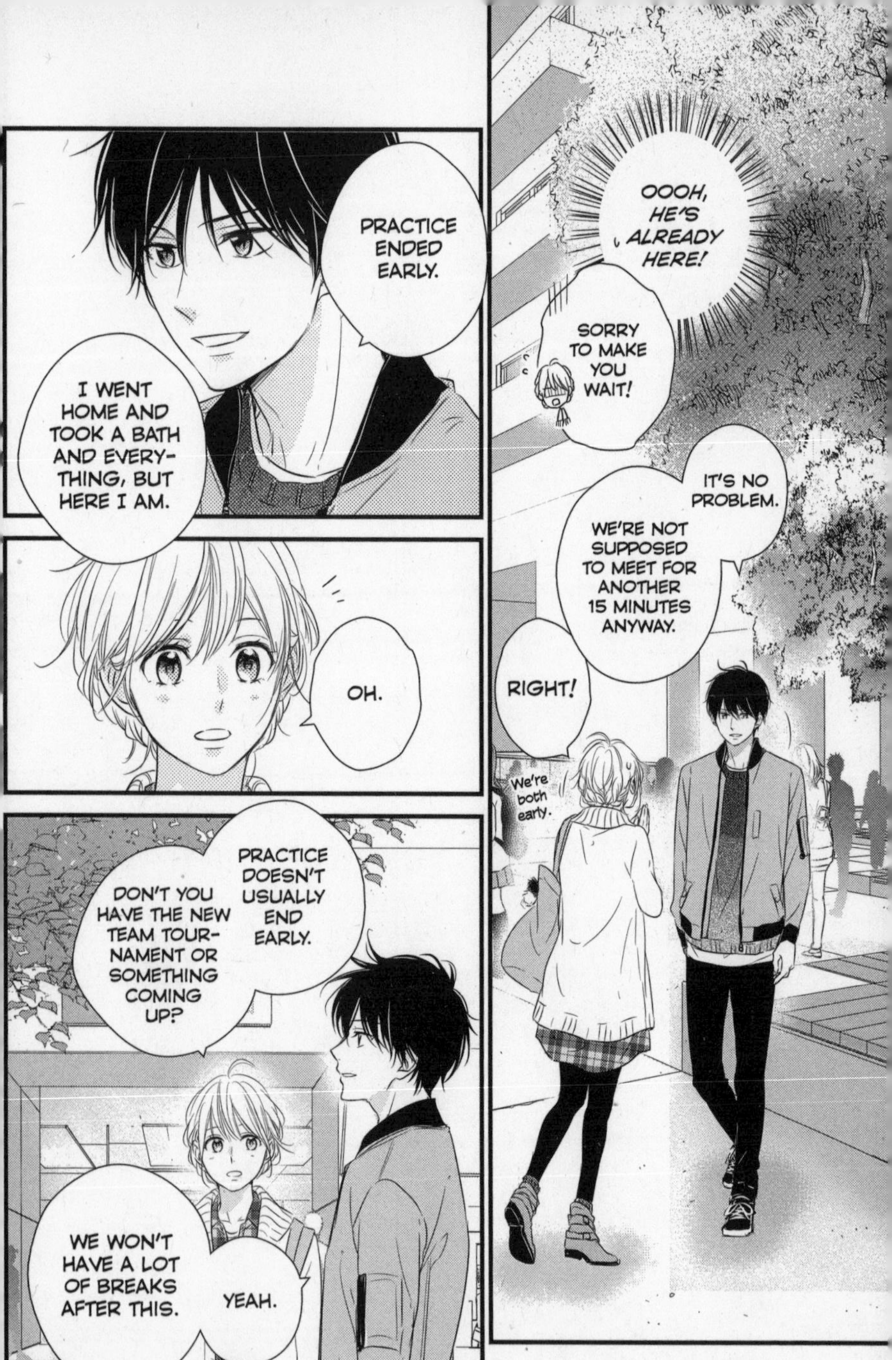
OOOH, HE'S ALREADY HERE!
SORRY TO MAKE YOU WAIT!
IT'S NO PROBLEM.
WE'RE NOT SUPPOSED TO MEET FOR ANOTHER 15 MINUTES ANYWAY.
RIGHT!
We're both early.
PRACTICE ENDED EARLY.
I WENT HOME AND TOOK A BATH AND EVERYTHING, BUT HERE I AM.
OH.
PRACTICE DOESN'T USUALLY END EARLY.
DON'T YOU HAVE THE NEW TEAM TOURNAMENT OR SOMETHING COMING UP?
YEAH.
WE WON'T HAVE A LOT OF BREAKS AFTER THIS.

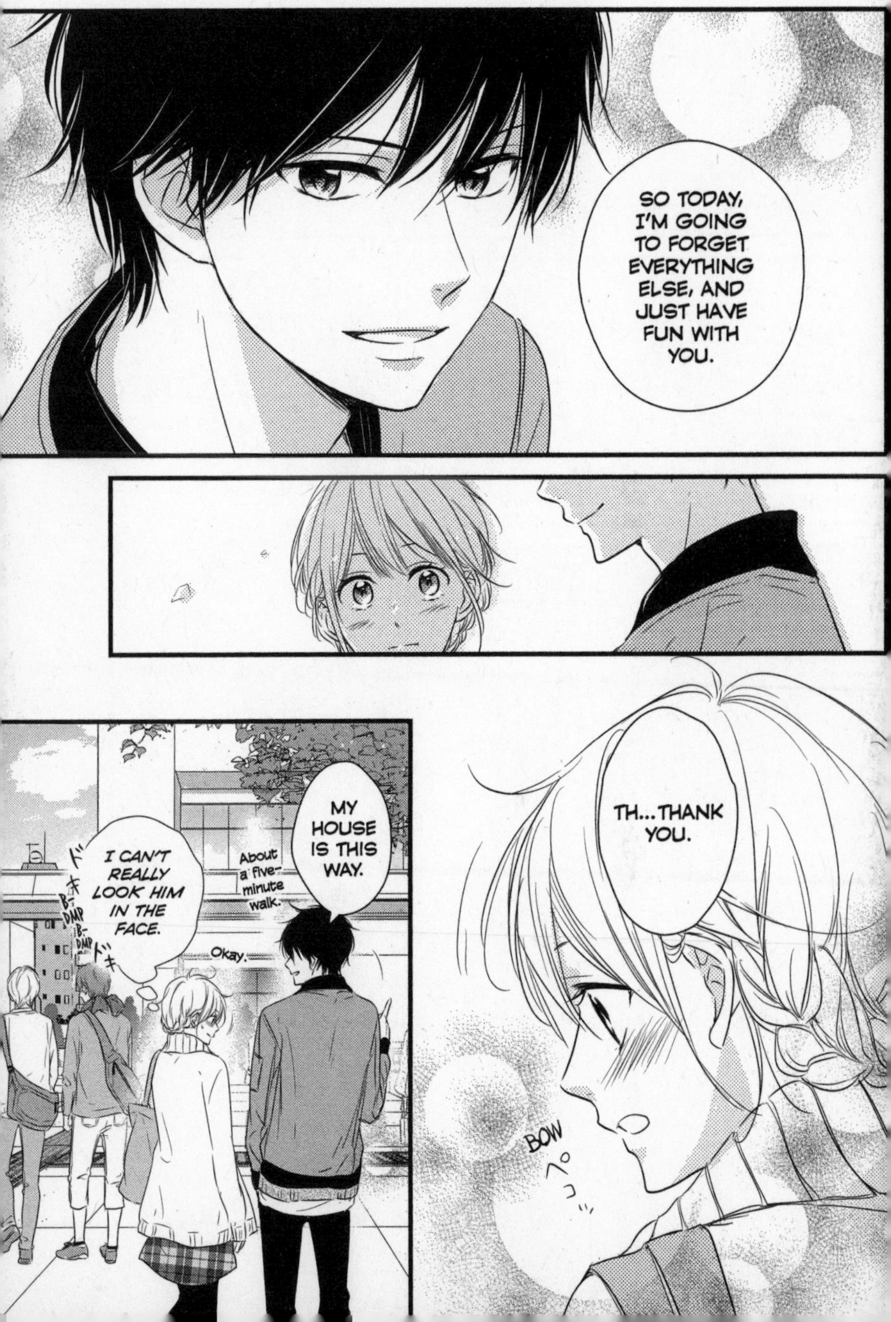
SO TODAY, I'M GOING TO FORGET EVERYTHING ELSE, AND JUST HAVE FUN WITH YOU.
TH...THANK YOU.
BOW
MY HOUSE IS THIS WAY.
About a five-minute walk.
Okay.
I CAN'T REALLY LOOK HIM IN THE FACE.
B-DMP B-DMP

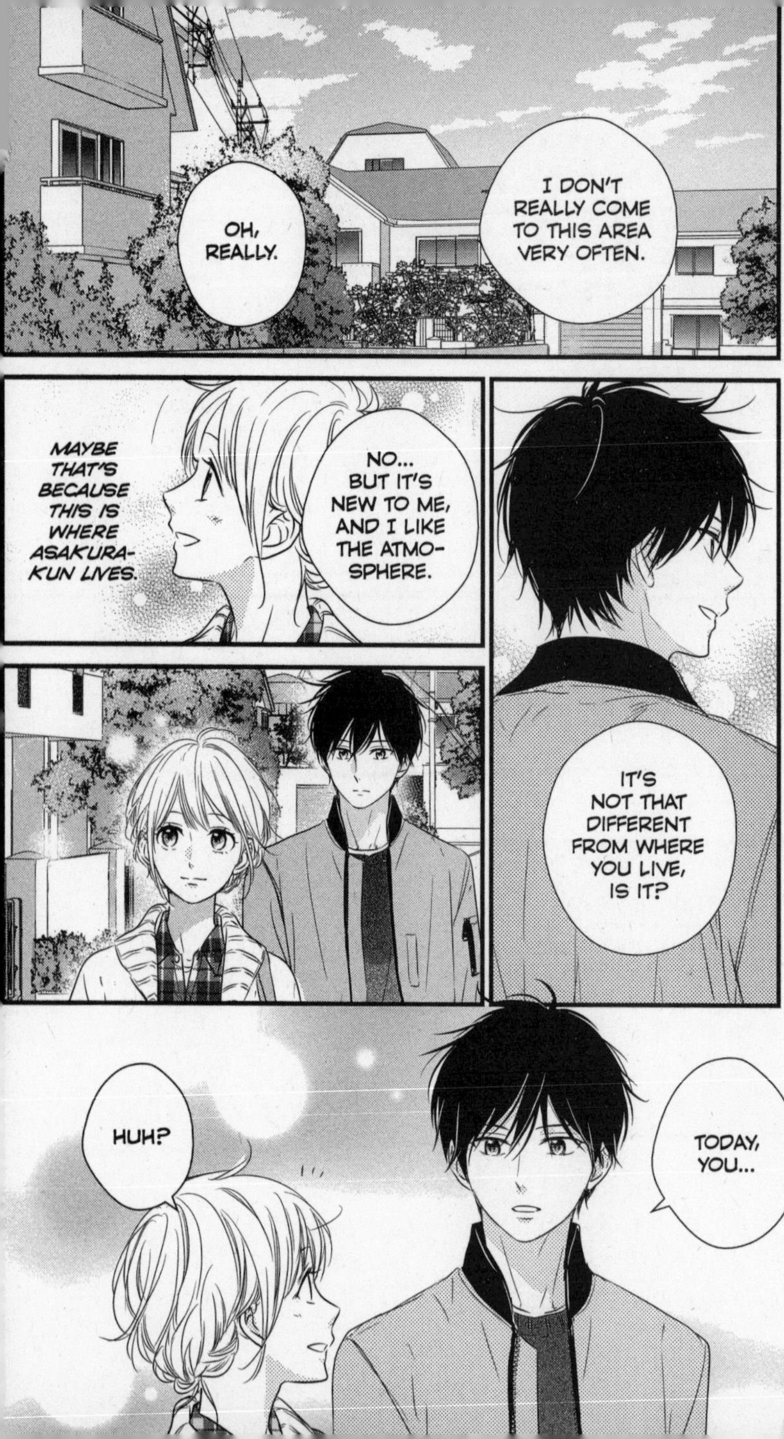
I DON'T REALLY COME TO THIS AREA VERY OFTEN.
OH, REALLY.
IT'S NOT THAT DIFFERENT FROM WHERE YOU LIVE, IS IT?
NO... BUT IT'S NEW TO ME, AND I LIKE THE ATMO-SPHERE.
MAYBE THAT'S BECAUSE THIS IS WHERE ASAKURA-KUN LIVES.
TODAY, YOU...
HUH?

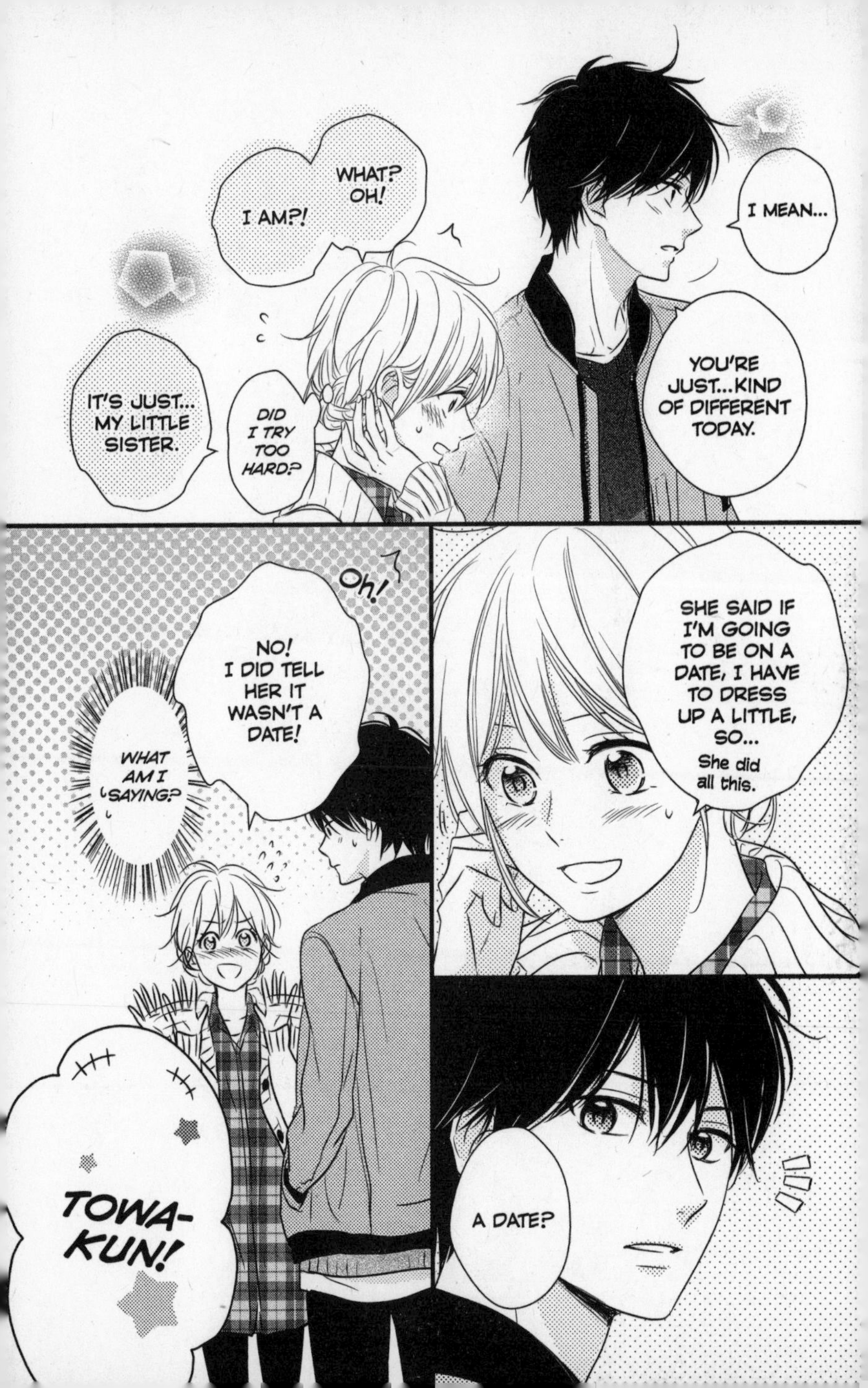
I MEAN...
YOU'RE JUST...KIND OF DIFFERENT TODAY.
WHAT? OH!
I AM?!
DID I TRY TOO HARD?
IT'S JUST... MY LITTLE SISTER.
SHE SAID IF I'M GOING TO BE ON A DATE, I HAVE TO DRESS UP A LITTLE, SO...
She did all this.
A DATE?
Oh!
NO! I DID TELL HER IT WASN'T A DATE!
WHAT AM I SAYING?
TOWA-KUN!

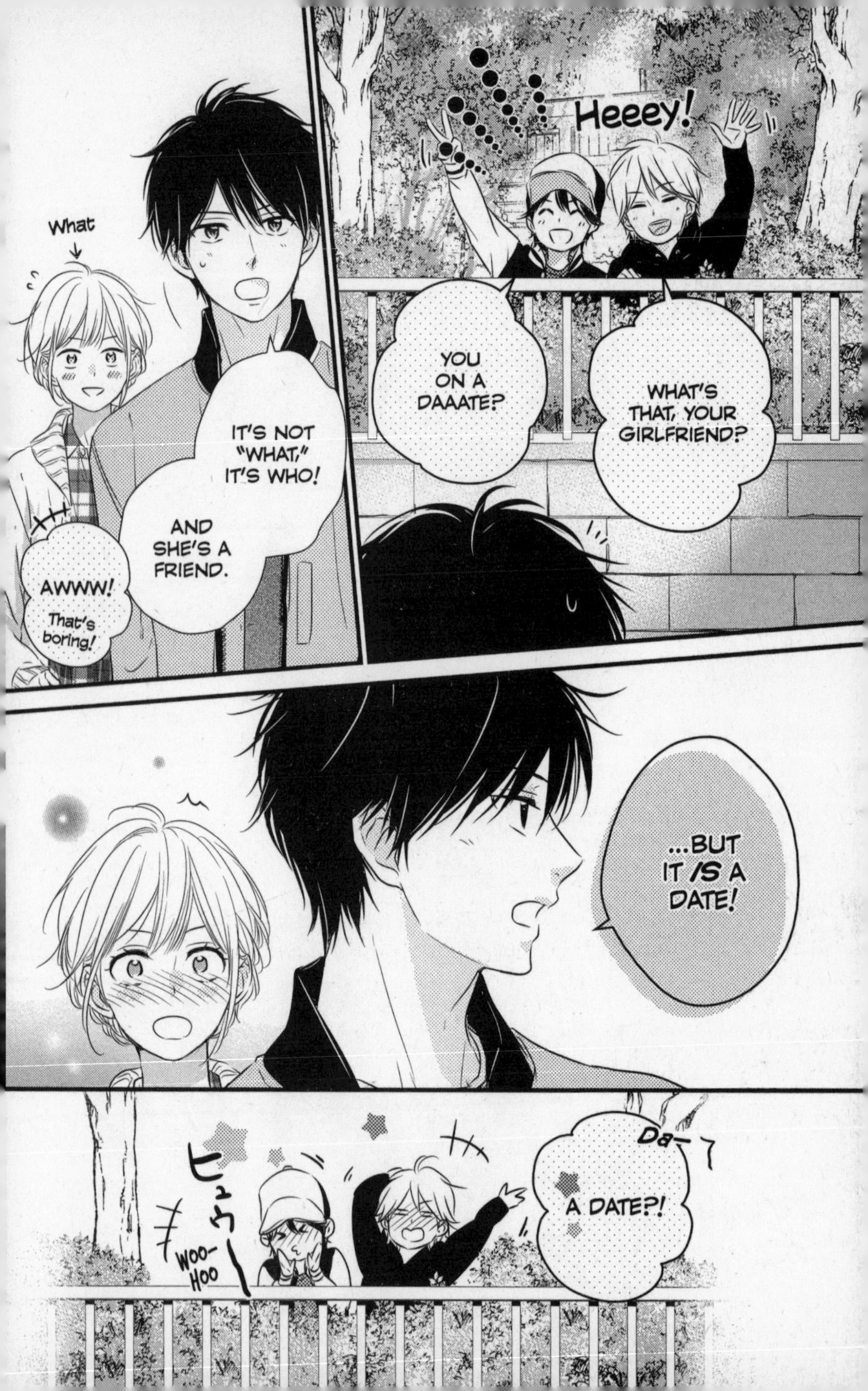
Heeey!
WHAT'S THAT, YOUR GIRLFRIEND?
YOU ON A DAAATE?
What
IT'S NOT "WHAT," IT'S WHO!
AND SHE'S A FRIEND.
AWWW! That's boring!
...BUT IT IS A DATE!
Da—
A DATE?!
WOO-HOO

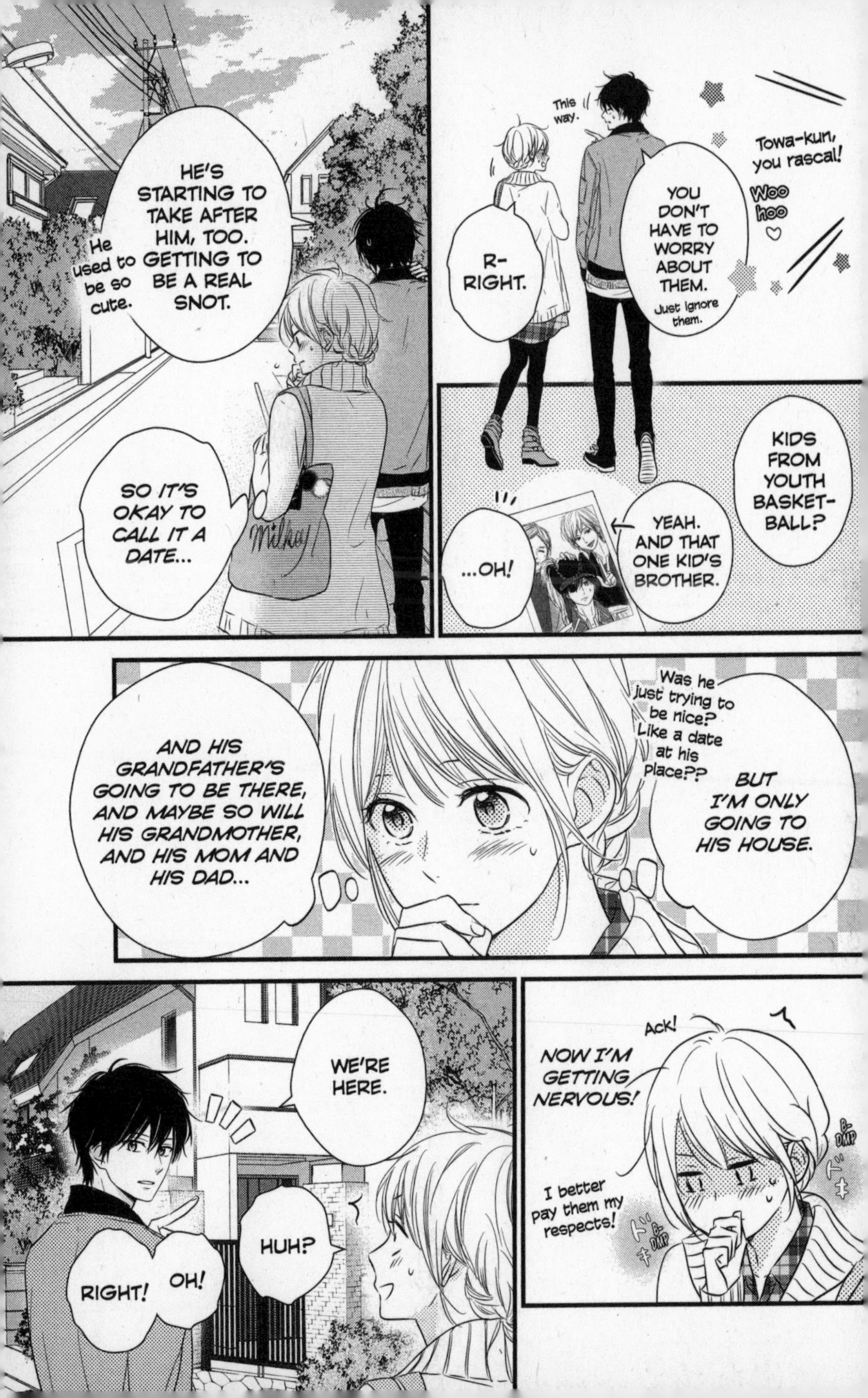

Towa-kun, you rascal!
Woo hoo
This way.
YOU DON'T HAVE TO WORRY ABOUT THEM.
Just ignore them.
R-RIGHT.
KIDS FROM YOUTH BASKET-BALL?
YEAH. AND THAT ONE KID'S BROTHER.
...OH!
HE'S STARTING TO TAKE AFTER HIM, TOO. GETTING TO BE A REAL SNOT.
He used to be so cute.
SO IT'S OKAY TO CALL IT A DATE...
Was he just trying to be nice? Like a date at his place??
BUT I'M ONLY GOING TO HIS HOUSE.
AND HIS GRANDFATHER'S GOING TO BE THERE, AND MAYBE SO WILL HIS GRANDMOTHER, AND HIS MOM AND HIS DAD...
Ack!
NOW I'M GETTING NERVOUS!
B-DMP
I better pay them my respects!
B-DMP
WE'RE HERE.
HUH?
OH!
RIGHT!

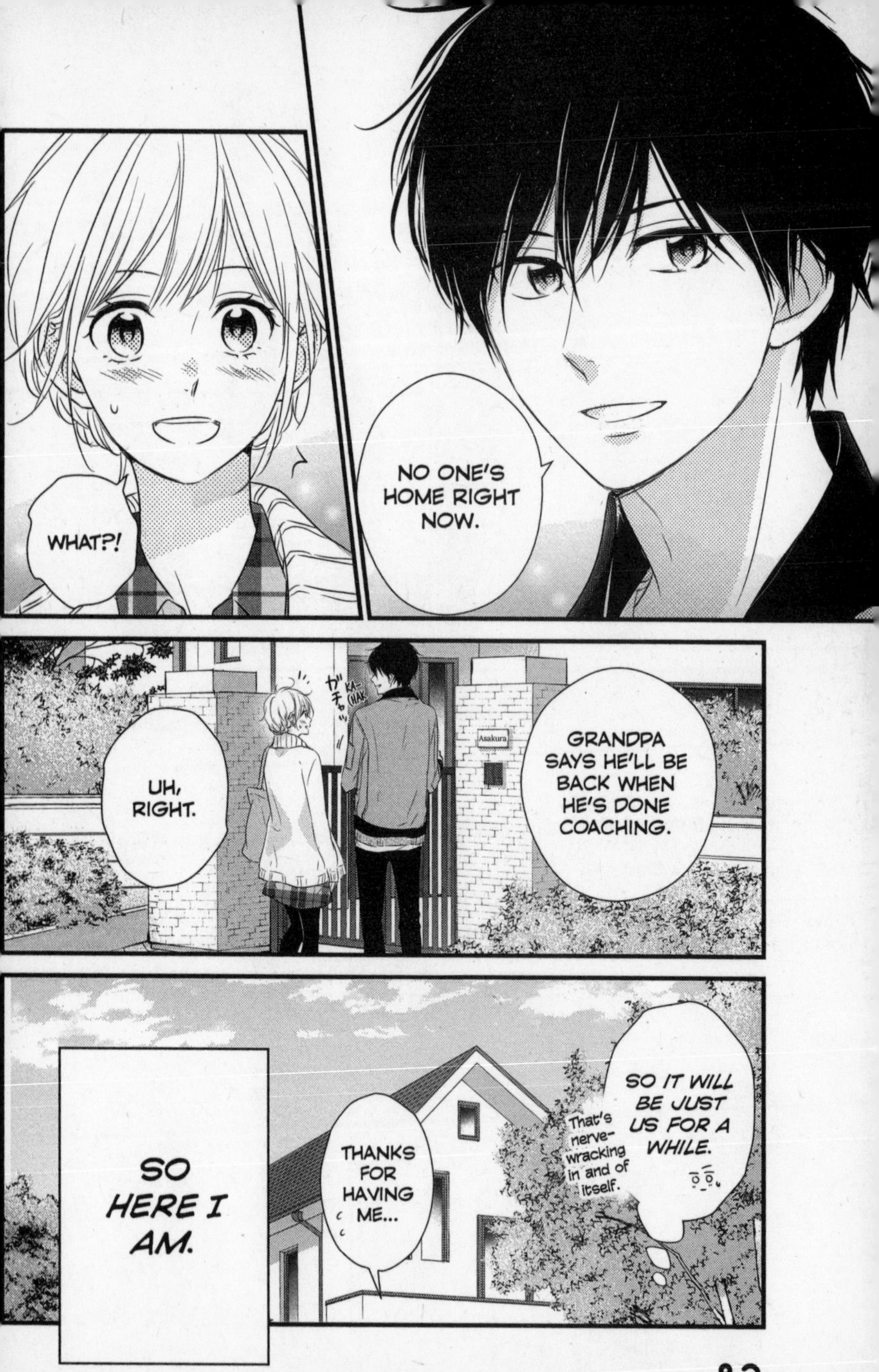
NO ONE'S HOME RIGHT NOW.
WHAT?!
GRANDPA SAYS HE'LL BE BACK WHEN HE'S DONE COACHING.
ガチャ
KA-CHAK
UH, RIGHT.
SO IT WILL BE JUST US FOR A WHILE.
That's nerve-wracking in and of itself.
THANKS FOR HAVING ME...
SO HERE I AM.

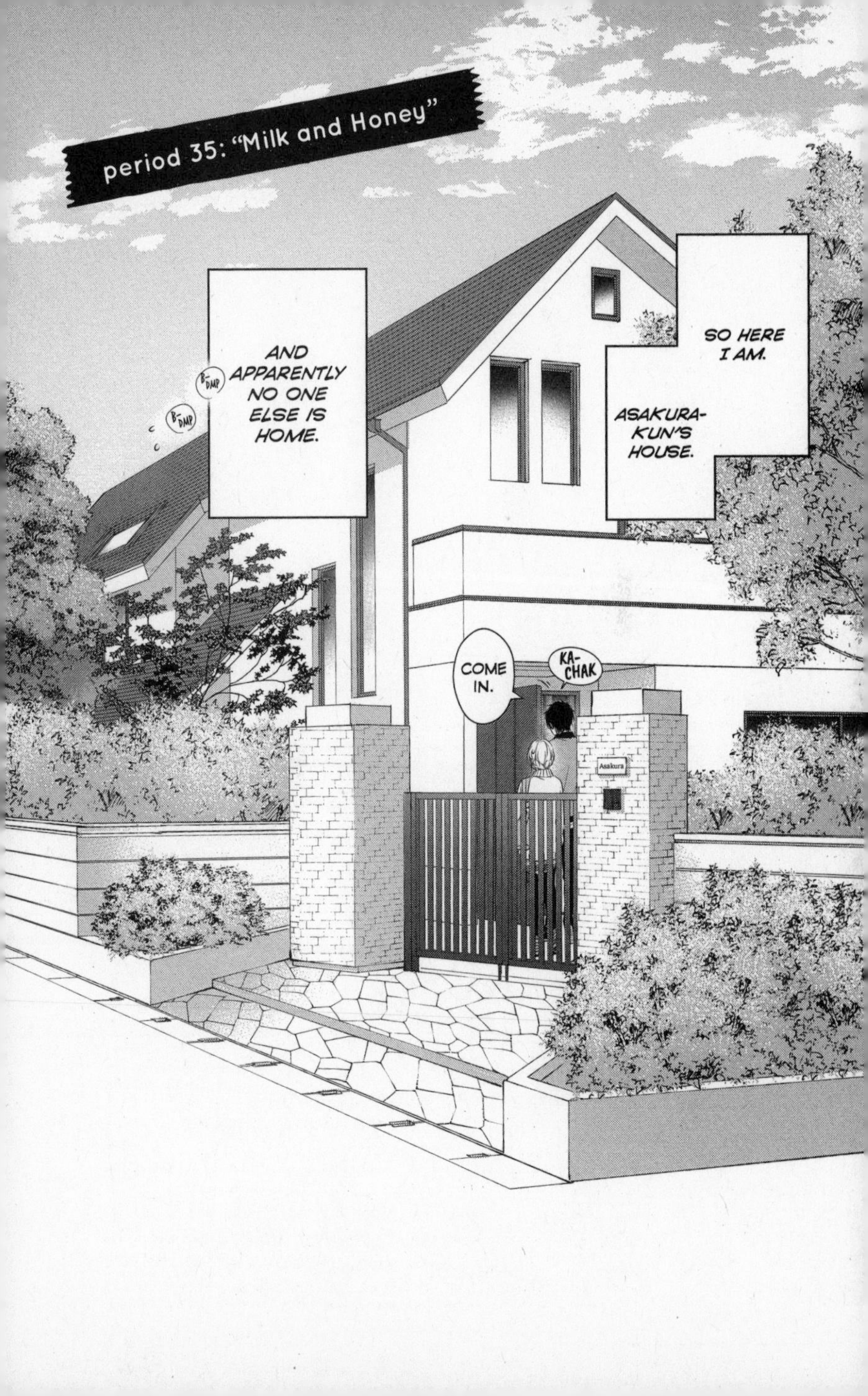
period 35: "Milk and Honey"
SO HERE I AM.
ASAKURA-KUN'S HOUSE.
AND APPARENTLY NO ONE ELSE IS HOME.
B-DMP
B-DMP
KA-CHAK
COME IN.
Asakura

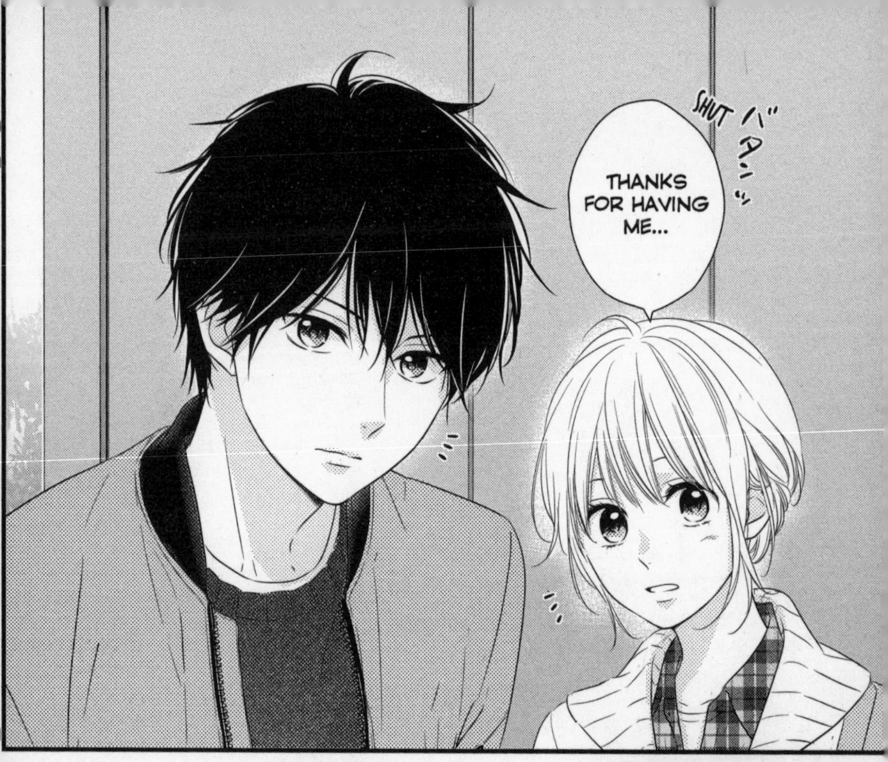
SHUT
バタ…
THANKS FOR HAVING ME...

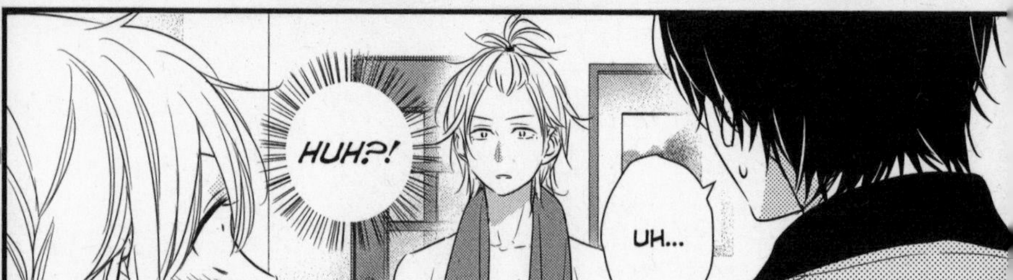
UH...
HUH?!

Design from before the series started

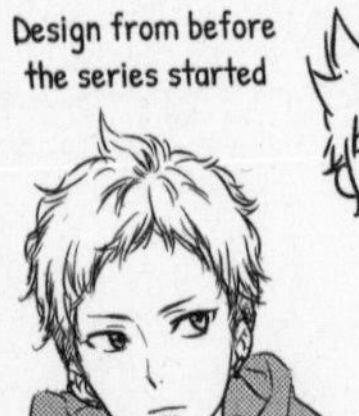

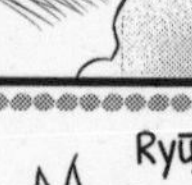

Ryūji

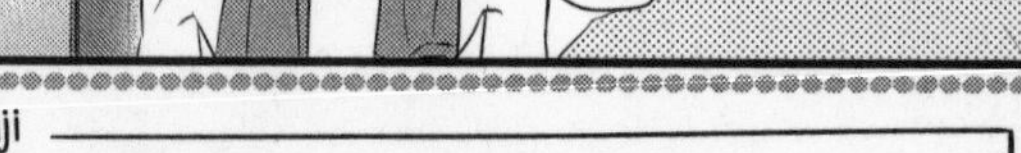

Family: Father, Mother, older brother, Ryūji
Apparently his brother (23) is extremely cool...
and Ryūji adores his big bro.

They pick on him a lot, but he has a brave soul, and he always comes through when it counts, which is something he got from his brother. Basketball, pierced ears, fashion—he copied his brother since he was little, and now here we are...is kind of how it went. At first, I called him "Sakuya."

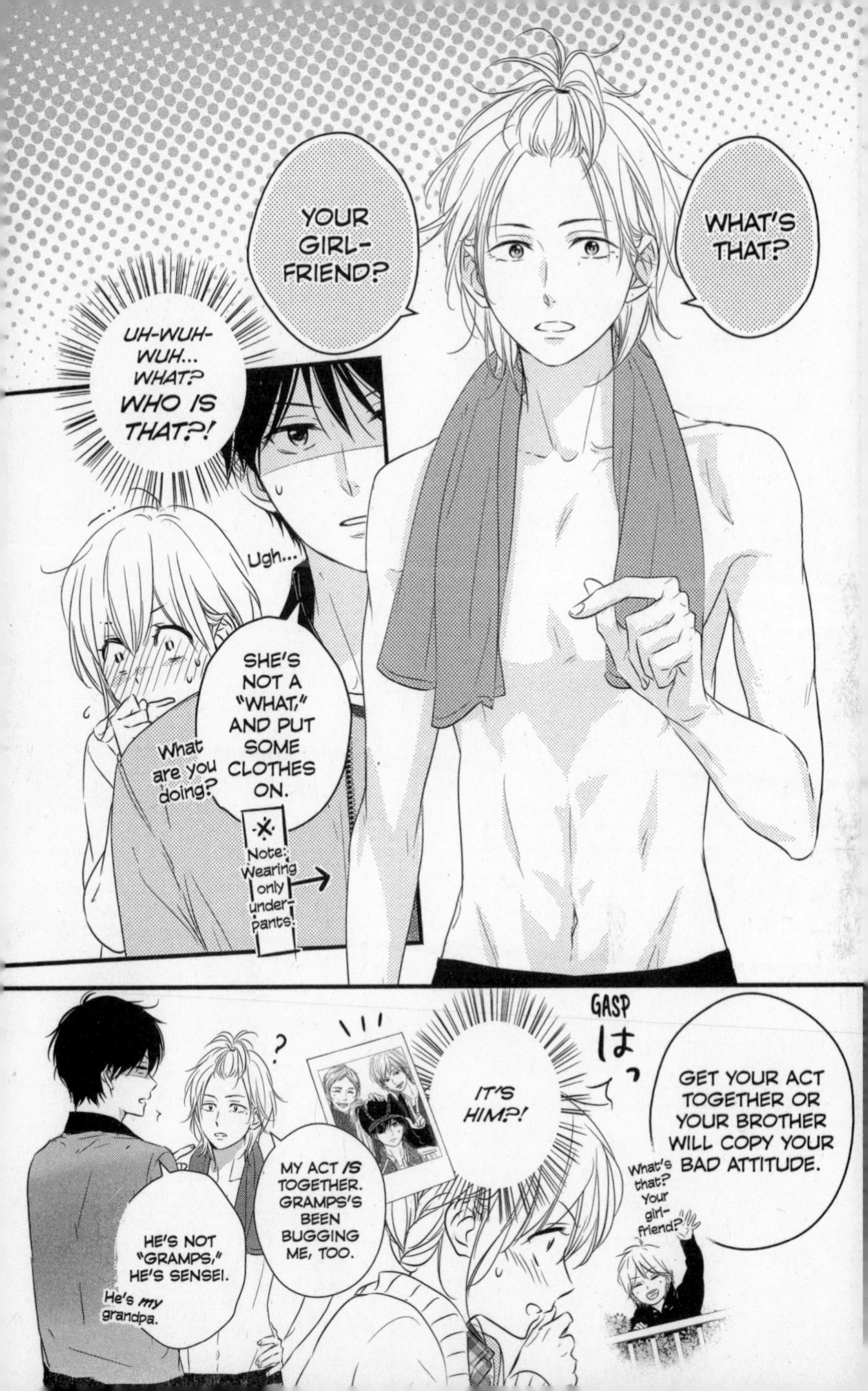
WHAT'S THAT?
YOUR GIRL-FRIEND?
UH-WUH-WUH... WHAT? WHO IS THAT?!
Ugh...
SHE'S NOT A "WHAT," AND PUT SOME CLOTHES ON.
What are you doing?
Note: Wearing only under-pants!
GET YOUR ACT TOGETHER OR YOUR BROTHER WILL COPY YOUR BAD ATTITUDE.
What's that? Your girl-friend?
GASP
は
IT'S HIM?!
MY ACT IS TOGETHER. GRAMPS'S BEEN BUGGING ME, TOO.
HE'S NOT "GRAMPS," HE'S SENSEI.
He's my grandpa.

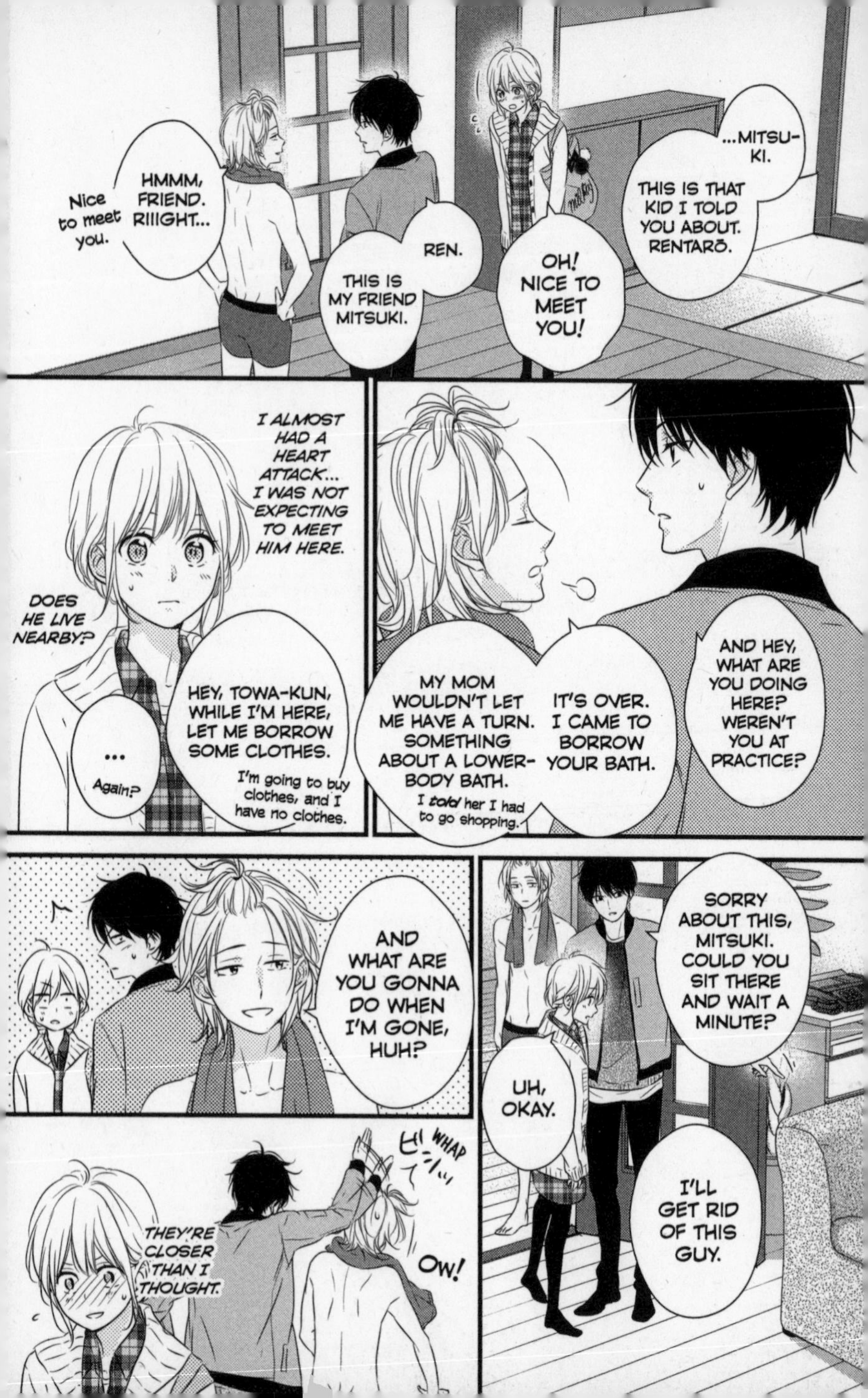
...MITSU-KI.
THIS IS THAT KID I TOLD YOU ABOUT. RENTARŌ.
OH! NICE TO MEET YOU!
REN.
THIS IS MY FRIEND MITSUKI.
HMMM, FRIEND. RIIIGHT...
Nice to meet you.
AND HEY, WHAT ARE YOU DOING HERE? WEREN'T YOU AT PRACTICE?
IT'S OVER. I CAME TO BORROW YOUR BATH.
MY MOM WOULDN'T LET ME HAVE A TURN. SOMETHING ABOUT A LOWER-BODY BATH.
I *told* her I had to go shopping.
I ALMOST HAD A HEART ATTACK... I WAS NOT EXPECTING TO MEET HIM HERE.
DOES HE LIVE NEARBY?
HEY, TOWA-KUN, WHILE I'M HERE, LET ME BORROW SOME CLOTHES.
I'm going to buy clothes, and I have no clothes.
...
Again?
SORRY ABOUT THIS, MITSUKI. COULD YOU SIT THERE AND WAIT A MINUTE?
UH, OKAY.
I'LL GET RID OF THIS GUY.
AND WHAT ARE YOU GONNA DO WHEN I'M GONE, HUH?
WHAP
OW!
THEY'RE CLOSER THAN I THOUGHT.

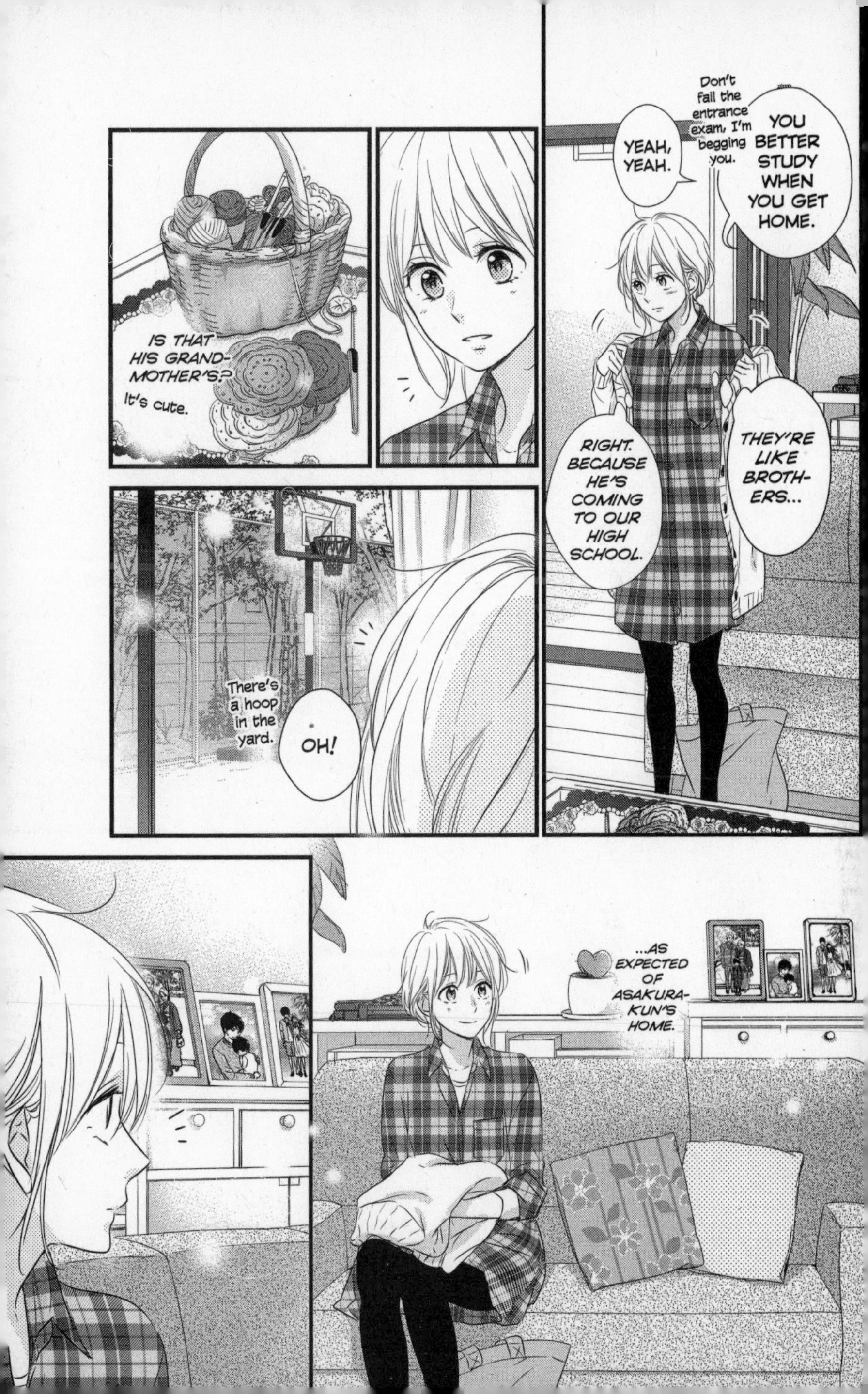
YOU BETTER STUDY WHEN YOU GET HOME.
Don't fail the entrance exam, I'm begging you.
YEAH, YEAH.
THEY'RE LIKE BROTHERS...
RIGHT. BECAUSE HE'S COMING TO OUR HIGH SCHOOL.
IS THAT HIS GRANDMOTHER'S?
It's cute.
OH!
There's a hoop in the yard.
...AS EXPECTED OF ASAKURA-KUN'S HOME.

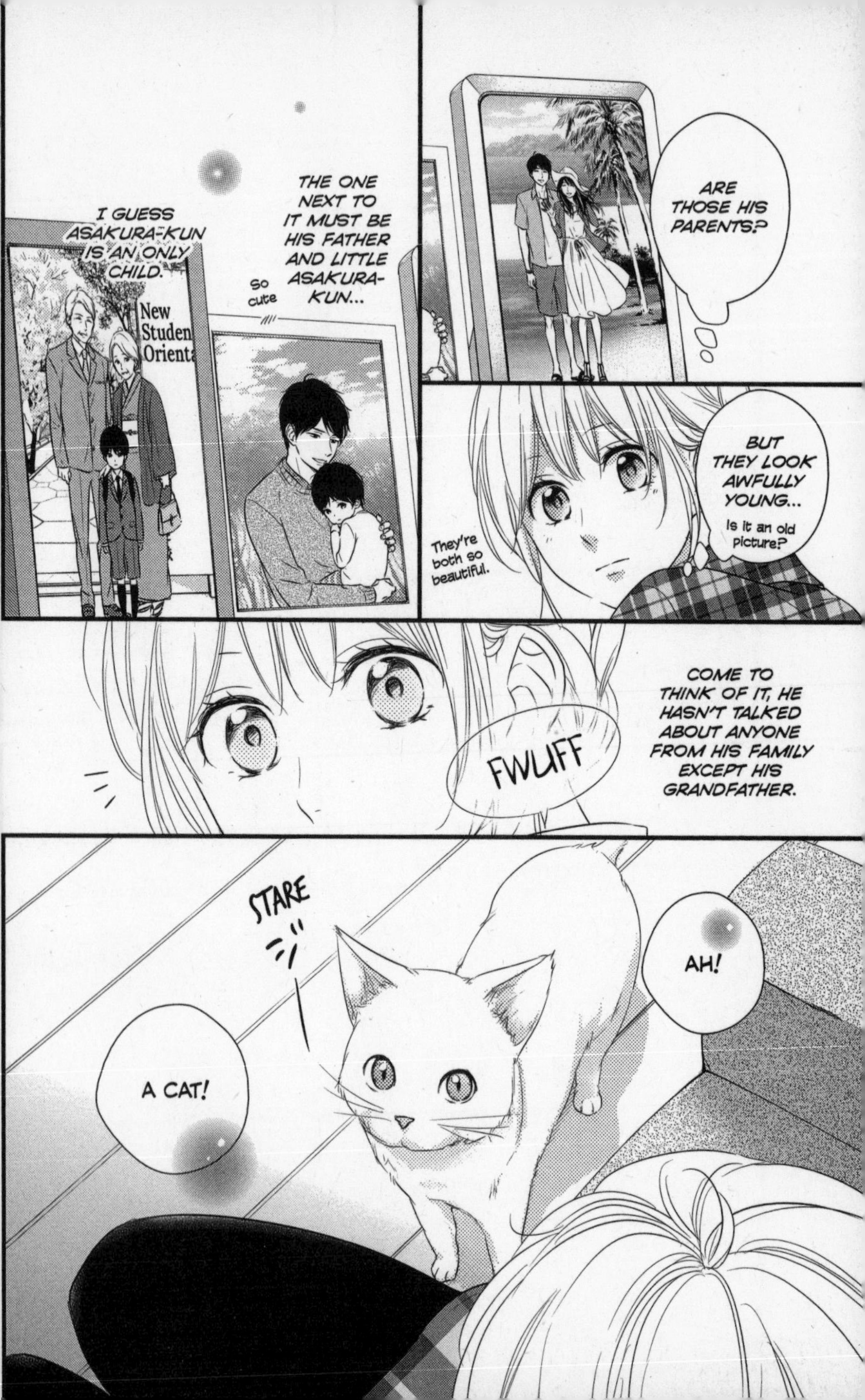
ARE THOSE HIS PARENTS?
BUT THEY LOOK AWFULLY YOUNG...
Is it an old picture?
They're both so beautiful.
THE ONE NEXT TO IT MUST BE HIS FATHER AND LITTLE ASAKURA-KUN...
So cute
I GUESS ASAKURA-KUN IS AN ONLY CHILD.
New Studen Orienta
COME TO THINK OF IT, HE HASN'T TALKED ABOUT ANYONE FROM HIS FAMILY EXCEPT HIS GRANDFATHER.
FWUFF
AH!
STARE
A CAT!

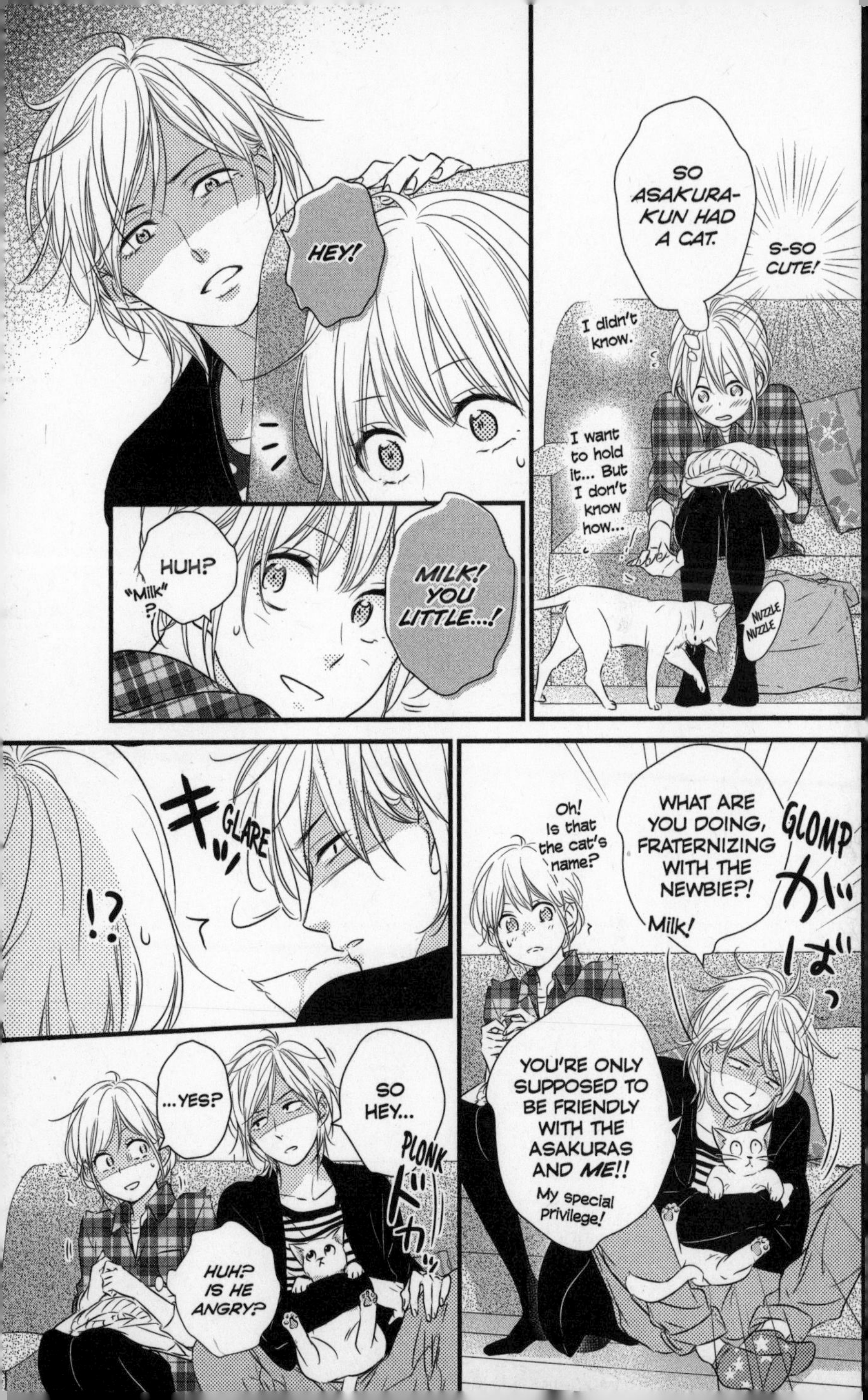
SO ASAKURA-KUN HAD A CAT.
S-SO CUTE!
I didn't know.
I want to hold it... But I don't know how...
NUZZLE NUZZLE
HEY!
MILK! YOU LITTLE...!
HUH?
"Milk"?
WHAT ARE YOU DOING, FRATERNIZING WITH THE NEWBIE?!
Milk!
GLOMP
Oh! Is that the cat's name?
YOU'RE ONLY SUPPOSED TO BE FRIENDLY WITH THE ASAKURAS AND ME!!
My special privilege!
GLARE
!?
SO HEY...
...YES?
PLONK
HUH? IS HE ANGRY?

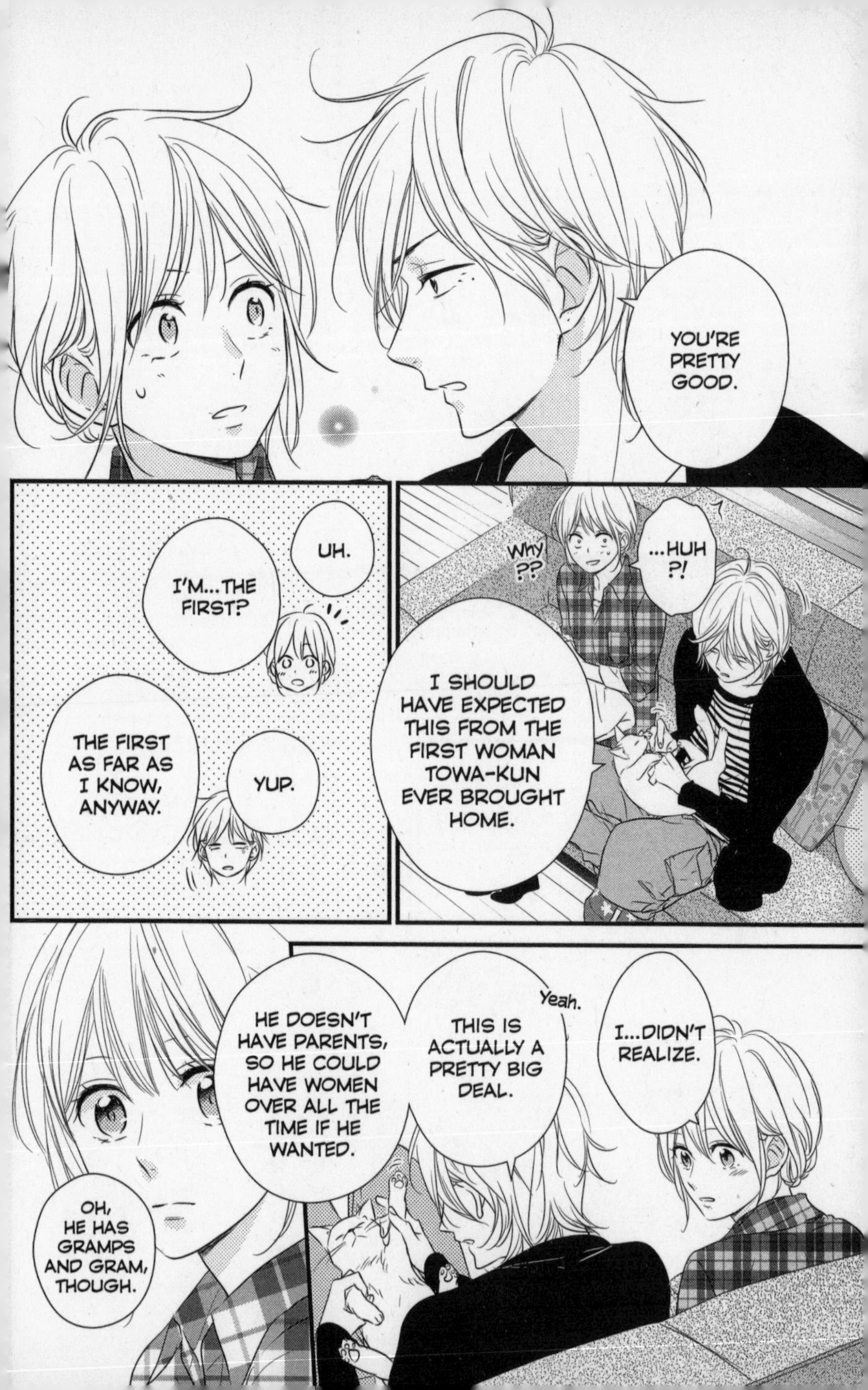
YOU'RE PRETTY GOOD.
...HUH ?!
Why ??
I SHOULD HAVE EXPECTED THIS FROM THE FIRST WOMAN TOWA-KUN EVER BROUGHT HOME.
UH.
I'M...THE FIRST?
THE FIRST AS FAR AS I KNOW, ANYWAY.
YUP.
I...DIDN'T REALIZE.
Yeah.
THIS IS ACTUALLY A PRETTY BIG DEAL.
HE DOESN'T HAVE PARENTS, SO HE COULD HAVE WOMEN OVER ALL THE TIME IF HE WANTED.
OH, HE HAS GRAMPS AND GRAM, THOUGH.

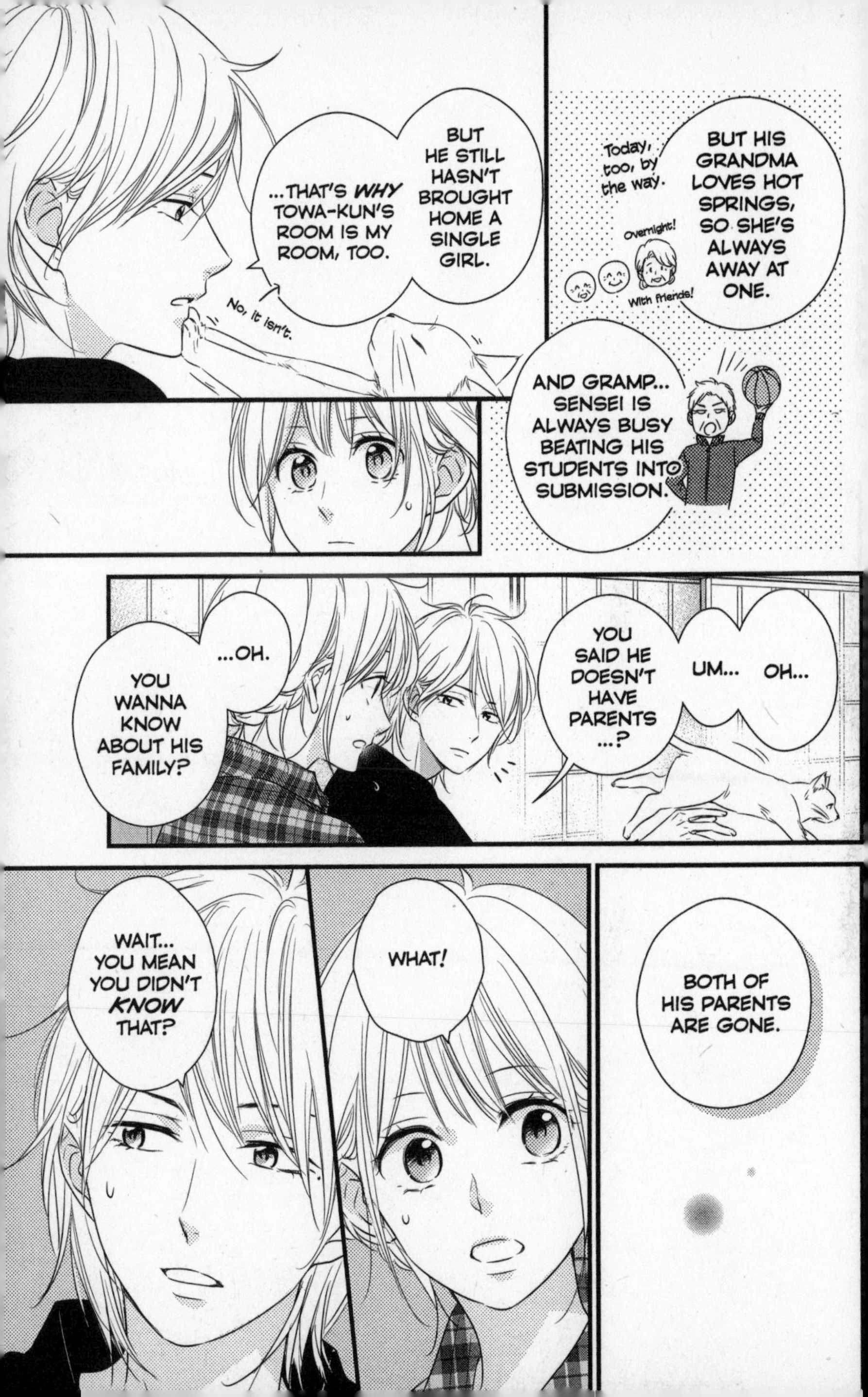
BUT HIS GRANDMA LOVES HOT SPRINGS, SO SHE'S ALWAYS AWAY AT ONE.
Today, too, by the way.
Overnight!
With friends!
AND GRAMP... SENSEI IS ALWAYS BUSY BEATING HIS STUDENTS INTO SUBMISSION.
BUT HE STILL HASN'T BROUGHT HOME A SINGLE GIRL.
...THAT'S *WHY* TOWA-KUN'S ROOM IS MY ROOM, TOO.
No, it isn't.
UM... OH...
YOU SAID HE DOESN'T HAVE PARENTS ...?
...OH.
YOU WANNA KNOW ABOUT HIS FAMILY?
BOTH OF HIS PARENTS ARE GONE.
WHAT!
WAIT... YOU MEAN YOU DIDN'T *KNOW* THAT?

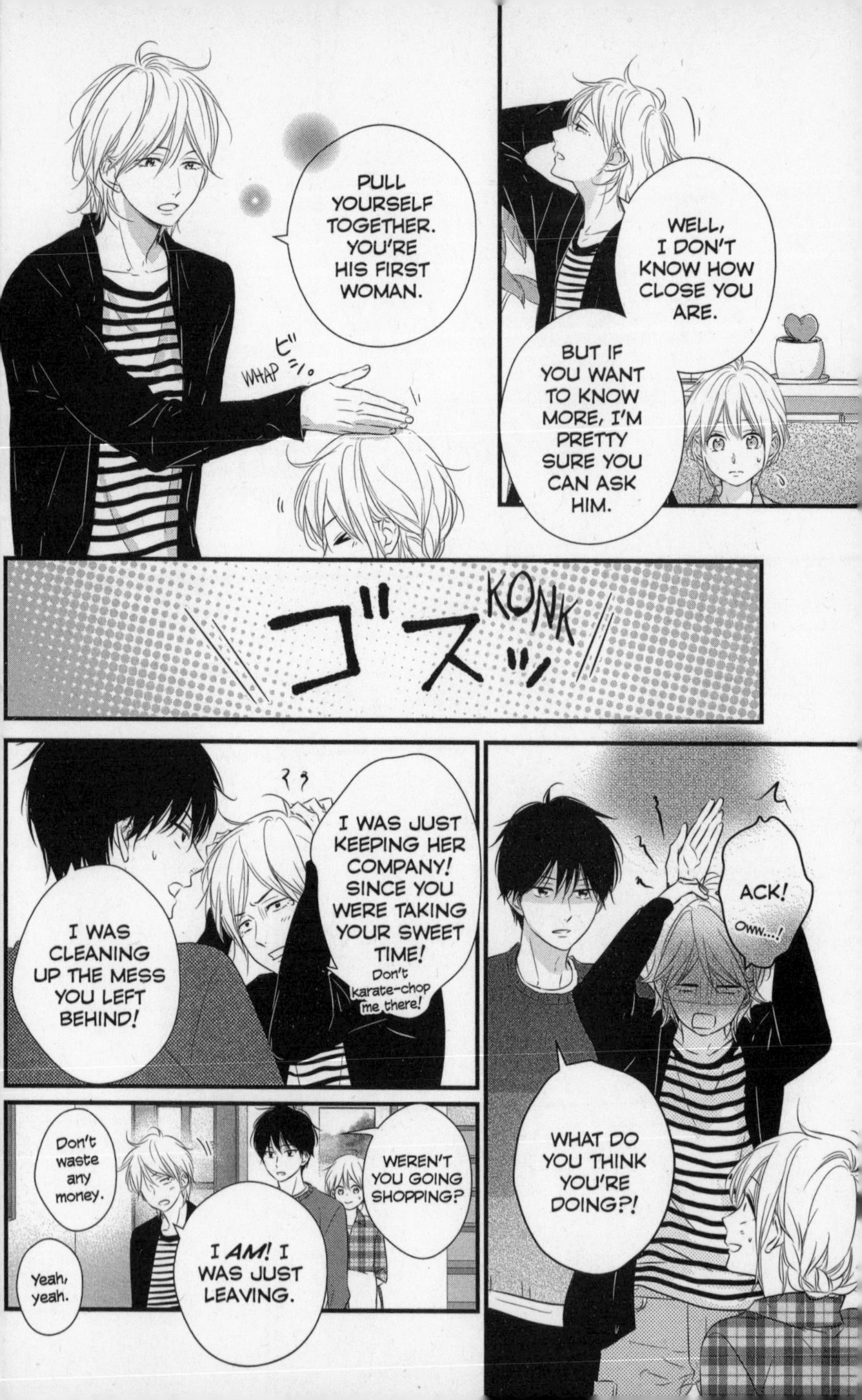
WELL, I DON'T KNOW HOW CLOSE YOU ARE.
BUT IF YOU WANT TO KNOW MORE, I'M PRETTY SURE YOU CAN ASK HIM.
PULL YOURSELF TOGETHER. YOU'RE HIS FIRST WOMAN.
WHAP
ゴスッ
KONK
ACK!
Oww...!
WHAT DO YOU THINK YOU'RE DOING?!
I WAS JUST KEEPING HER COMPANY! SINCE YOU WERE TAKING YOUR SWEET TIME!
Don't karate-chop me there!
I WAS CLEANING UP THE MESS YOU LEFT BEHIND!
WEREN'T YOU GOING SHOPPING?
I AM! I WAS JUST LEAVING.
Don't waste any money.
Yeah, yeah.

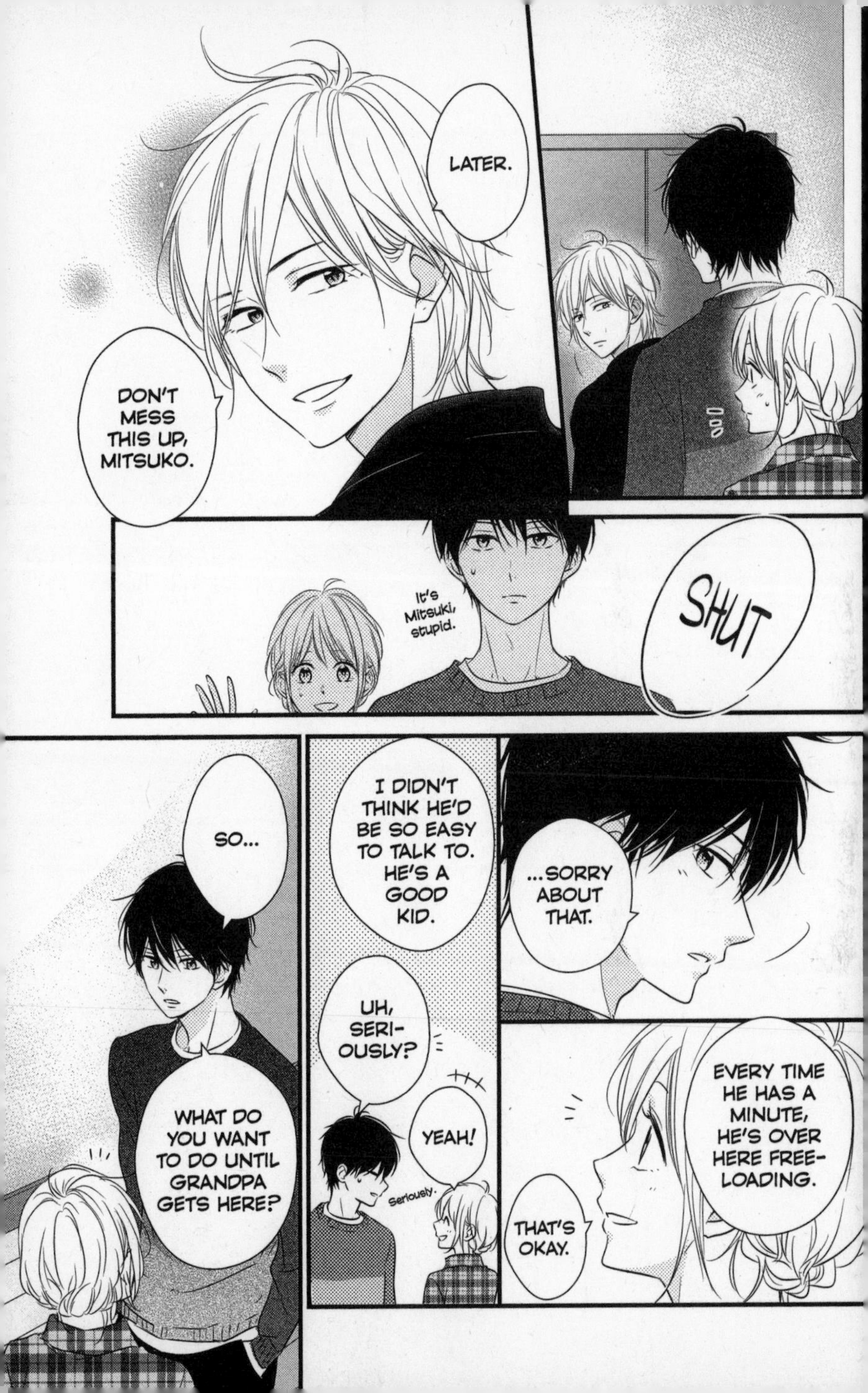
LATER.
DON'T MESS THIS UP, MITSUKO.
SHUT
It's Mitsuki, stupid.
...SORRY ABOUT THAT.
EVERY TIME HE HAS A MINUTE, HE'S OVER HERE FREE-LOADING.
THAT'S OKAY.
I DIDN'T THINK HE'D BE SO EASY TO TALK TO. HE'S A GOOD KID.
UH, SERI-OUSLY?
YEAH!
Seriously.
SO...
WHAT DO YOU WANT TO DO UNTIL GRANDPA GETS HERE?

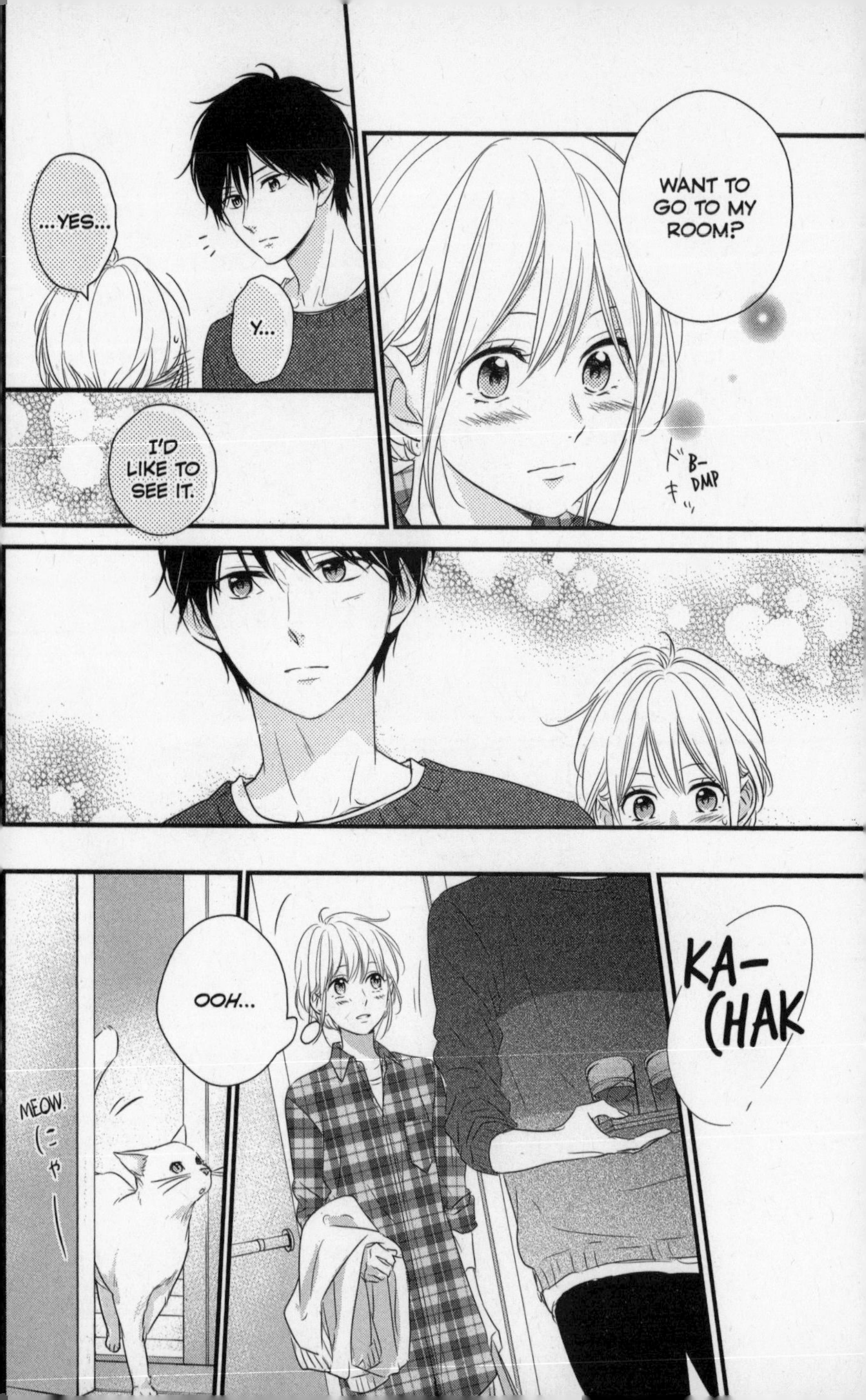
WANT TO GO TO MY ROOM?
B-DMP
ドキッ
Y...
...YES...
I'D LIKE TO SEE IT.
KA-CHAK
OOH...
MEOW.
にゃー

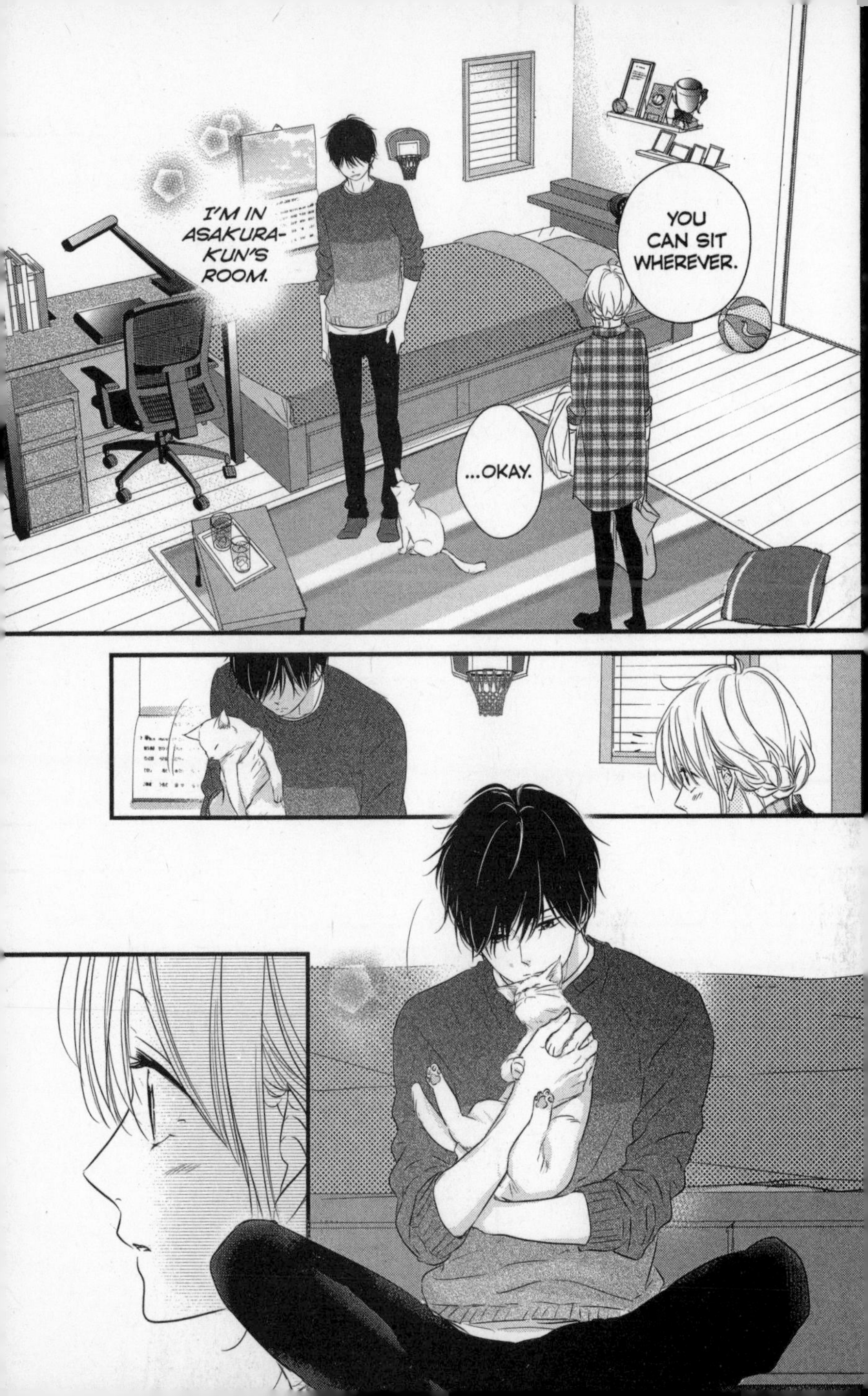
YOU CAN SIT WHEREVER.
I'M IN ASAKURA-KUN'S ROOM.
...OKAY.

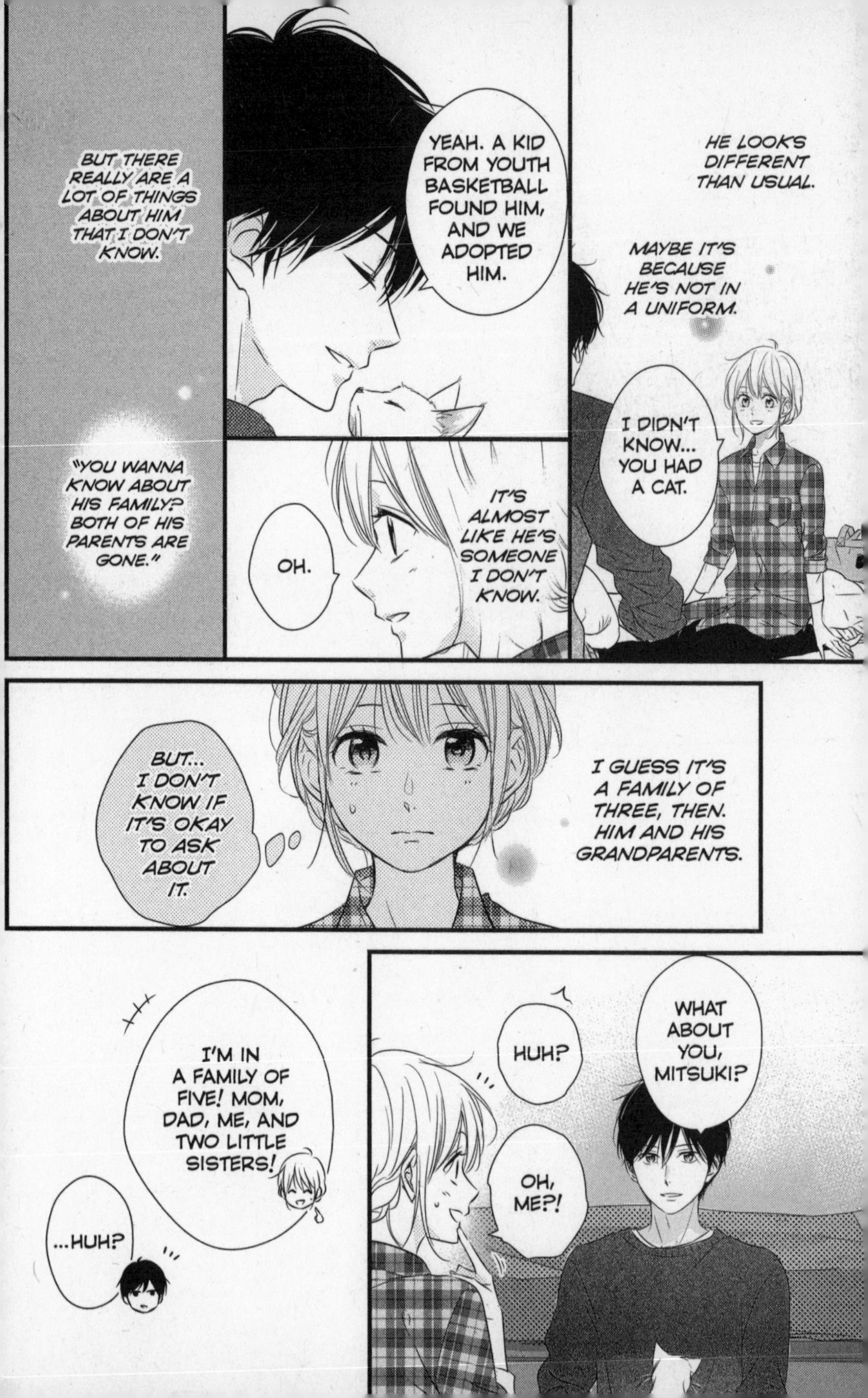
HE LOOKS DIFFERENT THAN USUAL.
MAYBE IT'S BECAUSE HE'S NOT IN A UNIFORM.
I DIDN'T KNOW... YOU HAD A CAT.
YEAH. A KID FROM YOUTH BASKETBALL FOUND HIM, AND WE ADOPTED HIM.
IT'S ALMOST LIKE HE'S SOMEONE I DON'T KNOW.
OH.
BUT THERE REALLY ARE A LOT OF THINGS ABOUT HIM THAT I DON'T KNOW.
"YOU WANNA KNOW ABOUT HIS FAMILY? BOTH OF HIS PARENTS ARE GONE."
I GUESS IT'S A FAMILY OF THREE, THEN. HIM AND HIS GRANDPARENTS.
BUT... I DON'T KNOW IF IT'S OKAY TO ASK ABOUT IT.
WHAT ABOUT YOU, MITSUKI?
HUH?
OH, ME?!
I'M IN A FAMILY OF FIVE! MOM, DAD, ME, AND TWO LITTLE SISTERS!
...HUH?

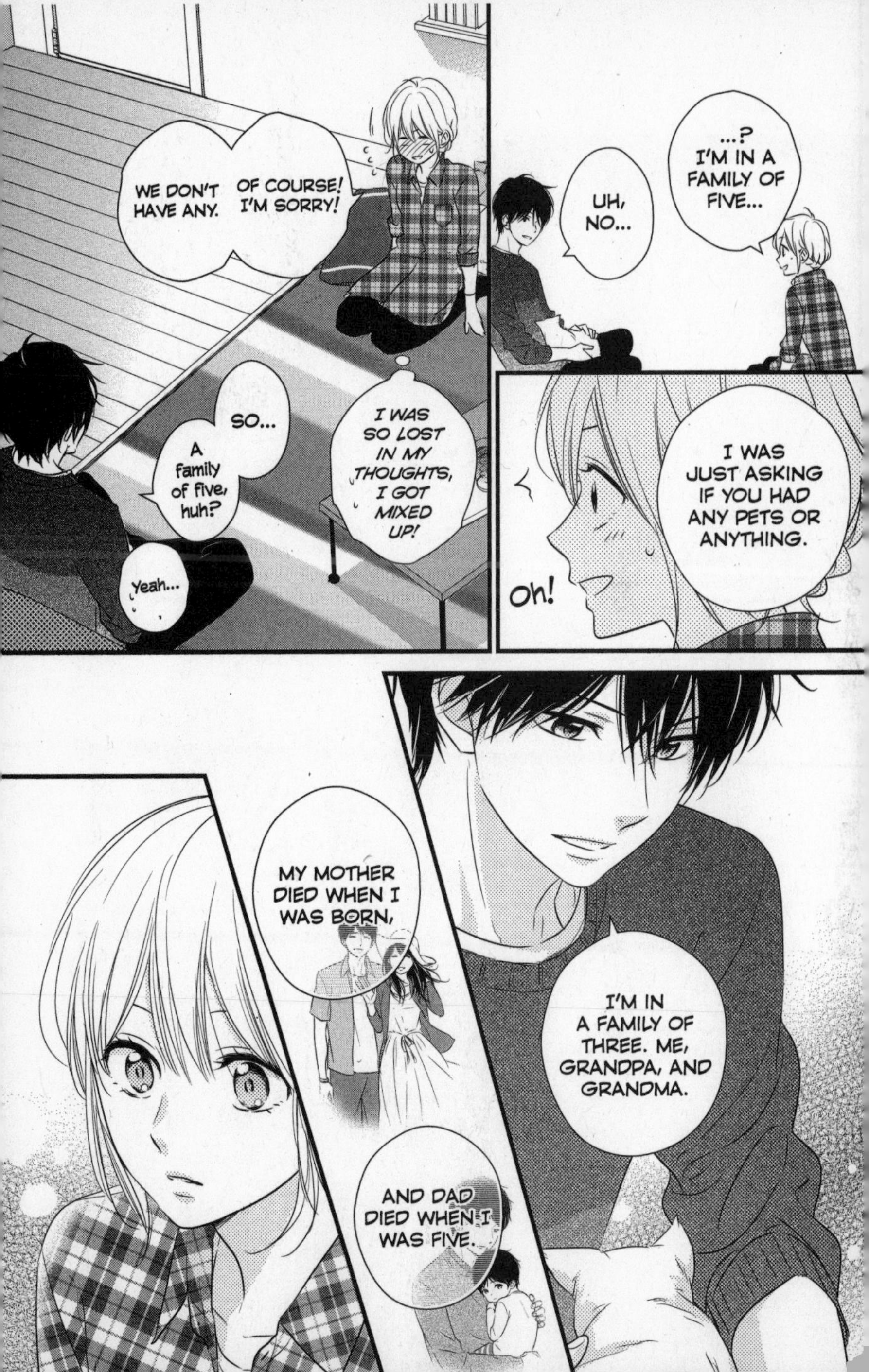
...? I'M IN A FAMILY OF FIVE...
UH, NO...
I WAS JUST ASKING IF YOU HAD ANY PETS OR ANYTHING.
Oh!
OF COURSE! I'M SORRY!
WE DON'T HAVE ANY.
I WAS SO LOST IN MY THOUGHTS, I GOT MIXED UP!
SO...
A family of five, huh?
Yeah...
I'M IN A FAMILY OF THREE. ME, GRANDPA, AND GRANDMA.
MY MOTHER DIED WHEN I WAS BORN,
AND DAD DIED WHEN I WAS FIVE.

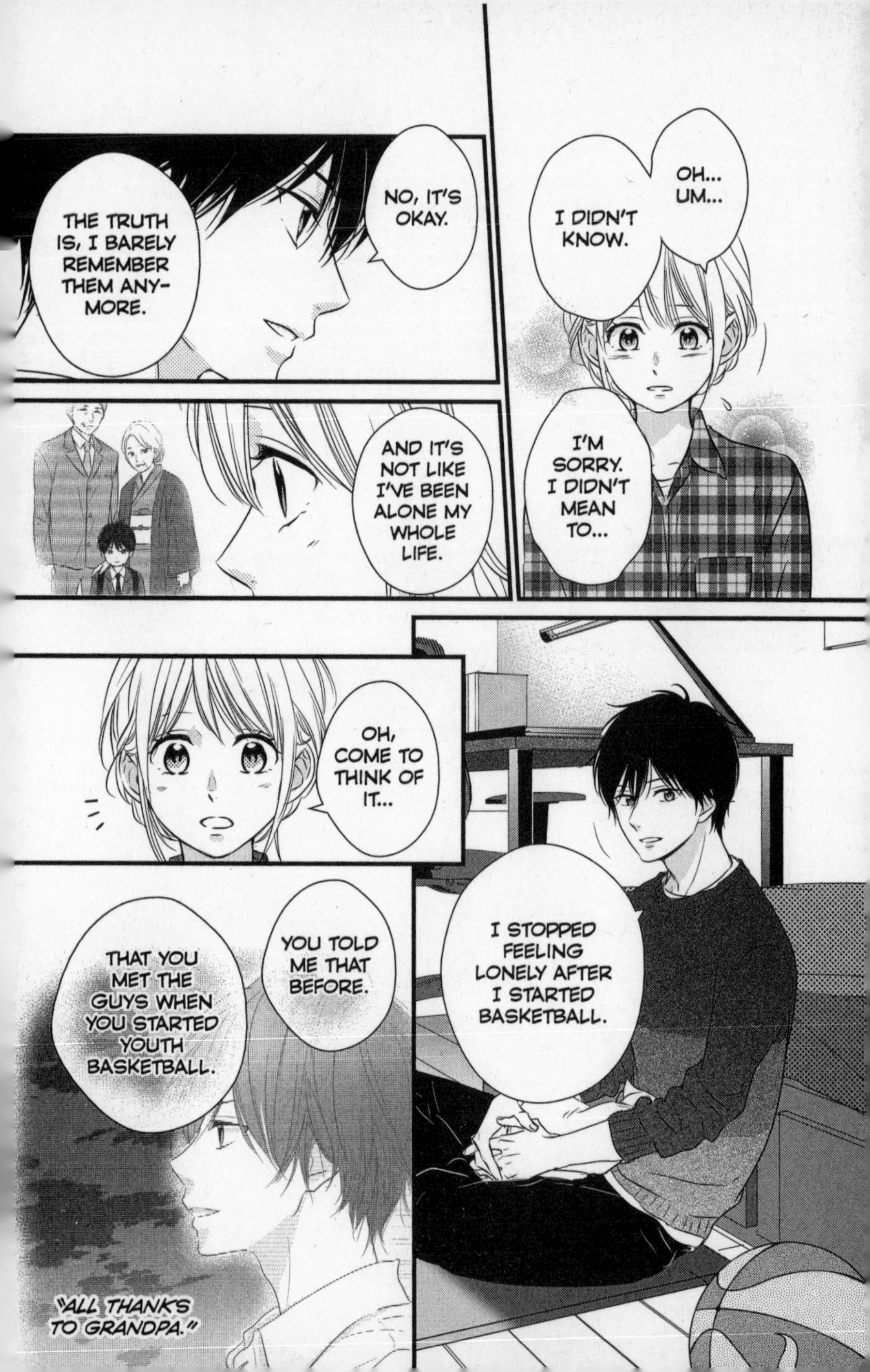
OH... UM...
I DIDN'T KNOW.
I'M SORRY. I DIDN'T MEAN TO...
NO, IT'S OKAY.
THE TRUTH IS, I BARELY REMEMBER THEM ANY-MORE.
AND IT'S NOT LIKE I'VE BEEN ALONE MY WHOLE LIFE.
I STOPPED FEELING LONELY AFTER I STARTED BASKETBALL.
OH, COME TO THINK OF IT...
YOU TOLD ME THAT BEFORE.
THAT YOU MET THE GUYS WHEN YOU STARTED YOUTH BASKETBALL.
"ALL THANKS TO GRANDPA."

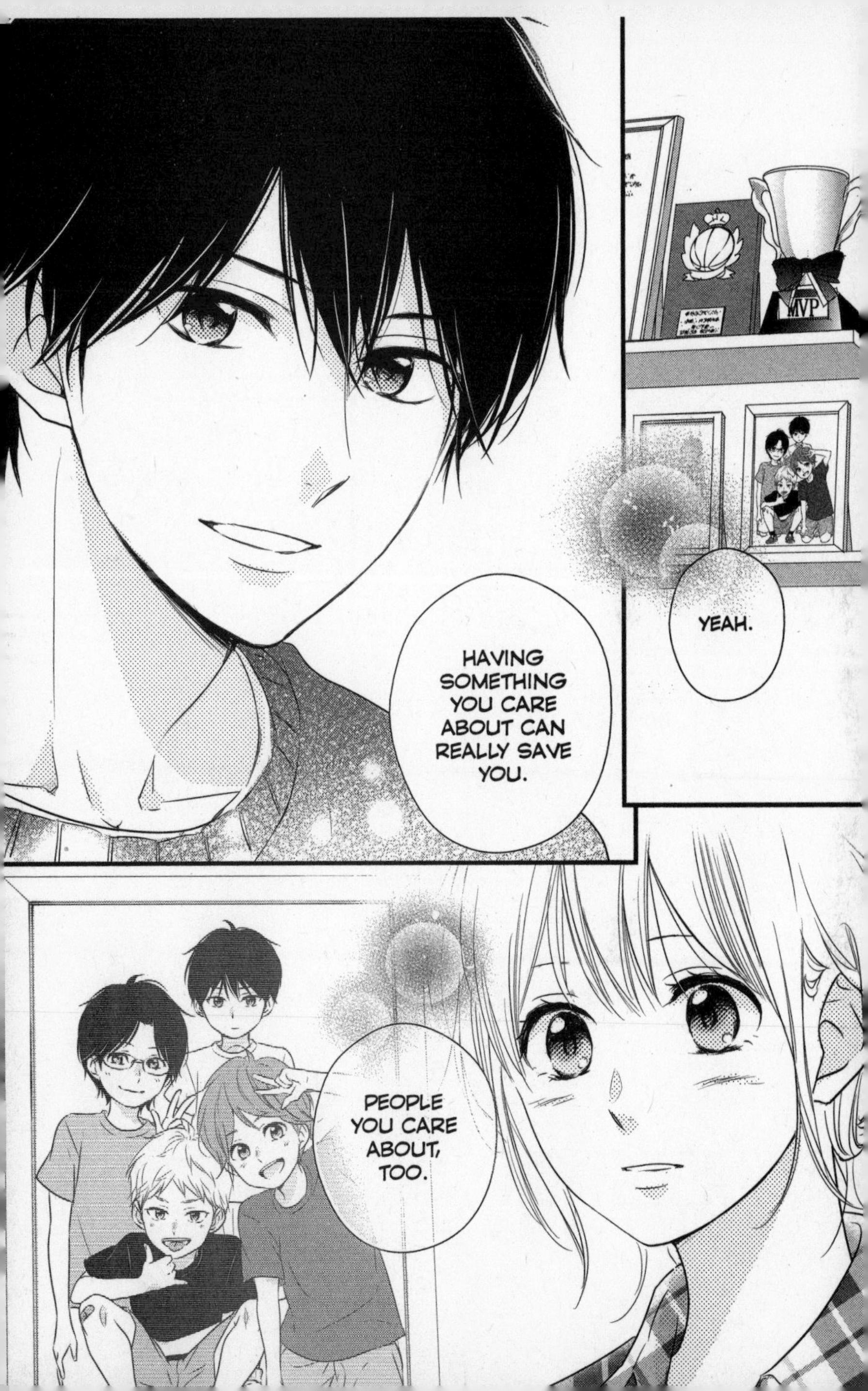
MVP
YEAH.
HAVING SOMETHING YOU CARE ABOUT CAN REALLY SAVE YOU.
PEOPLE YOU CARE ABOUT, TOO.

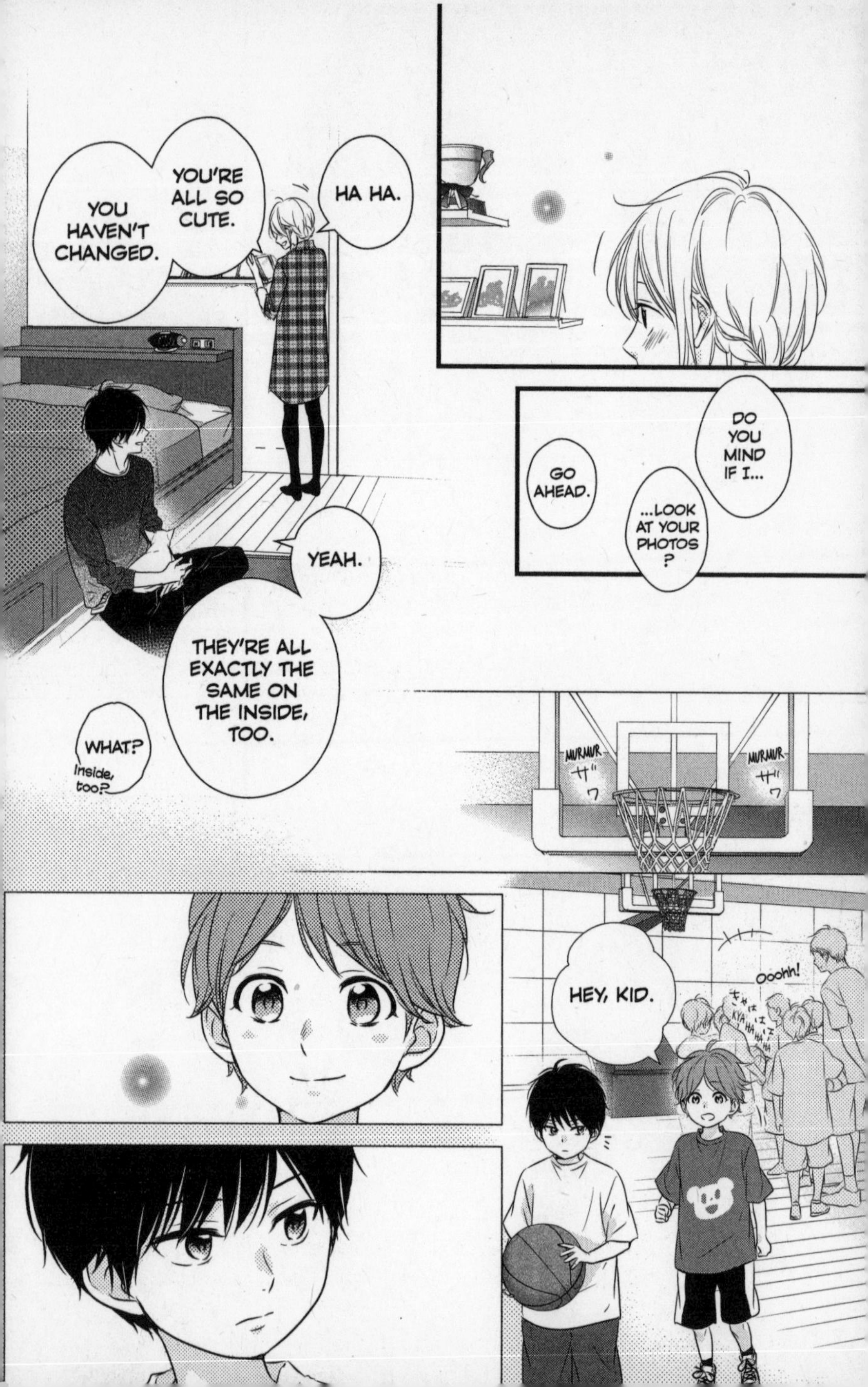
DO YOU MIND IF I...
...LOOK AT YOUR PHOTOS?
GO AHEAD.
HA HA.
YOU'RE ALL SO CUTE.
YOU HAVEN'T CHANGED.
YEAH.
THEY'RE ALL EXACTLY THE SAME ON THE INSIDE, TOO.
WHAT?
Inside, too?
MURMUR
ザワ
MURMUR
ザワ
Ooohh!
KYA HA HA
HEY, KID.

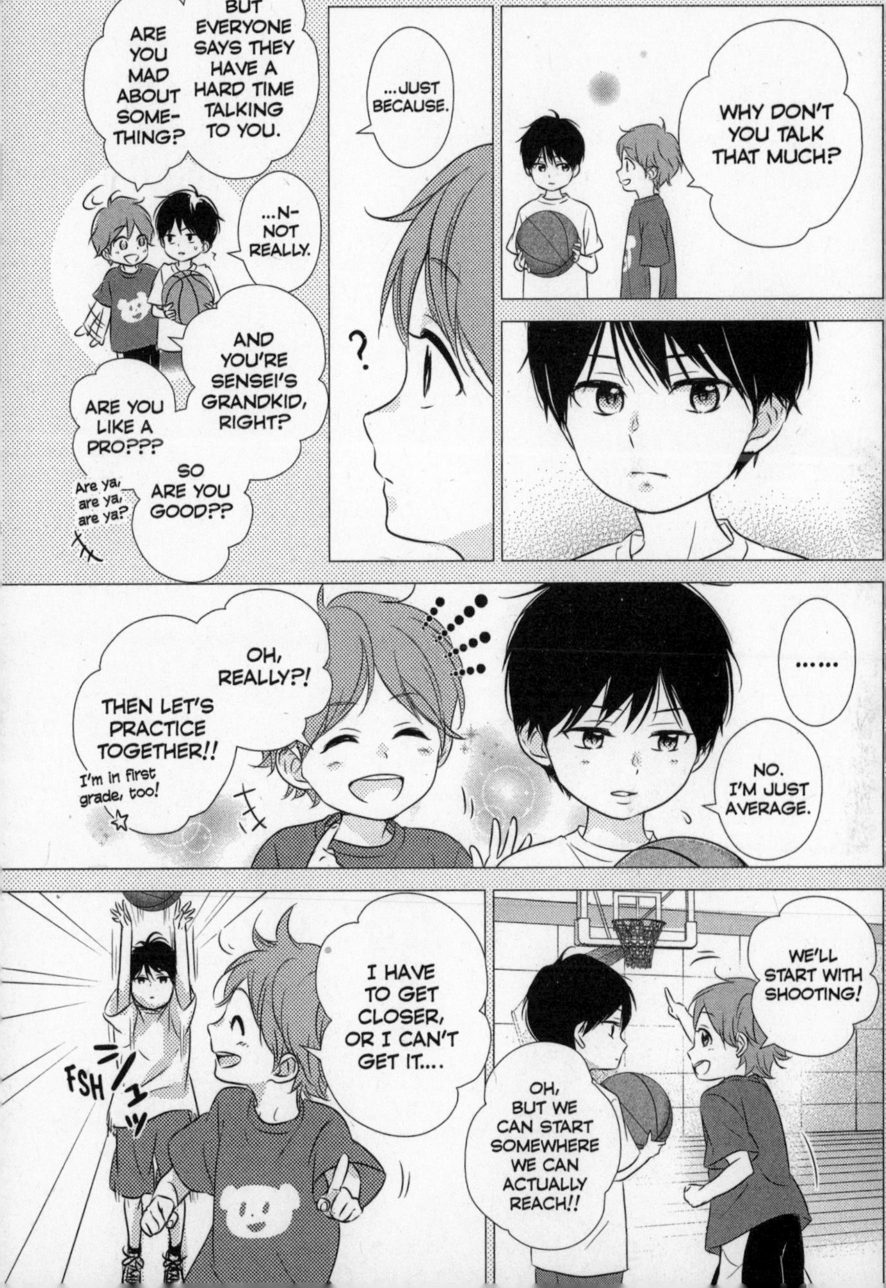
WHY DON'T YOU TALK THAT MUCH?
...JUST BECAUSE.
?
BUT EVERYONE SAYS THEY HAVE A HARD TIME TALKING TO YOU.
ARE YOU MAD ABOUT SOME-THING?
...N-NOT REALLY.
AND YOU'RE SENSEI'S GRANDKID, RIGHT?
ARE YOU LIKE A PRO???
SO ARE YOU GOOD??
Are ya, are ya, are ya?
......
NO. I'M JUST AVERAGE.
OH, REALLY?!
THEN LET'S PRACTICE TOGETHER!!
I'm in first grade, too!
WE'LL START WITH SHOOTING!
OH, BUT WE CAN START SOMEWHERE WE CAN ACTUALLY REACH!!
I HAVE TO GET CLOSER, OR I CAN'T GET IT....
FSH

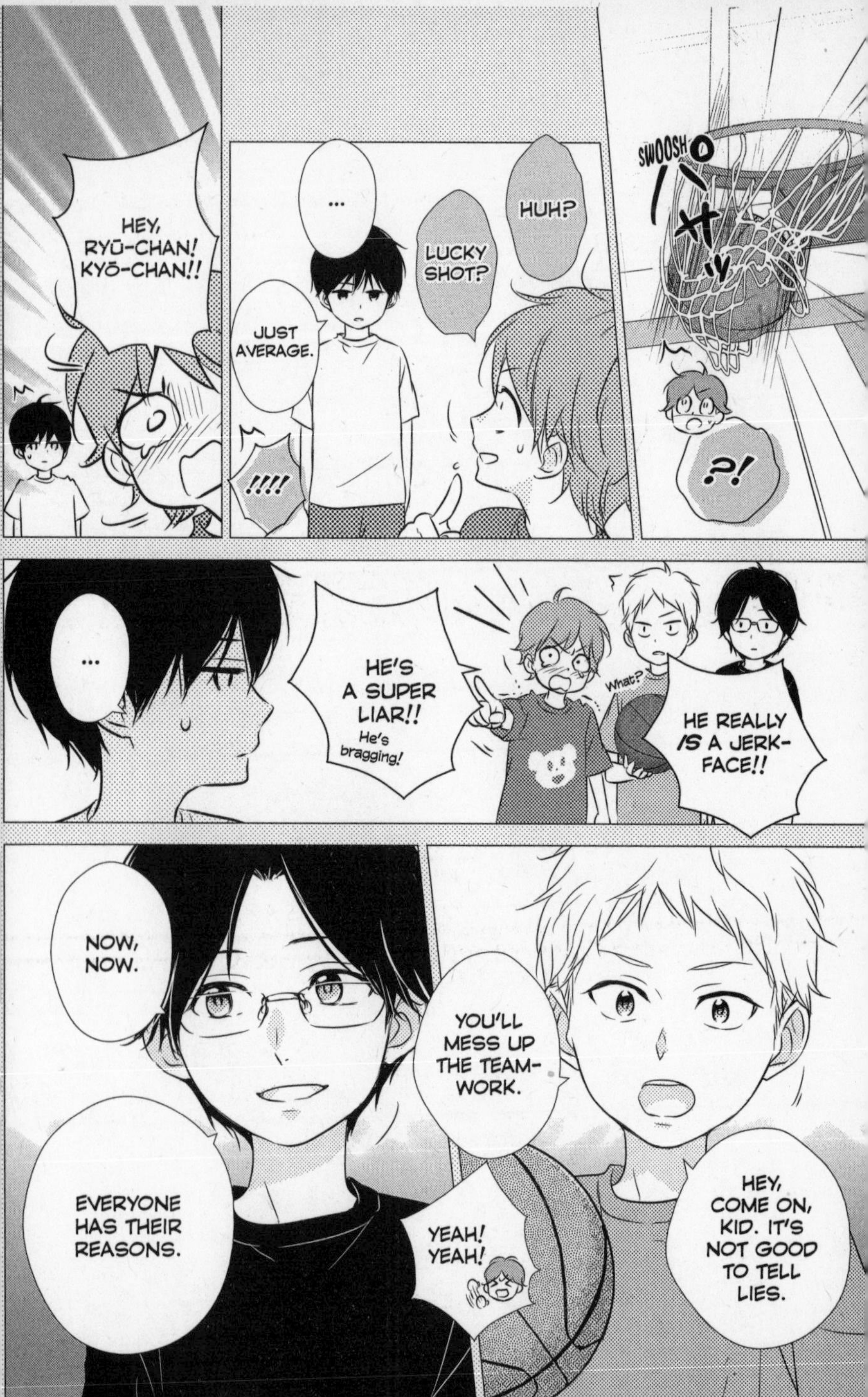
SWOOSH
?!
HUH?
LUCKY SHOT?
...
JUST AVERAGE.
!!!!
HEY, RYŪ-CHAN! KYŌ-CHAN!!
HE REALLY IS A JERK-FACE!!
What?
HE'S A SUPER LIAR!!
He's bragging!
...
HEY, COME ON, KID. IT'S NOT GOOD TO TELL LIES.
YOU'LL MESS UP THE TEAM-WORK.
YEAH! YEAH!
NOW, NOW.
EVERYONE HAS THEIR REASONS.

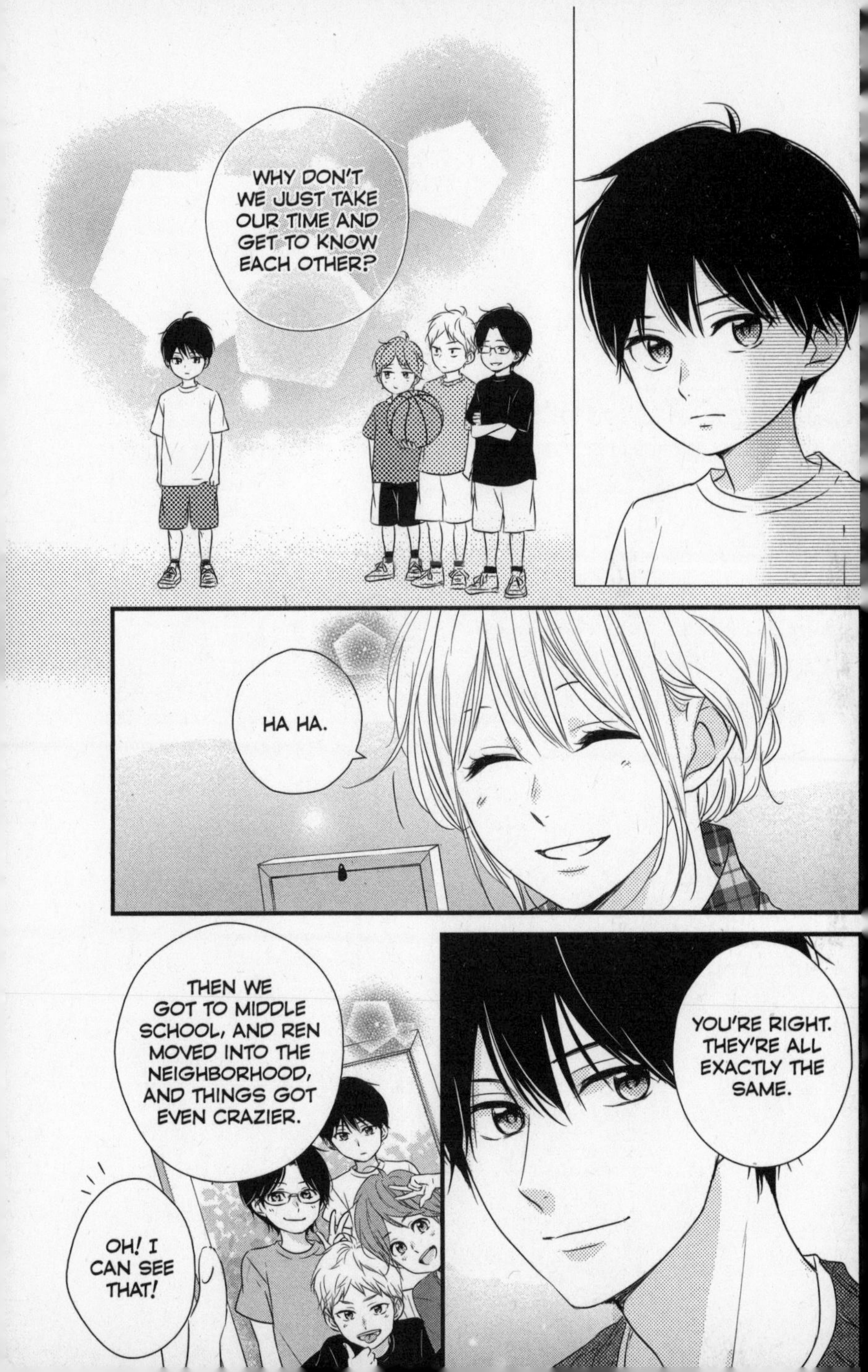
WHY DON'T WE JUST TAKE OUR TIME AND GET TO KNOW EACH OTHER?
HA HA.
YOU'RE RIGHT. THEY'RE ALL EXACTLY THE SAME.
THEN WE GOT TO MIDDLE SCHOOL, AND REN MOVED INTO THE NEIGHBORHOOD, AND THINGS GOT EVEN CRAZIER.
OH! I CAN SEE THAT!

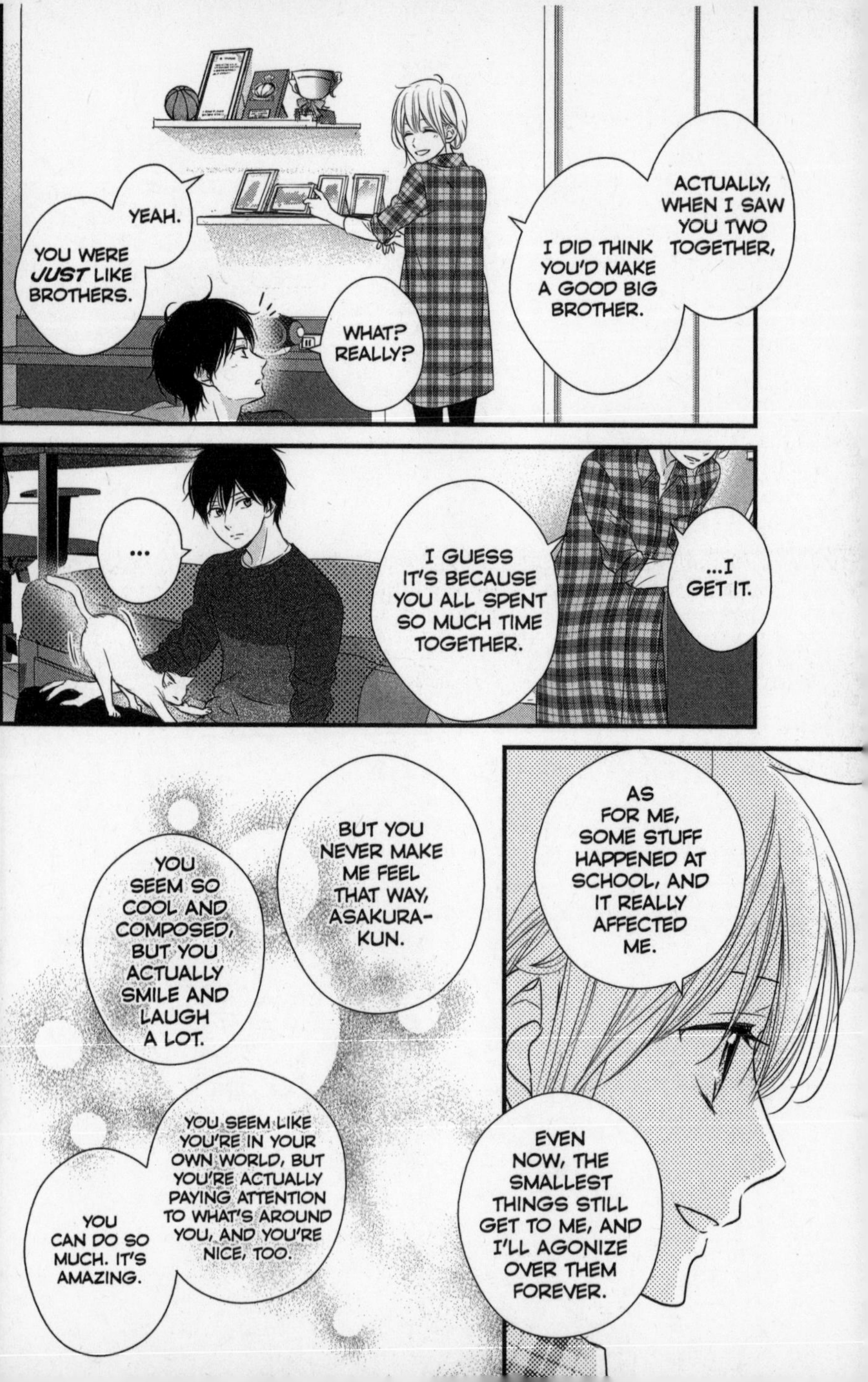
ACTUALLY, WHEN I SAW YOU TWO TOGETHER,
I DID THINK YOU'D MAKE A GOOD BIG BROTHER.
WHAT? REALLY?
YEAH.
YOU WERE *JUST* LIKE BROTHERS.
...I GET IT.
I GUESS IT'S BECAUSE YOU ALL SPENT SO MUCH TIME TOGETHER.
...
AS FOR ME, SOME STUFF HAPPENED AT SCHOOL, AND IT REALLY AFFECTED ME.
EVEN NOW, THE SMALLEST THINGS STILL GET TO ME, AND I'LL AGONIZE OVER THEM FOREVER.
BUT YOU NEVER MAKE ME FEEL THAT WAY, ASAKURA-KUN.
YOU SEEM SO COOL AND COMPOSED, BUT YOU ACTUALLY SMILE AND LAUGH A LOT.
YOU SEEM LIKE YOU'RE IN YOUR OWN WORLD, BUT YOU'RE ACTUALLY PAYING ATTENTION TO WHAT'S AROUND YOU, AND YOU'RE NICE, TOO.
YOU CAN DO SO MUCH. IT'S AMAZING.

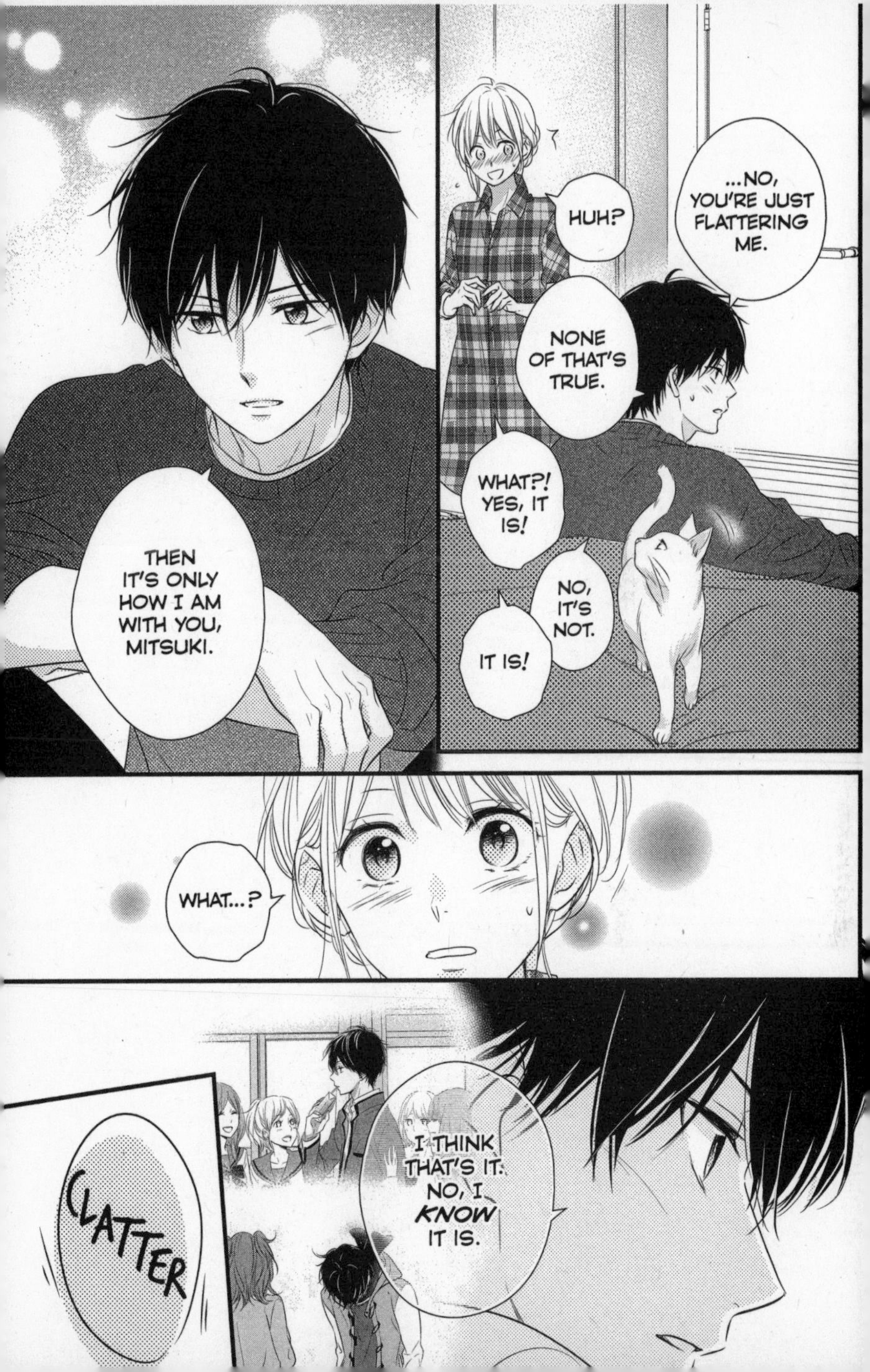
...NO, YOU'RE JUST FLATTERING ME.
HUH?
NONE OF THAT'S TRUE.
WHAT?! YES, IT IS!
NO, IT'S NOT.
IT IS!
THEN IT'S ONLY HOW I AM WITH YOU, MITSUKI.
WHAT...?
I THINK THAT'S IT. NO, I *KNOW* IT IS.
CLATTER

...I'VE NEVER WANTED TO BE WITH SOMEONE LIKE THIS BEFORE.

RATTLE RATTLE

ROLL

ACK!

FW

Look out!

...HUH?

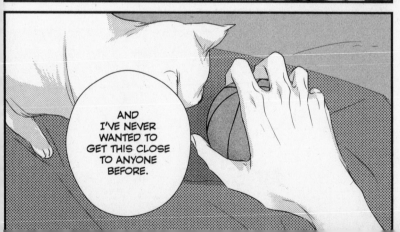

AND I'VE NEVER WANTED TO GET THIS CLOSE TO ANYONE BEFORE.

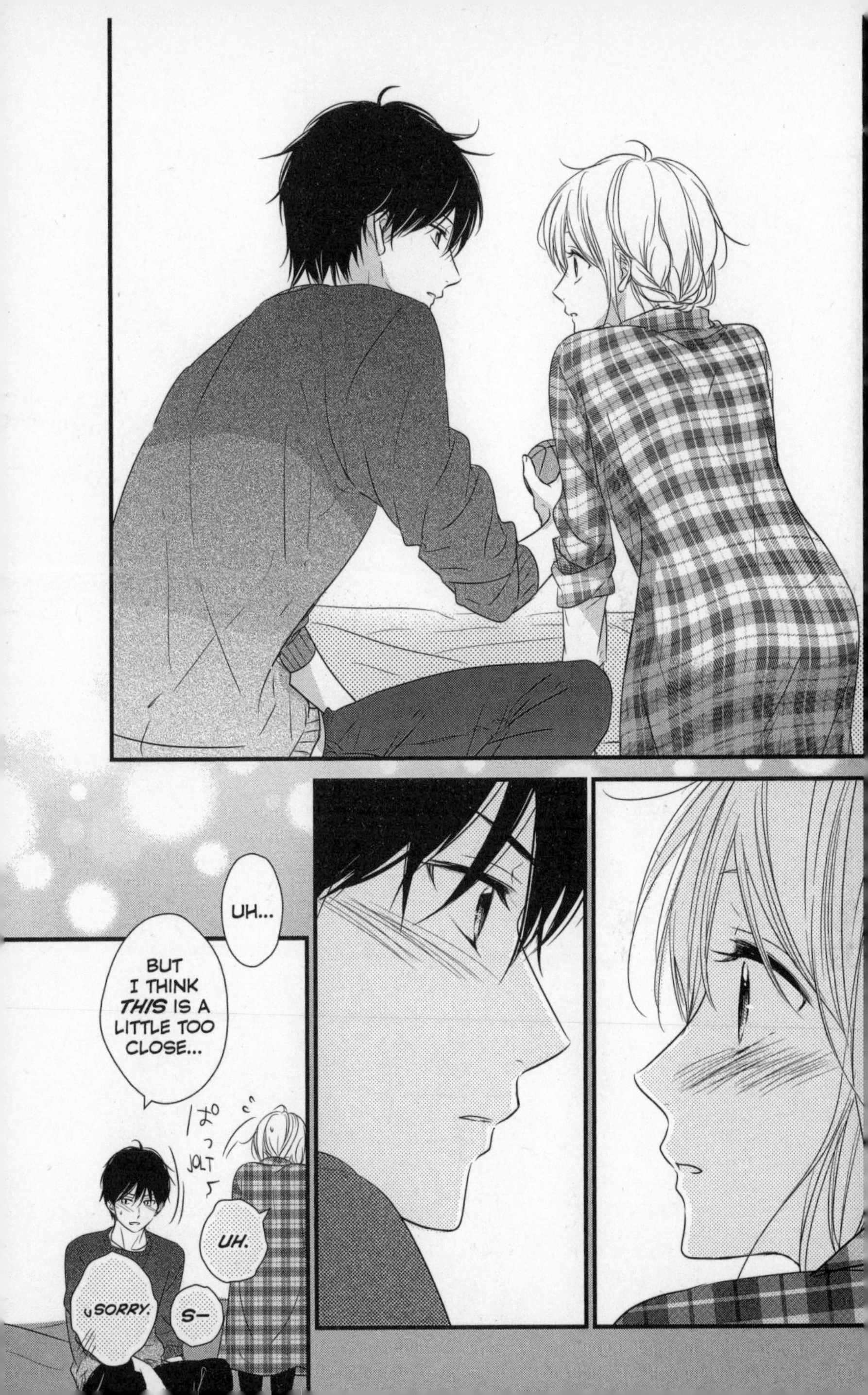
UH...
BUT I THINK *THIS* IS A LITTLE TOO CLOSE...
ぱっ
JOLT
UH.
S—
SORRY.

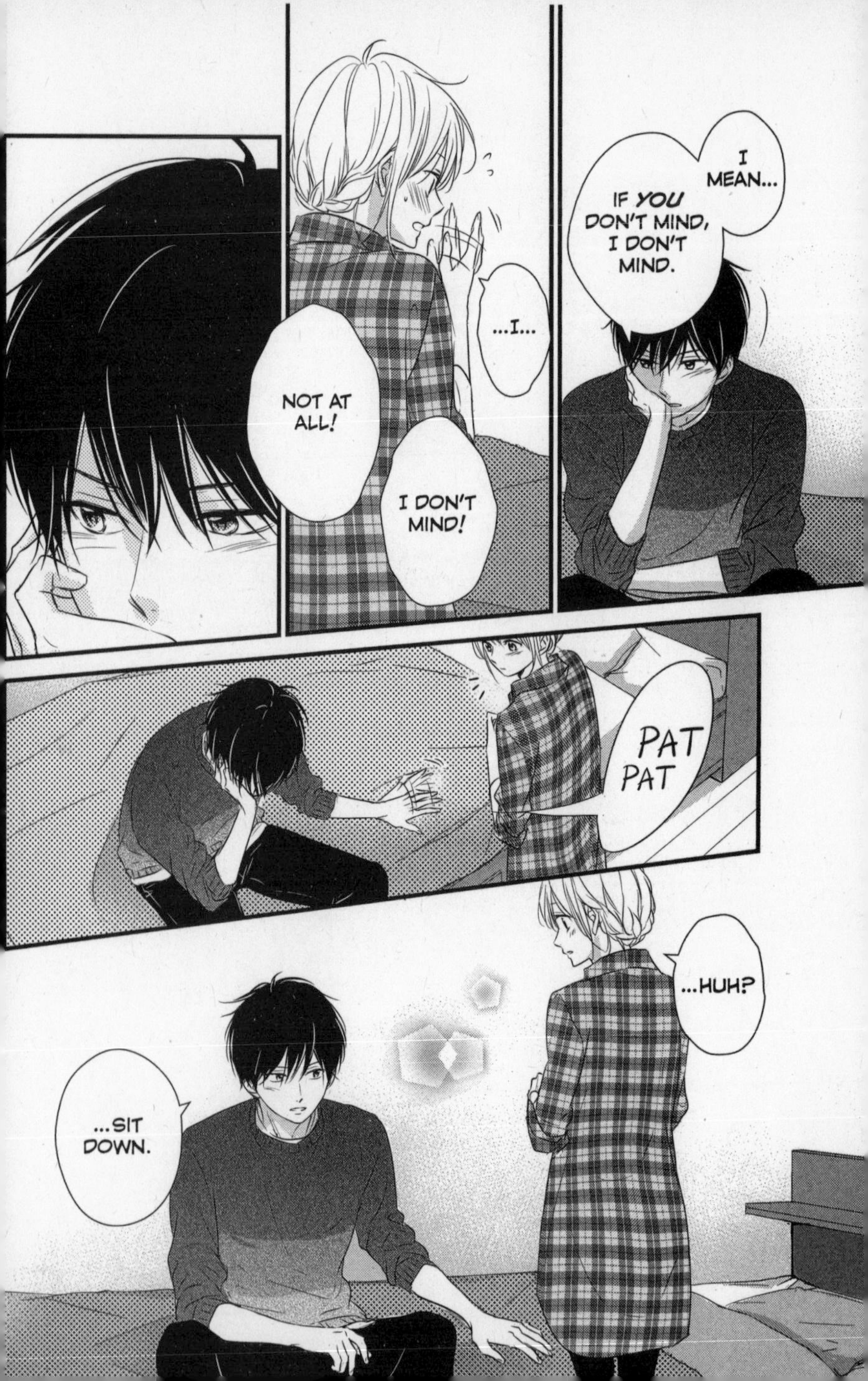
I MEAN...
IF *YOU* DON'T MIND, I DON'T MIND.
...I...
NOT AT ALL!
I DON'T MIND!
PAT PAT
...HUH?
...SIT DOWN.

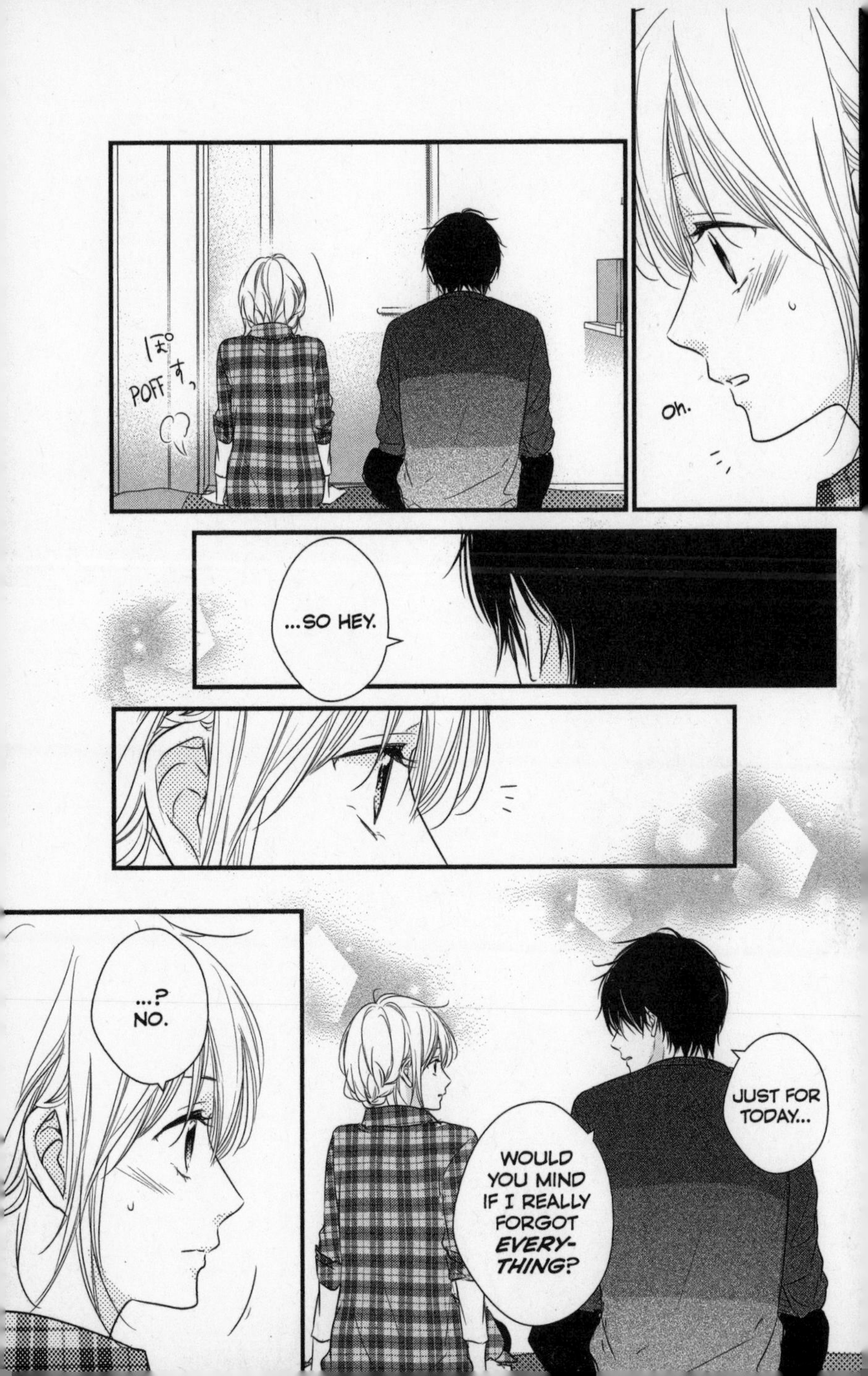
Oh.
ぽすっ
POFF
...SO HEY.
JUST FOR TODAY...
WOULD YOU MIND IF I REALLY FORGOT *EVERYTHING?*
...? NO.

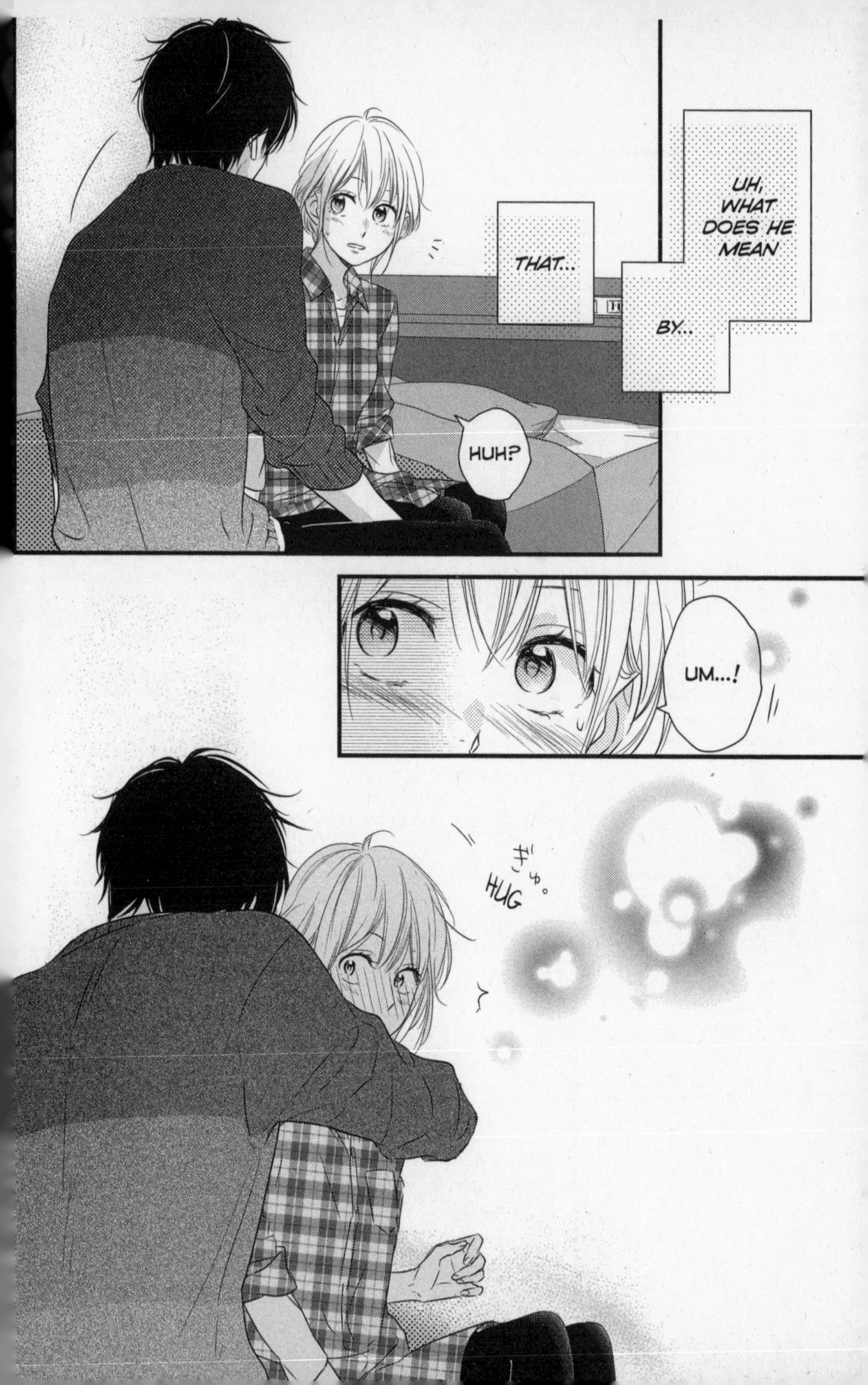
UH, WHAT DOES HE MEAN
BY...
THAT...
HUH?
UM...!
ぎゅ。
HUG

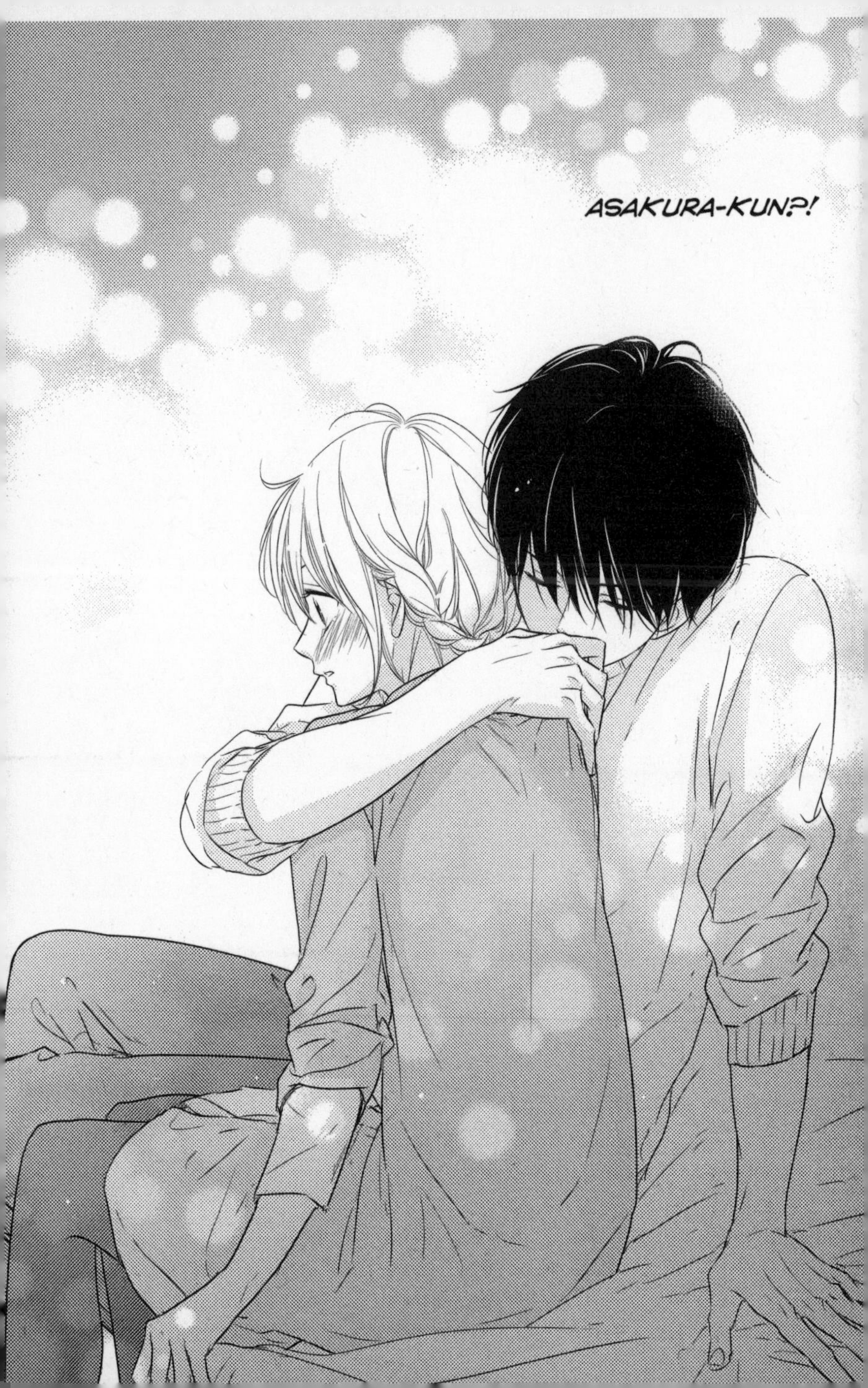
ASAKURA-KUN?!

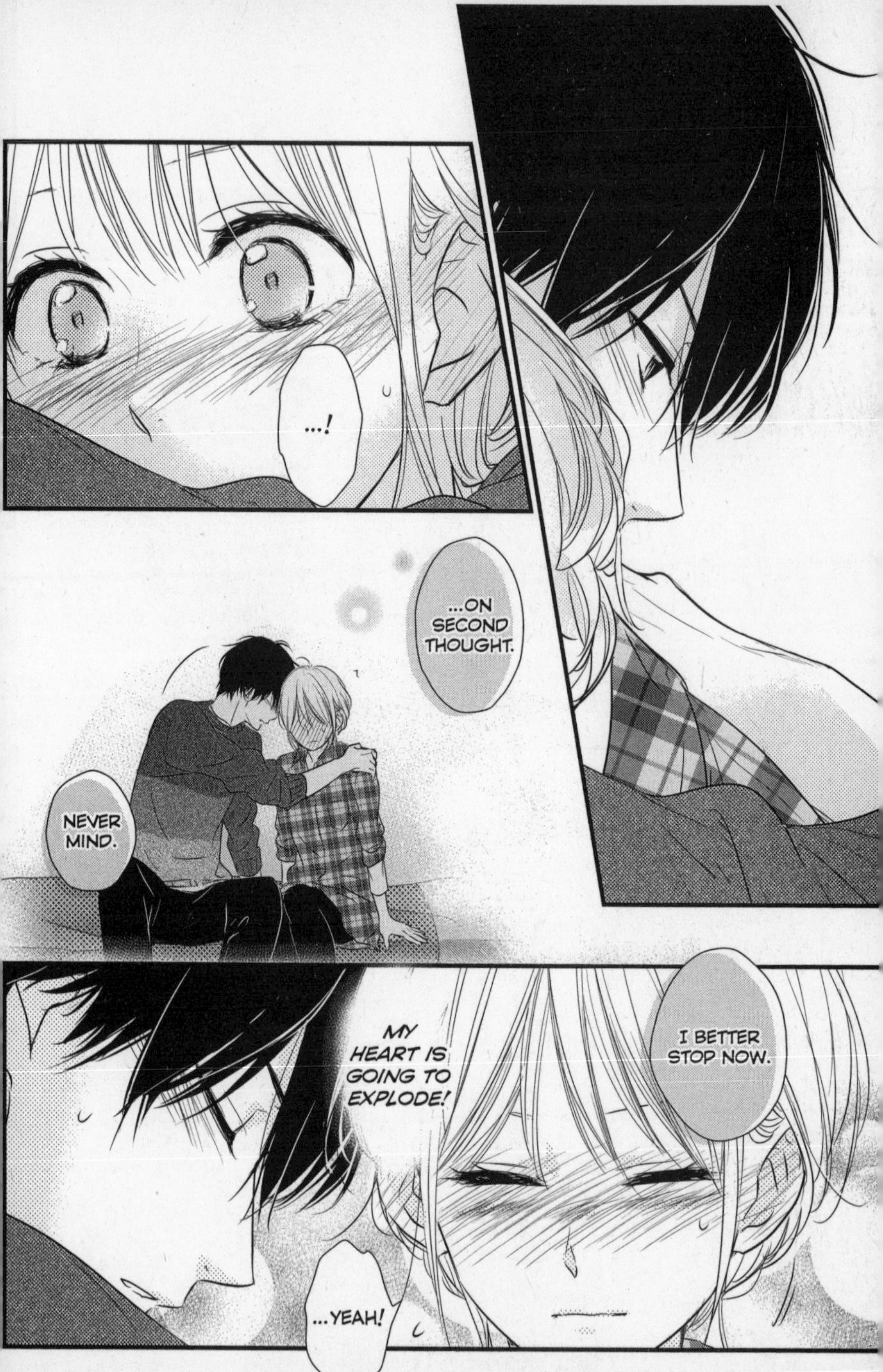
...!
...ON SECOND THOUGHT.
NEVER MIND.
I BETTER STOP NOW.
MY HEART IS GOING TO EXPLODE!
...YEAH!

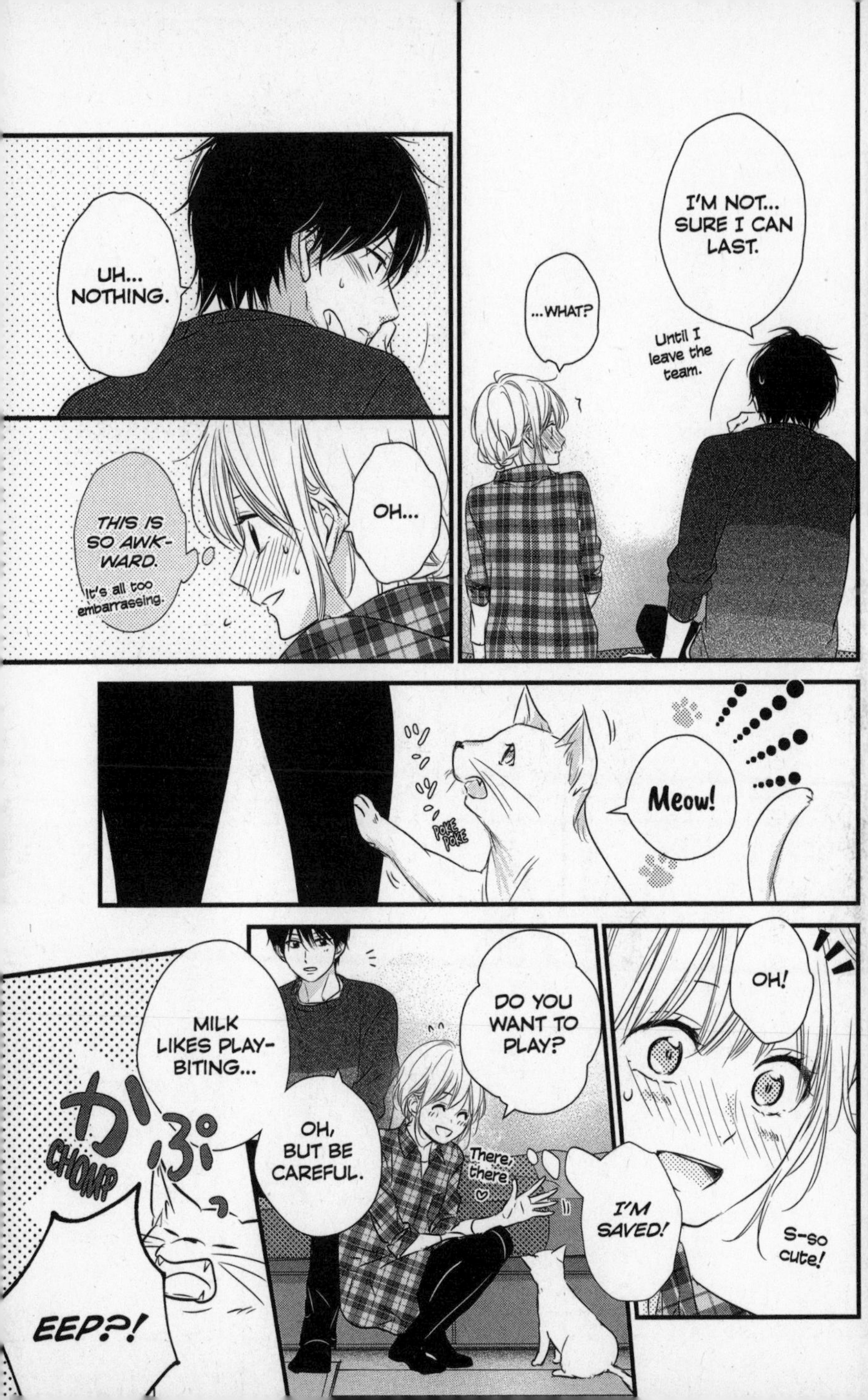
I'M NOT... SURE I CAN LAST.
Until I leave the team.
...WHAT?
UH... NOTHING.
OH...
THIS IS SO AWK-WARD.
It's all too embarrassing.
Meow!
POKE POKE
OH!
I'M SAVED!
S-so cute!
DO YOU WANT TO PLAY?
There, there ♡
OH, BUT BE CAREFUL.
MILK LIKES PLAY-BITING...
かぷ
CHOMP
EEP?!

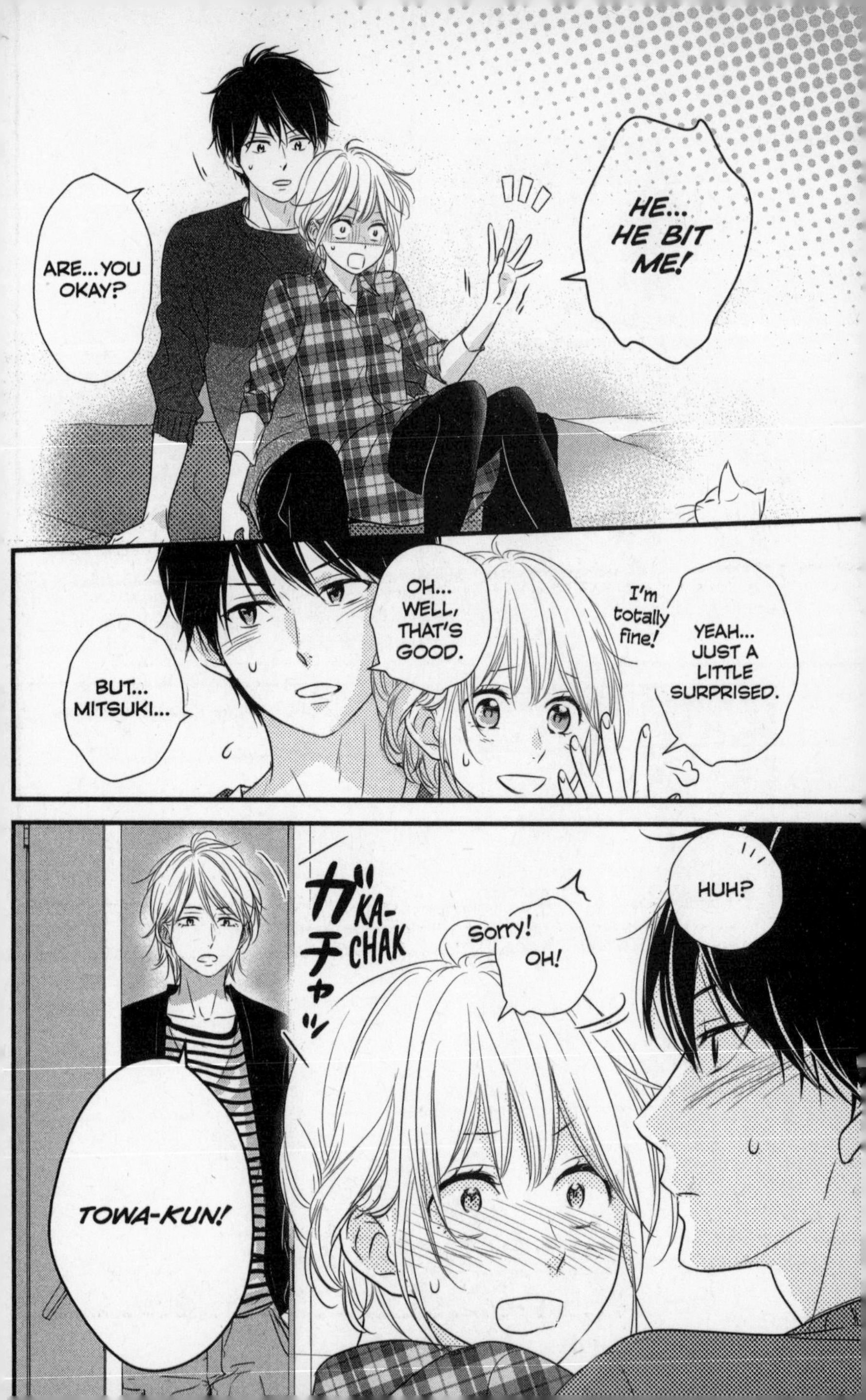
HE... HE BIT ME!
ARE...YOU OKAY?
YEAH... JUST A LITTLE SURPRISED.
I'm totally fine!
OH... WELL, THAT'S GOOD.
BUT... MITSUKI...
HUH?
OH!
Sorry!
ガチャッ KA-CHAK
TOWA-KUN!

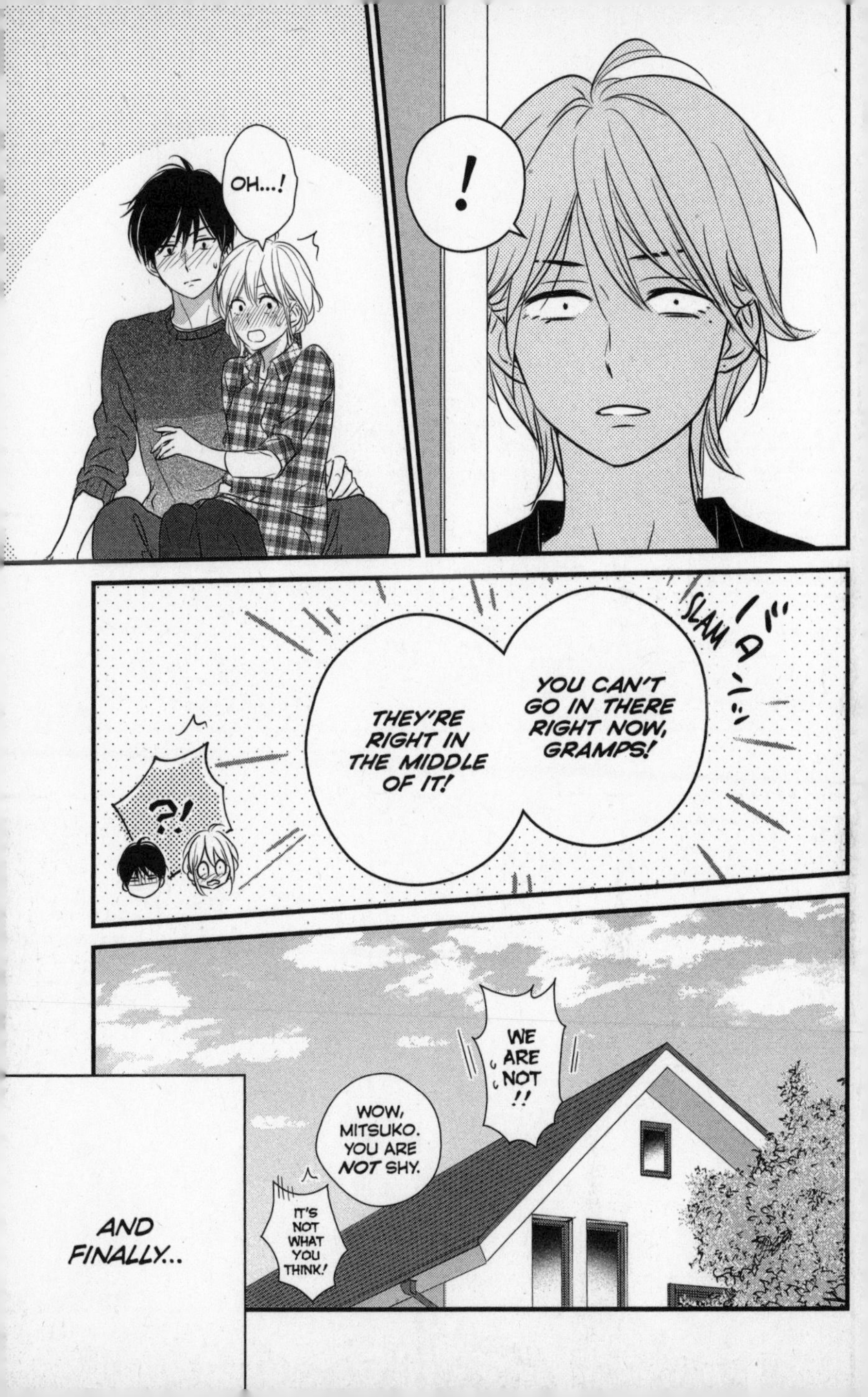
!
OH...!
SLAM
YOU CAN'T GO IN THERE RIGHT NOW, GRAMPS!
THEY'RE RIGHT IN THE MIDDLE OF IT!
?!
WE ARE NOT!!
WOW, MITSUKO. YOU ARE NOT SHY.
IT'S NOT WHAT YOU THINK!
AND FINALLY...

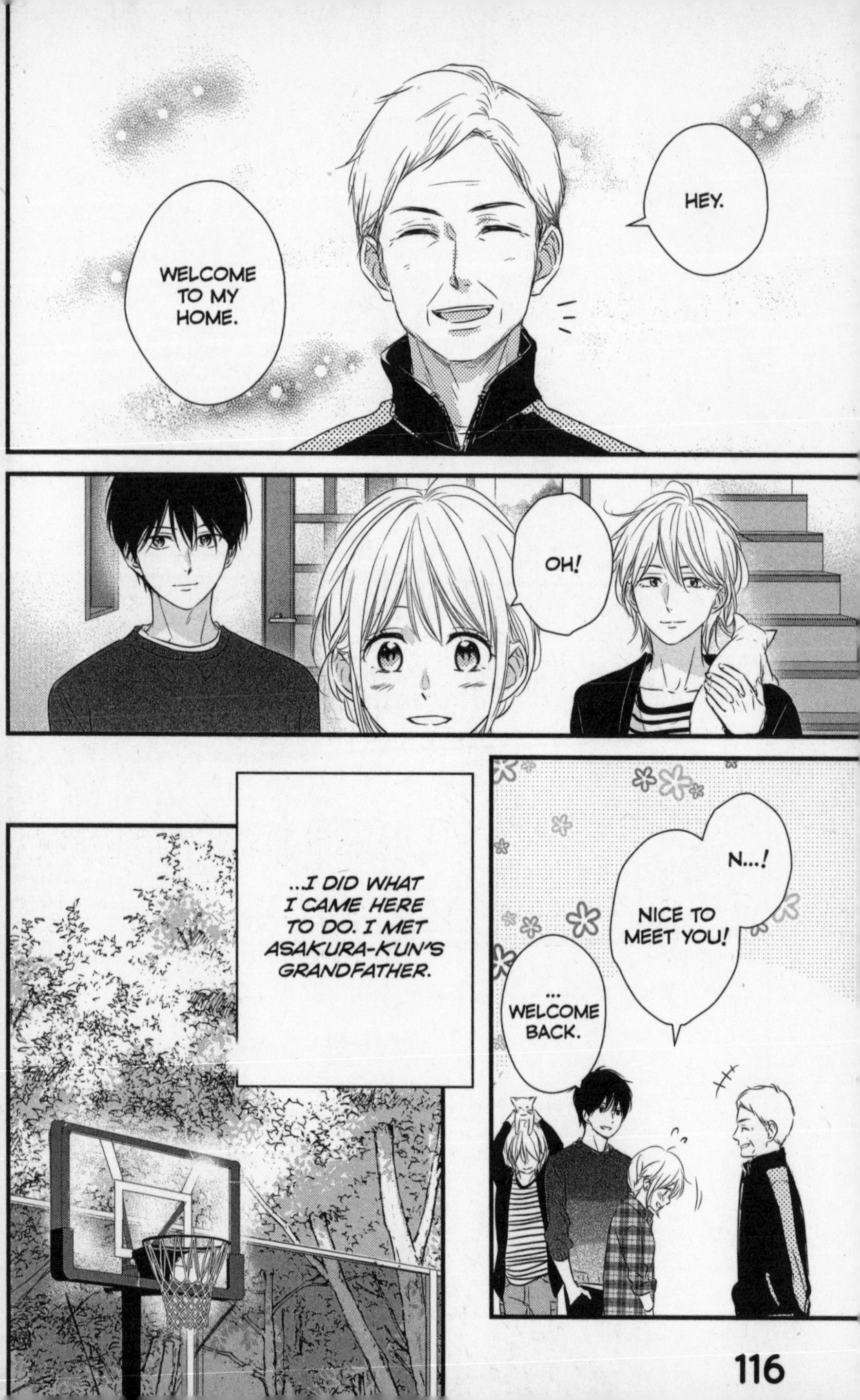
HEY.
WELCOME TO MY HOME.
OH!
N...!
NICE TO MEET YOU!
... WELCOME BACK.
...I DID WHAT I CAME HERE TO DO. I MET ASAKURA-KUN'S GRANDFATHER.

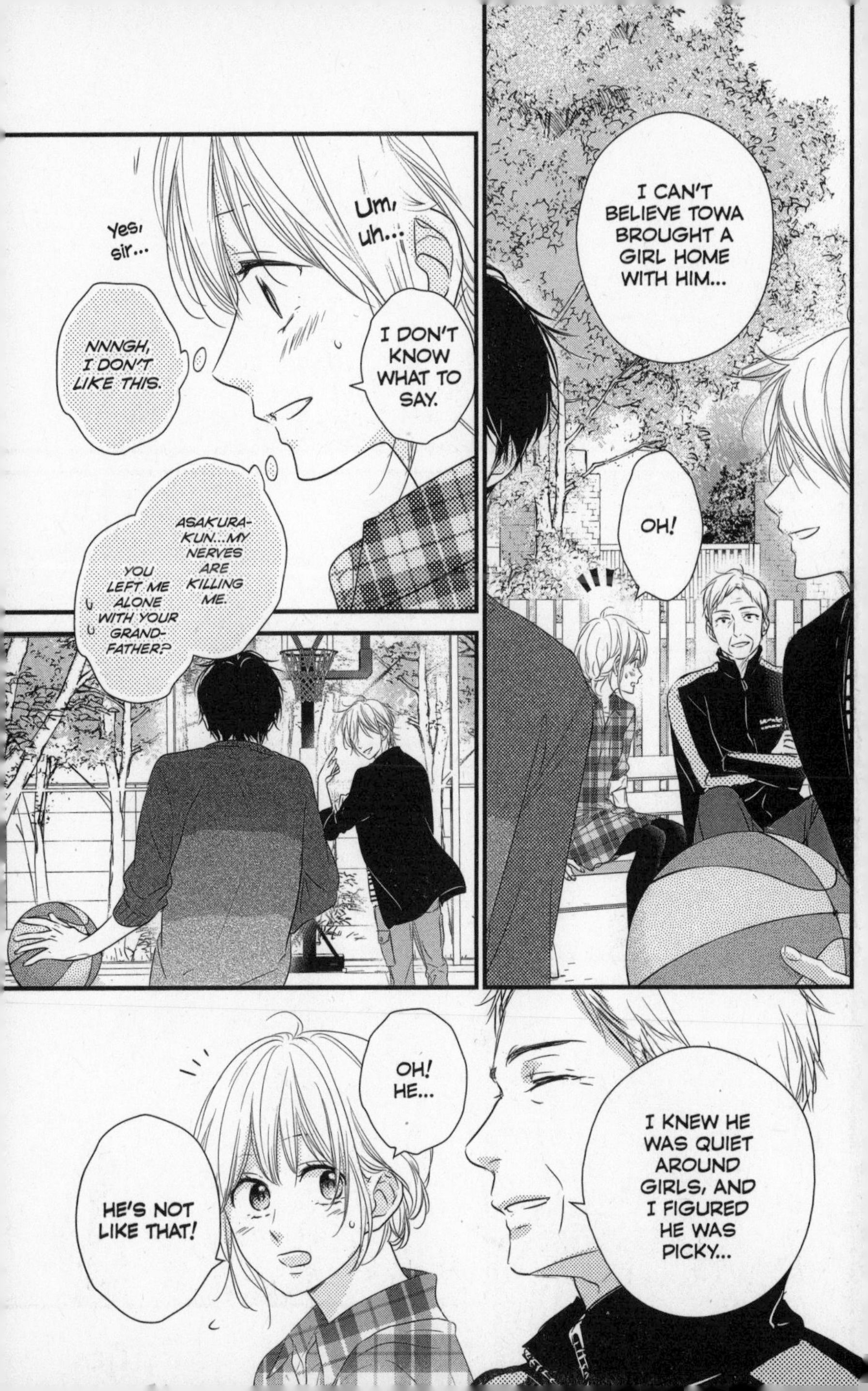

I CAN'T BELIEVE TOWA BROUGHT A GIRL HOME WITH HIM...
OH!
Um, uh...
I DON'T KNOW WHAT TO SAY.
Yes, sir...
NNNGH, I DON'T LIKE THIS.
ASAKURA-KUN...MY NERVES ARE KILLING ME.
YOU LEFT ME ALONE WITH YOUR GRANDFATHER?
I KNEW HE WAS QUIET AROUND GIRLS, AND I FIGURED HE WAS PICKY...
OH! HE...
HE'S NOT LIKE THAT!

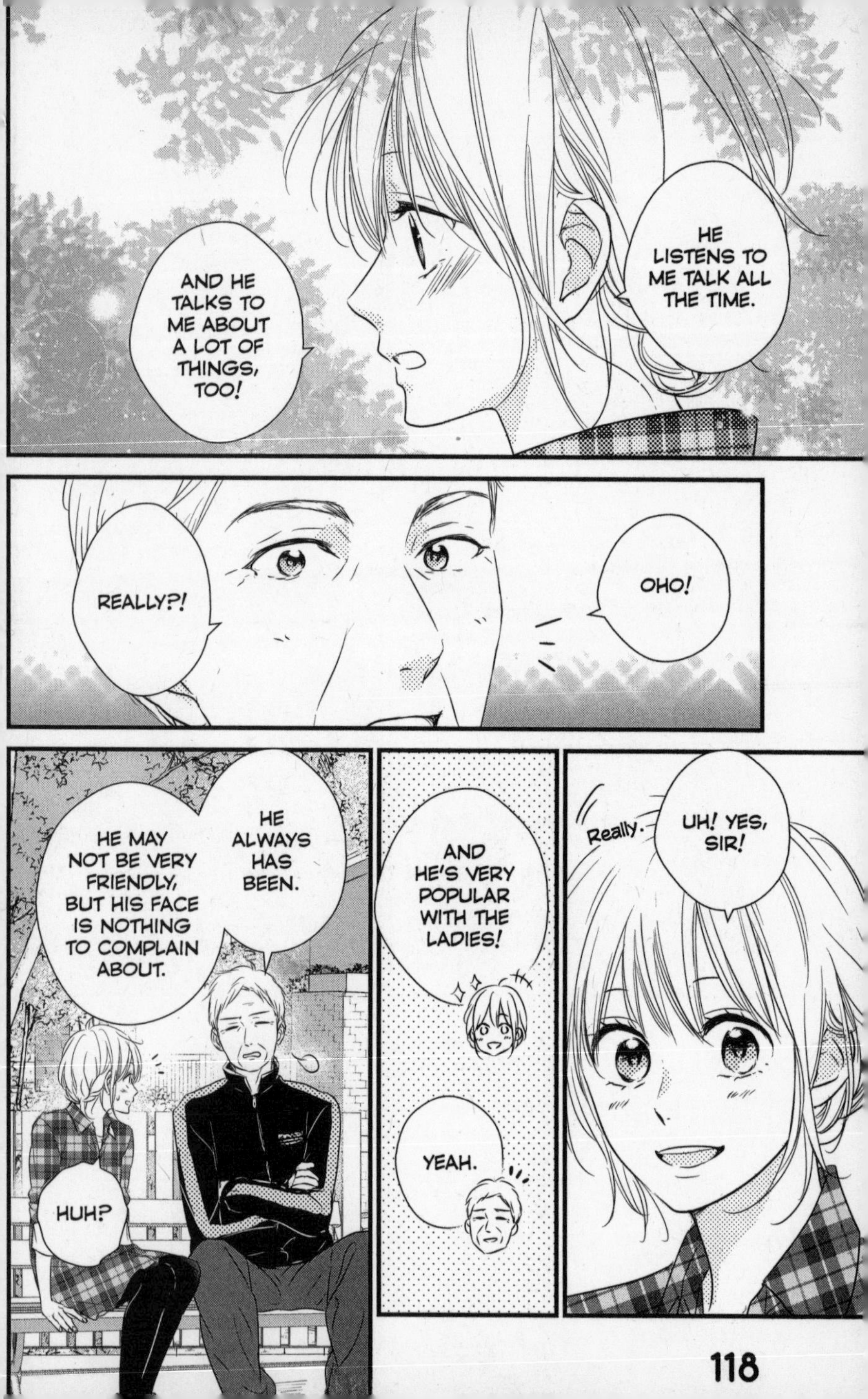
HE LISTENS TO ME TALK ALL THE TIME.
AND HE TALKS TO ME ABOUT A LOT OF THINGS, TOO!
OHO!
REALLY?!
UH! YES, SIR!
Really.
AND HE'S VERY POPULAR WITH THE LADIES!
YEAH.
HE ALWAYS HAS BEEN.
HE MAY NOT BE VERY FRIENDLY, BUT HIS FACE IS NOTHING TO COMPLAIN ABOUT.
HUH?

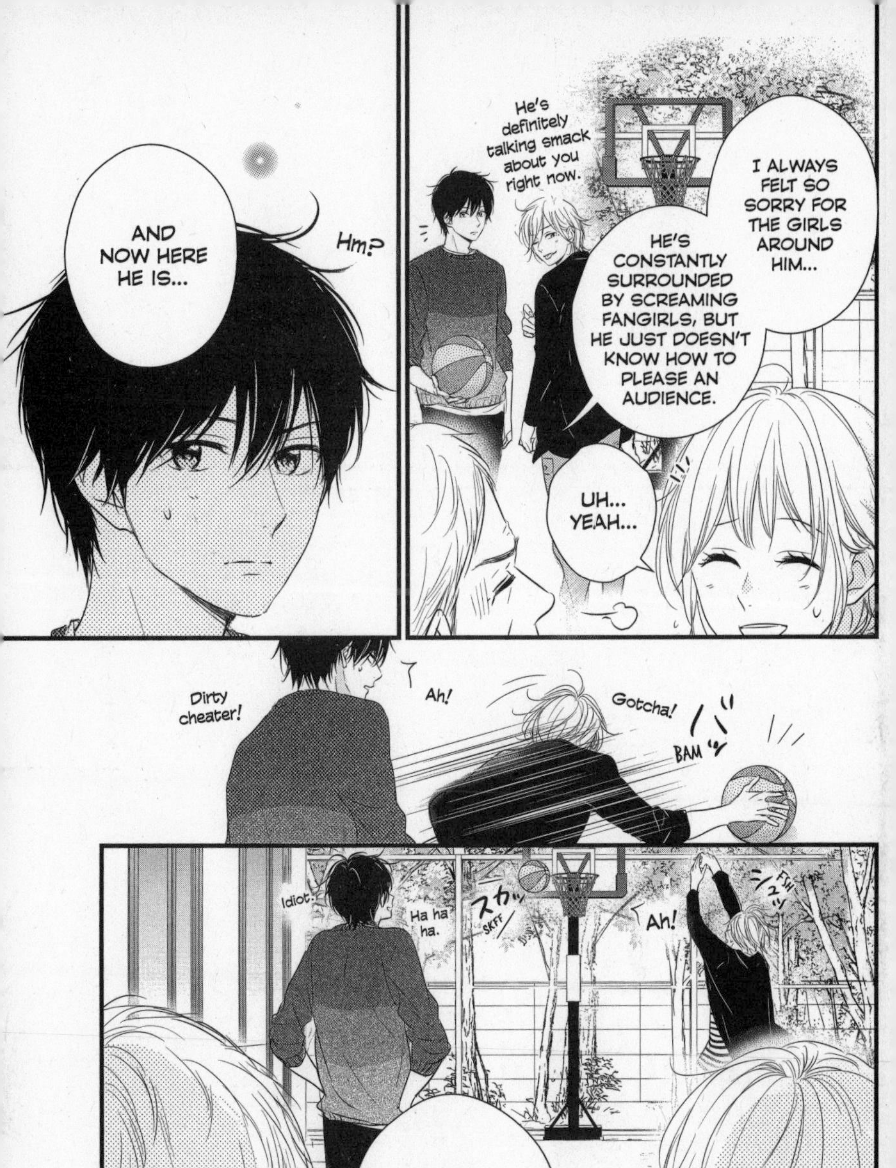
I ALWAYS FELT SO SORRY FOR THE GIRLS AROUND HIM...
HE'S CONSTANTLY SURROUNDED BY SCREAMING FANGIRLS, BUT HE JUST DOESN'T KNOW HOW TO PLEASE AN AUDIENCE.
He's definitely talking smack about you right now.
UH... YEAH...
Hm?
AND NOW HERE HE IS...
Gotcha!
BAM
Ah!
Dirty cheater!
Ah!
FSH
SKFF
Ha ha ha.
Idiot.
IT'S BEST WHEN HE'S HONEST WITH HIMSELF.

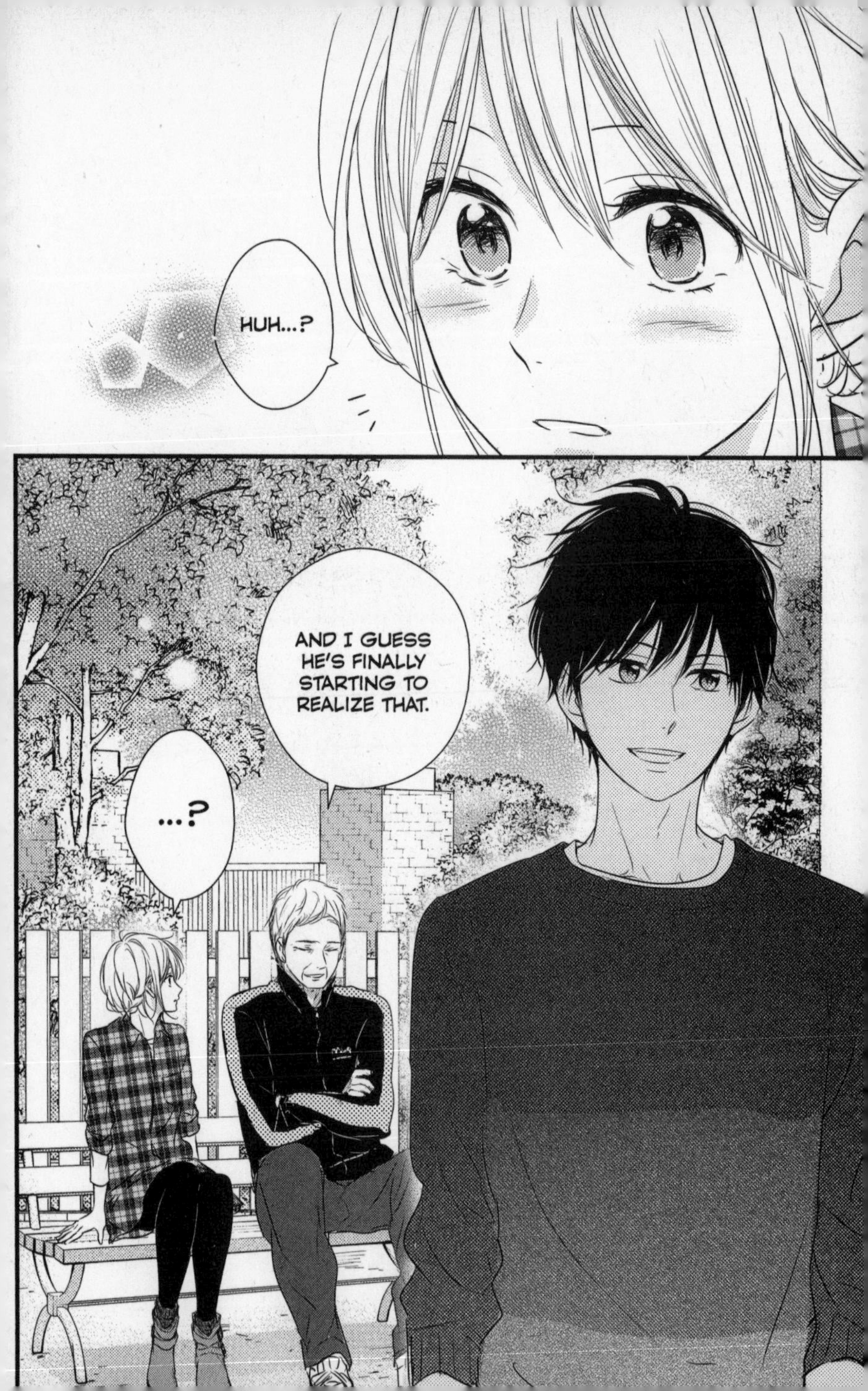
HUH...?
AND I GUESS HE'S FINALLY STARTING TO REALIZE THAT.
...?

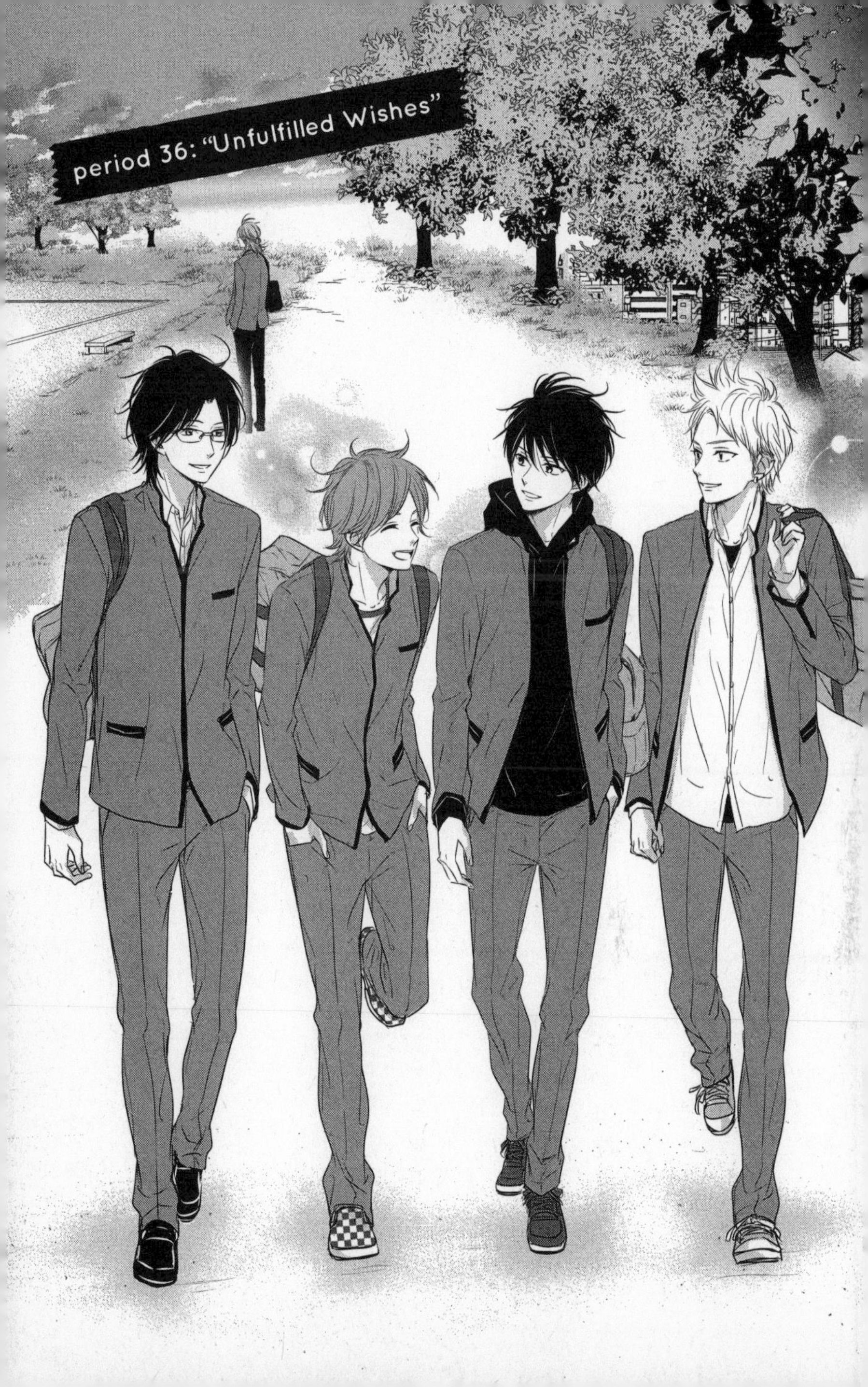
period 36: "Unfulfilled Wishes"

"IT'S BEST WHEN HE'S HONEST WITH HIMSELF."
"AND I GUESS HE'S FINALLY STARTING TO REALIZE THAT."
...?
UM...
WHAT DO YOU MEAN?

Towa

Family: Grandfather, Grandmother, Towa, cat

Towa likes milk, so the white cat's name is Milk.

Design from before the series started

I started with "he's a grandma and grandpa's boy," and then his personality evolved from there. At first, he had (gasp!) white hair! I wanted to avoid black hair because it takes so much time to do... (ha ha). But ultimately, at the suggestion of my editor, I gave him black hair. At first, I called him "Riku."

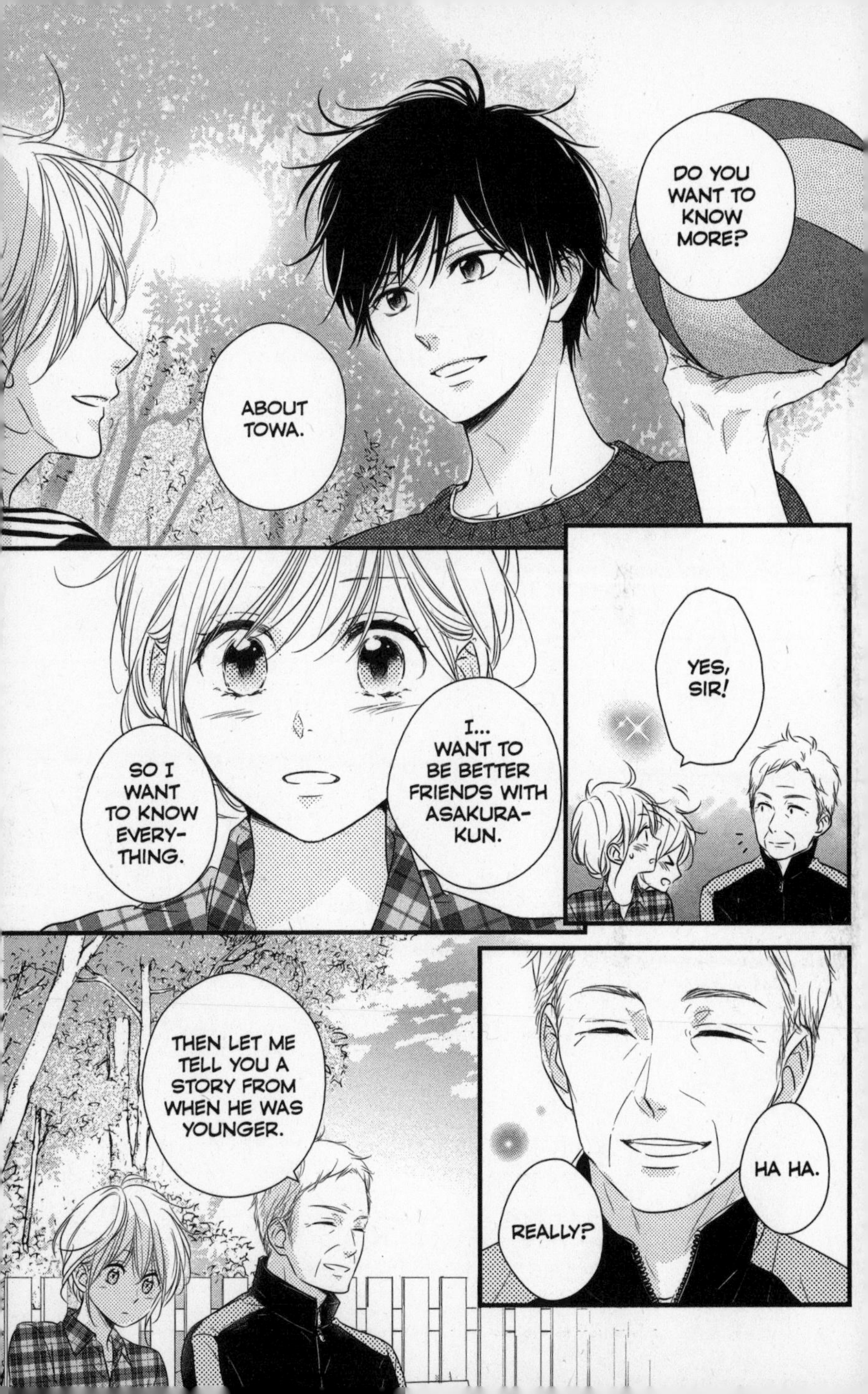
DO YOU WANT TO KNOW MORE?
ABOUT TOWA.
YES, SIR!
I... WANT TO BE BETTER FRIENDS WITH ASAKURA-KUN.
SO I WANT TO KNOW EVERYTHING.
HA HA.
REALLY?
THEN LET ME TELL YOU A STORY FROM WHEN HE WAS YOUNGER.

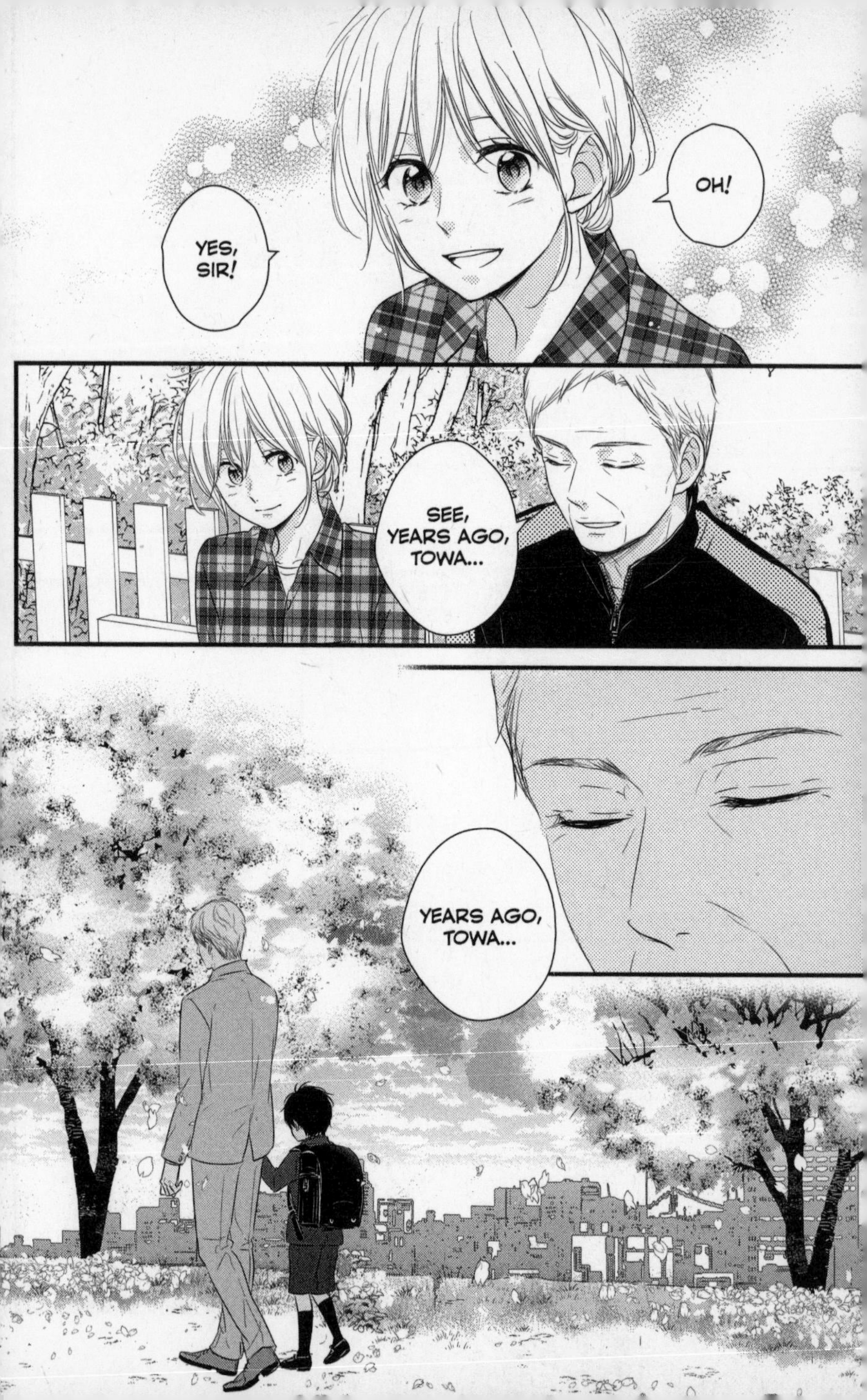

OH!
YES, SIR!
SEE, YEARS AGO, TOWA...
YEARS AGO, TOWA...

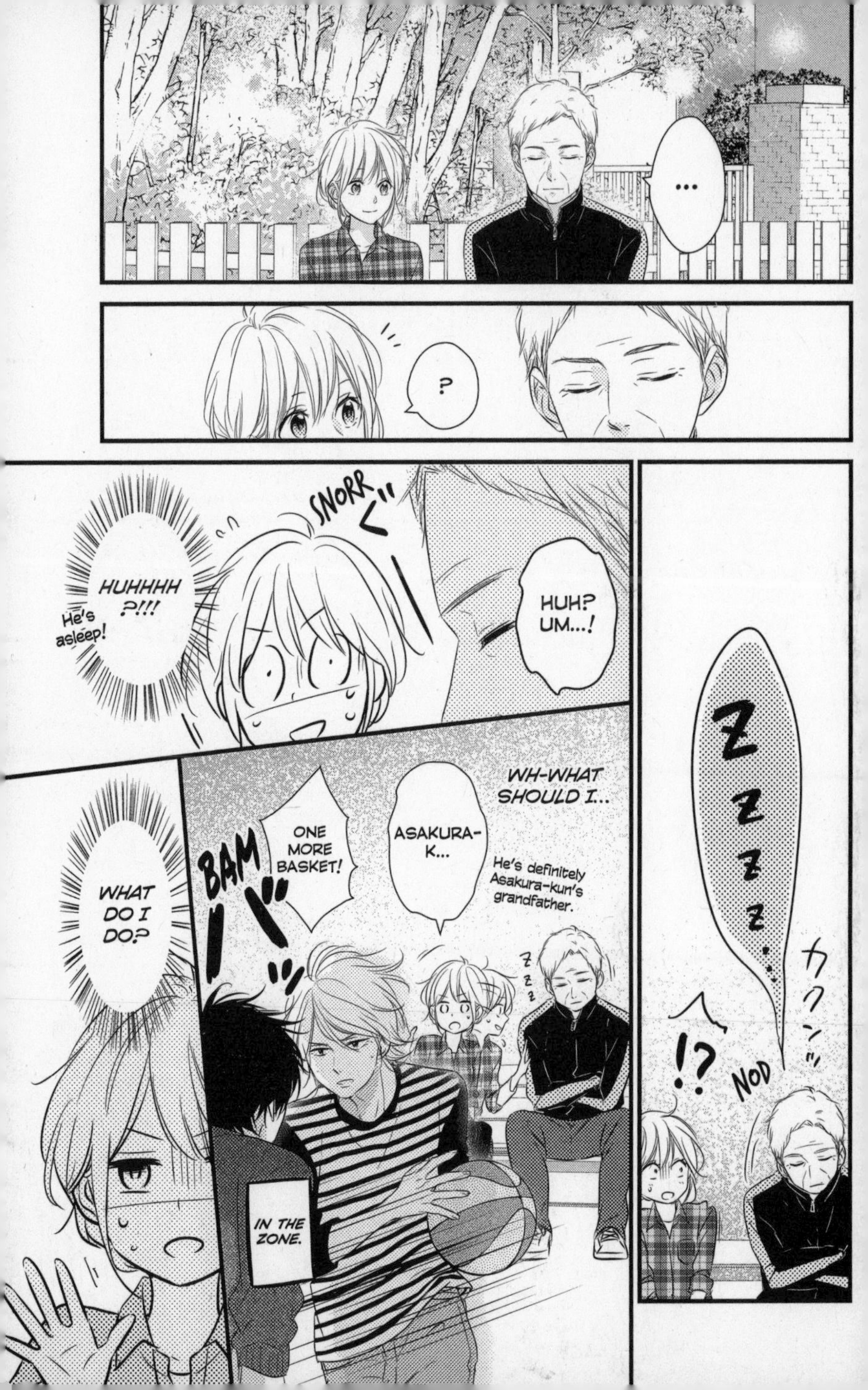
...
?
ZZZZ...
!?
NOD
SNORR
HUH? UM...!
HUHHHH?!!!
He's asleep!
WH-WHAT SHOULD I...
He's definitely Asakura-kun's grandfather.
ASAKURA-K...
ONE MORE BASKET!
BAM
WHAT DO I DO?
IN THE ZONE.

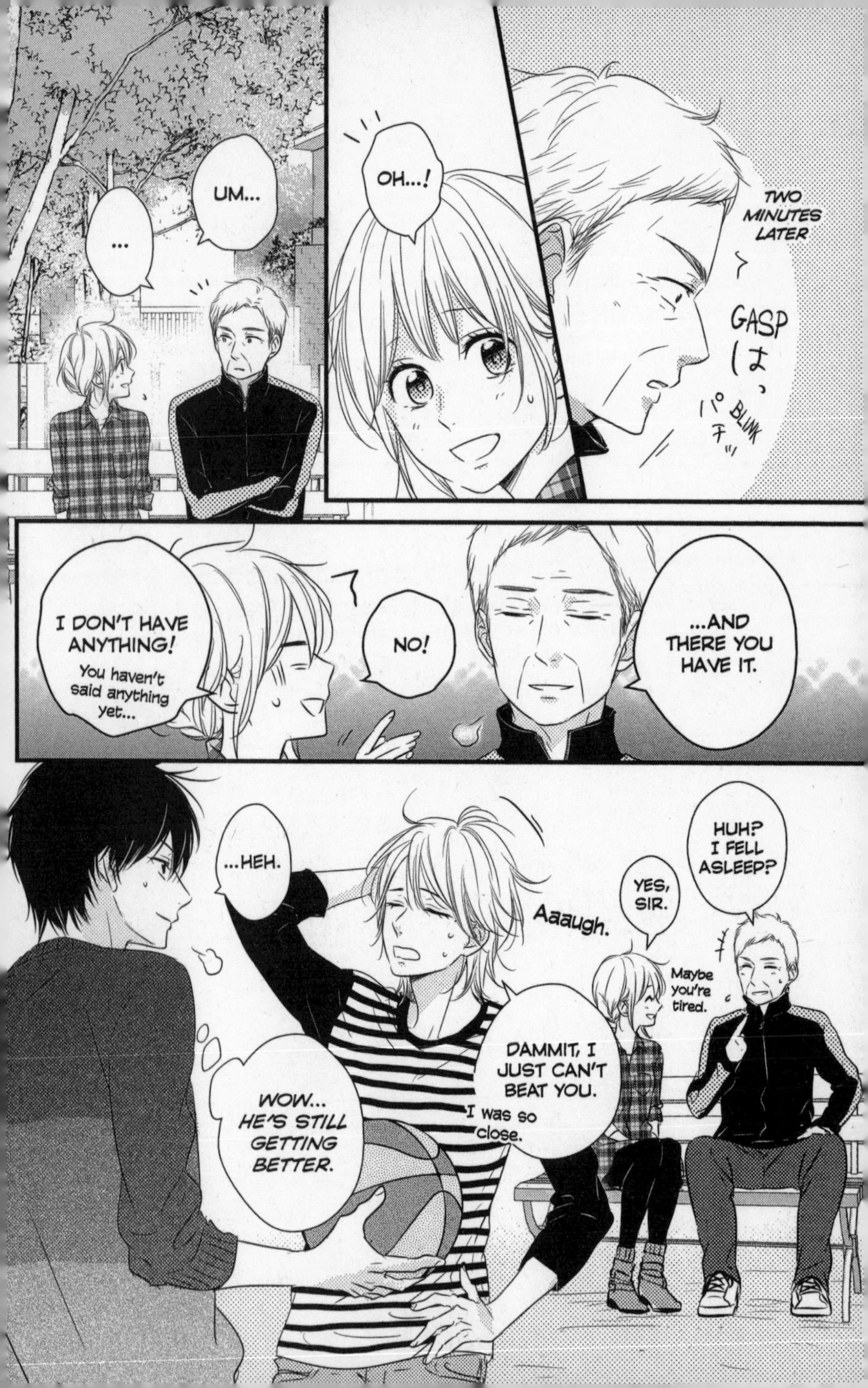
TWO MINUTES LATER
GASP
は、
BLINK
パチッ
OH...!
UM...
...
...AND THERE YOU HAVE IT.
NO!
I DON'T HAVE ANYTHING!
You haven't said anything yet...
HUH? I FELL ASLEEP?
YES, SIR.
Maybe you're tired.
Aaaugh.
DAMMIT, I JUST CAN'T BEAT YOU.
I was so close.
...HEH.
WOW... HE'S STILL GETTING BETTER.

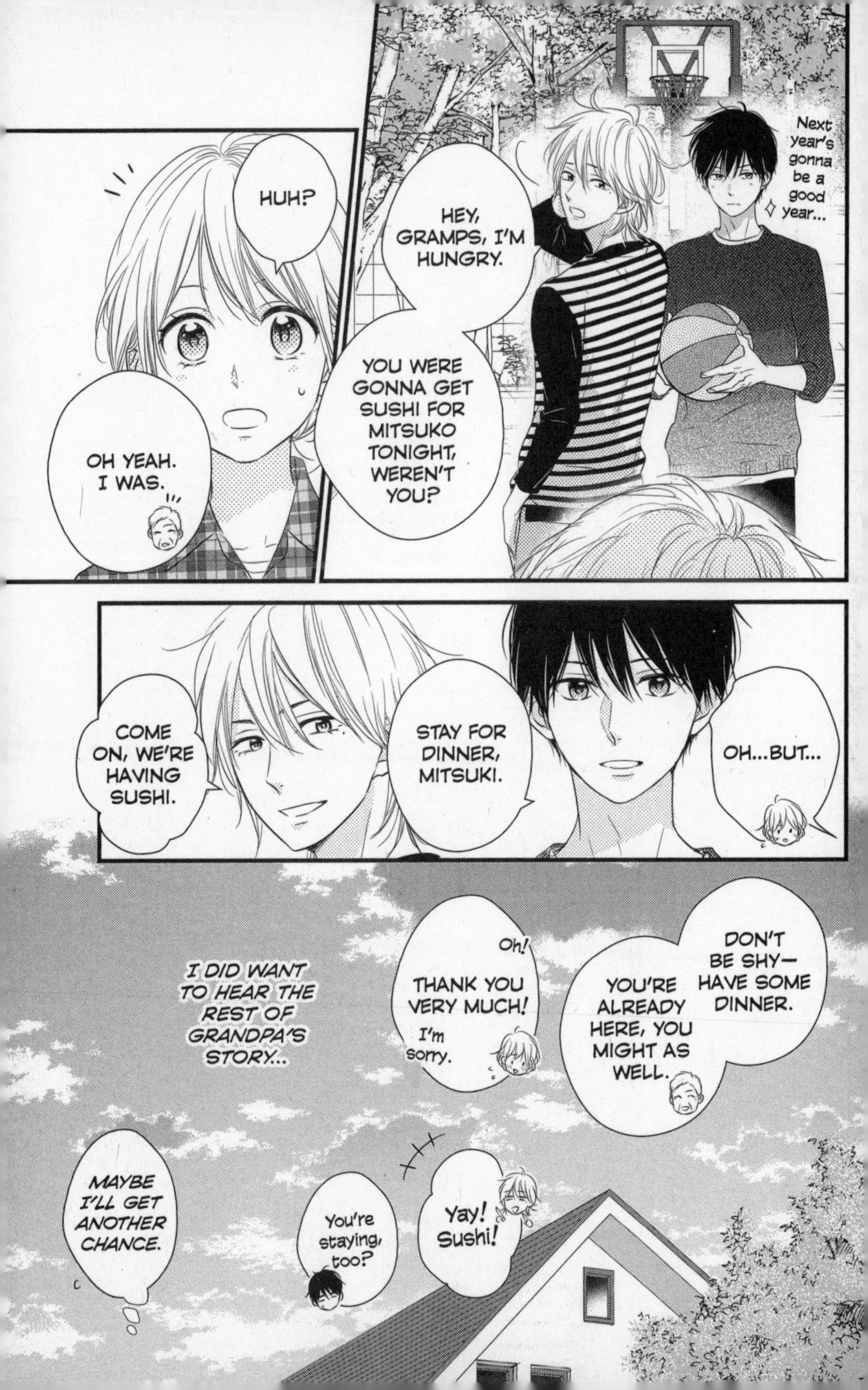
Next year's gonna be a good year...
HEY, GRAMPS, I'M HUNGRY.
YOU WERE GONNA GET SUSHI FOR MITSUKO TONIGHT, WEREN'T YOU?
HUH?
OH YEAH. I WAS.
OH...BUT...
STAY FOR DINNER, MITSUKI.
COME ON, WE'RE HAVING SUSHI.
DON'T BE SHY— HAVE SOME DINNER.
YOU'RE ALREADY HERE, YOU MIGHT AS WELL.
Oh!
THANK YOU VERY MUCH!
I'm sorry.
I DID WANT TO HEAR THE REST OF GRANDPA'S STORY...
Yay! Sushi!
You're staying, too?
MAYBE I'LL GET ANOTHER CHANCE.

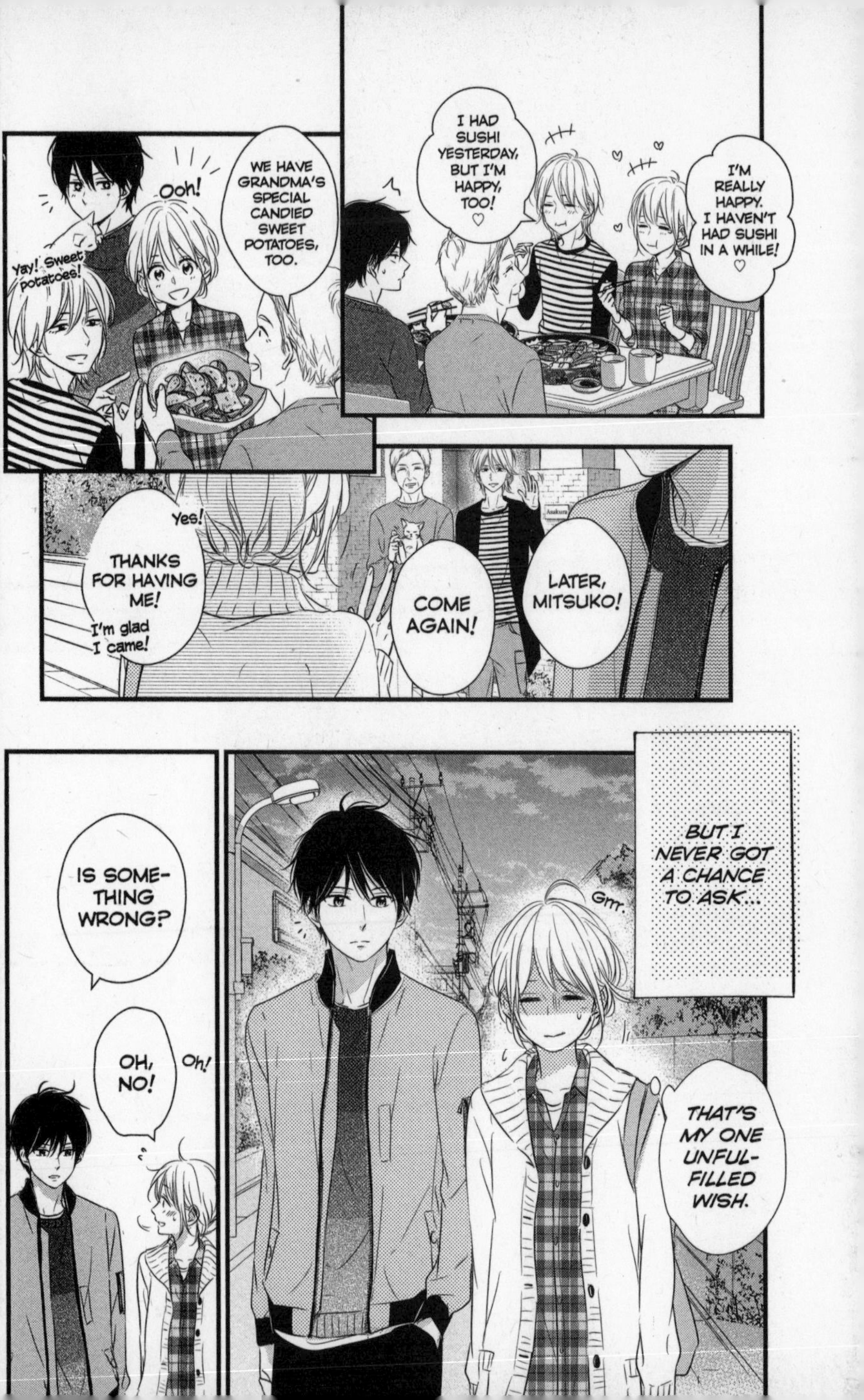
I'M REALLY HAPPY. I HAVEN'T HAD SUSHI IN A WHILE! ♡
I HAD SUSHI YESTERDAY, BUT I'M HAPPY, TOO! ♡
WE HAVE GRANDMA'S SPECIAL CANDIED SWEET POTATOES, TOO.
Ooh!
Yay! Sweet potatoes!
LATER, MITSUKO!
COME AGAIN!
Yes!
THANKS FOR HAVING ME!
I'm glad I came!
BUT I NEVER GOT A CHANCE TO ASK...
Grrr.
THAT'S MY ONE UNFUL-FILLED WISH.
IS SOME-THING WRONG?
Oh!
OH, NO!

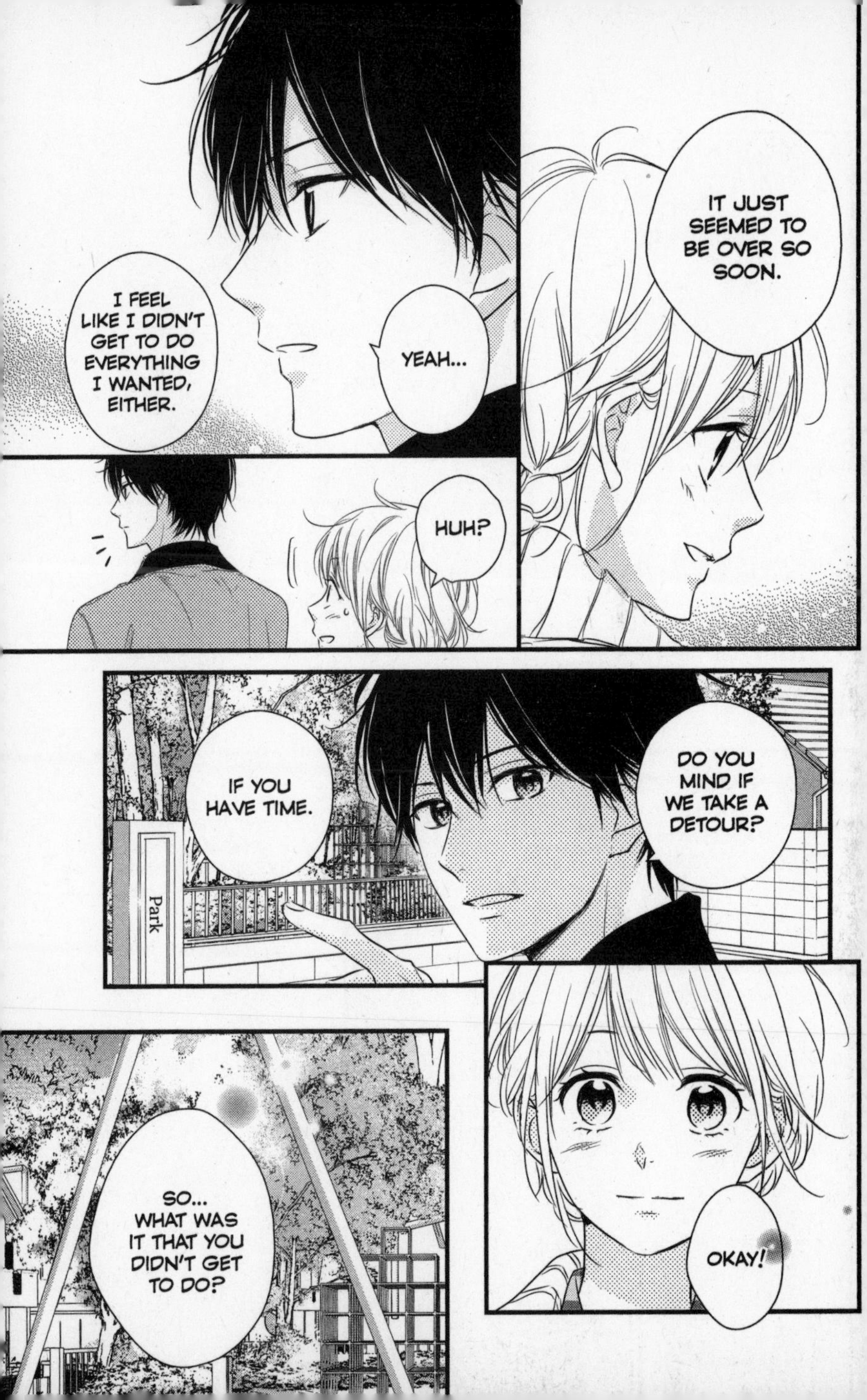
IT JUST SEEMED TO BE OVER SO SOON.
YEAH...
I FEEL LIKE I DIDN'T GET TO DO EVERYTHING I WANTED, EITHER.
HUH?
DO YOU MIND IF WE TAKE A DETOUR?
IF YOU HAVE TIME.
Park
OKAY!
SO... WHAT WAS IT THAT YOU DIDN'T GET TO DO?

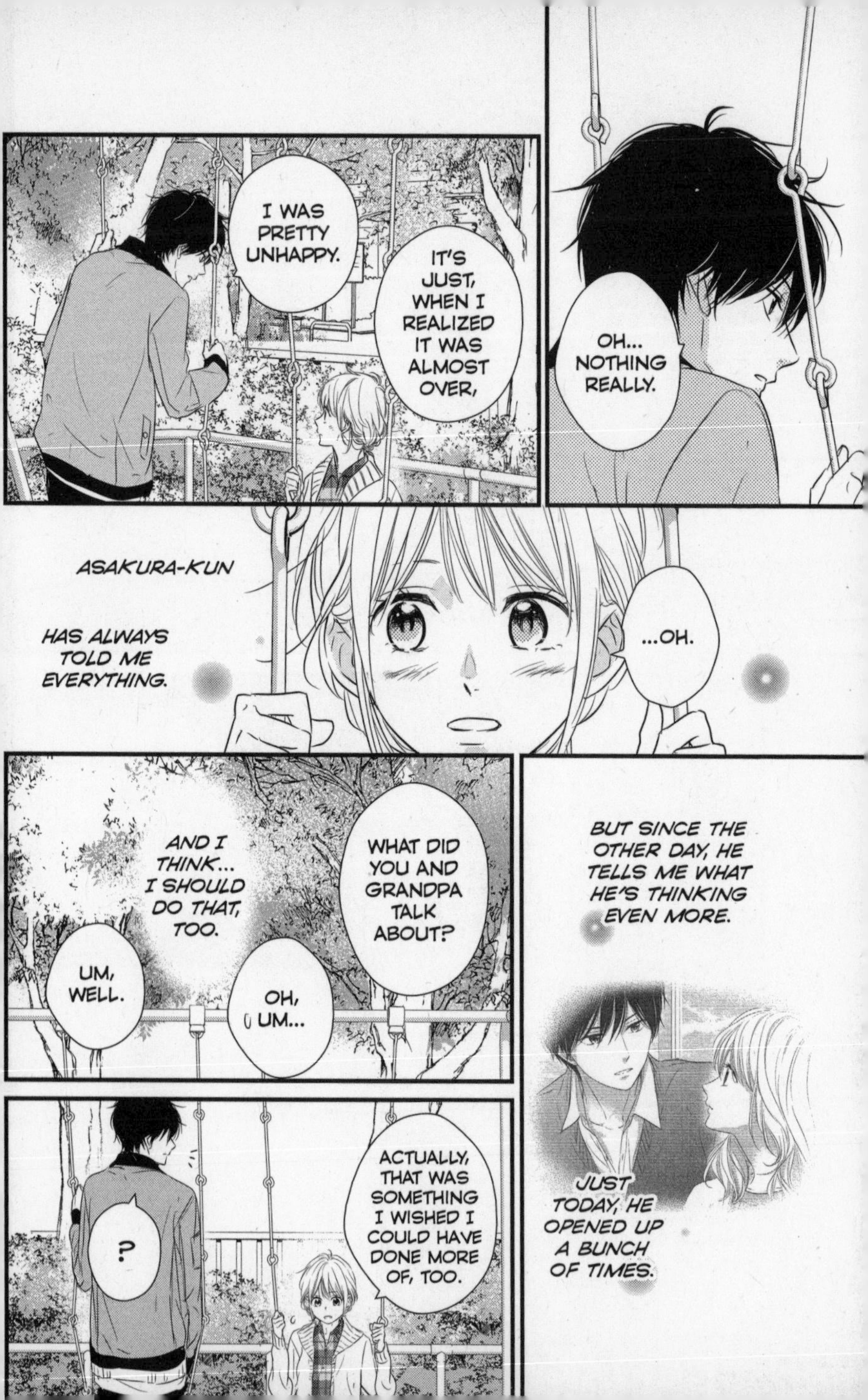
OH... NOTHING REALLY.
IT'S JUST, WHEN I REALIZED IT WAS ALMOST OVER,
I WAS PRETTY UNHAPPY.
...OH.
ASAKURA-KUN
HAS ALWAYS TOLD ME EVERYTHING.
BUT SINCE THE OTHER DAY, HE TELLS ME WHAT HE'S THINKING EVEN MORE.
JUST TODAY, HE OPENED UP A BUNCH OF TIMES.
WHAT DID YOU AND GRANDPA TALK ABOUT?
AND I THINK... I SHOULD DO THAT, TOO.
OH, UM...
UM, WELL.
ACTUALLY, THAT WAS SOMETHING I WISHED I COULD HAVE DONE MORE OF, TOO.
?

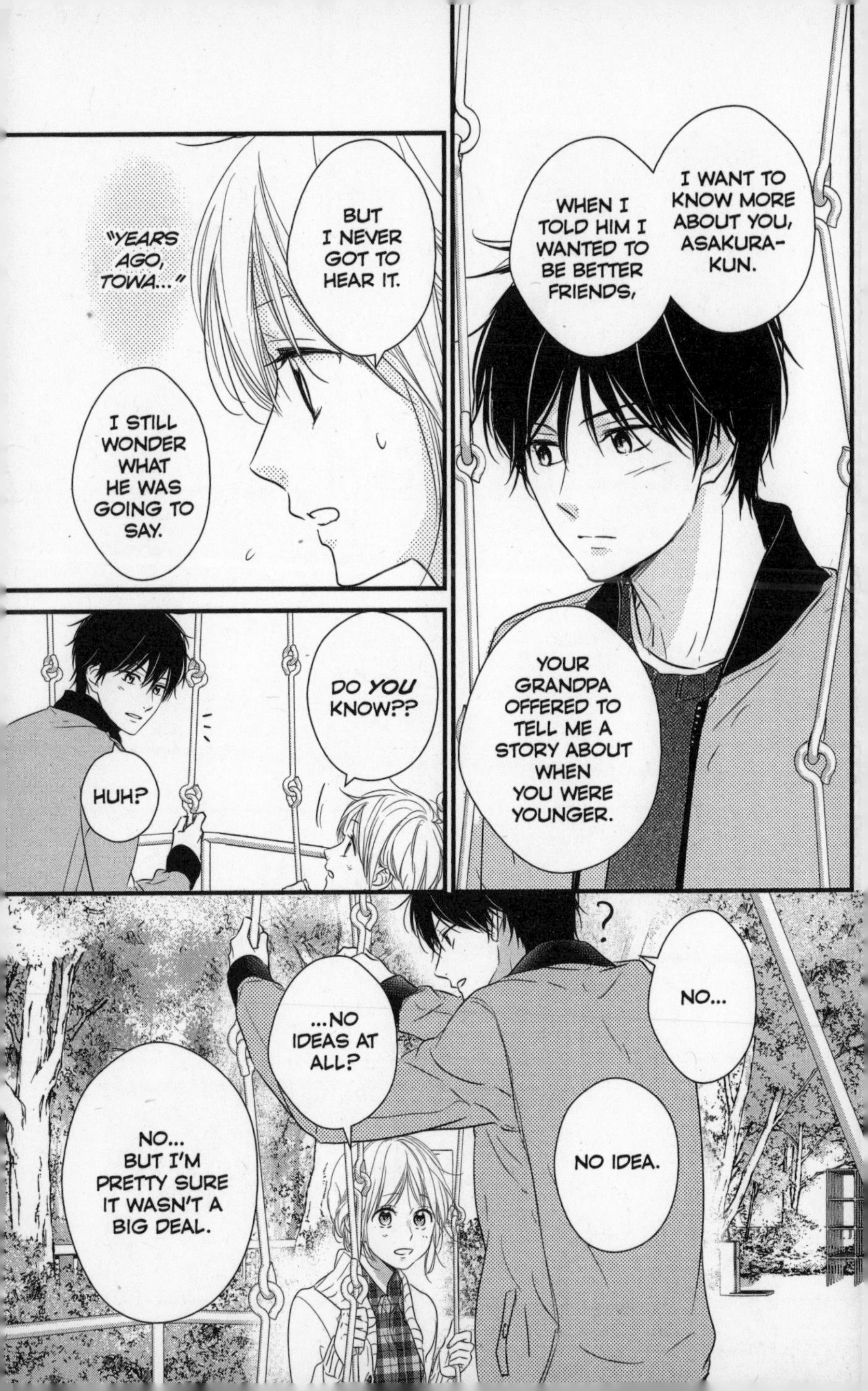
I WANT TO KNOW MORE ABOUT YOU, ASAKURA-KUN.
WHEN I TOLD HIM I WANTED TO BE BETTER FRIENDS,
YOUR GRANDPA OFFERED TO TELL ME A STORY ABOUT WHEN YOU WERE YOUNGER.
BUT I NEVER GOT TO HEAR IT.
"YEARS AGO, TOWA..."
I STILL WONDER WHAT HE WAS GOING TO SAY.
DO *YOU* KNOW??
HUH?
?
NO...
...NO IDEAS AT ALL?
NO IDEA.
NO... BUT I'M PRETTY SURE IT WASN'T A BIG DEAL.

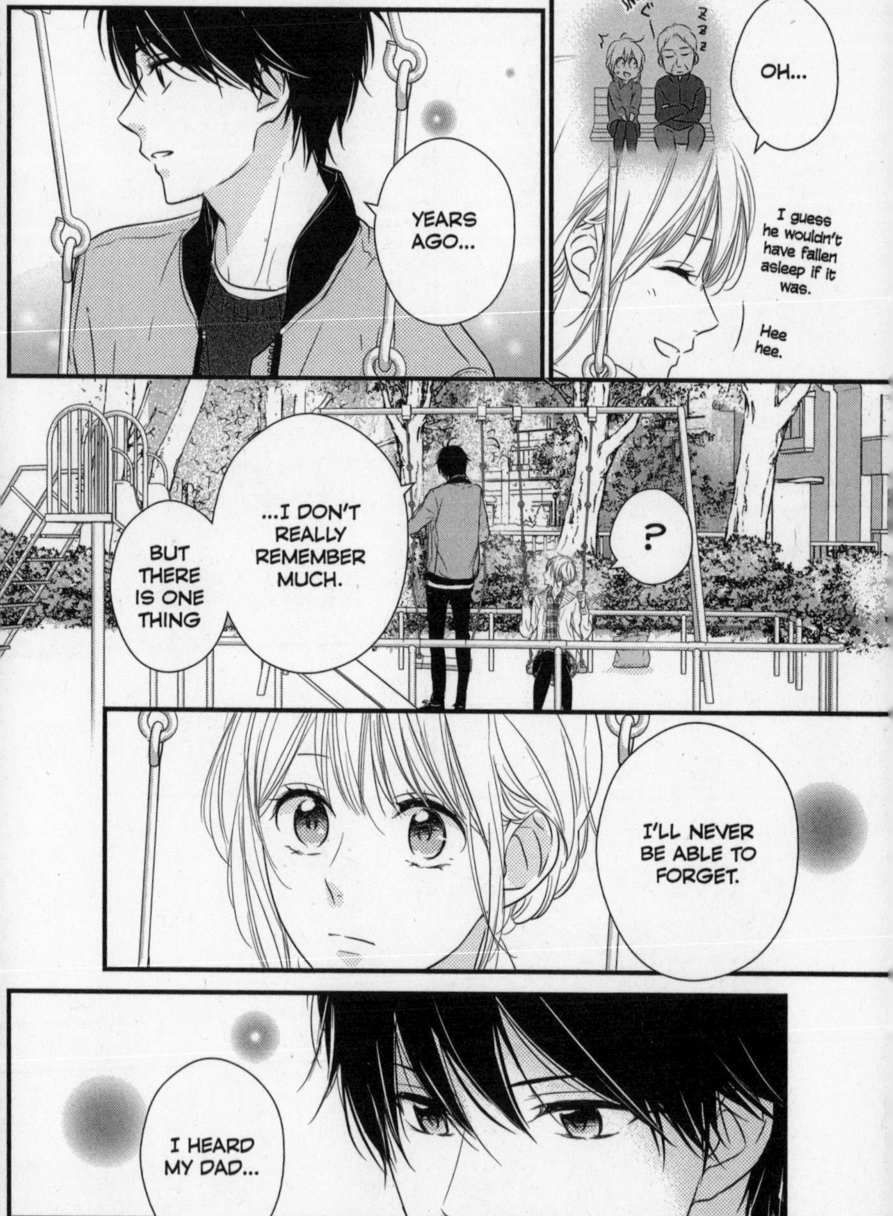

OH...
SNORR
I guess he wouldn't have fallen asleep if it was.
Hee hee.
YEARS AGO...
?
...I DON'T REALLY REMEMBER MUCH.
BUT THERE IS ONE THING
I'LL NEVER BE ABLE TO FORGET.
I HEARD MY DAD...

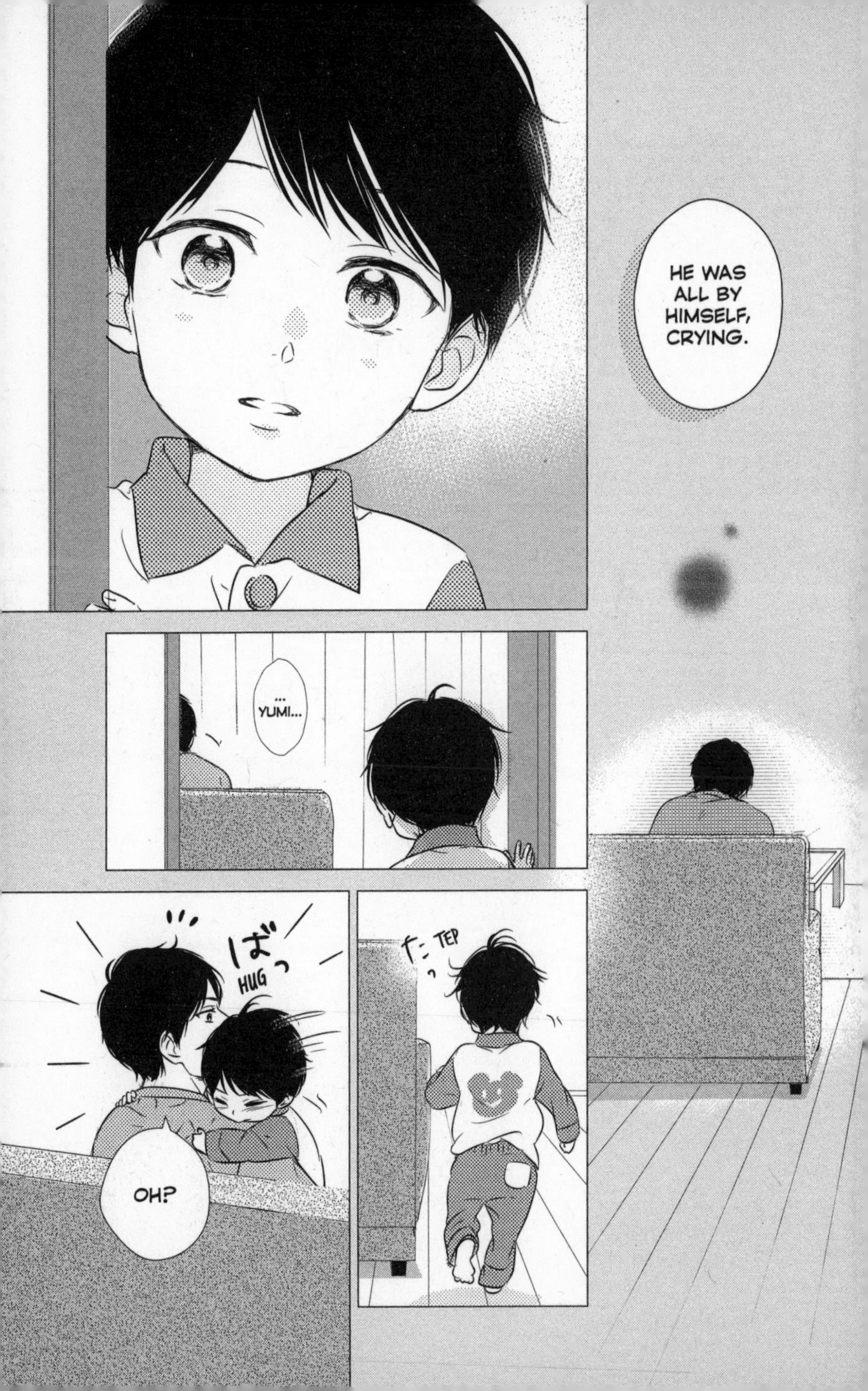
HE WAS ALL BY HIMSELF, CRYING.
... YUMI...
たっ TEP
ばっ HUG
OH?

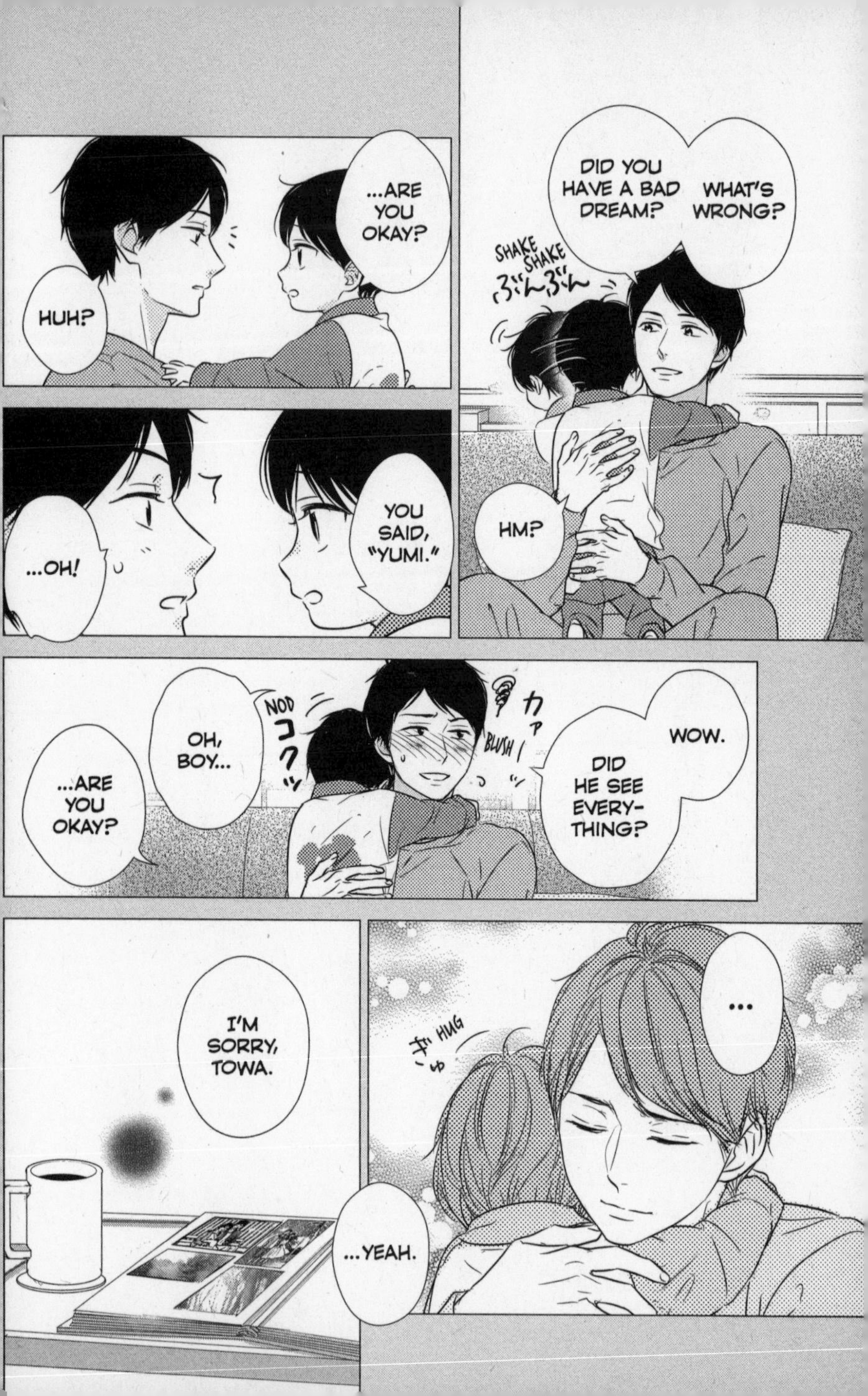
WHAT'S WRONG?
DID YOU HAVE A BAD DREAM?
SHAKE SHAKE
ぶんぶん
HM?
...ARE YOU OKAY?
HUH?
YOU SAID, "YUMI."
...OH!
WOW.
DID HE SEE EVERYTHING?
カァ
BLUSH!
NOD
コクッ
OH, BOY...
...ARE YOU OKAY?
...
HUG
ぎゅ
...YEAH.
I'M SORRY, TOWA.

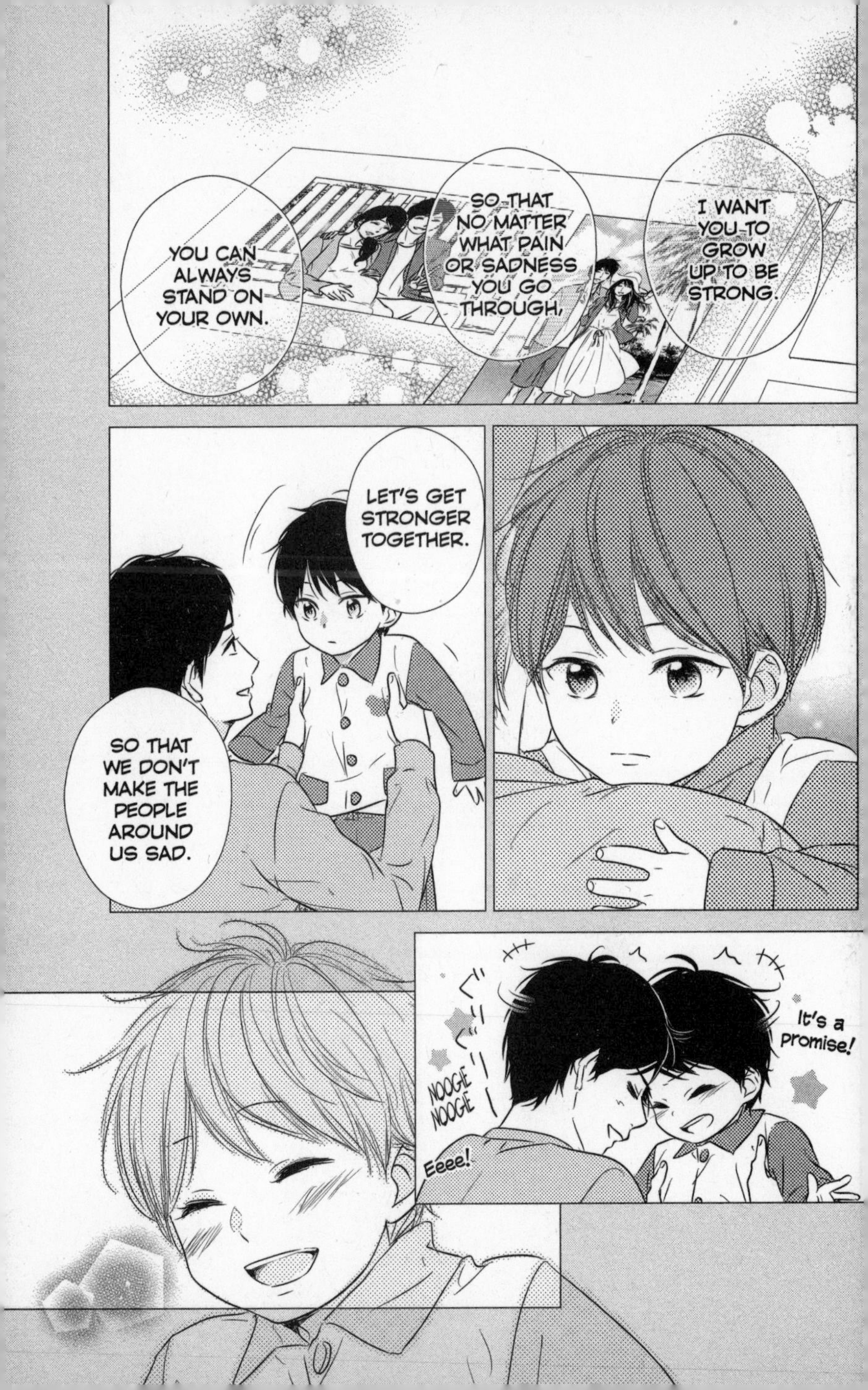
I WANT YOU TO GROW UP TO BE STRONG.
SO THAT NO MATTER WHAT PAIN OR SADNESS YOU GO THROUGH,
YOU CAN ALWAYS STAND ON YOUR OWN.
LET'S GET STRONGER TOGETHER.
SO THAT WE DON'T MAKE THE PEOPLE AROUND US SAD.
It's a promise!
NOOGIE NOOGIE
Eeee!

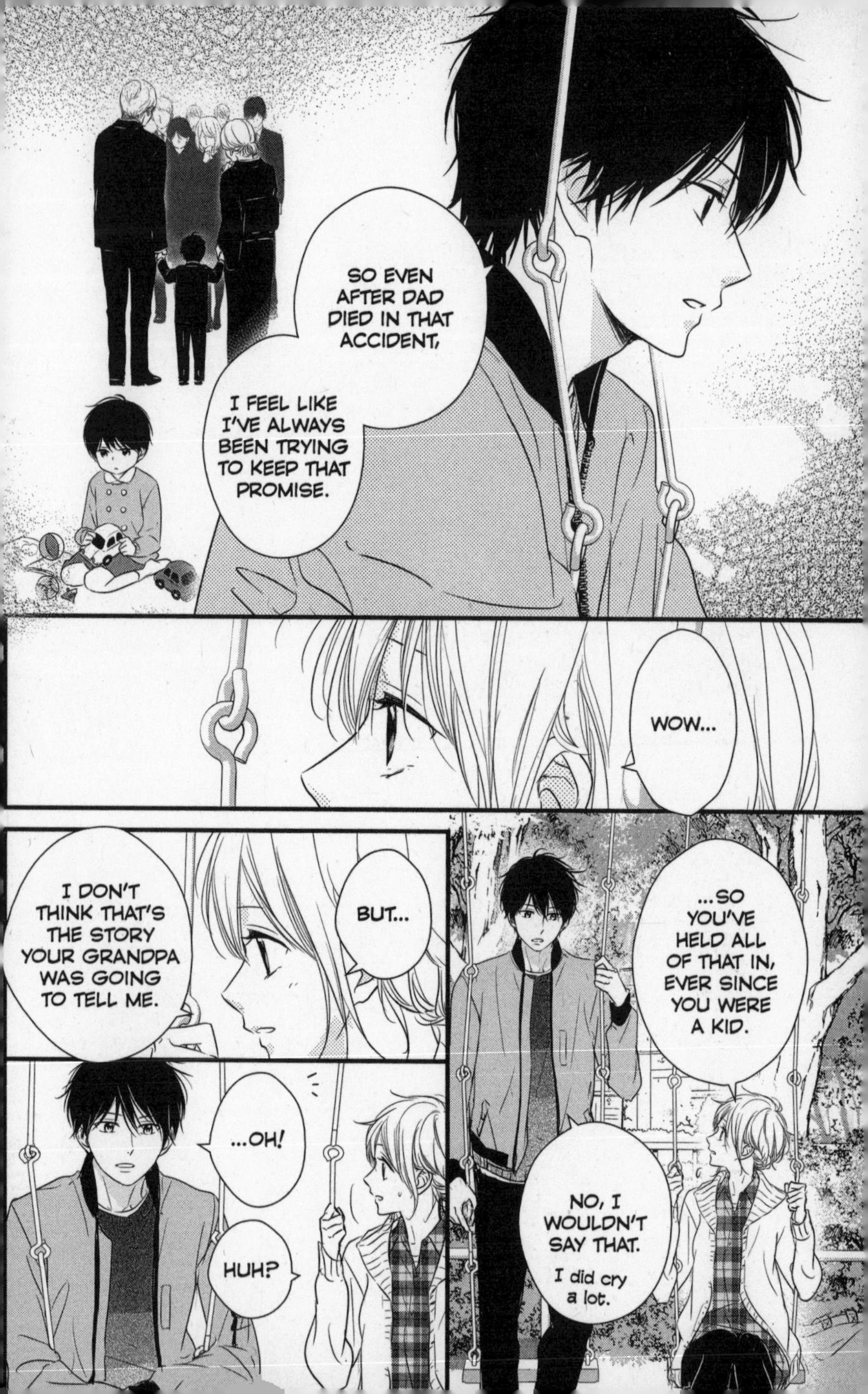
SO EVEN AFTER DAD DIED IN THAT ACCIDENT,
I FEEL LIKE I'VE ALWAYS BEEN TRYING TO KEEP THAT PROMISE.
WOW...
...SO YOU'VE HELD ALL OF THAT IN, EVER SINCE YOU WERE A KID.
NO, I WOULDN'T SAY THAT.
I did cry a lot.
BUT...
I DON'T THINK THAT'S THE STORY YOUR GRANDPA WAS GOING TO TELL ME.
...OH!
HUH?

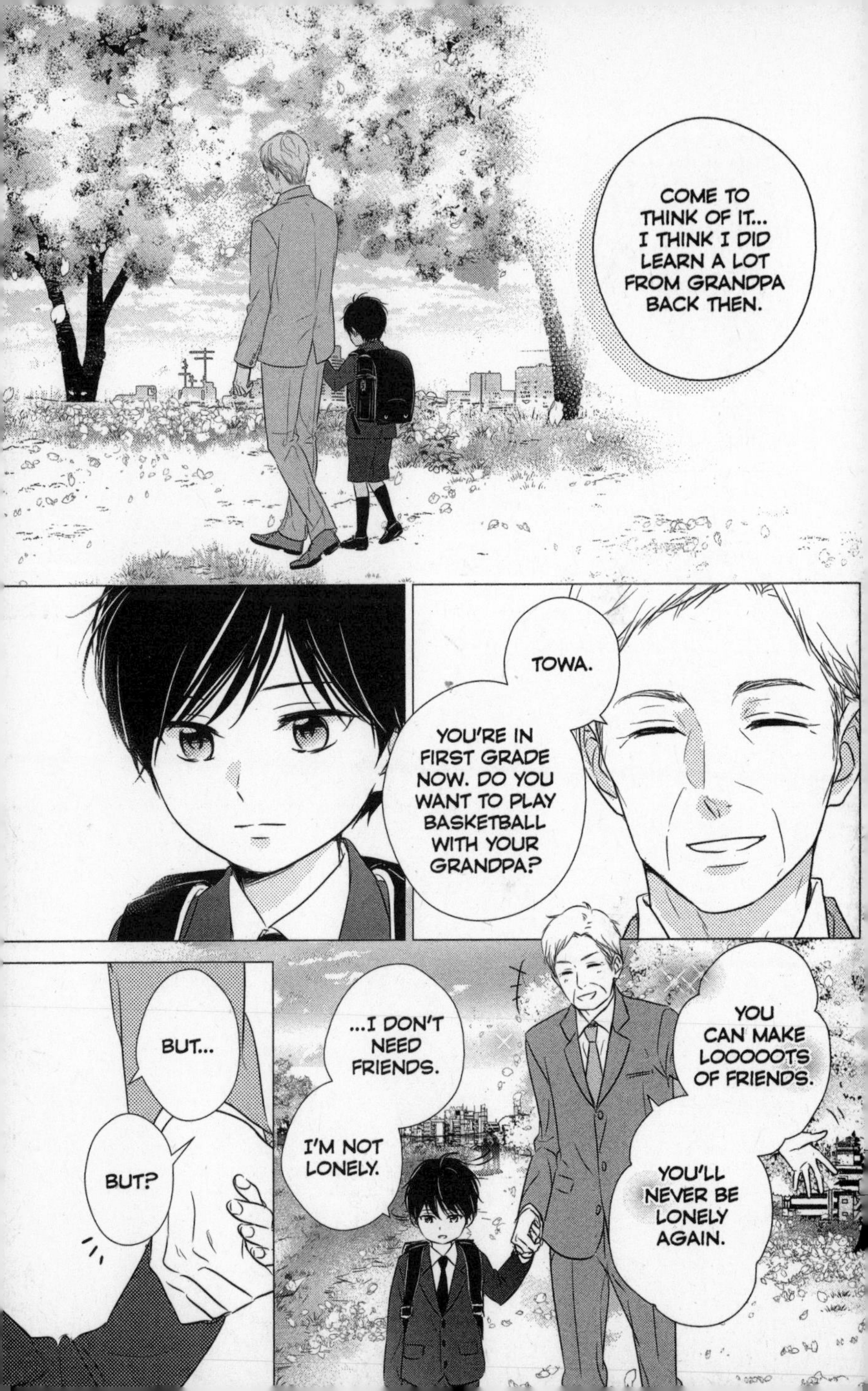
COME TO THINK OF IT... I THINK I DID LEARN A LOT FROM GRANDPA BACK THEN.
TOWA.
YOU'RE IN FIRST GRADE NOW. DO YOU WANT TO PLAY BASKETBALL WITH YOUR GRANDPA?
YOU CAN MAKE LOOOOOTS OF FRIENDS.
YOU'LL NEVER BE LONELY AGAIN.
...I DON'T NEED FRIENDS.
I'M NOT LONELY.
BUT...
BUT?

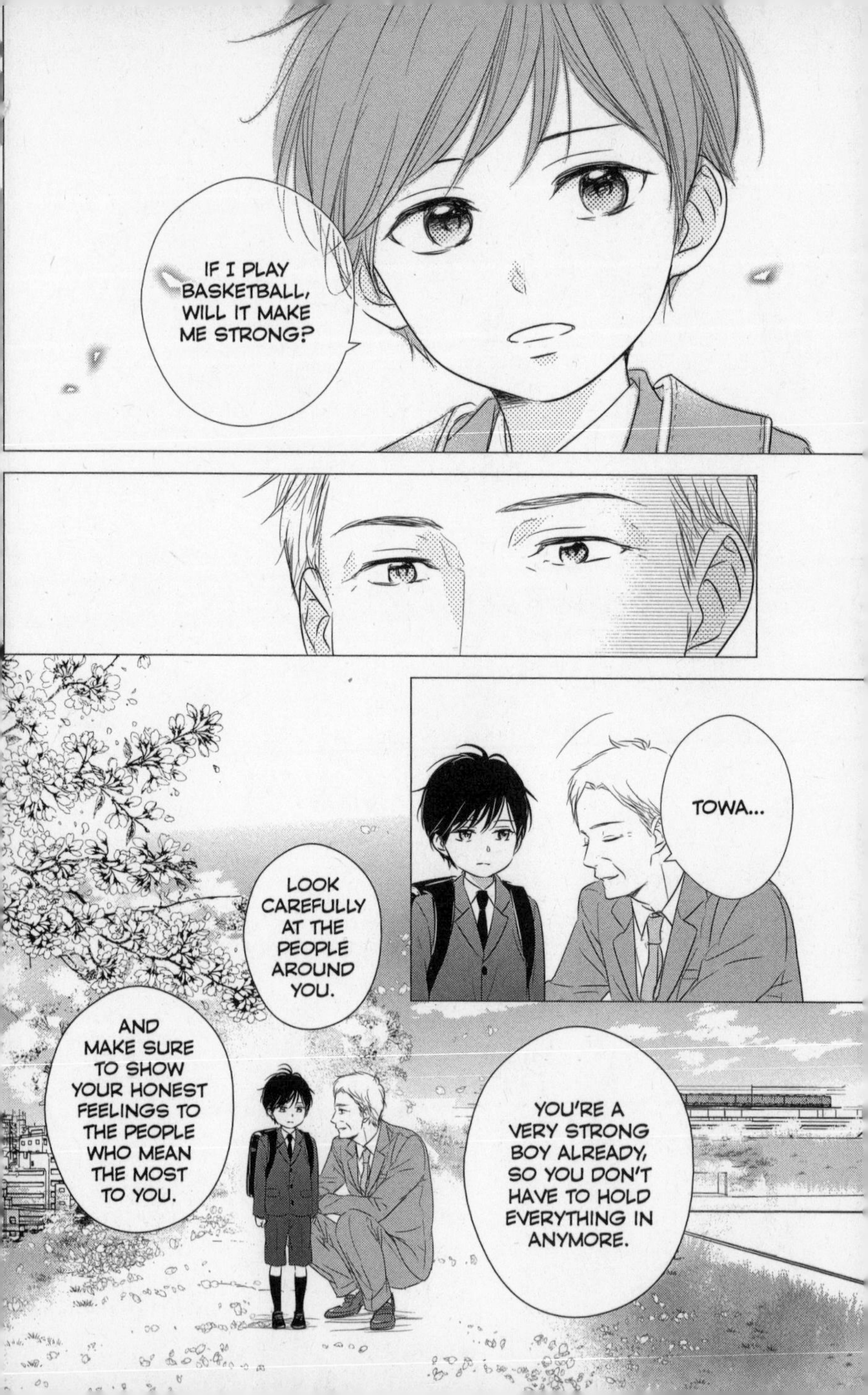
IF I PLAY BASKETBALL, WILL IT MAKE ME STRONG?
TOWA...
YOU'RE A VERY STRONG BOY ALREADY, SO YOU DON'T HAVE TO HOLD EVERYTHING IN ANYMORE.
LOOK CAREFULLY AT THE PEOPLE AROUND YOU.
AND MAKE SURE TO SHOW YOUR HONEST FEELINGS TO THE PEOPLE WHO MEAN THE MOST TO YOU.

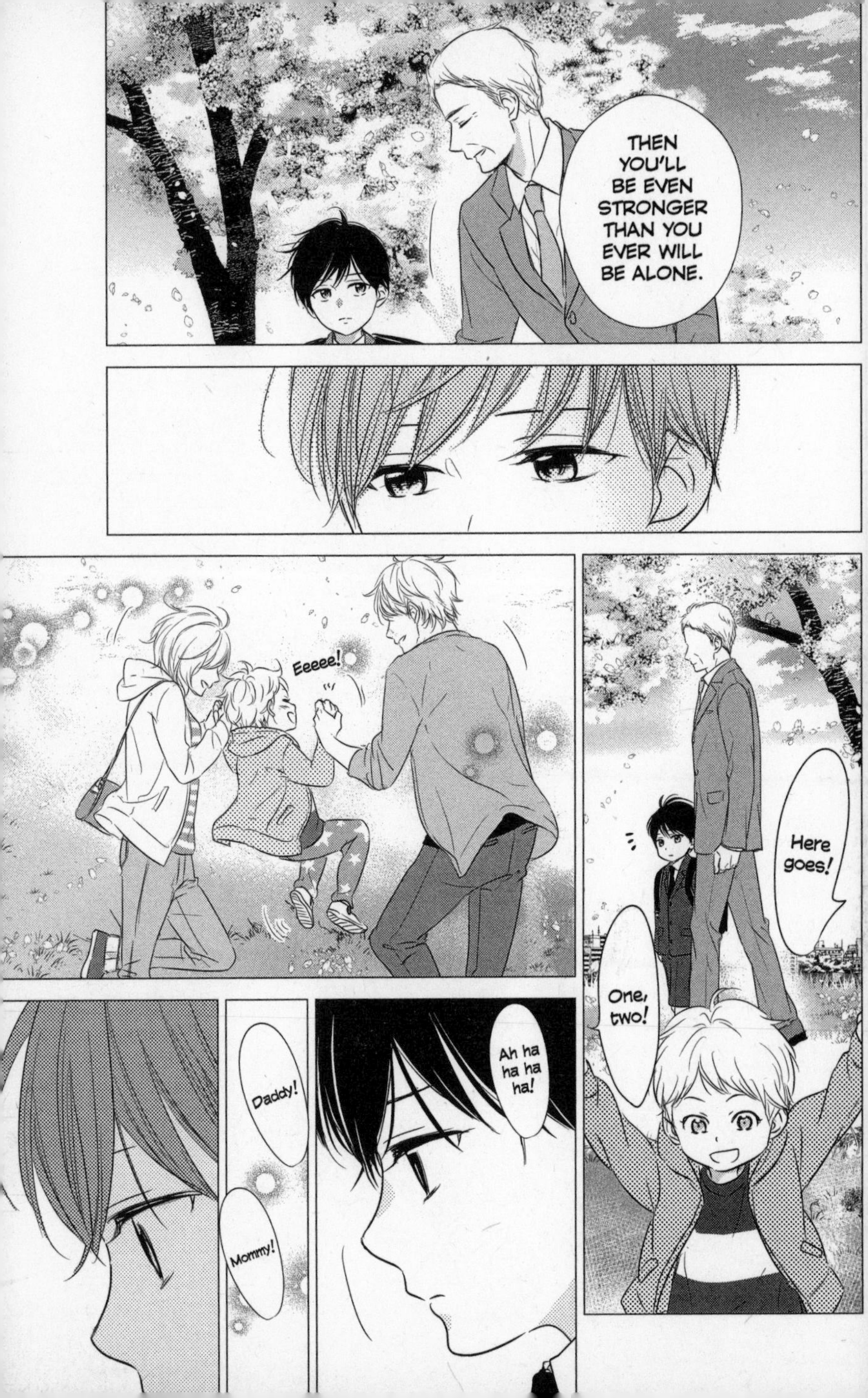
THEN YOU'LL BE EVEN STRONGER THAN YOU EVER WILL BE ALONE.
Here goes!
One, two!
Eeeee!
Ah ha ha ha!
Daddy!
Mommy!

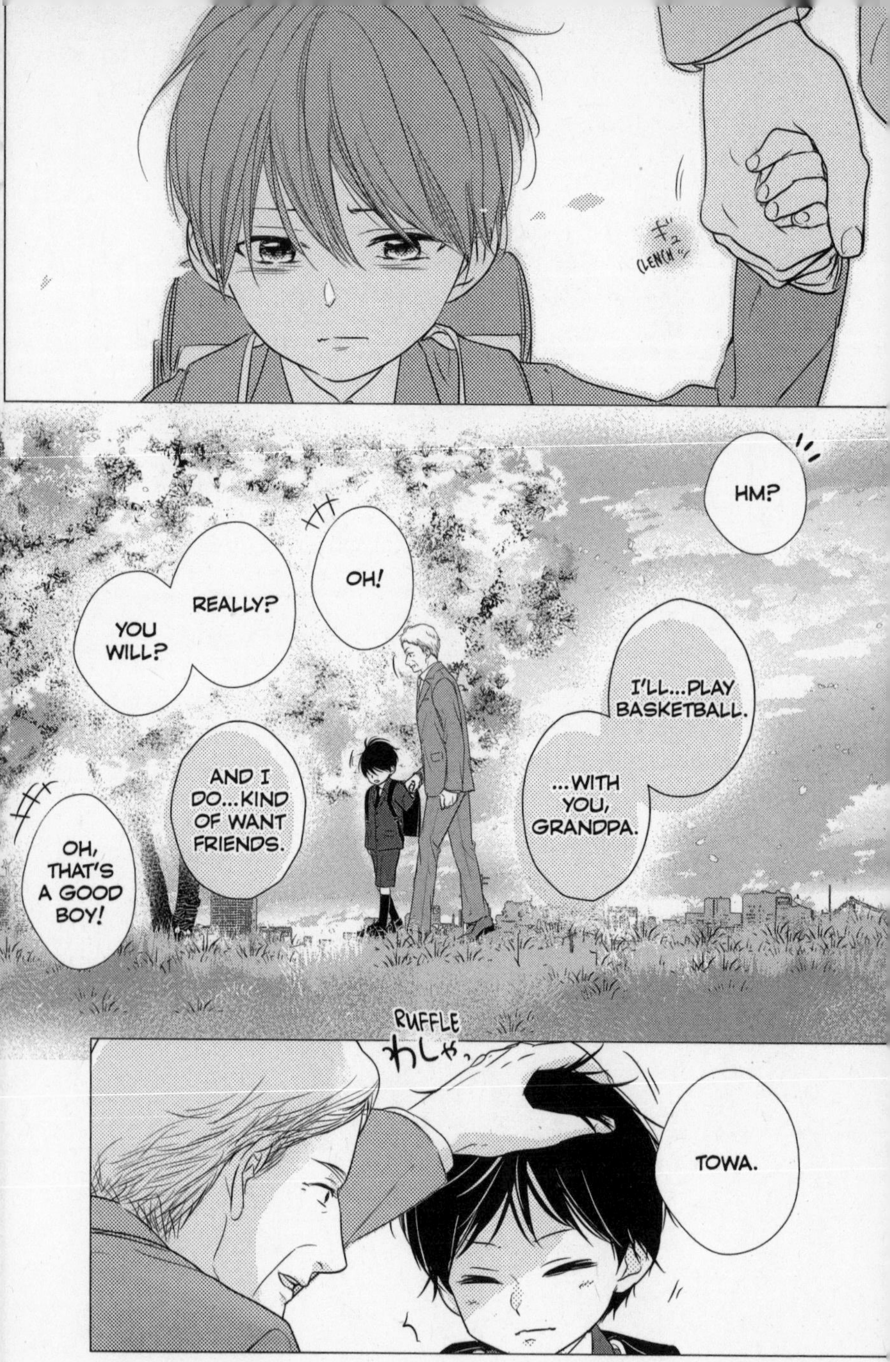
CLENCH
HM?
I'LL...PLAY BASKETBALL.
...WITH YOU, GRANDPA.
OH!
REALLY? YOU WILL?
AND I DO...KIND OF WANT FRIENDS.
OH, THAT'S A GOOD BOY!
RUFFLE
わしゃ
TOWA.

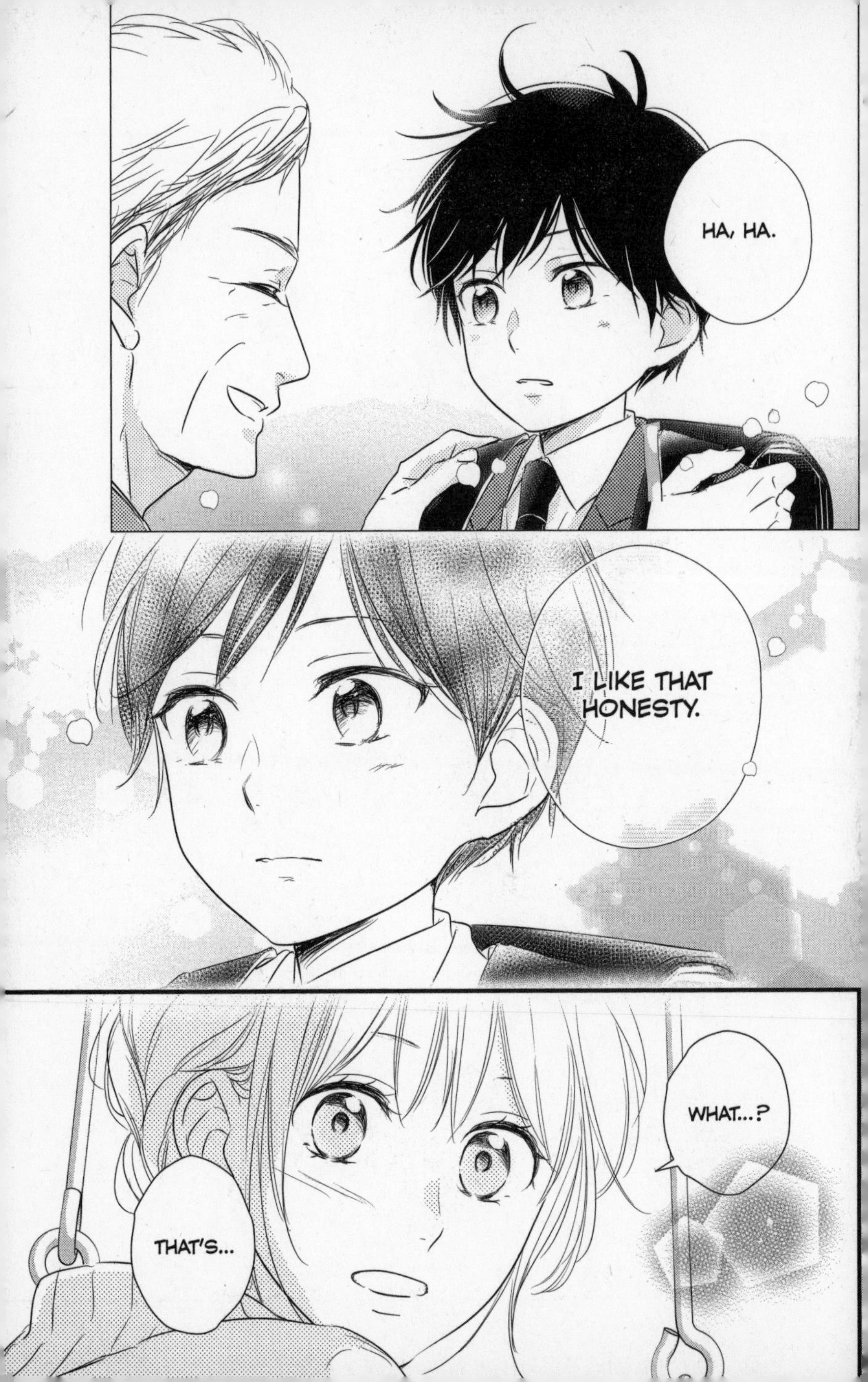
HA, HA.
I LIKE THAT HONESTY.
WHAT...?
THAT'S...

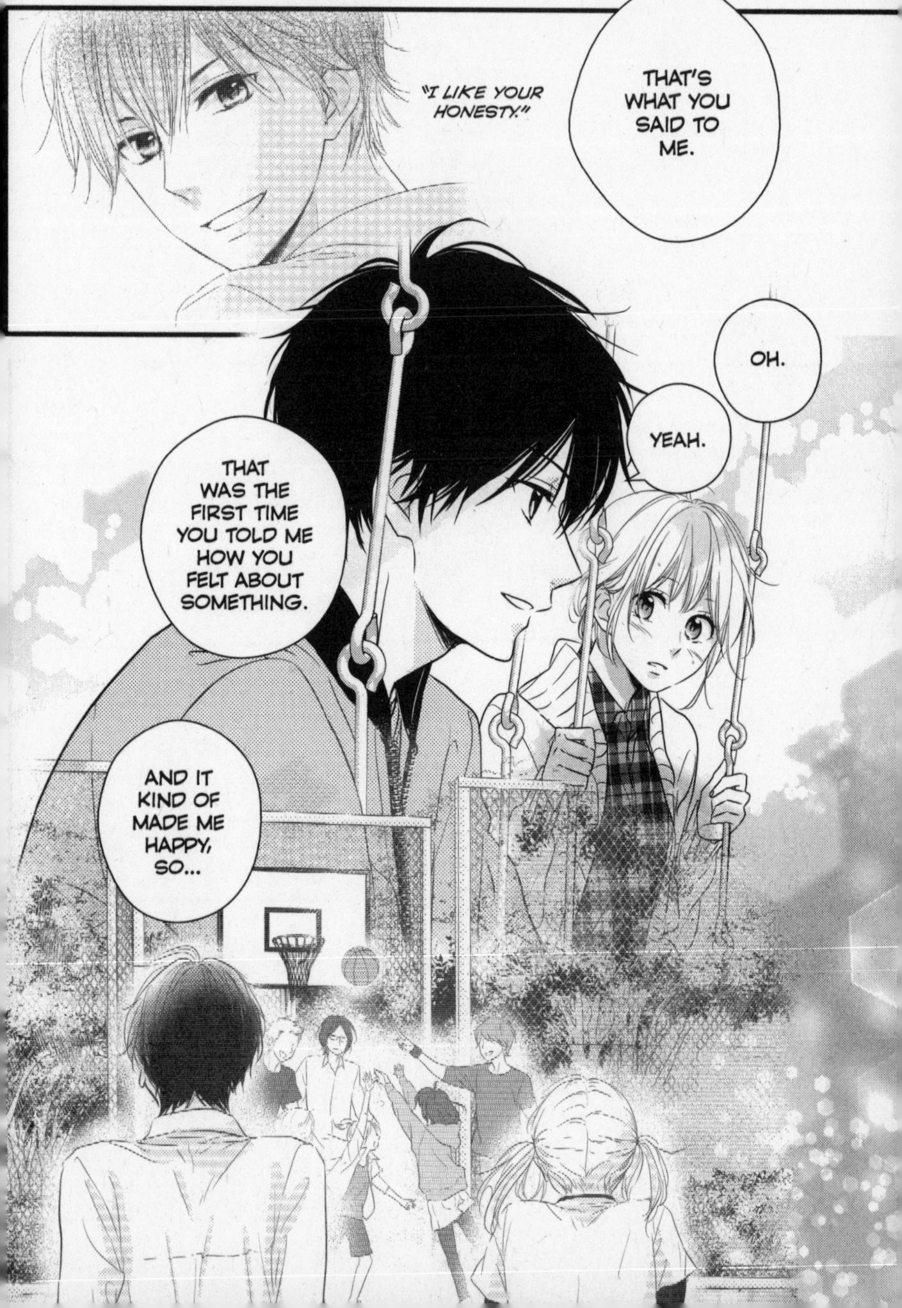
THAT'S WHAT YOU SAID TO ME.
"I LIKE YOUR HONESTY."
OH.
YEAH.
THAT WAS THE FIRST TIME YOU TOLD ME HOW YOU FELT ABOUT SOMETHING.
AND IT KIND OF MADE ME HAPPY, SO...

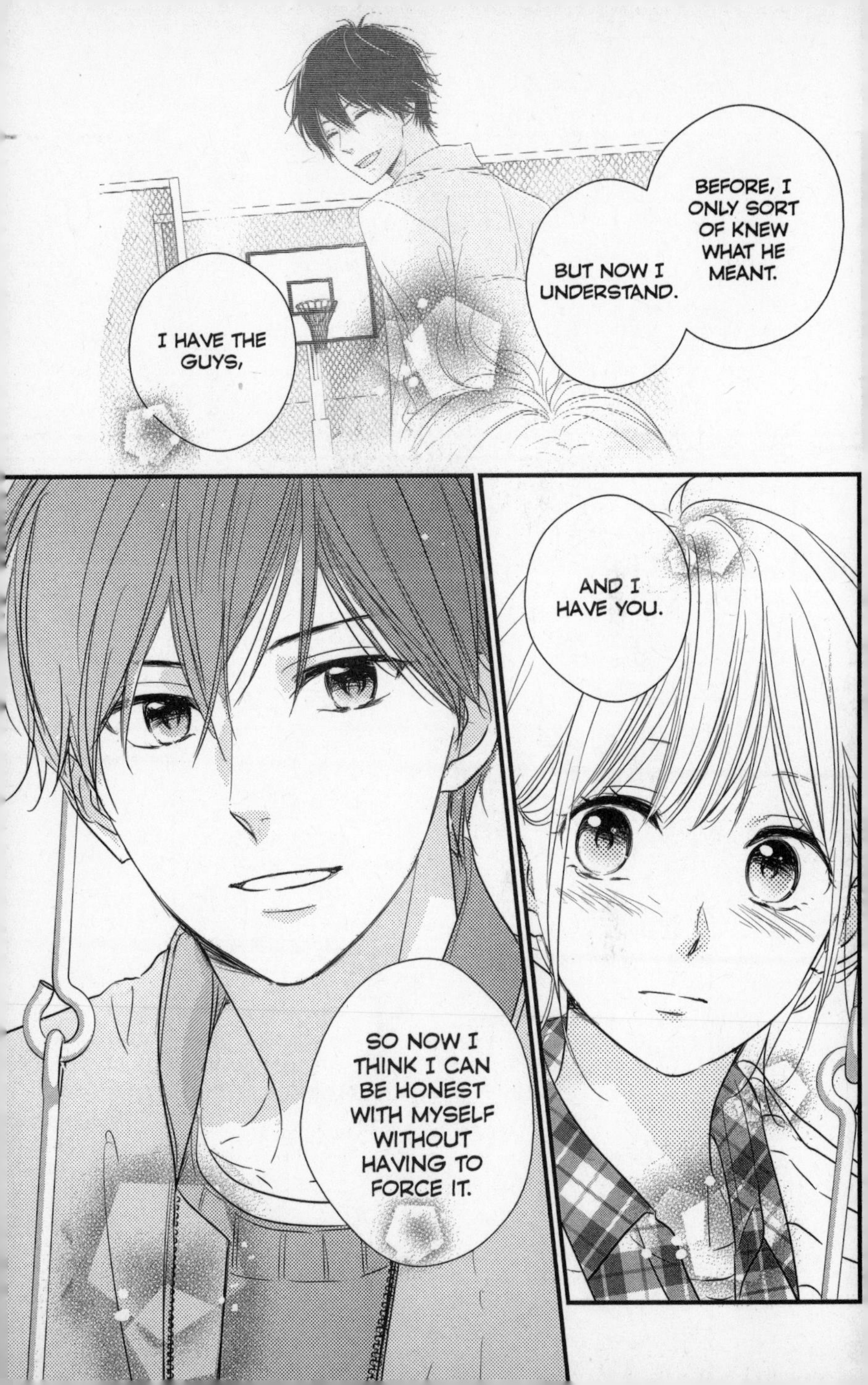
BEFORE, I ONLY SORT OF KNEW WHAT HE MEANT.
BUT NOW I UNDERSTAND.
I HAVE THE GUYS,
AND I HAVE YOU.
SO NOW I THINK I CAN BE HONEST WITH MYSELF WITHOUT HAVING TO FORCE IT.

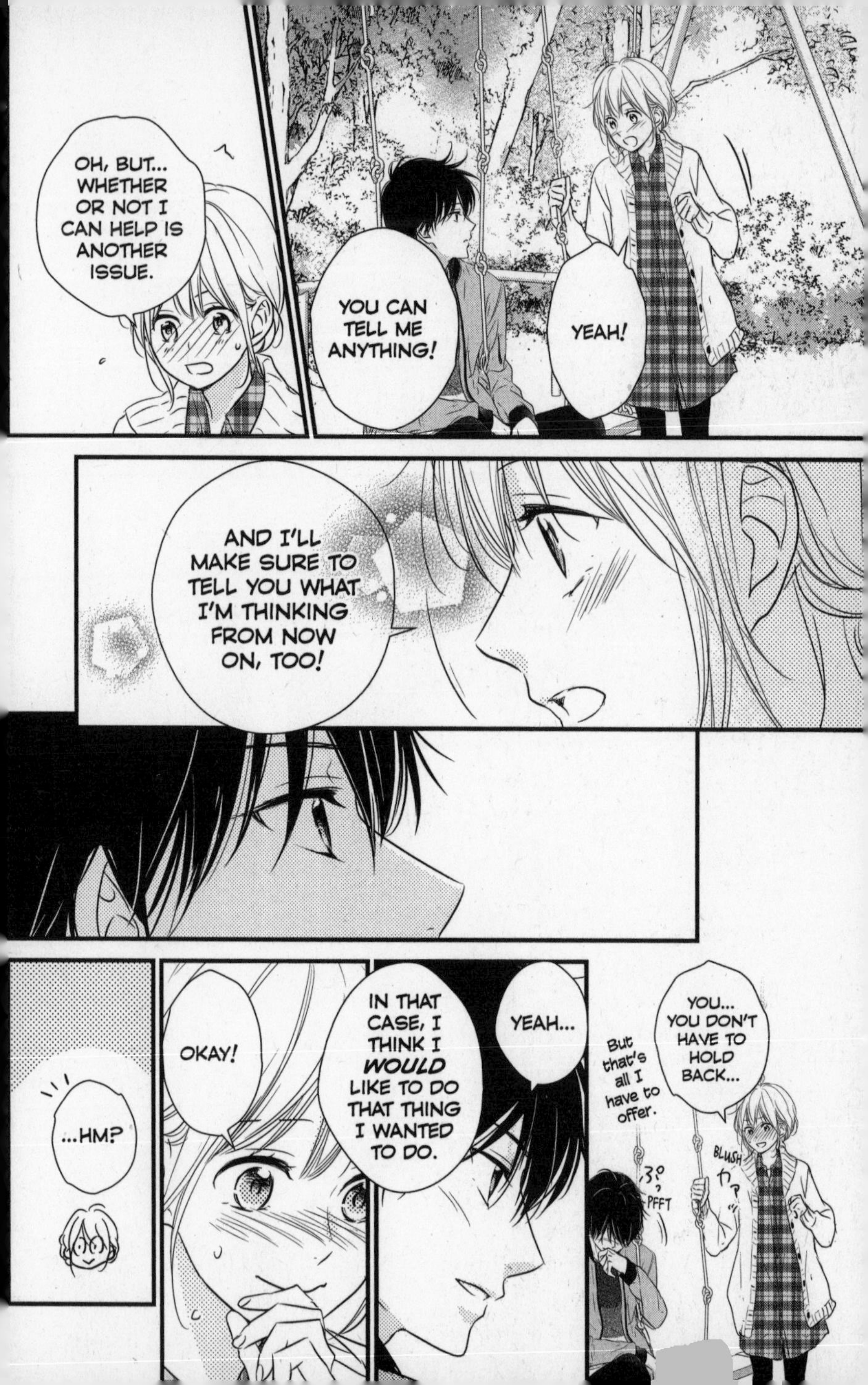
YEAH!
YOU CAN TELL ME ANYTHING!
OH, BUT... WHETHER OR NOT I CAN HELP IS ANOTHER ISSUE.
AND I'LL MAKE SURE TO TELL YOU WHAT I'M THINKING FROM NOW ON, TOO!
YOU... YOU DON'T HAVE TO HOLD BACK...
But that's all I have to offer.
BLUSH
PFFT
YEAH...
IN THAT CASE, I THINK I *WOULD* LIKE TO DO THAT THING I WANTED TO DO.
OKAY!
...HM?

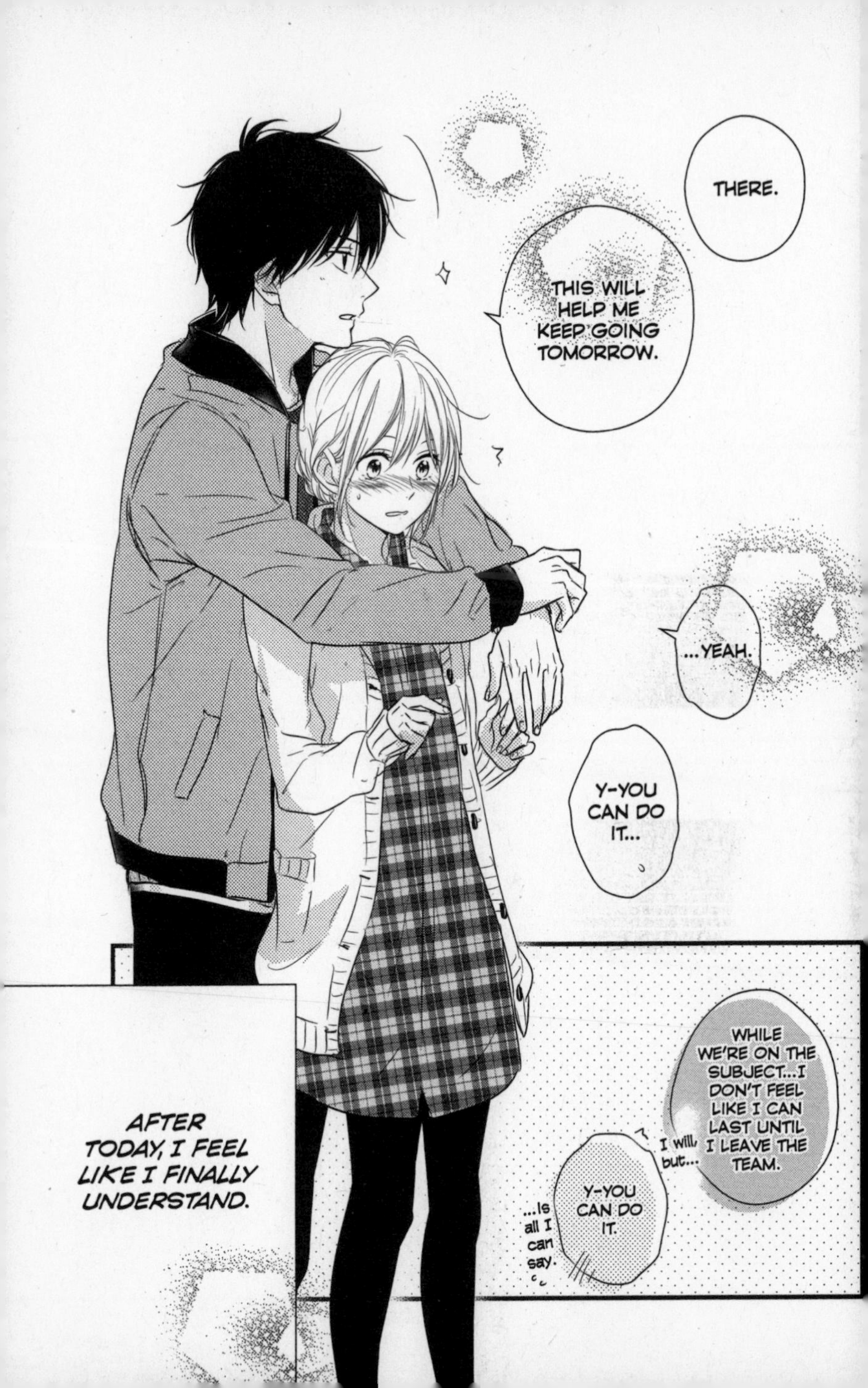
THERE.
THIS WILL HELP ME KEEP GOING TOMORROW.
...YEAH.
Y-YOU CAN DO IT...
WHILE WE'RE ON THE SUBJECT...I DON'T FEEL LIKE I CAN LAST UNTIL I LEAVE THE TEAM.
I will, but...
Y-YOU CAN DO IT.
...Is all I can say.
AFTER TODAY, I FEEL LIKE I FINALLY UNDERSTAND.

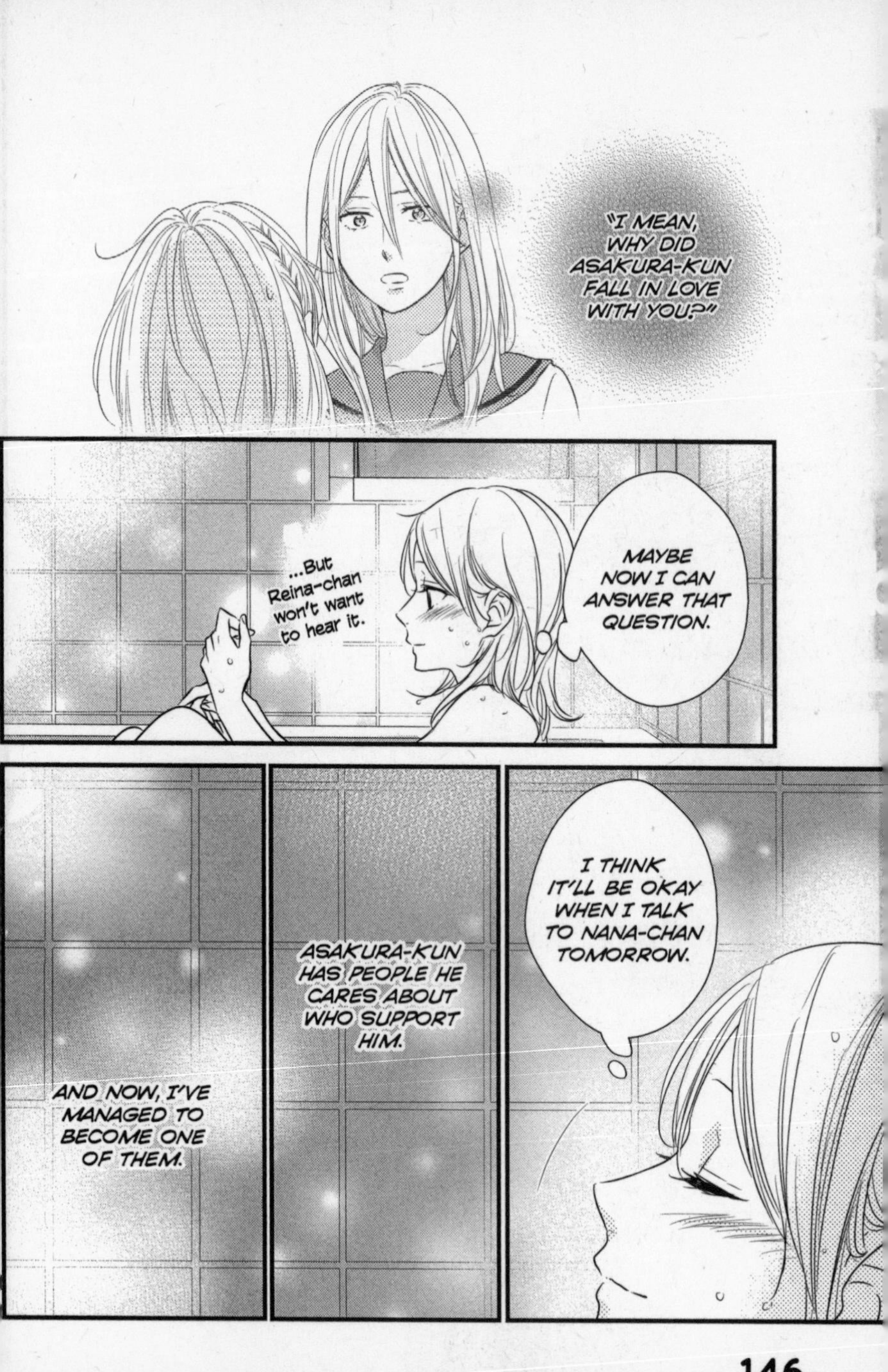
"I MEAN, WHY DID ASAKURA-KUN FALL IN LOVE WITH YOU?"
MAYBE NOW I CAN ANSWER THAT QUESTION.
...But Reina-chan won't want to hear it.
I THINK IT'LL BE OKAY WHEN I TALK TO NANA-CHAN TOMORROW.
ASAKURA-KUN HAS PEOPLE HE CARES ABOUT WHO SUPPORT HIM.
AND NOW, I'VE MANAGED TO BECOME ONE OF THEM.

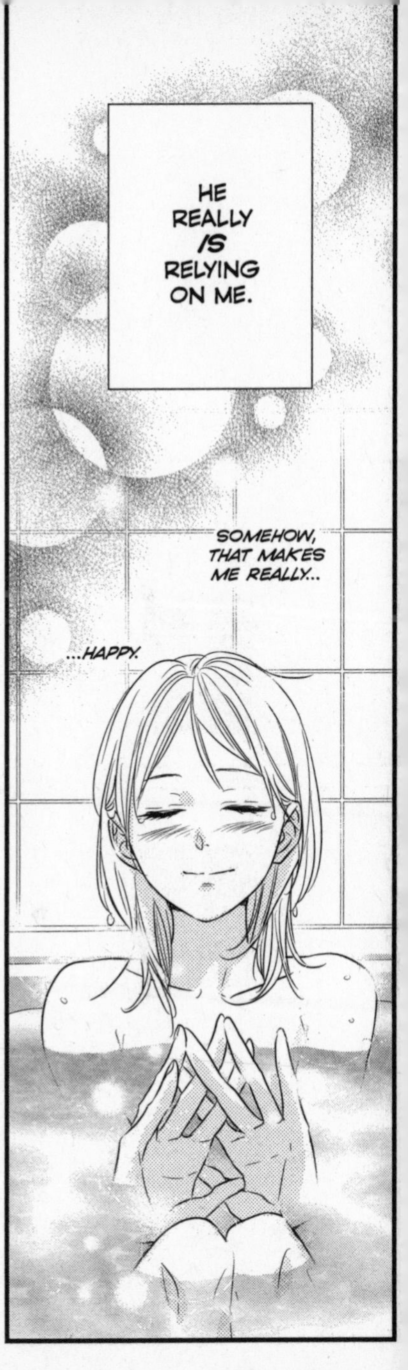
HE REALLY *IS* RELYING ON ME.
SOMEHOW, THAT MAKES ME REALLY...
...HAPPY.

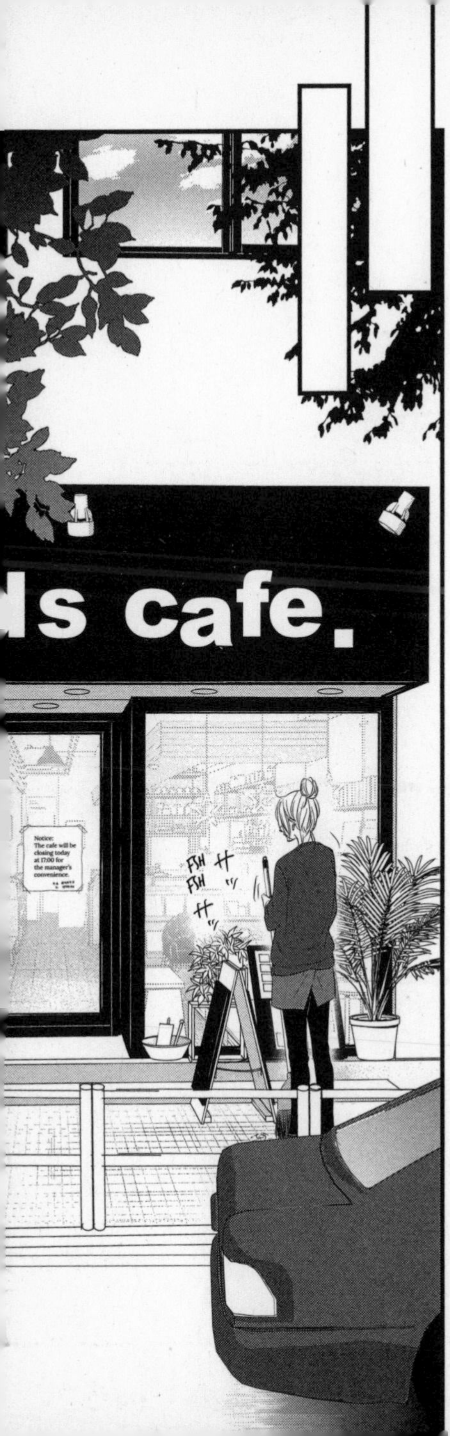
ls cafe.
Notice: The cafe will be closing today at 17:00 for the manager's convenience.
FSH FSH

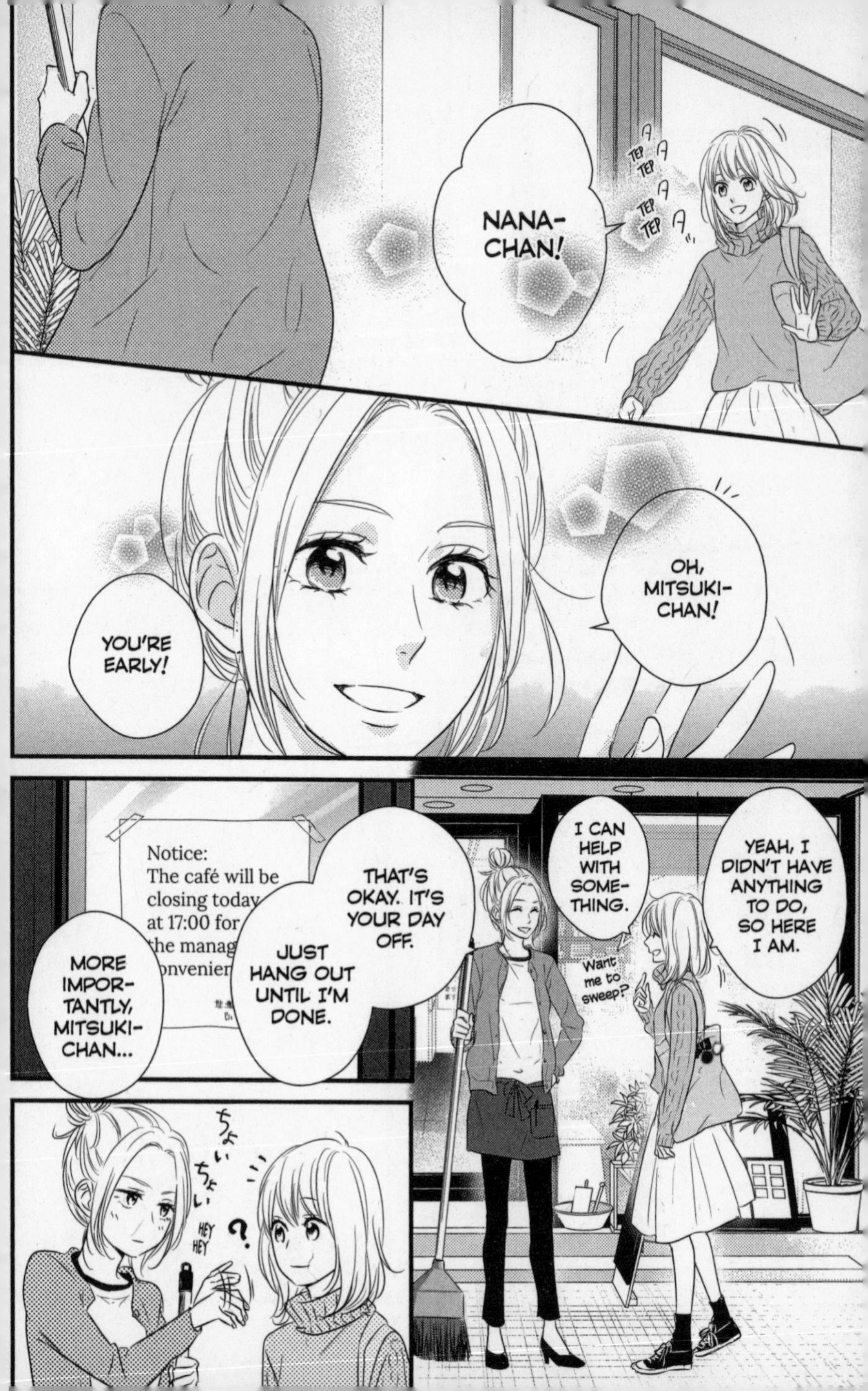
TEP TEP TEP TEP
NANA-CHAN!
OH, MITSUKI-CHAN!
YOU'RE EARLY!
YEAH, I DIDN'T HAVE ANYTHING TO DO, SO HERE I AM.
I CAN HELP WITH SOME-THING.
Want me to sweep?
THAT'S OKAY. IT'S YOUR DAY OFF.
JUST HANG OUT UNTIL I'M DONE.
Notice:
The café will be
closing today
at 17:00 for
the manag
onvenien
MORE IMPOR-TANTLY, MITSUKI-CHAN...
ちょいちょい
HEY HEY
?

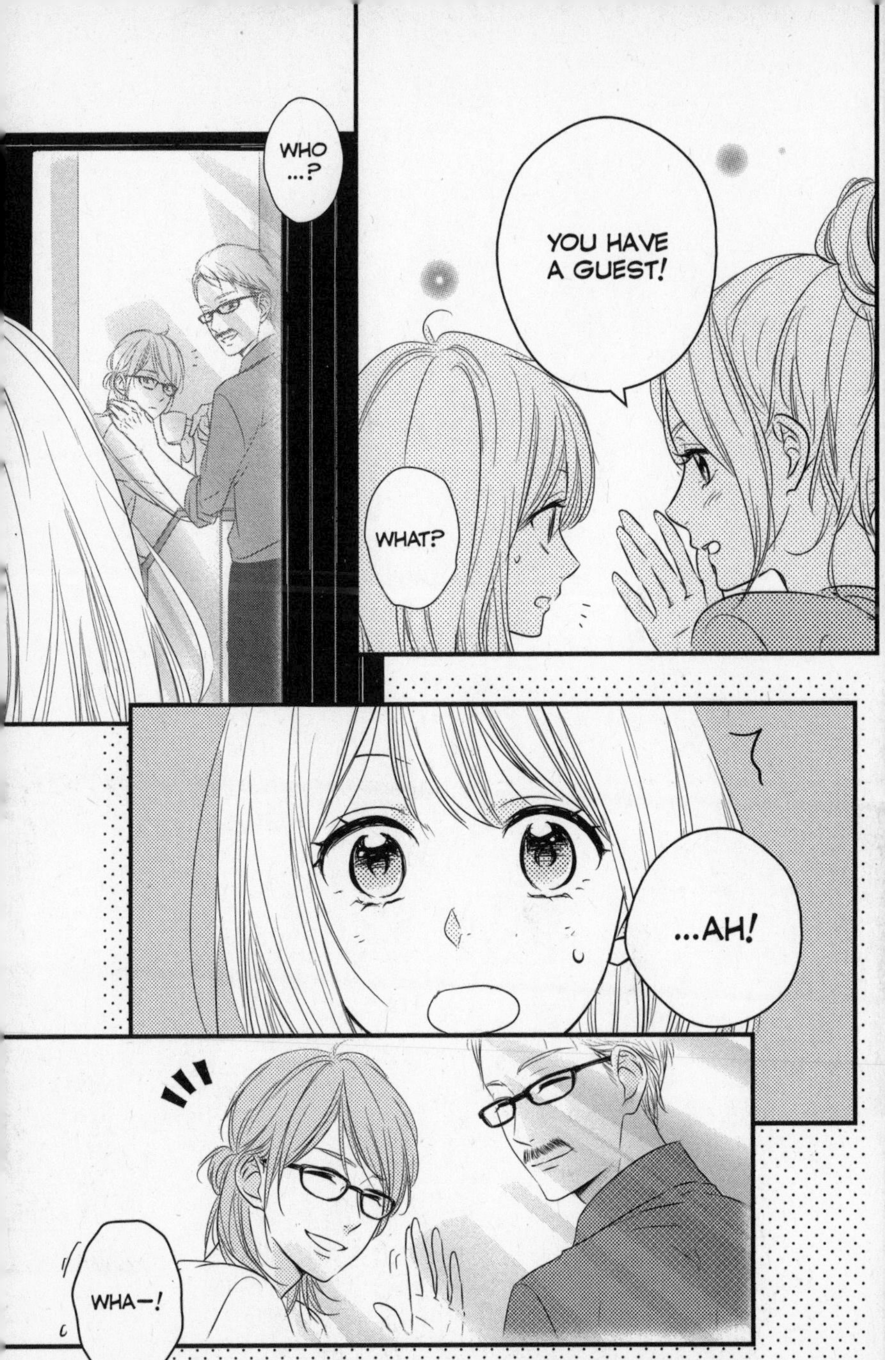
YOU HAVE A GUEST!
WHAT?
WHO ...?
...AH!
WHA—!

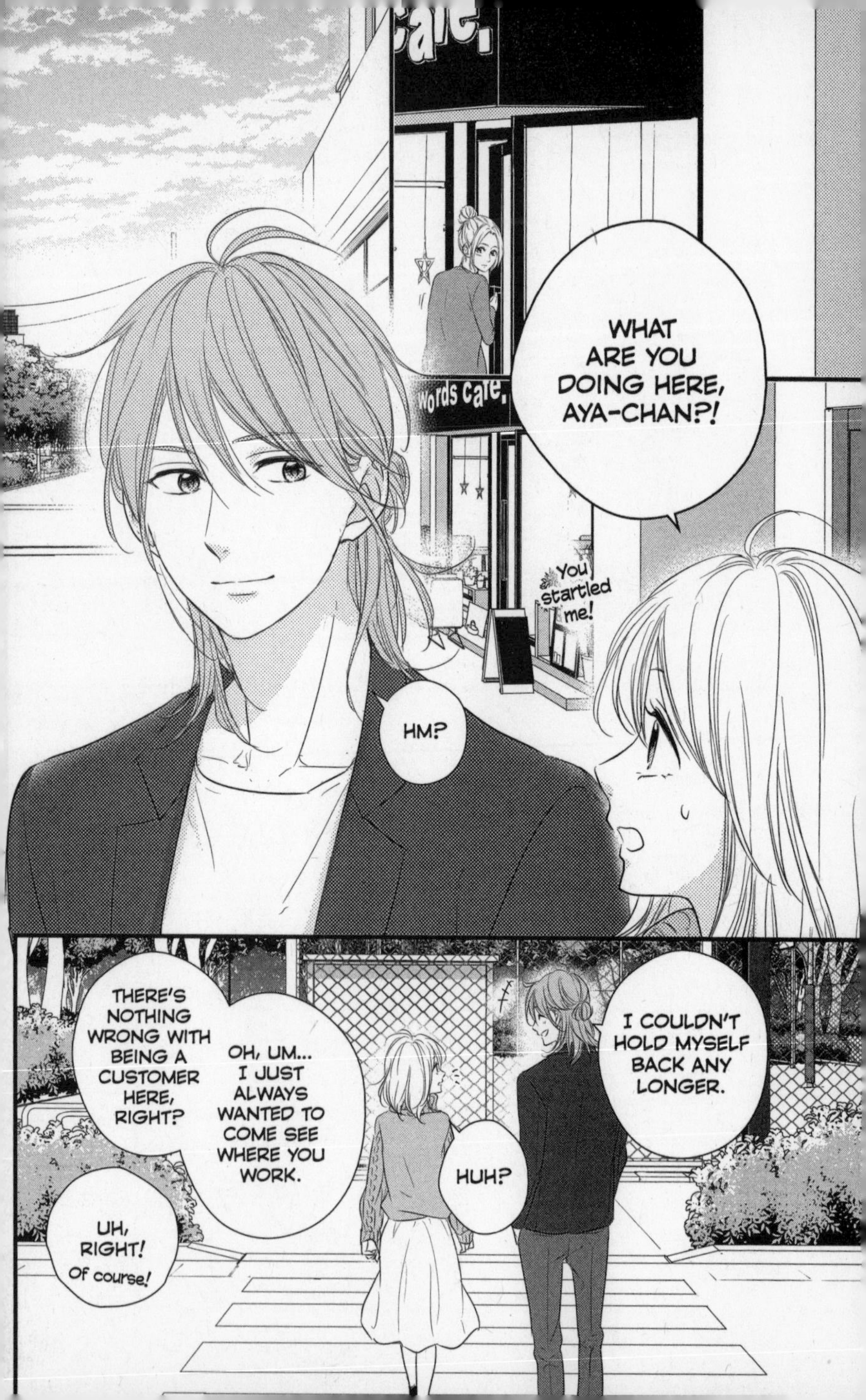

WHAT ARE YOU DOING HERE, AYA-CHAN?!
words cafe.
You startled me!
HM?
I COULDN'T HOLD MYSELF BACK ANY LONGER.
HUH?
OH, UM... I JUST ALWAYS WANTED TO COME SEE WHERE YOU WORK.
THERE'S NOTHING WRONG WITH BEING A CUSTOMER HERE, RIGHT?
UH, RIGHT! Of course!

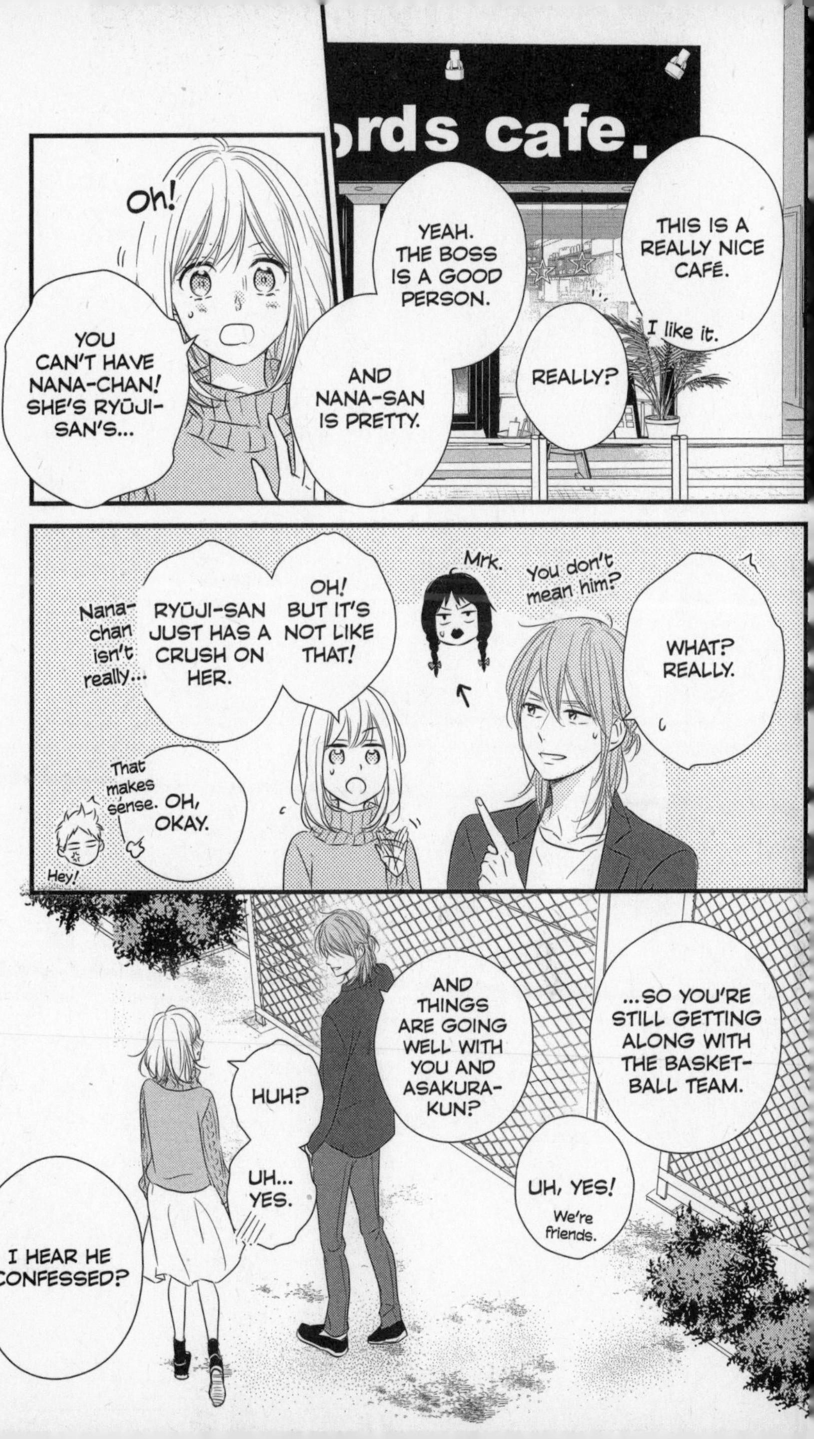
ords cafe.
THIS IS A REALLY NICE CAFÉ.
I like it.
REALLY?
YEAH. THE BOSS IS A GOOD PERSON.
AND NANA-SAN IS PRETTY.
Oh!
YOU CAN'T HAVE NANA-CHAN! SHE'S RYŪJI-SAN'S...
WHAT? REALLY.
You don't mean him?
Mrk.
OH! BUT IT'S NOT LIKE THAT!
RYŪJI-SAN JUST HAS A CRUSH ON HER.
Nana-chan isn't really...
OH, OKAY.
That makes sense.
Hey!
...SO YOU'RE STILL GETTING ALONG WITH THE BASKET-BALL TEAM.
UH, YES!
We're friends.
AND THINGS ARE GOING WELL WITH YOU AND ASAKURA-KUN?
HUH?
UH... YES.
I HEAR HE CONFESSED?

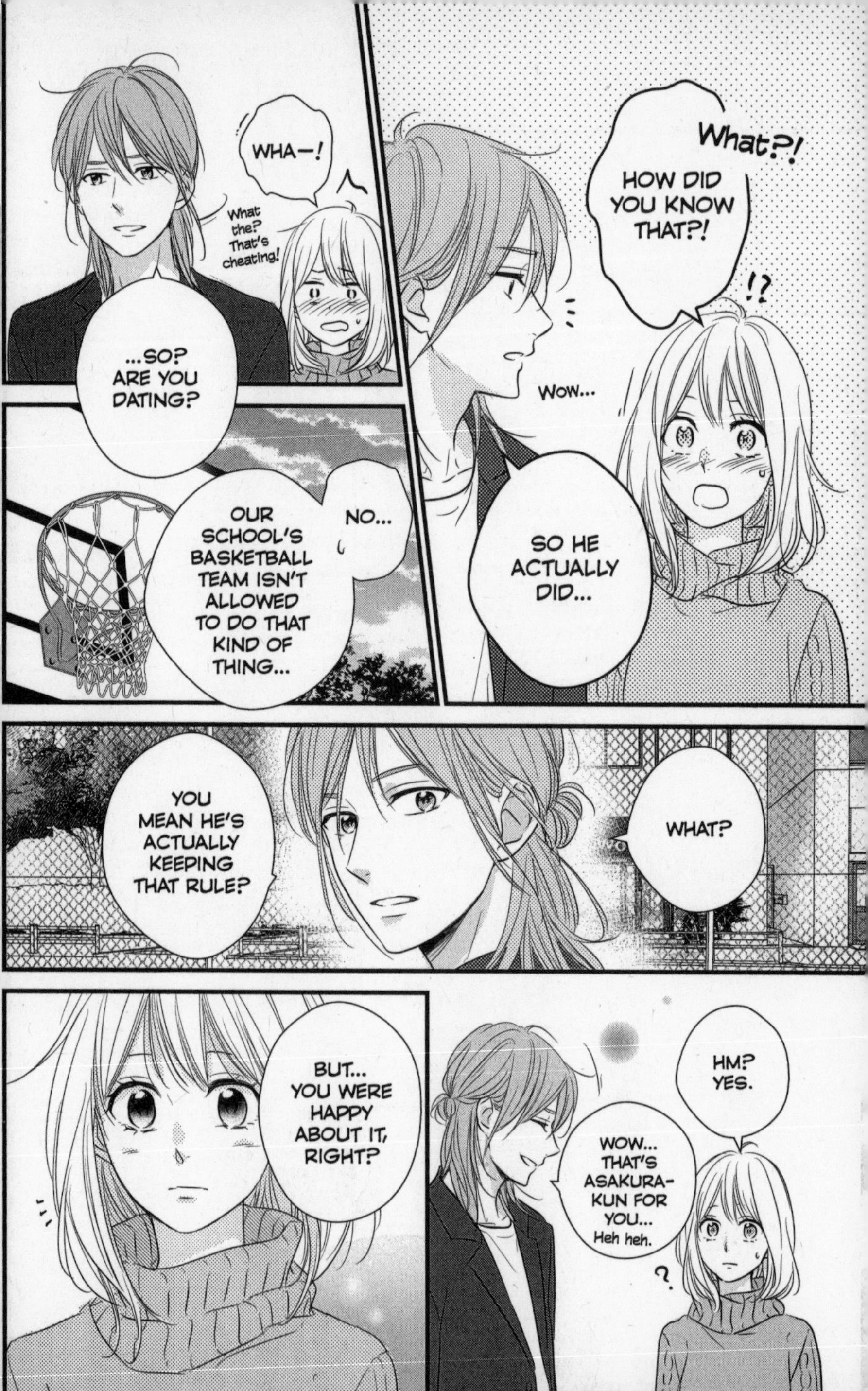
What?!
HOW DID YOU KNOW THAT?!
!?
WOW...
SO HE ACTUALLY DID...
WHA-!
What the? That's cheating!
...SO? ARE YOU DATING?
NO...
OUR SCHOOL'S BASKETBALL TEAM ISN'T ALLOWED TO DO THAT KIND OF THING...
WHAT?
YOU MEAN HE'S ACTUALLY KEEPING THAT RULE?
HM? YES.
WOW... THAT'S ASAKURA-KUN FOR YOU... Heh heh.
?
BUT... YOU WERE HAPPY ABOUT IT, RIGHT?

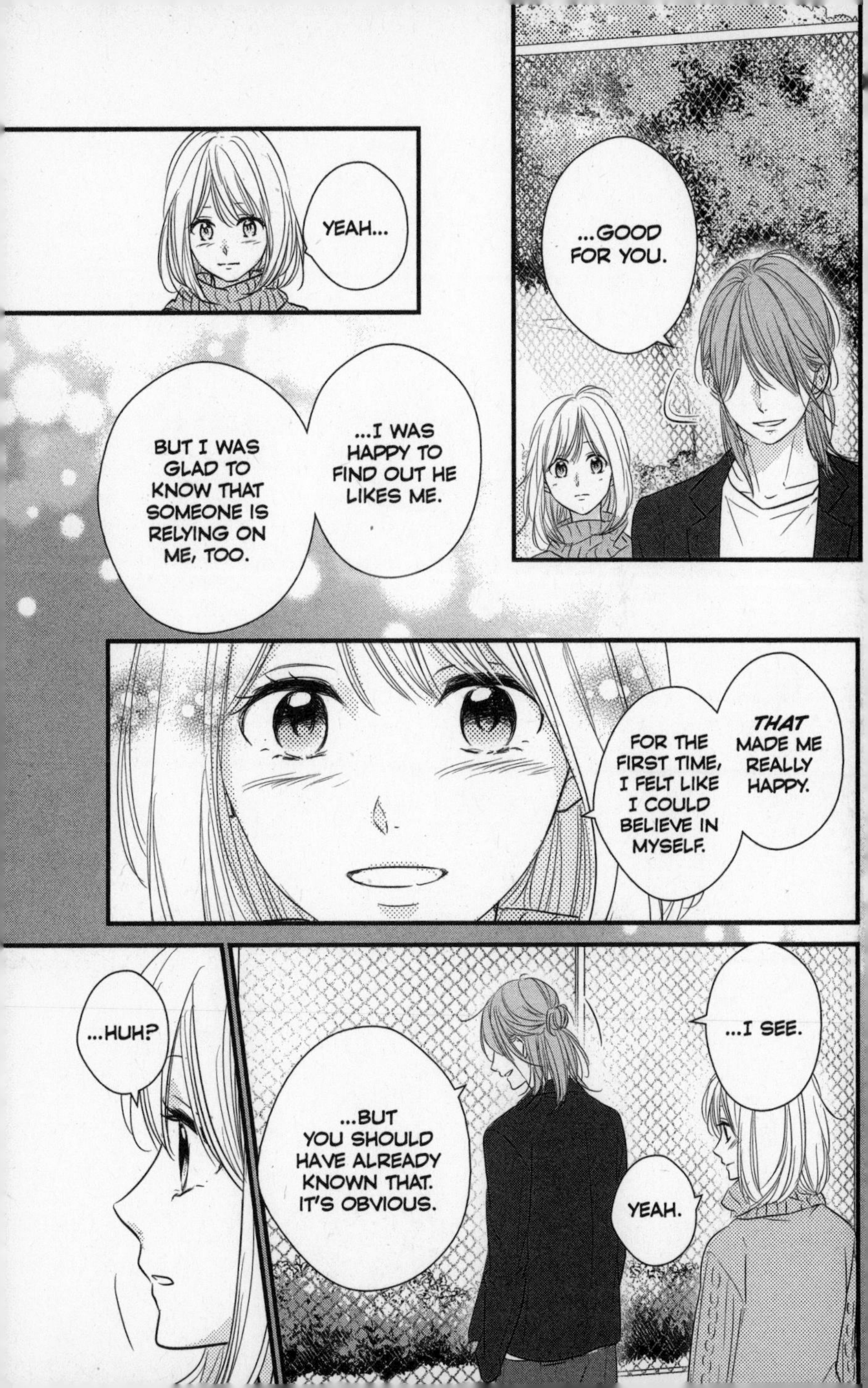
...GOOD FOR YOU.
YEAH...
...I WAS HAPPY TO FIND OUT HE LIKES ME.
BUT I WAS GLAD TO KNOW THAT SOMEONE IS RELYING ON ME, TOO.
THAT MADE ME REALLY HAPPY.
FOR THE FIRST TIME, I FELT LIKE I COULD BELIEVE IN MYSELF.
...I SEE.
YEAH.
...BUT YOU SHOULD HAVE ALREADY KNOWN THAT. IT'S OBVIOUS.
...HUH?

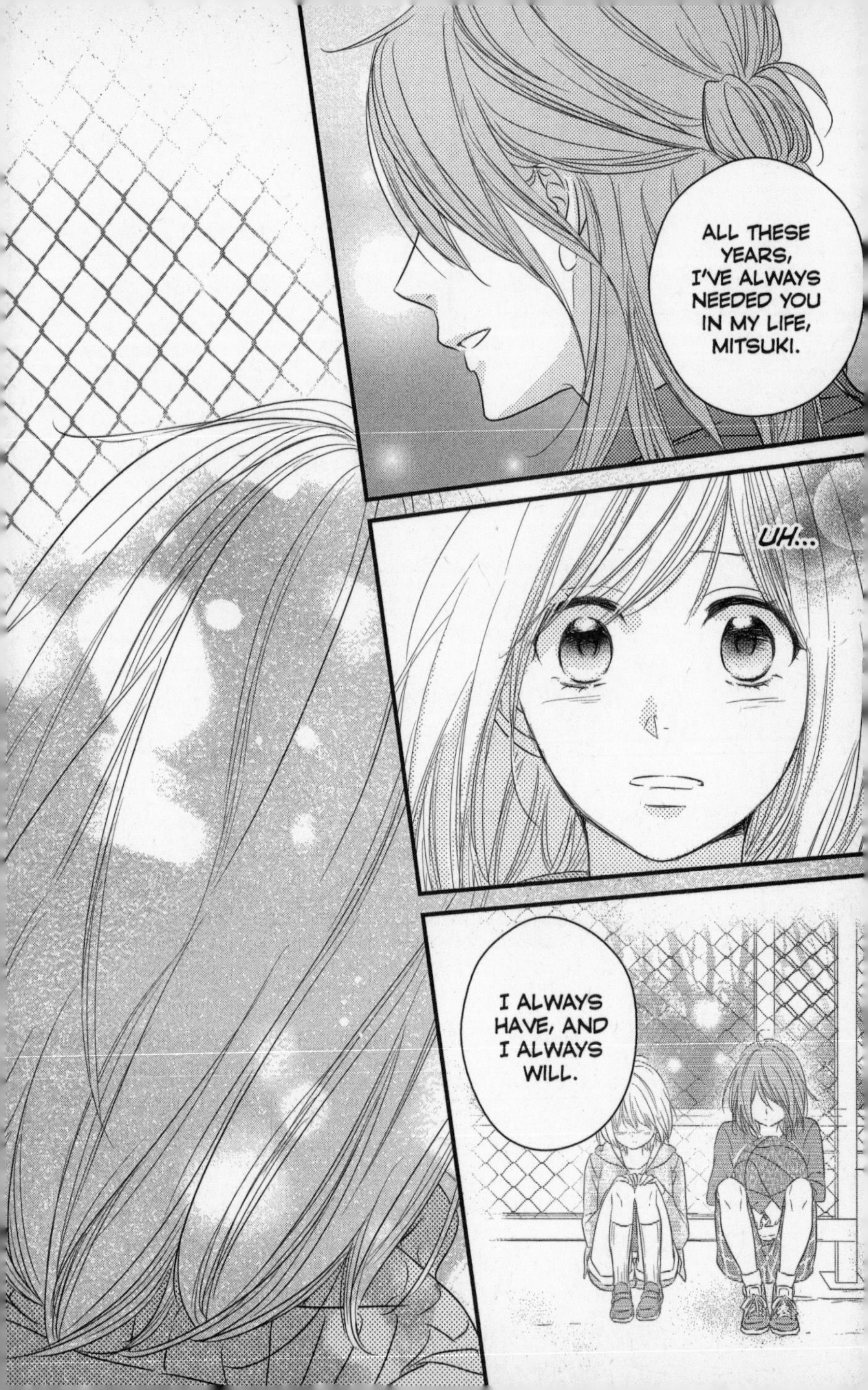

ALL THESE YEARS, I'VE ALWAYS NEEDED YOU IN MY LIFE, MITSUKI.
UH...
I ALWAYS HAVE, AND I ALWAYS WILL.

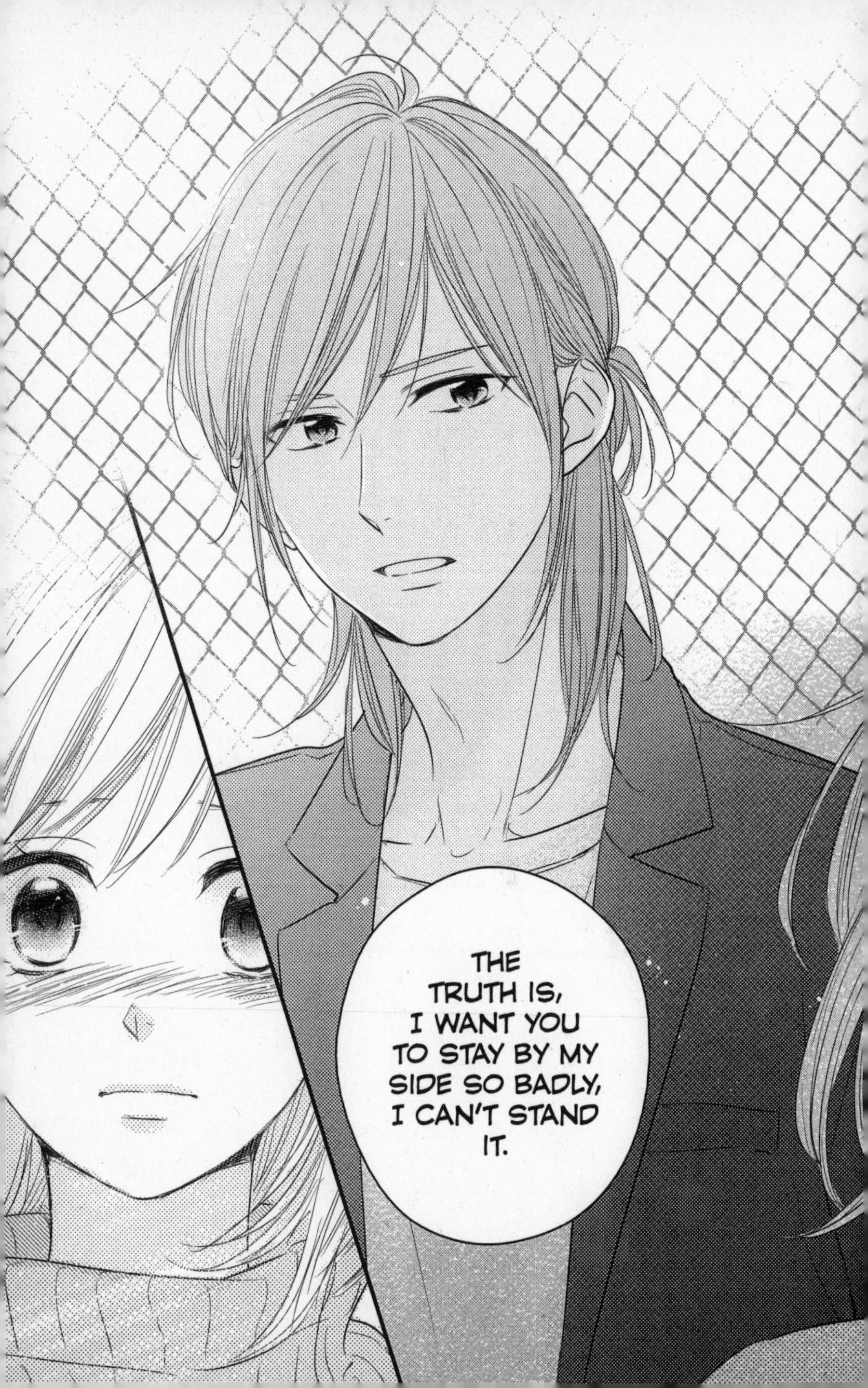
THE TRUTH IS, I WANT YOU TO STAY BY MY SIDE SO BADLY, I CAN'T STAND IT.

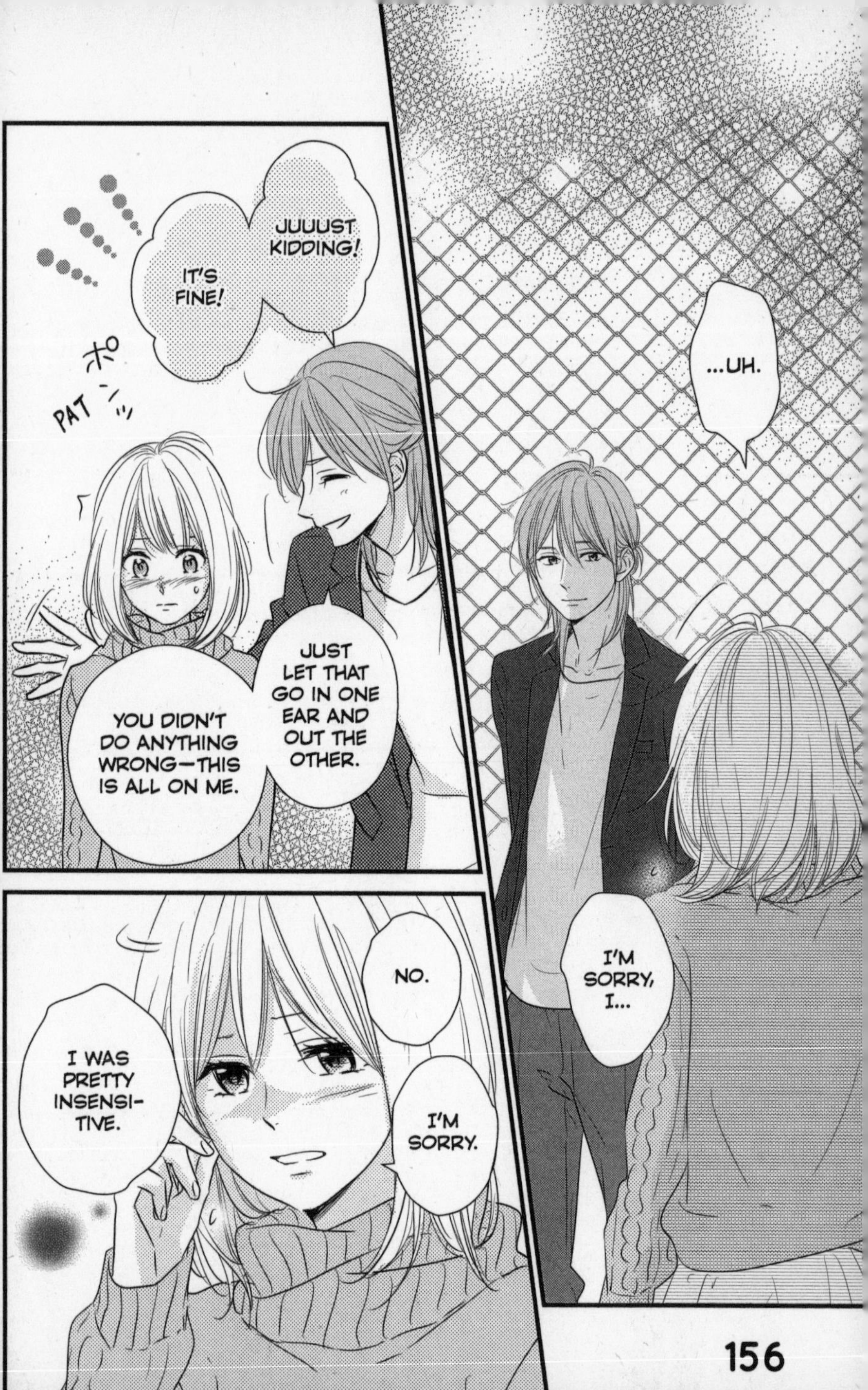
...UH.
I'M SORRY, I...
JUUUST KIDDING!
IT'S FINE!
PAT
JUST LET THAT GO IN ONE EAR AND OUT THE OTHER.
YOU DIDN'T DO ANYTHING WRONG—THIS IS ALL ON ME.
NO.
I'M SORRY.
I WAS PRETTY INSENSITIVE.

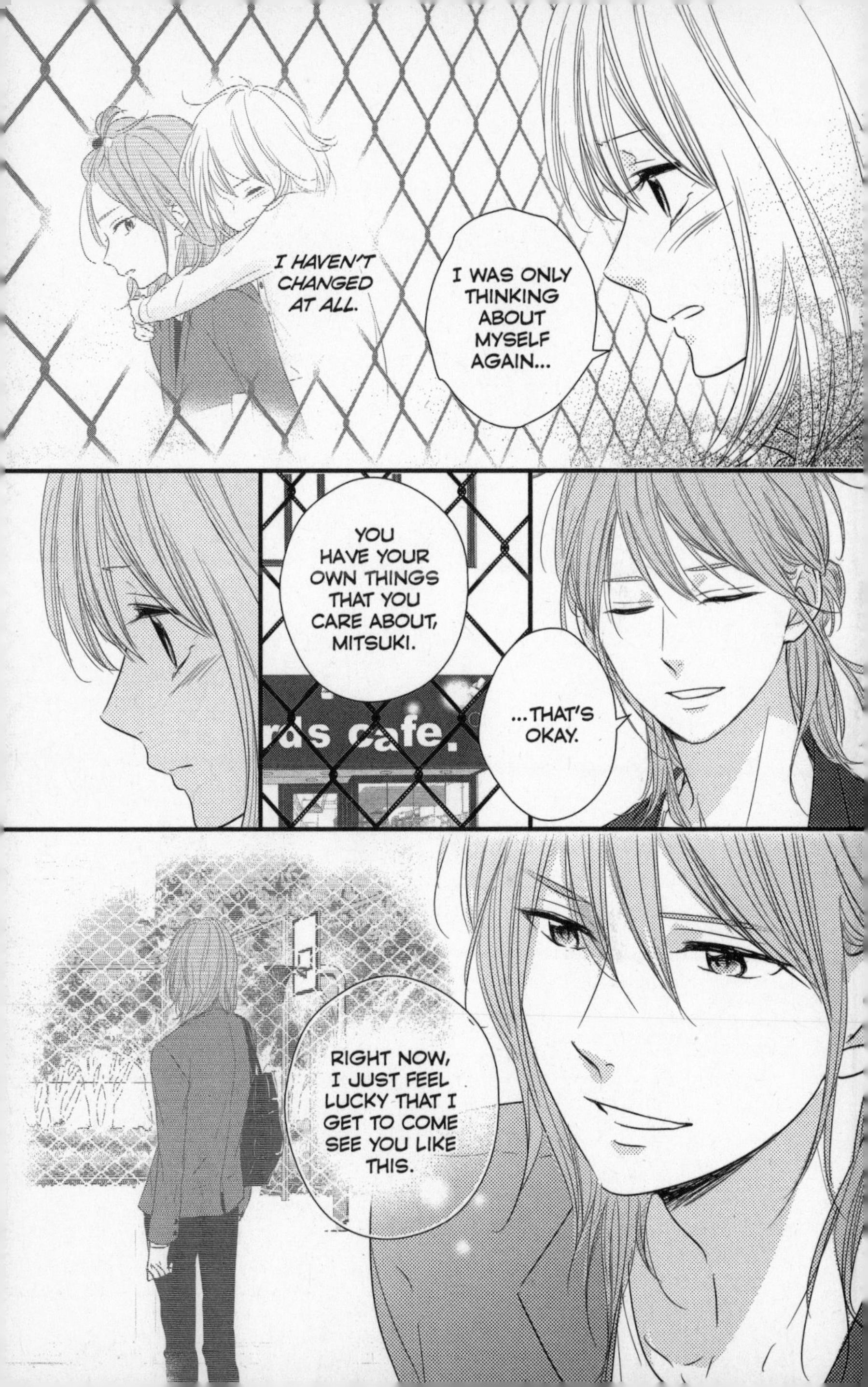

I WAS ONLY THINKING ABOUT MYSELF AGAIN...
I HAVEN'T CHANGED AT ALL.
...THAT'S OKAY.
YOU HAVE YOUR OWN THINGS THAT YOU CARE ABOUT, MITSUKI.
RIGHT NOW, I JUST FEEL LUCKY THAT I GET TO COME SEE YOU LIKE THIS.

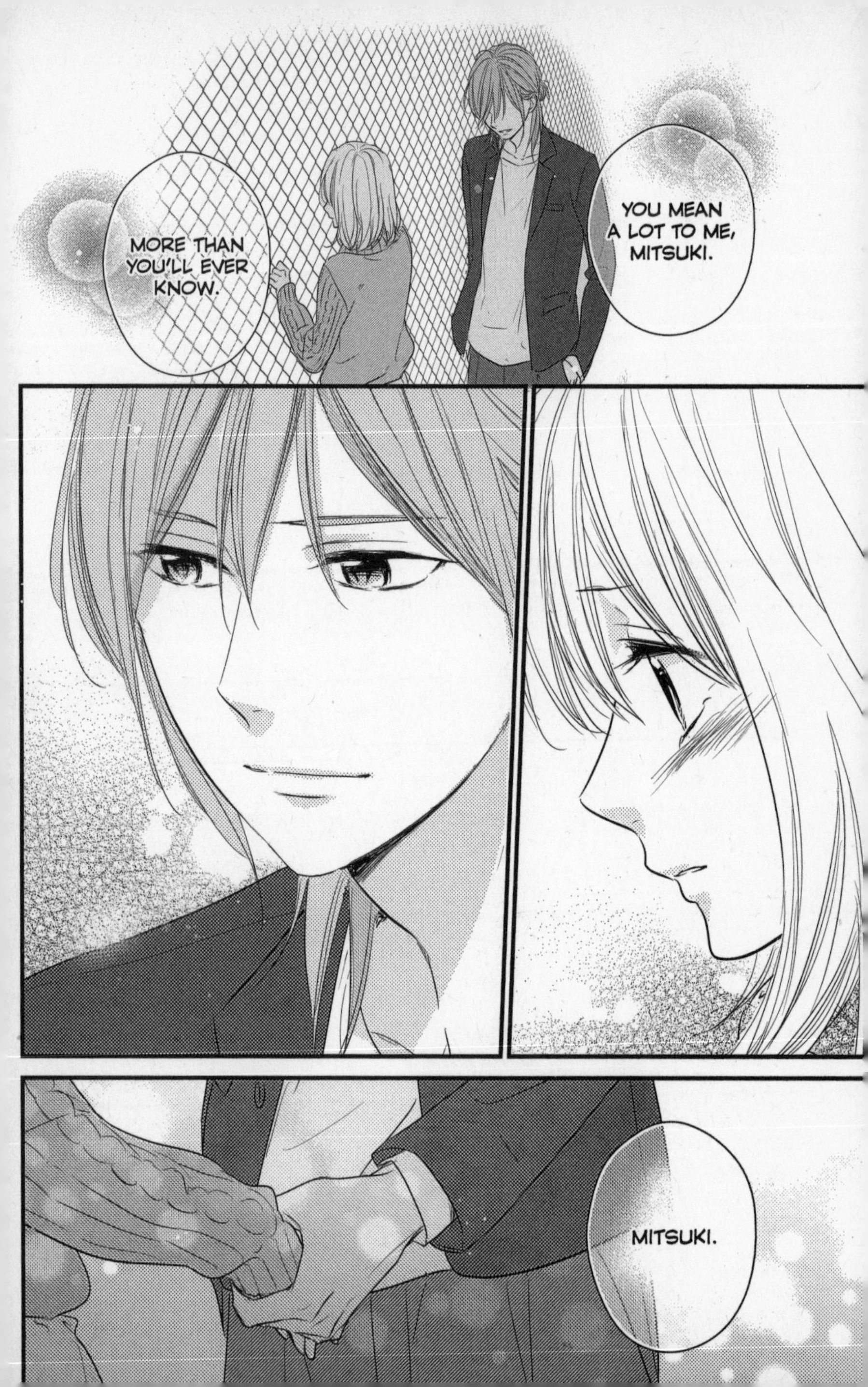
YOU MEAN A LOT TO ME, MITSUKI.
MORE THAN YOU'LL EVER KNOW.
MITSUKI.

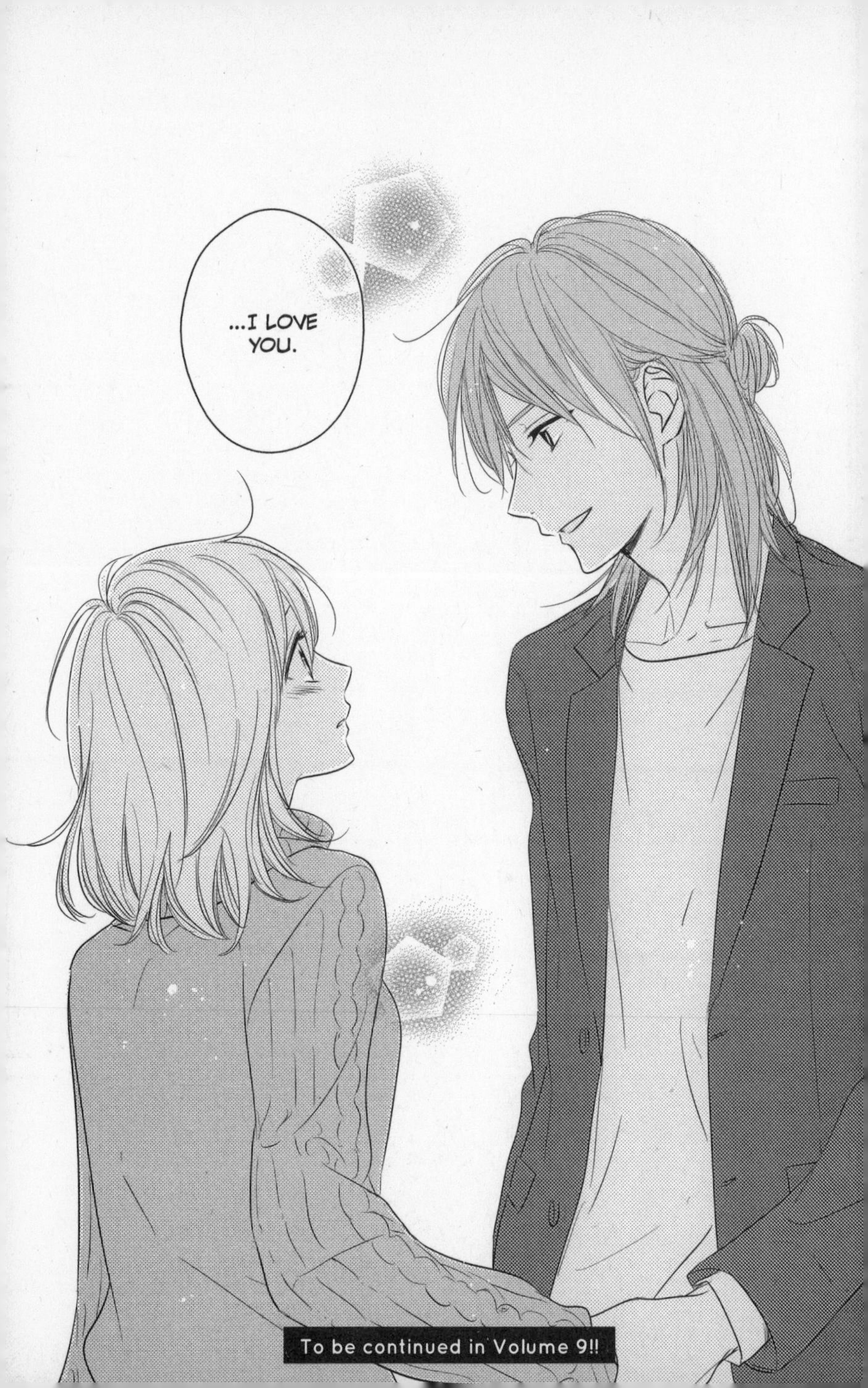
...I LOVE YOU.
To be continued in Volume 9!!

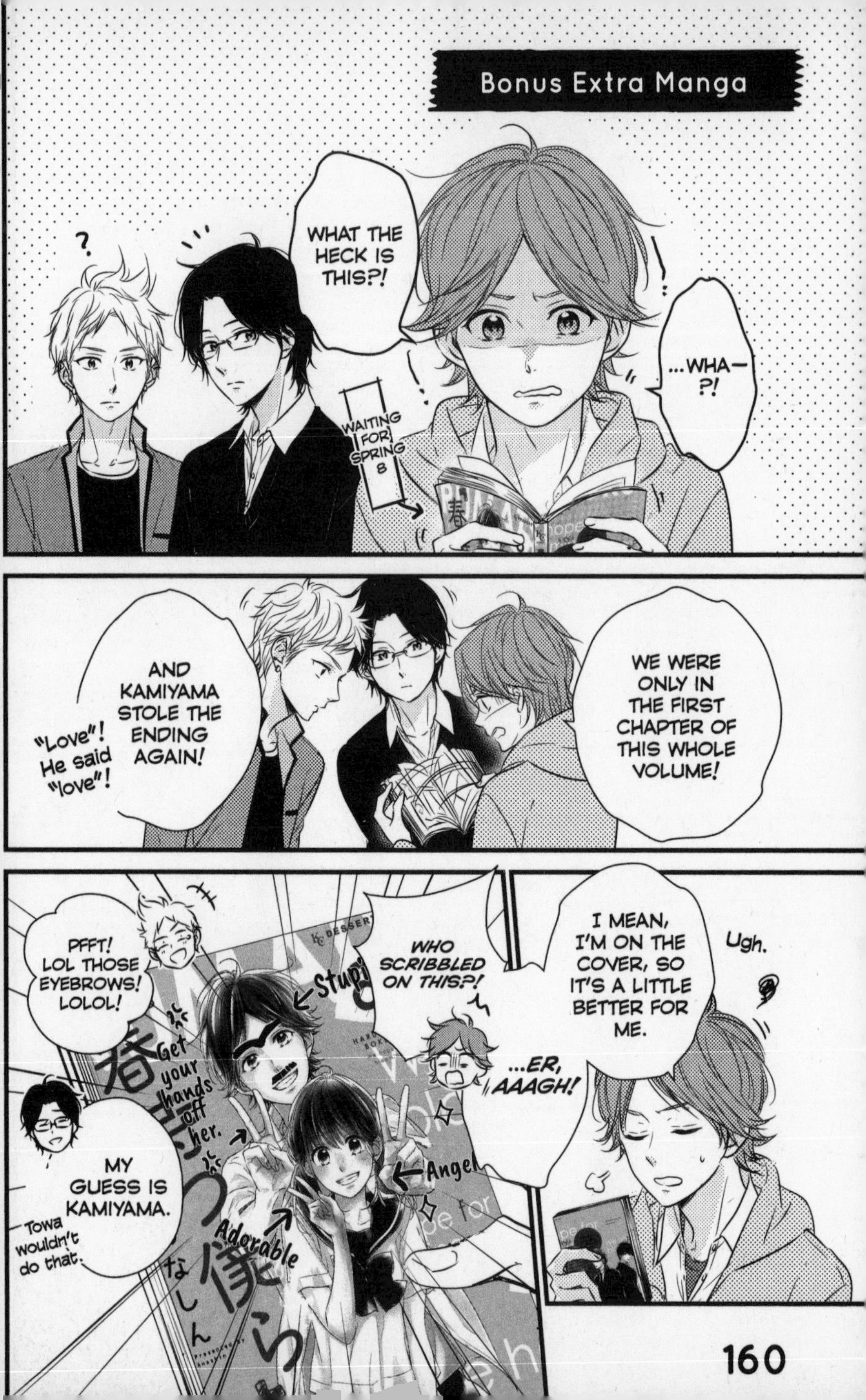
Bonus Extra Manga
...WHA— ?!
WHAT THE HECK IS THIS?!
WAITING FOR SPRING 8
WE WERE ONLY IN THE FIRST CHAPTER OF THIS WHOLE VOLUME!
AND KAMIYAMA STOLE THE ENDING AGAIN!
"Love"! He said "love"!
Ugh.
I MEAN, I'M ON THE COVER, SO IT'S A LITTLE BETTER FOR ME.
...ER, AAAGH!
WHO SCRIBBLED ON THIS?!
PFFT! LOL THOSE EYEBROWS! LOLOL!
Stupi
Get your hands off her.
Angel
Adorable
MY GUESS IS KAMIYAMA.
Towa wouldn't do that.

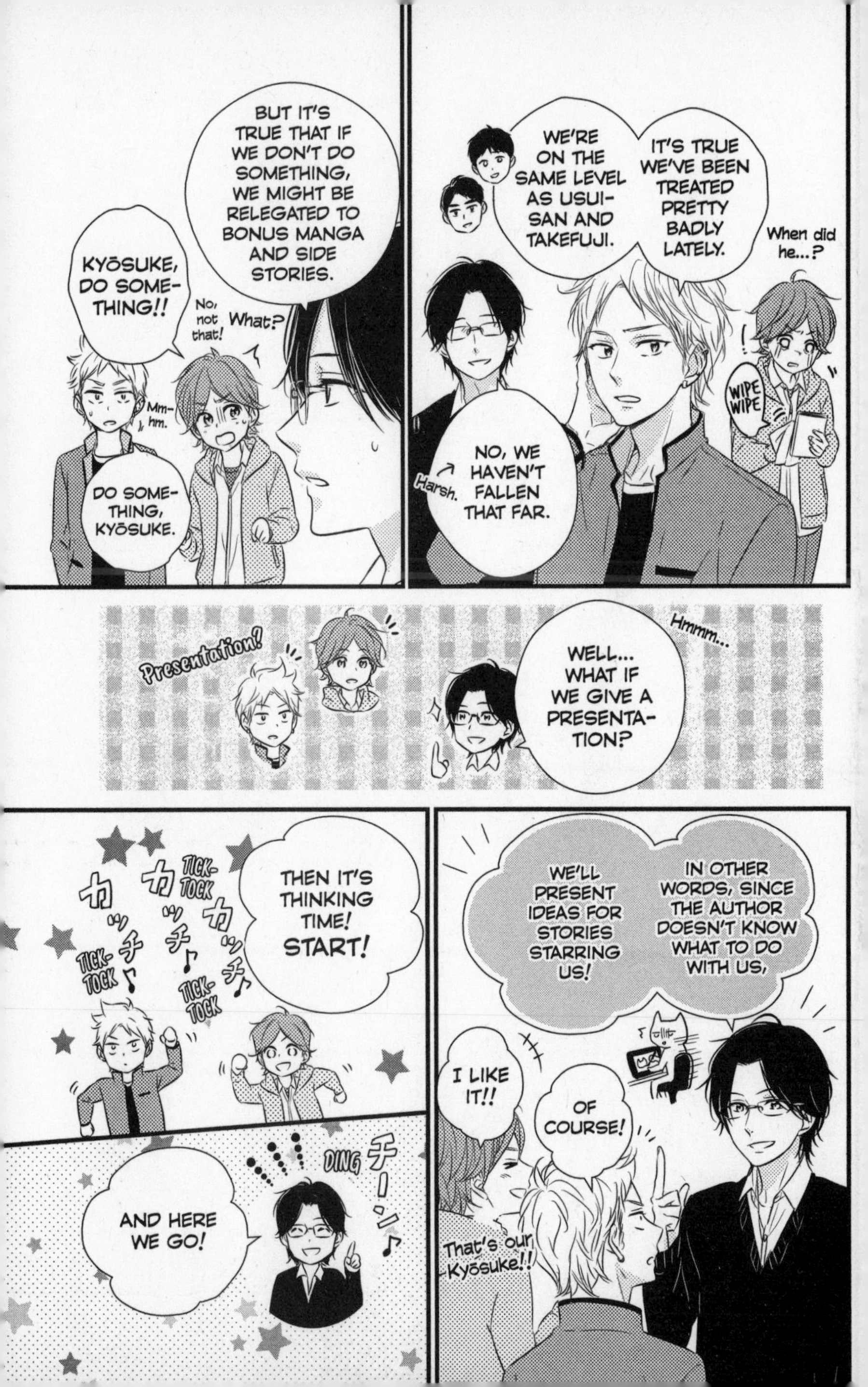
IT'S TRUE WE'VE BEEN TREATED PRETTY BADLY LATELY.
When did he...?
WE'RE ON THE SAME LEVEL AS USUI-SAN AND TAKEFUJI.
WIPE WIPE
NO, WE HAVEN'T FALLEN THAT FAR.
Harsh.
BUT IT'S TRUE THAT IF WE DON'T DO SOMETHING, WE MIGHT BE RELEGATED TO BONUS MANGA AND SIDE STORIES.
What?
No, not that!
KYŌSUKE, DO SOME-THING!!
Mm-hm.
DO SOME-THING, KYŌSUKE.
Hmmm...
WELL... WHAT IF WE GIVE A PRESENTATION?
Presentation!?
IN OTHER WORDS, SINCE THE AUTHOR DOESN'T KNOW WHAT TO DO WITH US,
WE'LL PRESENT IDEAS FOR STORIES STARRING US!
I LIKE IT!!
OF COURSE!
That's our Kyōsuke!!
THEN IT'S THINKING TIME! START!
カッチ
TICK-TOCK
カッチ
TICK-TOCK
カッチ
TICK-TOCK
DING
チーン
AND HERE WE GO!

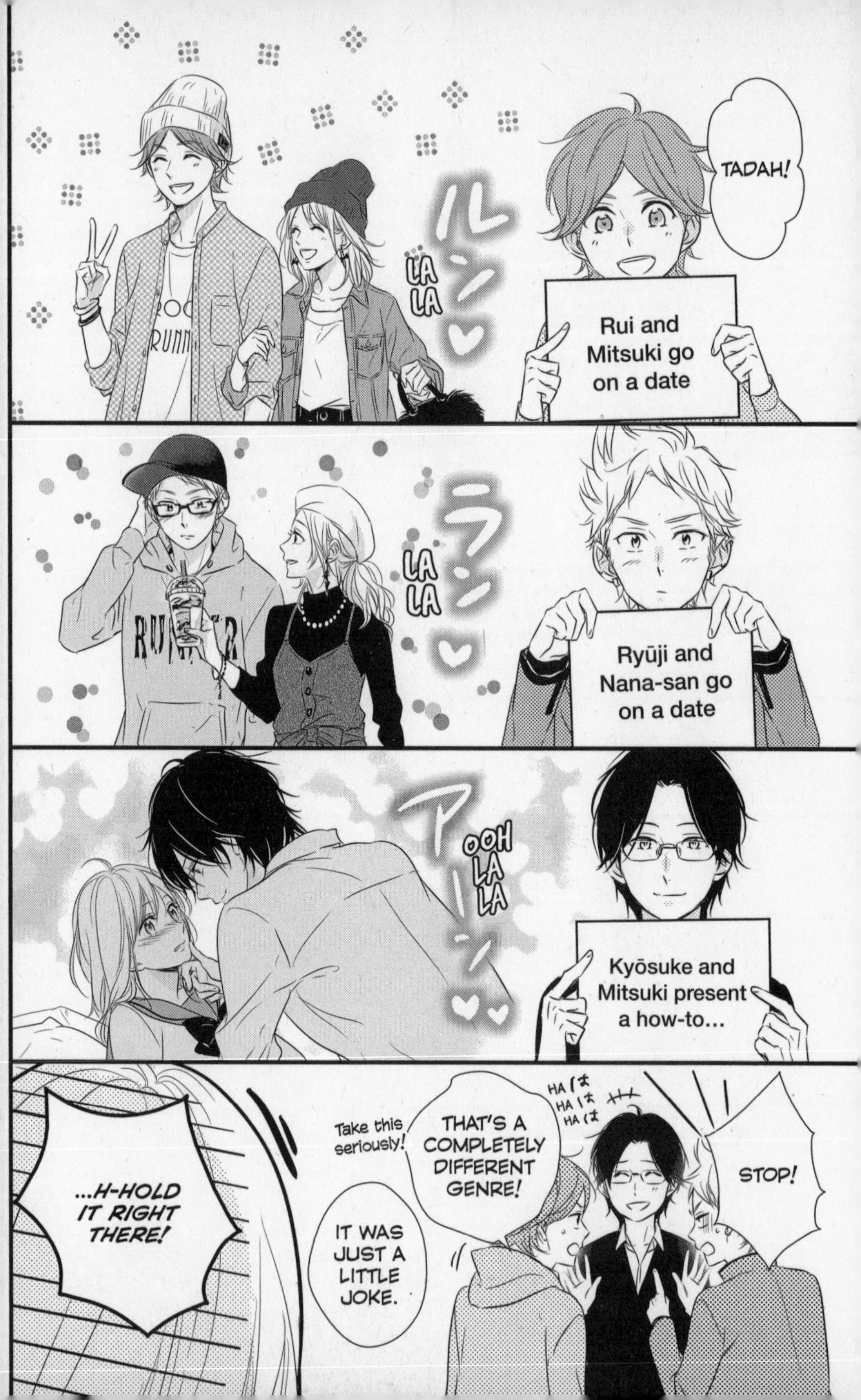
TADAH!
Rui and Mitsuki go on a date
ルン
LA LA
Ryūji and Nana-san go on a date
ラン
LA LA
Kyōsuke and Mitsuki present a how-to...
アーン
OOH LA LA
STOP!
HA は HA は HA は
THAT'S A COMPLETELY DIFFERENT GENRE!
Take this seriously!
IT WAS JUST A LITTLE JOKE.
...H-HOLD IT RIGHT THERE!

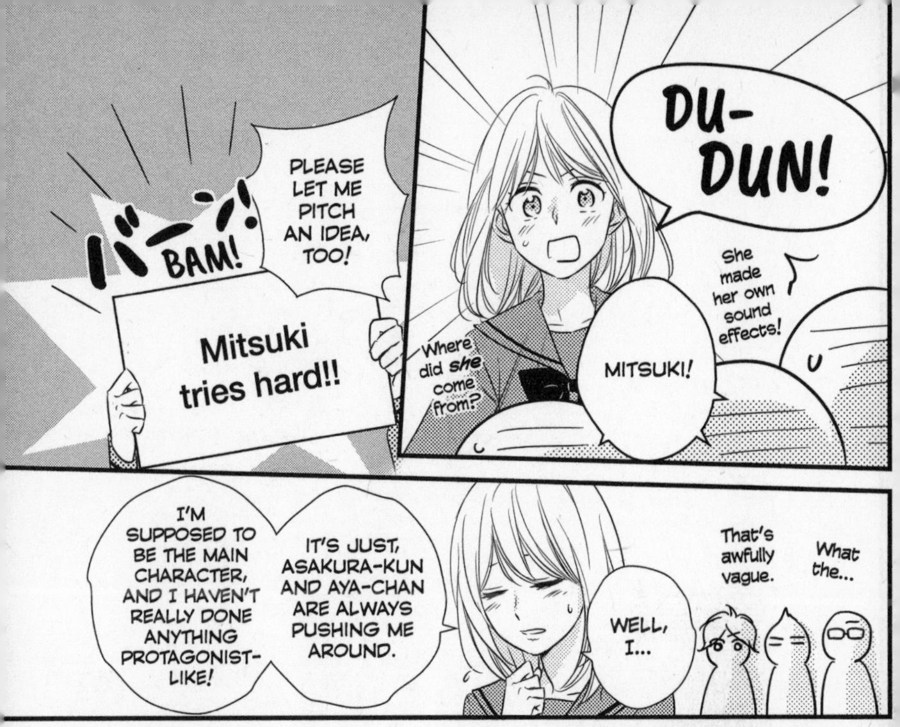
DU-DUN!
She made her own sound effects!
MITSUKI!
Where did *she* come from?
PLEASE LET ME PITCH AN IDEA, TOO!
BAM!
Mitsuki tries hard!!
What the...
That's awfully vague.
WELL, I...
IT'S JUST, ASAKURA-KUN AND AYA-CHAN ARE ALWAYS PUSHING ME AROUND.
I'M SUPPOSED TO BE THE MAIN CHARACTER, AND I HAVEN'T REALLY DONE ANYTHING PROTAGONIST-LIKE!

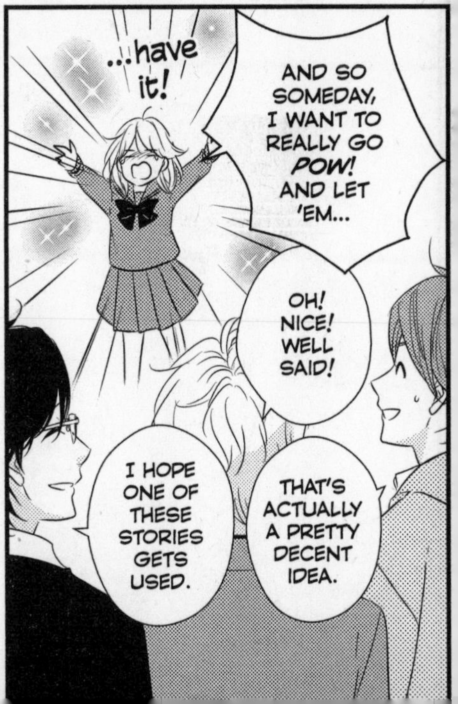
AND SO SOMEDAY, I WANT TO REALLY GO *POW!* AND LET 'EM...
...have it!
OH! NICE! WELL SAID!
THAT'S ACTUALLY A PRETTY DECENT IDEA.
I HOPE ONE OF THESE STORIES GETS USED.

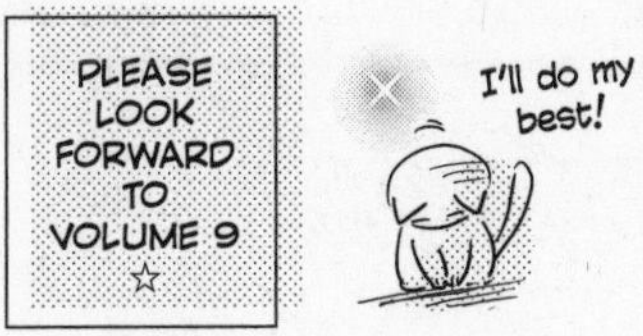
PLEASE LOOK FORWARD TO VOLUME 9 ☆
I'll do my best!

~ SPECIAL ★ THANKS ~

To my editor; the Designer-sama; everyone on the Dessert editorial team; everyone who was involved in the creation of this work;
Words Cafe-sama
My assistants Masuda-san,
Aki-chan, my family,
And to all my readers. Thank you with all my heart.

Anashin

9/2017

True Feelings

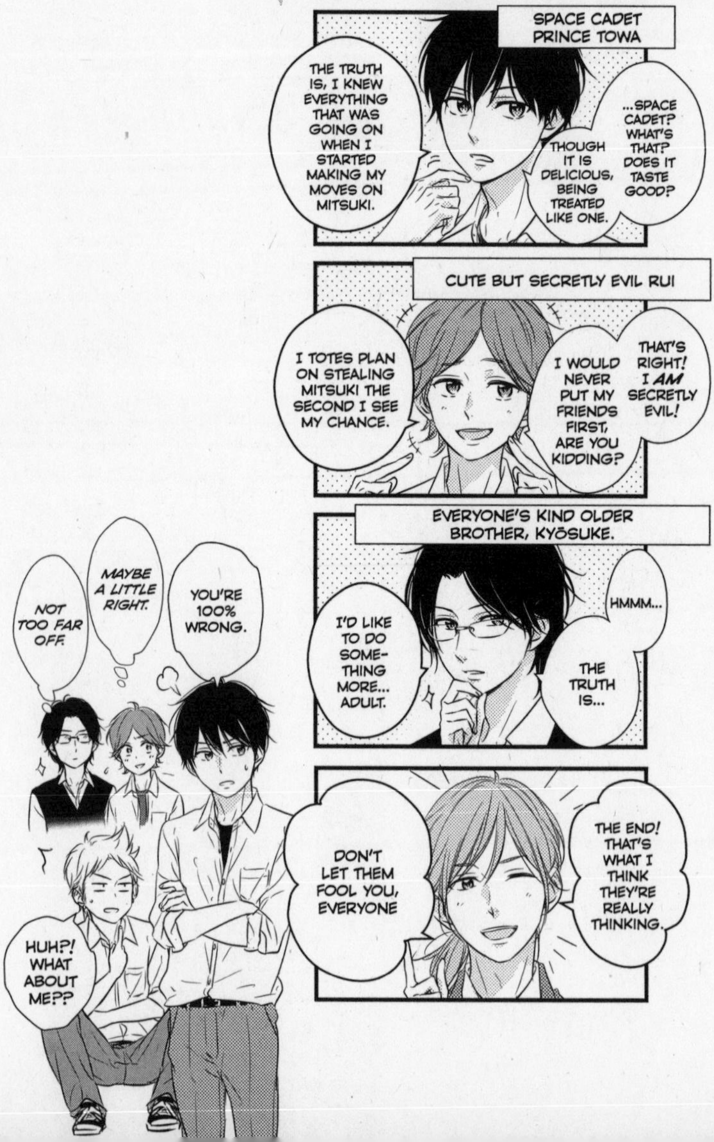
SPACE CADET PRINCE TOWA
...SPACE CADET? WHAT'S THAT? DOES IT TASTE GOOD?
THOUGH IT IS DELICIOUS, BEING TREATED LIKE ONE.
THE TRUTH IS, I KNEW EVERYTHING THAT WAS GOING ON WHEN I STARTED MAKING MY MOVES ON MITSUKI.
CUTE BUT SECRETLY EVIL RUI
THAT'S RIGHT! I *AM* SECRETLY EVIL!
I WOULD NEVER PUT MY FRIENDS FIRST, ARE YOU KIDDING?
I TOTES PLAN ON STEALING MITSUKI THE SECOND I SEE MY CHANCE.
EVERYONE'S KIND OLDER BROTHER, KYŌSUKE.
HMMM...
THE TRUTH IS...
I'D LIKE TO DO SOME-THING MORE... ADULT.
THE END! THAT'S WHAT I THINK THEY'RE REALLY THINKING.
DON'T LET THEM FOOL YOU, EVERYONE
YOU'RE 100% WRONG.
MAYBE A LITTLE RIGHT.
NOT TOO FAR OFF.
HUH?! WHAT ABOUT ME??

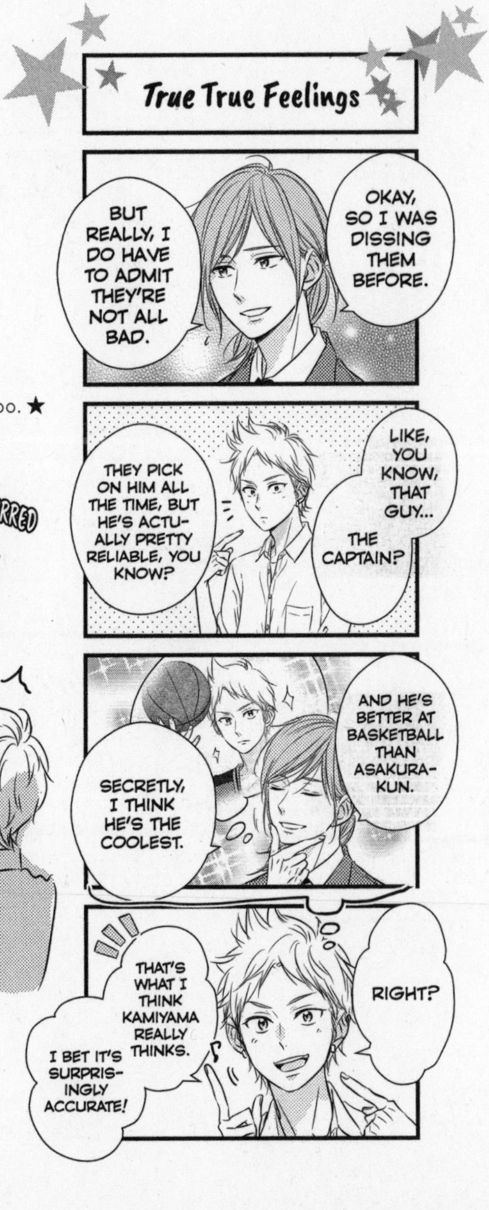
True True Feelings
OKAY, SO I WAS DISSING THEM BEFORE.
BUT REALLY, I DO HAVE TO ADMIT THEY'RE NOT ALL BAD.
LIKE, YOU KNOW, THAT GUY... THE CAPTAIN?
THEY PICK ON HIM ALL THE TIME, BUT HE'S ACTU-ALLY PRETTY RELIABLE, YOU KNOW?
AND HE'S BETTER AT BASKETBALL THAN ASAKURA-KUN.
SECRETLY, I THINK HE'S THE COOLEST.
RIGHT?
THAT'S WHAT I THINK KAMIYAMA REALLY THINKS.
I BET IT'S SURPRIS-INGLY ACCURATE!

★ Please read Volume 9, too. ★

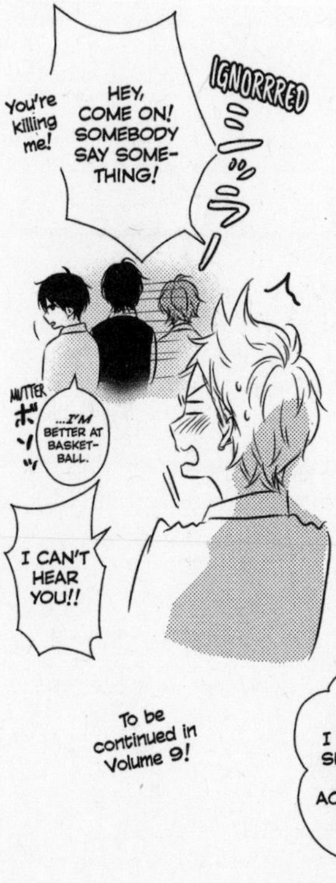
HEY, COME ON! SOMEBODY SAY SOME-THING!
You're killing me!
IGNORRRED
MUTTER
...I'M BETTER AT BASKET-BALL.
I CAN'T HEAR YOU!!

To be continued in Volume 9!

Translation Notes

Thanks for the food, page 8
In Japan, it is customary at meal times to express gratitude before and after a meal. Before a meal, the polite thing to say is *itadakimasu*, which means "I humbly partake," and can be more loosely translated to "thanks for the food," or even, "let's eat." The idea is to express appreciation for the meal. After a meal, the polite thing to say is *gochisō-sama*, which can translate roughly to "I have been fed."

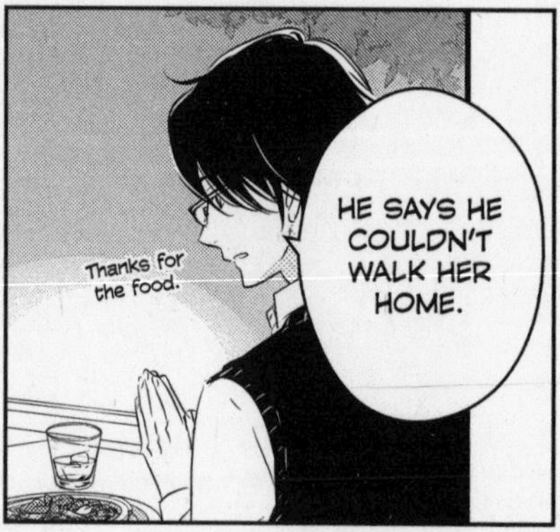
HE SAYS HE COULDN'T WALK HER HOME.
Thanks for the food.

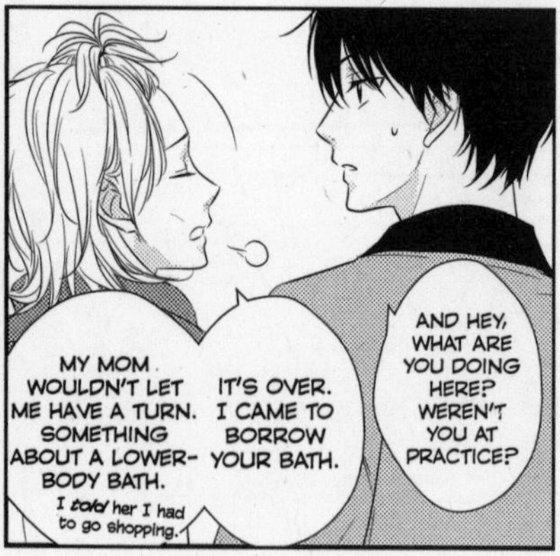
AND HEY, WHAT ARE YOU DOING HERE? WEREN'T YOU AT PRACTICE?
IT'S OVER. I CAME TO BORROW YOUR BATH.
MY MOM WOULDN'T LET ME HAVE A TURN. SOMETHING ABOUT A LOWER-BODY BATH.
I told her I had to go shopping.

Lower-body bath, page 86
A bath where one would sit in warm water between 38 to 39°C (100.4 to 102.2 °F) for about 20-30 minutes. The bath water level should reach a bit above the belly button. It is said to be a suitable type of bath for older individuals or those with heart issues. This is because the heart only needs to work hard enough to regulate the heat and body temperature for the lower half of the body, as opposed to the whole body in a full bath.

Waiting for Spring

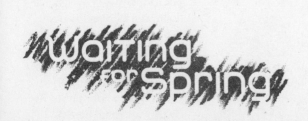

complex age

yui sakuma

26-year-old Nagisa Kataura has a secret. Transforming into her favorite anime and manga characters is her passion in life, and she's earned great respect amongst her fellow cospayers. But to the rest of society, her hobby is a silly fantasy. As demands from both her office job and cosplaying begin to increase, she may one day have to make a tough choice—what's more important to her, cosplay or being "normal"?

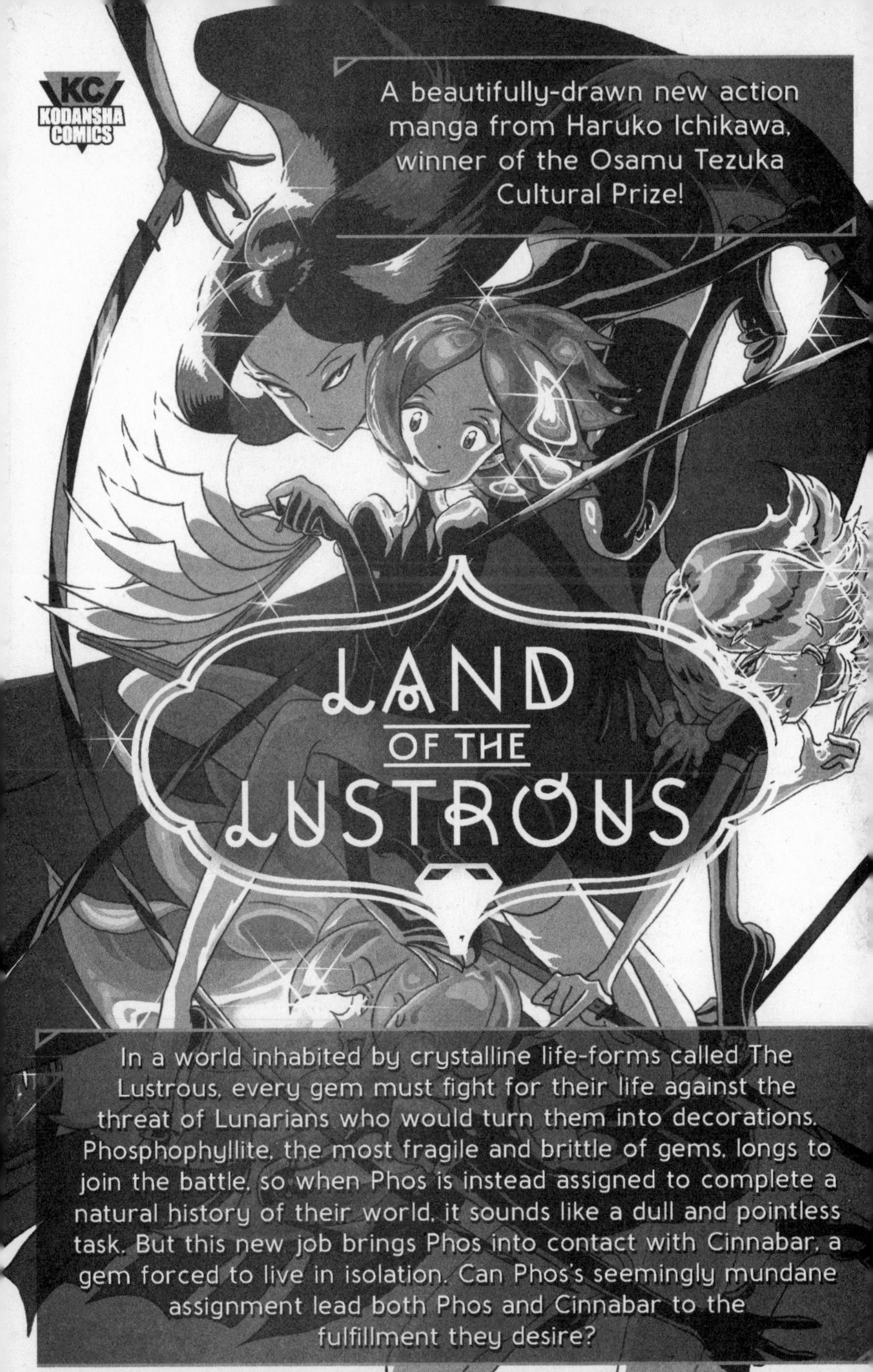
KC KODANSHA COMICS
A beautifully-drawn new action manga from Haruko Ichikawa, winner of the Osamu Tezuka Cultural Prize!
LAND OF THE LUSTROUS
In a world inhabited by crystalline life-forms called The Lustrous, every gem must fight for their life against the threat of Lunarians who would turn them into decorations. Phosphophyllite, the most fragile and brittle of gems, longs to join the battle, so when Phos is instead assigned to complete a natural history of their world, it sounds like a dull and pointless task. But this new job brings Phos into contact with Cinnabar, a gem forced to live in isolation. Can Phos's seemingly mundane assignment lead both Phos and Cinnabar to the fulfillment they desire?

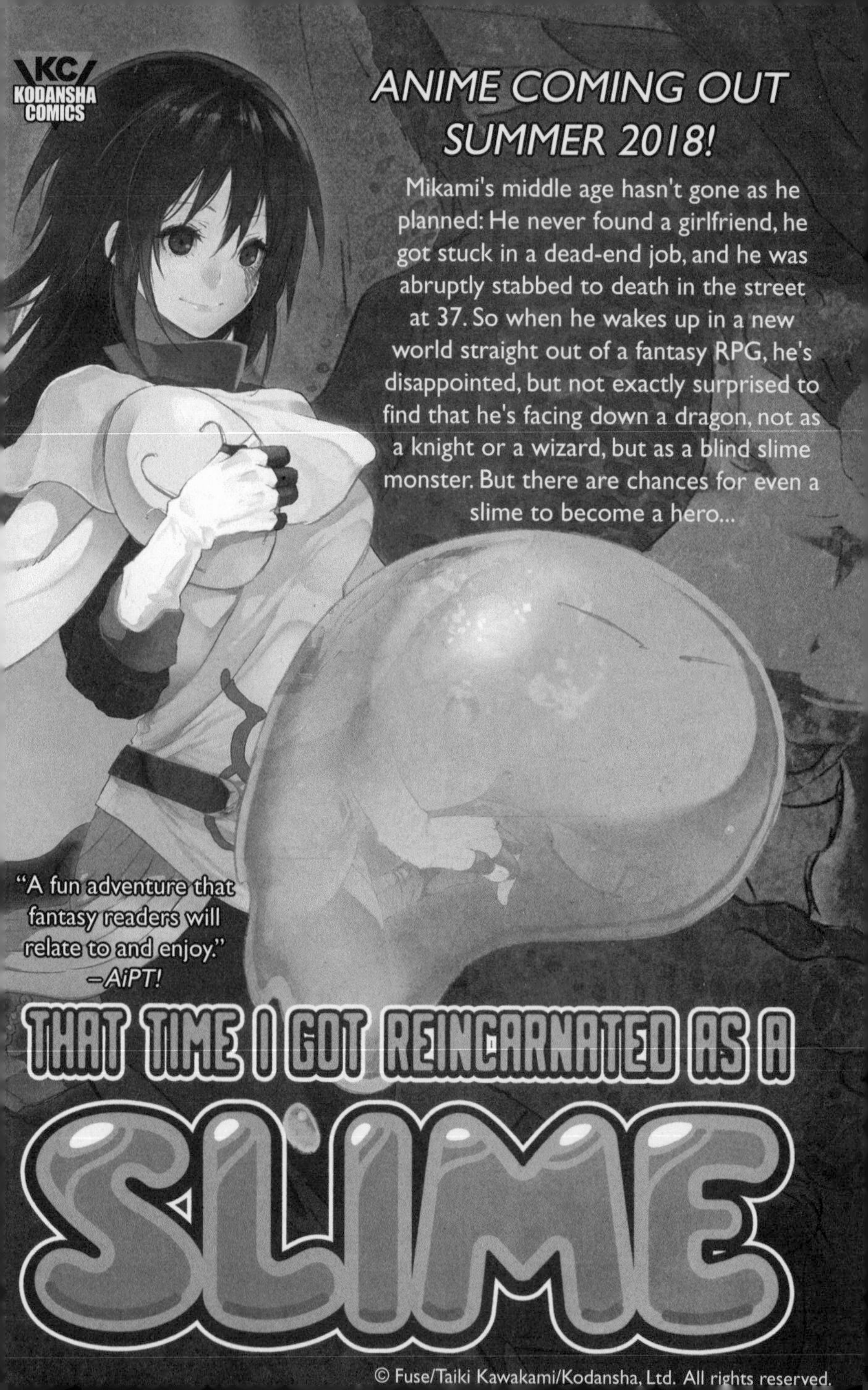
KC
KODANSHA COMICS
ANIME COMING OUT SUMMER 2018!
Mikami's middle age hasn't gone as he planned: He never found a girlfriend, he got stuck in a dead-end job, and he was abruptly stabbed to death in the street at 37. So when he wakes up in a new world straight out of a fantasy RPG, he's disappointed, but not exactly surprised to find that he's facing down a dragon, not as a knight or a wizard, but as a blind slime monster. But there are chances for even a slime to become a hero...
"A fun adventure that fantasy readers will relate to and enjoy."
–AiPT!
THAT TIME I GOT REINCARNATED AS A
SLIME
© Fuse/Taiki Kawakami/Kodansha, Ltd. All rights reserved.

KC

KODANSHA
COMICS

"I'm pleasantly
surprised to find
modern shojo using
cross-dressing as a
dramatic device to deliver
social commentary...
Recommended."

-Otaku USA
Magazine

The prince in his dark days

By Hico Yamanaka

A drunkard for a father, a household of poverty... For 17-year-old Atsuko, misfortune is all she knows and believes in. Until one day, a chance encounter with Itaru-the wealthy heir of a huge corporation-changes everything. The two look identical, uncannily so. When Itaru curiously goes missing, Atsuko is roped into being his stand-in. There, in his shoes, Atsuko must parade like a prince in a palace. She encounters many new experiences, but at what cost...?

Say I Love You.

KC KODANSHA COMICS

Mei Tachibana has no friends — and says she doesn't need them!
But everything changes when she accidentally roundhouse kicks the most popular boy in school! However, Yamato Kurosawa isn't angry in the slightest— in fact, he thinks his ordinary life could use an unusual girl like Mei. But winning Mei's trust will be a tough task. How long will she refuse to say, "I love you"?

a Silent Voice

The New York Times bestselling manga and Eisner Award nominee— now available in a complete box set!

Now a feature-length animation from Kyoto Animation!

KC
KODANSHA COMICS

- Exclusive 2-sided poster
- Replica of Shoko's notebook
- Preview of Yoshitoki Oima's new series, To Your Eternity

Shoya is a bully. When Shoko, a girl who can't hear, enters his elementary school class, she becomes their favorite target, and Shoya and his friends goad each other into devising new tortures for her. But the children's cruelty goes too far. Shoko is forced to leave the school, and Shoya ends up shouldering all the blame. Six years later, the two meet again. Can Shoya make up for his past mistakes, or is it too late?